UNDERSTANDING THE WORKING COLLEGE STUDENT

UNDERSTANDING THE WORKING COLLEGE STUDENT

New Research and Its Implications
for Policy and Practice

Edited by Laura W. Perna

Foreword by Glenn DuBois

STERLING, VIRGINIA

Published by Stylus Publishing, LLC
22883 Quicksilver Drive
Sterling, Virginia 20166-2102

Library of Congress Cataloging-in-Publication-Data
Understanding the working college student : new research and its implications for policy and practice / edited by Laura W. Perna ; foreword by Glenn DuBois.—1st ed.
    p.   cm.
Includes index.
ISBN 978-1-57922-426-4 (cloth : alk. paper)
ISBN 978-1-57922-427-1 (pbk. : alk. paper)
1. Undergraduates—Employment—United States.
2. Undergraduates—United States—Psychology.
3. Undergraduates—United States—Economic conditions.   I. Perna, Laura W. (Laura Walter)
HD6276.52.U5U64   2010
331.5—dc22   20090332418

13-digit ISBN: 978-1-57922-426-4 (cloth)
13-digit ISBN: 978-1-57922-427-1 (paper)

Printed in the United States of America

All first editions printed on acid free paper
that meets the American National Standards Institute
Z39-48 Standard.

> **Bulk Purchases**
>
> Quantity discounts are available for use in workshops and for staff development.
> Call 1-800-232-0223

First Edition, 2010

10   9   8   7   6   5   4   3   2   1

*This book is dedicated to
anyone who is striving
to complete an educational program
while also juggling the demands
of employment and other responsibilities.
I hope that this volume will lead to
improved support for and benefits from your efforts.*

CONTENTS

ACKNOWLEDGMENTS

D uring the preparation of this volume, I benefited tremendously from the encouragement and support of many individuals. Most notably, Ed St. John, now Algo D. Henderson College Professor of Higher Education at the University of Michigan, and Don Hossler, Professor of Educational Leadership and Policy Studies at Indiana University, focused my attention on this topic when they invited me to speak with, and write a paper for, campus leaders about the meaning and implications of employment for undergraduate students as part of the Indiana Project on Academic Success (IPAS). Current and former students Michelle Cooper, Chunyan Li, and Valerie Lundy-Wagner provided essential assistance with gathering relevant background material for understanding this topic. My colleagues at the University of Pennsylvania, especially Joni Finney, Marybeth Gasman, Shaun Harper, and Matthew Hartley, were also invaluable sources of support.

I also greatly appreciate the time and effort that the authors of each chapter invested in this volume. These individuals not only trusted me to produce this volume, but also were wonderful to work with. A number of the chapter authors further contributed to this final product by discussing preliminary versions of their chapters at the 2007 and 2008 annual meetings of the Association for the Study of Higher Education.

This book would not have been possible without the encouragement and assistance of Stylus President and Publisher John von Knorring. He was supportive and encouraging when this volume was no more than a set of developing ideas. John provided me with not only the opportunity to edit this volume, but also invaluable support and feedback at each step in the process.

On a more personal note, words cannot adequately express my appreciation for my parents' unwavering confidence in me and my three sisters, and the sacrifices that they made to promote our educational attainment. Finally, I am forever grateful for the support, encouragement, and inspiration that I receive from my husband, Len Perna, and my children, Madison and Jonah.

FOREWORD

America has been resting on its educational laurels for too long. The consequences of that will be revealed as the education level of our nation's workforce declines over the next generation. Areas of opportunity once dominated by the United States will probably become the property of nations that are more aggressively cultivating their peoples' talents, knowledge, and skills.

International comparisons, national test scores, and parental anecdotes all indicate the same thing: the U.S. educational system is stagnating. And that malaise threatens our ability to compete globally.

The world in which our children are growing up bears scant resemblance to the world in which today's education leaders grew up.

Is our education system keeping up? Can its traditions meet today's demands? Is lifelong learning now a requirement for everybody, and if so, what does that mean for our community colleges and universities?

These questions should drive the agendas and conversations of every board and every education policymaker in our country. I applaud Laura Perna for giving us a good place to begin that discussion with *Understanding the Working College Student: New Research and Its Implications for Policy and Practice.*

The United States shares with Germany the dubious distinction of the being the world's only developed nation to be replacing its current generation of workers with a generation that is less educated.

Perhaps if I were trendier, I would suggest that what we need is Education 2.0 or 3.0, or I would suggest that our education system is "flat." Instead, I think what we need is a sober look at what our education system is really doing for individuals, not only at the beginning of their lives but throughout their lives and to ask whether that is truly enough. This book provides a good starting point for that conversation.

Glenn DuBois, Chancellor
Virginia Community College System

INTRODUCTION

Laura W. Perna

W ork is a fundamental part of life for many undergraduate students. The average college student is now not only employed but also working a substantial number of hours. In 2003–2004, about 75% of dependent undergraduates and 80% of independent undergraduates worked while enrolled (Perna, Cooper, & Li, 2007). Working dependent undergraduates averaged 24 hours of employment per week while enrolled, and working independent undergraduates averaged 34.5 hours per week (Perna et al., 2007). Employment is now the norm even among traditional undergraduates, as nearly half (46.5%) of undergraduates who were enrolled full time and under the age of 25 worked some number of hours in 2006 (U.S. Department of Education, 2008a). Nearly 1 in 10 (8%) undergraduates under the age of 25 and enrolled full time was employed at least 35 hours per week (U.S. Department of Education, 2008a).

The high prevalence and intensity of working among both dependent and independent students raise a number of important questions for public policymakers and college administrators, including: Why do so many college students work so many hours? What are the characteristics of undergraduates who work? What are the implications of working for students' educational experiences and outcomes? And how can public and institutional policymakers promote the educational success of undergraduate students who work?

Available data and research provide few answers to these questions. Drawing on the limited available research, college administrators, faculty, and researchers have generally assumed that undergraduates should simply work no more than 10 to 20 hours per week at a job on campus, on the theory that such an experience will increase their integration into and subsequent persistence at a campus (King, 2002; Pascarella & Terenzini, 2005; Swail, Redd, & Perna, 2003).

However, the frequency and prevalence of employment suggest that this recommendation is unrealistic for many undergraduates, particularly adult students. About one third of all undergraduates are age 25 and older (U.S. Department of Education, 2008b). As described in several chapters in this volume, working is just one of several identities for many college students, especially adult learners (see Carol Kasworm, in chapter 2; John Levin, Virginia Montero-Hernandez, and Christine Cerven, in chapter 3; and Mary Ziskin, Vasti Torres, Don Hossler, and Jacob P. K. Gross, in chapter 4, in this volume). This recommendation also presumes to "fix" nontraditional students to fit the pattern of the "ideal" traditional undergraduate, thereby ignoring the realities and complexities of adult students' lives. Moreover, a careful read of existing research (as summarized in the chapters in this volume) shows the mixed empirical support for this recommendation, with some research suggesting that working negatively affects student outcomes and other research showing no or even positive effects (Pascarella & Terenzini, 2005; Perna et al., 2007).

Especially when considered in light of the prevalence of employment, the ambiguity in available research and the absence of more appropriate recommendations regarding student employment underscore the need to know more about the nature and consequences of employment for today's undergraduates. A better understanding of the reasons that undergraduate students work and the effects of working on students' educational outcomes is an obvious prerequisite for identifying the public and institutional policies that can ensure a high-quality educational experience for all students, including the substantial number who work while enrolled.

This volume describes the need to reconsider the appropriateness of policies and practices that were created for traditional-age students who work on campus for 10 to 15 hours per week and offers suggestions for policies and practices that more completely reflect the experiences of today's working undergraduates. The chapters draw on a range of theoretical perspectives that together provide a more complete and comprehensive conceptualization of the "working college student." The chapters also use both quantitative and qualitative research methodologies and data from national and single institution sources to paint a comprehensive picture of the characteristics, experiences, and challenges of working college students. Together, the chapters provide a more complete understanding of the heterogeneity underlying the label "undergraduates who work" and the implications of working for undergraduate students' educational experiences and outcomes. The volume offers recommendations for public and institutional policymakers to recognize the tendency of students to work and act in ways that maximize the benefits of working while minimizing the disadvantages.

Importance of Improving Our Understanding of the Working College Student

Understanding the experiences of students who work, the implications of working for students' educational outcomes, and variations in experiences and implications for traditional and adult students adds one piece to the puzzle for raising the nation's educational attainment. Improving college enrollment and degree attainment is critical to ensuring the nation's continued economic and social prosperity because a growing share of jobs calls for workers who have a college education (Carnevale & Desrochers, 2003). Although increasingly important, educational attainment in the United States has fallen behind that of other developed nations (Baum & Ma, 2007; National Center for Public Policy and Higher Education, 2008). The Organisation for Economic Co-operation and Development (OECD, 2006) predicts that, because the United States is experiencing both slower enrollment and lower rates of college completion than some other nations, the share of college graduates in OECD nations produced by the United States will decline over the next decade.

Recognizing these trends, in a nationally televised, prime-time address to a joint session of Congress in February 2009, President Barack Obama specified an ambitious goal: "By 2020, America will once again have the highest proportion of college graduates in the world." Along the same lines, Lumina Foundation for Education (2009) has a goal of increasing the percentage of young adults in the United States who have attained an associate's or bachelor's degree from the current 40% to 60% by 2025. The first goal in the State Higher Education Executive Officers' (SHEEO, 2008) "national agenda for higher education" is to increase the percentage of young adults who earn at least an associate's degree to 55% by 2025. Realizing this goal requires producing an additional 3 million degrees each year between now and 2025 (SHEEO, 2008).

To raise degree production to the level of leading nations, the United States must improve educational attainment of both traditional-age and adult students. The Council for Adult and Experiential Learning (CAEL, 2008) warns that "32 states cannot catch up to the educational attainment levels of the best performing countries internationally by relying solely on strategies related to traditional-age students . . . educating adults must be part of the solution" (p. 7). About one third of the U.S. adult population (i.e., more than 59 million individuals) has no postsecondary education and 20% of U.S. adults have some postsecondary education but no college degree (CAEL, 2008).

Given differences in financial resources, family responsibilities, and other circumstances, work is likely to play a different role in the college enrollment of a traditional student who enrolls in college full time in the fall after graduating from high school than it is for adult or nontraditional students. In a much-cited definition, Horn (1996) defines a nontraditional student based on enrollment patterns (e.g., not enrolling in college immediately after high school, attending part time), financial and family status (having dependents other than a spouse, being a single parent, working full time while enrolled, being financially independent from parents), and high school graduation status (received a certificate rather than a standard high school diploma).

Although the role of work in promoting and limiting degree completion is unclear for both traditional and nontraditional students, relatively more attention has been focused on the implications of work for traditional students. For example, the Advisory Committee on Student Financial Assistance (2006) points to the high "work and loan burden caused by rising college prices and insufficient need-based grant aid" (p. iv) as a primary barrier to college enrollment for college-qualified high school graduates from low- and moderate-income families. Defining the work–loan burden as the net price or the total cost of attendance less grant aid, the Advisory Committee reports that the "work and loan burden" as a percentage of family income increased at public four-year institutions from 75% in 1990 to 87% in 2004 for those with family incomes below $20,000 (Advisory Committee on Student Financial Assistance, 2006).

Although some share of students may work to finance lifestyle choices (King, 2002), many students must work to pay college prices. The prevalence of working is not surprising given trends in tuition, financial aid, and family incomes (College Board, 2008a, 2008b). Between 1998–1999 and 2008–2009, average tuition and fees increased in constant dollars by 50% at public four-year institutions (College Board, 2008a). Over the same period, average grant aid per full-time equivalent (FTE) student increased by 47% (College Board, 2008b) and average family income increased by just 3% for families in the bottom quintile and 5% for families in the second lowest quintile (College Board, 2008a). Traditional-age students may also work when their parents are unable or unwilling to help them pay college prices (Stern & Nakata, 1991; Stringer, Cunningham, O'Brien, & Merisotis, 1998).

Although it enables students to pay college expenses, working is often assumed to have negative consequences for students' educational experiences. Noting that time is finite, some (e.g., Baum, 2005; Pascarella & Terenzini, 2005; Stinebrickner & Stinebrickner, 2004) argue that spending time working necessarily restricts the availability of time for engaging in educational activities. This assumption is supported by theories of student integration and engagement. For example, Tinto's (1993) model assumes that a student decides to leave or persist in a college or university based on the student's academic and social interactions with the institution. Along the same lines, Kuh, Kinzie, Bridges, and Hayek's (2006) model assumes that students who are engaged in "educationally effective practices" will persist and graduate from an institution. Working off campus is one force that is expected to mediate the relationship between students' college experiences and engagement (Kuh et al., 2006). Drawing on qualitative and quantitative data to compare the experiences of low-income, high-achieving minority students who received Gates Millennium Scholars awards with the experiences of nonrecipients, St. John (2008) concludes that finances, including the need to work, should be included in any examination of academic and social integration because lack of adequate financial support limits students' integration opportunities.

However, before this volume, few have considered how working influences the integration and engagement experiences of students who work, especially those who work full time. Although some models have been developed to recognize that forces other than integration and engagement influence the college outcomes of adult students (e.g., Donaldson & Graham, 1999), few models focus specifically on the college experiences of working adults. Moreover, little is known about the benefits that may accrue to students who work or how the benefits and costs of working are different for traditional-age students than for adult students. Understanding the nature of work for adult students is especially important given the substantial and growing size of this population. Nearly half (42%) of students enrolled at two-year institutions and more than one third (38%) of students enrolled at four-year institutions in fall 2005 were age 25 or older (U.S. Department of Education, 2008b). Descriptive data show that, on average, independent students not only are more likely than dependent students to work but also average a higher number of hours per week working (Perna et al., 2007).

Understanding the Experiences of Students Who Work

This volume has three goals:

1. Develop a comprehensive understanding of the working college student
2. Provide a more complete assessment of both the positive and negative implications of working for students' educational experiences and outcomes
3. Offer recommendations for public policymakers, campus administrators, and researchers to improve the educational experiences and outcomes of undergraduates who work

The insights offered in this volume have particular relevance for public policymakers, faculty, academic advisors, student services and financial aid staff, and institutional and educational researchers.

The volume attempts to achieve these goals by using several strategies. First, the volume assumes that, although student agency plays a role, public policymakers and campus administrators have an obligation to promote the educational outcomes (including degree attainment) of students who work. As described more completely later in this volume (see Pusser in chapter 7), public policymakers have a responsibility to address this issue in part because of the public good aspects of higher education. Increased educational attainment benefits not only individual degree recipients but also society more generally. The benefits of higher education to individuals include higher earnings, better working conditions, lower probability of unemployment, better health, and longer life, while the benefits to society include greater national economic productivity, lower expenditures on social welfare programs, lower crime, and greater civic involvement (Baum & Ma, 2007; Bowen, 1997). This "public good" characteristic is one reason that federal and state governments "intervene" in the higher education market with policies designed to promote college enrollment and attainment (Paulsen, 2001).

Campus administrators also have an obligation to ensure that institutional resources and structures support the educational success of all students, including those who work. The role of institutions in promoting student success is implicit in many prevailing conceptual frameworks. For example, Kuh et al.'s (2006) model assigns responsibility for student success both to students for allocating time and effort to engage in educational practices and to institutions for encouraging students to participate in these practices. Nonetheless, as the authors in this volume observe, often institutional policies and practices approach students who work (particularly adult workers who are undergraduates) from the perspective of what works for traditional undergraduate students, failing to recognize that higher education is generally not the primary life environment of working students.

Second, collectively, the chapters provide a comprehensive conceptualization of the working college student by drawing on multiple theoretical and conceptual frameworks. Some chapters (e.g., chapter 9 by Alexander McCormick, John Moore, and George Kuh; chapter 10 by Lamont Flowers; and chapter 11 by Paul Umbach, Ryan Padgett, and Ernest Pascarella) conceptualize work as a force that may mediate students' engagement in effective educational practices. Others show the potential contributions of such perspectives as identity theory (chapter 2 by Carol Kasworm), economic production functions (chapter 6 by Doug Lynch, Michael Gottfried, Wendy Green, and Chris Allen Thomas), labor economics and retention theory (chapter 12 by Marvin Titus), social reproduction and stratification theories (chapter 7 by Brian Pusser; chapter 4 by Mary Ziskin, Vasti Torres, Don Hossler, and Jacob Gross), models of nontraditional undergraduate student attrition (chapter 5 by Heather Rowan-Kenyon, Amy Swan, Nancy Deutsch, and Bruce Gansneder), and organizational and cultural theory (chapter 3 by John Levin, Virginia Montero-Hernandez, and Christine Cerven).

Third, the volume considers the consequences of working for a range of student outcomes including student learning, grades, and persistence, as well as such intermediary outcomes as student engagement and interactions with faculty. The volume also considers both the costs as well as the benefits that may result from working. Some chapter authors consider the ways that working may promote student learning (e.g., Lewis in chapter 8 and Lynch et al. in chapter 6), while others (e.g., Titus in chapter 12) assume that work and study time may be complements in the process of building human capital.

Fourth, the volume also generates a wide-ranging assessment of the implications of working for students' educational experiences by using a range of methodological approaches and sources of data. The chapters draw on both quantitative and qualitative methods and national, regional, and institutional samples of students. The quantitative analyses identify the relationship between common and readily measured dimensions of working (e.g., number of hours worked) and particular student outcomes, while the qualitative analyses provide depth and insight into the nature of work and the challenges associated with working for today's undergraduates. Whereas the national samples offer broad representation and generalizable findings, regional and institutional samples recognize the potential roles of contextual forces.

Finally, the volume also explicitly recognizes that the experiences of traditional-age undergraduates who work part time at on-campus jobs are typically fundamentally different from the experiences of adult students who work full time at jobs off campus. The volume also stresses the importance of recognizing the value and contribution of adult learners to higher education. Several authors explicitly note the problems associated with labeling this group "nontraditional" (e.g., Lynch et al. in chapter 6 and Rowan-Keyon et al. in chapter 5). Lynch and colleagues argue that "nontraditional" is not only pejorative but also inappropriate, given the high representation of this group in higher education. Lynch and colleagues also contend that "nontraditional" may be a red herring that allows higher education institutions to avoid considering changes that can meet the needs of this population, including changes in course offerings, course scheduling, financial aid, and pedagogy. Although the label *nontraditional* is occasionally used in the volume, the reader is urged to recognize the problematic nature of this label.

Organization of the Volume

These strategies are evident throughout this volume's chapters, which are organized to reflect attention to the following five dimensions of college student employment: (1) work as a form of student financial aid, (2) work as a component of student identity, (3) work as a vehicle for promoting students' cognitive development and learning, (4) work as a vehicle for improving student engagement, and (5) work as a vehicle for improving educational and economic attainment.

The first section explores work as a form of student financial aid. In the first chapter, Sandy Baum examines work-study as a component of the federal student aid system, the impact of student earnings on financial aid awards for both dependent and independent students, and the tension between work that is considered financial aid and work that is not. The chapter identifies the challenges of the Federal Work-Study Program from the perspective of students, including the relatively small number of students who receive work-study awards, the relatively low average earnings of recipients, and the disproportionate targeting of work-study aid to students attending private nonprofit four-year institutions. The chapter argues that work-study awards should not be considered "aid" because students must work to earn these dollars and because work-study awards reduce students' eligibility for aid in the form of grants.

The next four chapters of the volume include attention to a second dimension of work: work as one of a student's many identities. Attention to multiple identities is especially important for understanding the experiences of adult learners. To recognize the multiple identities of adult workers who are also undergraduate students, Carol Kasworm offers the Adult Undergraduate Student Identity model. This conceptual framework assumes that adult workers engage in education through adult worker identity and student identity and act based on complex beliefs and understandings that are coconstructed through their lives, roles, identity anchors, and interactions with their various worlds. Drawing on her own and others' prior research, Kasworm argues that, although important, participation in higher education is only one of four to six competing life identity roles for adult students because many also have substantial roles and responsibilities pertaining to work, family, and community. The chapter suggests that the "life meaning identity anchors" of adult undergraduates influence their understandings and actions toward collegiate participation, engagement in learning, and sense of place and identity vis-à-vis student roles. The chapter also explores the different cultural contexts of collegiate and workplace environments to identify the characteristics and policies that may influence adult working students' participation and persistence.

Recognizing the high representation of adults among community college students, the next chapter explores how community colleges can support the development of working students' identities. Drawing on organizational and culture theory, authors John Levin, Virginia Montero-Hernandez, and Christine Cerven argue that, by offering sustained support and encouraging interactions that promote the acquisition of new resources, skills, and perspectives, community colleges can help students develop their identities as well as achieve social mobility and educational attainment. Levin and colleagues use quantitative data from national, state, and institutional sources and qualitative data from various community colleges to describe working community college students' patterns of enrollment and attendance, goals, social interactions, sources of support, academic engagement, and outcomes. The chapter also examines the programs, curriculum structures, student services, organizational resources, and policy frameworks that enable community colleges to develop (or not) behaviors that are responsive to working students' needs. The chapter concludes by identifying what community colleges are doing to address working students' needs and what new understandings and strategies of action can be developed to create colleges that not only are flexible and responsive but also provide social justice on the basis of students' personal conditions.

Adult students also represent a sizeable percentage of students at many four-year colleges and universities—particularly less-selective and "commuter" campuses. In chapter 4, Mary Ziskin, Vasti Torres, Don Hossler, and Jacob Gross describe the multiple roles and demands facing working students attending three commuter colleges in one metropolitan region. Drawing on rich qualitative data collected from focus groups and interviews with more than 90 working students at these three institutions, their analyses paint a compelling picture of the variety and intensity of students' daily work and family obligations; the strategies students use to balance work, family, and college; and the ways that these students believe they are connected (or not) to their campuses. The chapter also explores how the demands of college, work, and family influence the academic success of mobile working students. The findings provide a foundation for developing institutional policies and practices that are based on the experiences and enrollment patterns of adult workers who are also students.

In the final chapter in this section, Heather Rowan-Kenyon, Amy Swan, Nancy Deutsch, and Bruce Gansneder use mixed methods to examine the academic experiences of adult working students. The quantitative analyses draw on data from more than a thousand students collected as part of the 2007 National Study on Non-Traditional Students to identify differences in the characteristics of adult students based on employment status (i.e., full time, part time, none) and the predictors of academic performance for adult students who work full time, part time, or not at all. The qualitative analyses draw on data from focus groups conducted at multiple institutions to examine the barriers to academic success facing adult students who work. The results illustrate differences in the academic experiences of adult students based on employment status and shed light on the ways that challenges related to time and money limit academic success for adult students. The chapter concludes by offering recommendations for policymakers and practitioners for supporting adult working students.

The third section of this volume considers work as a vehicle for promoting students' cognitive development and learning. In the first chapter in this section, Doug Lynch, Michael Gottfried, Wendy Green, and Chris Thomas propose that work should be conceptualized as a force that contributes to learning especially for adult undergraduate students. The chapter uses data on students, employers, and institutions; theoretical constructs from adult learning theory; and research on peer effects to propose an alternative economic model of education production. The authors argue that a traditional educational production function fails to recognize the ways that educational inputs (and the relative weights assigned to various inputs) may vary between traditional and adult students. Because of differences in workplace and life experience, traditional and adult students may differ in terms of their learning "endowments," needs, and goals. The chapter presents three hypothetical scenarios to illustrate how workplace and life experience may alter the education production function—and thus the postsecondary education decisions and outcomes—of adult students.

In chapter 7, Brian Pusser argues that, by limiting time for engagement in educational activities, working for pay is often viewed as being in conflict with the intellectual goals of higher education. Pusser draws on social and political theories, research on student engagement and institutional transformation, and qualitative data collected from a longitudinal study of adult learners to reconceptualize how work influences the lives of undergraduate students. The chapter argues that understanding why undergraduates work, the type of work students do (both on and off campus), and institutional incentives and disincentives for work is required to identify how colleges and universities may transform student employment into an endeavor that not only pays the price of attending college but also promotes students' intellectual development.

In the last chapter in this section, Jonathan Lewis encourages campus administrators to consider the ways that on-campus employment may be intentionally constructed so as to promote student learning. Lewis argues that students who work likely engage with many experiences, tasks, and processes while on the job that may be constructed not only to achieve organizational performance goals but also promote student learning. Drawing on data collected from a study of student employees at Northwestern University's college union, the chapter identifies workplace experiences that correlate with important learning outcomes, including career development, leadership, civic and community engagement, ethics and values, and responsible independence. Lewis concludes by recommending that employment supervisors include such practices as collaboration, peer feedback, informal supervisor interactions, and intuitive decision making in their student employment programs.

The next section explores a fourth dimension of work: work as a vehicle for improving student engagement. In their chapter, Alexander McCormick, John Moore, and George Kuh examine the assumption that working for pay—particularly working full time or off campus—may reduce both the time students can devote to their academic work, as well as their ability to participate in educational practices that are related to positive learning outcomes. Examples of effective practices that may be less available to working students include collaborations with other students outside of class, substantive interactions with students and faculty members, community-based experiences such as service-learning and internships, and study abroad. Heavy work commitments may also affect students' access to cocurricular offerings. Using descriptive and multilevel analyses of data from the National Survey of Student Engagement, the chapter examines how employment affects engagement and success for undergraduate students attending four-year colleges and universities. The results show that working both on and off campus is positively related to engagement, as measured by benchmarks of effective educational practice. The relationship is stronger for full-time than part-time students and the benefits are generally greater for on- rather than off-campus employment. The analyses also suggest that the relationship between employment and educational outcomes (e.g., self-reported gains, grade point average) is mediated by student engagement.

In the second chapter in this section, Lamont Flowers examines the relationship between working during college and engagement for African American students. Using descriptive and regression analyses of data from the National Survey of Student Engagement, this chapter examines the relationship between the number of hours spent working on and off campus and various academic engagement and educational outcomes. Taking into account individual and institutional variables, the results show that, for African American undergraduates, working on campus is positively related to engagement in the experiences that enhance students' intellectual growth in college. Although not to the same degree as working on campus, the findings also suggest that working off campus is positively related to African American students' engagement.

Also assuming the importance of student engagement in effective educational practices, Paul Umbach, Ryan Padgett, and Ernest Pascarella focus more specifically on the effects of employment on full-time students' interactions with faculty, perceptions of faculty interest in teaching and student development, participation in active classroom environments, and beliefs about teaching quality. The chapter uses regression analyses of data from the Wabash National Study of Liberal Arts Education (WNSLAE), a large longitudinal study examining the effects of liberal arts experiences on cognitive and personal outcomes. The results provide insights for understanding how working influences students' experiences with faculty and participation in effective instructional strategies. The chapter offers practical implications for faculty instruction, including how faculty may better promote learning for working students.

The final dimension of work that is considered in this volume is work as a vehicle for improving students' educational and economic attainment. In chapter 12, Marvin Titus examines the relationship between working while in college and both degree completion and salaries for undergraduates attending four-year colleges and universities. The chapter is informed by labor economics and retention theory and uses quantitative analyses of national data from the 2001 follow-up of the 1996 Beginning Postsecondary Students (BPS:96/01) survey. Using instrumental variable regression to address the endogenous nature of employment, Titus identifies a trade-off: After controlling for other variables, working more hours is associated with lower rates of bachelor's degree completion but higher average salaries. Moreover, although completing a bachelor's degree is positively related to salary, the economic payoff for working is greater than the payoff for bachelor's degree completion.

Finally, I conclude by summarizing the volume and offering recommendations. This final chapter describes the central findings and themes that cut across the volume. This final chapter also builds on the findings of the chapters to offer recommendations for public and institutional policy and practice, as well as future research.

References

Advisory Committee on Student Financial Assistance. (2006). *Mortgaging our future: How financial barriers to college undercut America's global competitiveness.* Washington, DC: Author.

Baum, S. (2005). *Financial barriers to college access and persistence: The current status of student reliance on grants, loans, and work.* Paper prepared for the Advisory Committee on Student Financial Assistance, Washington, DC.

Baum, S., & Ma, J. (2007). *Education pays.* Washington, DC: College Board.

Bowen, H. R. (1997). *Investment in learning: The individual and social value of American higher education* (2nd ed.). Baltimore: Johns Hopkins University Press.

Carnevale, A. P., & Desrochers, D. M. (2003). *Standards for what? The economic roots of K–16 reform.* Princeton, NJ: Educational Testing Service.

College Board. (2008a). *Trends in college pricing.* Washington, DC: Author.

College Board. (2008b). *Trends in student aid.* Washington, DC: Author.

Council for Adult and Experiential Learning. (2008). *Adult learning in focus: National and state-by-state data.* Retrieved February 24, 2009, from www.cael.org/pdf/publication_pdf/State_Indicators_Monograph.pdf

Donaldson, J. F., & Graham, S. (1999). A model of college outcomes for adults. *Adult Education Quarterly, 50*(1), 24–40.

Horn, L. (1996). *Nontraditional undergraduates: Trends in enrollment from 1986 to 1992 and persistence and attainment among 1989–90 beginning postsecondary students* (NCES 97–578). Washington, DC: National Center for Education Statistics.

King, J. E. (2002). *Crucial choices: How students' financial decisions affect their academic success.* Washington, DC: American Council on Education.

Kuh, G., Kinzie, J., Bridges, B. K., & Hayek, J. C. (2006). *What matters to student success: A review of the literature.* Washington, DC: National Postsecondary Education Cooperative.

Lumina Foundation for Education. (2009). Our goal. Retrieved January 23, 2009, from www.luminafoundation.org

National Center for Public Policy and Higher Education. (2008). *Measuring up 2008.* San Jose, CA: Author.

Organisation for Economic Co-operation and Development. (2006). *Education at a glance 2006.* Retrieved September 25, 2009, from www.oecd.org/dataoecd/51/20/37392850.pdf

Pascarella, E. T., & Terenzini, P. T. (2005). *How college affects students, volume 2: A third decade of research.* San Francisco, CA: Jossey-Bass.

Paulsen, M. B. (2001). The economics of the public sector: The nature and role of public policy in the finance of higher education. In M. B. Paulsen and J. C. Smart (Eds.), *The finance of higher education: Theory, research, policy, and practice* (pp. 95–132). New York: Agathon Press.

Perna, L. W., Cooper, M., & Li, C. (2007). Improving educational opportunities for students who work. E. P. St. John (Ed.), *Readings on equal education,22,* 109–160.

St. John, E. P. (2008). Financial inequality and academic success: Rethinking the foundations of research on college students. In E. P. St. John and W. T. Trent (Eds.), *Resources, assets, and strengths among successful diverse students: Understanding the contributions of the Gates Millennium Scholars program* (pp. 201–228). Brooklyn, NY: AMS Press.

State Higher Education Executive Officers. (2008, October). Second to none in attainment, discovery, and innovation: The national agenda for higher education. *Change,40*(5), 16–23.

Stern, D., Nakata, Y. F. (1991). Paid employment among U.S. college students: Trends, effects, and possible causes. *Journal of Higher Education, 62,* 25–43.

Stinebrickner, R., & Stinebrickner, T. R. (2004). Time-use and college outcomes. *Journal of Econometrics, 121*(1/2), 243–269.

Stringer, W. L., Cunningham, A. F., O'Brien, C. T., & Merisotis, J. (1998). *It's all relative: The role of parents in college financing and enrollment.* Indianapolis, IN: Lumina Foundation for Education, New Agenda Series.

Swail, W. S., with Redd, K., & Perna, L.W. (2003). Retaining minority students in higher education: A framework for success. *ASHE-ERIC Higher Education Report, 30*(2).

Tinto, V. (1993). *Leaving college: Rethinking the causes and cures of student attrition* (2nd ed.). Chicago: University of Chicago Press.

Turner, J. K., & Pusser, B. (2007). Advancing leadership as a public good: The challenge of postsecondary selectivity in Virginia. In S. Marginson (Ed.), *Prospects of higher education: Globalization, market competition, public goods and the future of the university.* Rotterdam: Sense Publishers.

U.S. Department of Education. (2008a). *Condition of education.* Washington, DC: Author.

U.S. Department of Education. (2008b). *Digest of education statistics.* Washington, DC: Author.

SECTION ONE

WORK AS A FORM OF FINANCIAL AID

I

STUDENT WORK AND THE FINANCIAL AID SYSTEM

Sandy Baum

As noted in this volume's introduction, almost half of all full-time undergraduates and 81% of part-time undergraduates are employed while enrolled in college (U.S. Department of Education, 2008). Students may work to meet their tuition and fee charges, to pay for basic living costs, to increase their available spending money, or to gain employment experience. As the price of college increases more rapidly than incomes, more students are certain to find work a necessity rather than a choice. Other chapters in this volume address the implications of student employment for academic success and persistence. The focus here is on the relationship between student aid and student work and, in particular, the role of the Federal Work-Study Program in increasing students' ability to pay for college.

The distinction between work-study jobs that are allocated through the financial aid system and other student employment is frequently neglected in discussion of the pros and cons of term-time employment. From a student's perspective, the hours worked, the nature and location of the work, and the wages are the critical factors. If working in certain types of jobs enhances the college experience, this is likely to be the case whether or not the job falls under work-study. The fact that work-study jobs are partially funded by the government matters quite a bit to the institution, but not at all to the student. Similarly, if workplace demands interfere with academic success, it is likely to be the number of hours devoted to employment, not the source of the funding, that is relevant. What does matter to the student—although surely few students understand this reality—is that earnings from work-study jobs and earnings from other employment are treated very differently by the financial aid system.

This chapter begins with an overview of student work patterns and then provides a history of the Federal Work-Study (FWS) Program, as well as information on the distribution of these funds. This is followed by a discussion of the relationship between student earnings and financial aid eligibility. The conclusion makes suggestions for improvements in the way student work is incorporated into the student aid system. These perspectives are important for both government and institutional policymakers.

Who Works and How Much Do They Work?

The image of college students washing dishes or driving taxis to put themselves through school has long been part of the legend associated with the American dream. Among some segments of the current generation, shelving books in the library or working at the Gap puts gas in the car or permits more frequent nights out. But for a sizeable fraction of today's college students, long hours of work are the only option for paying the tuition bill. A $4,731 Pell Grant, a $5,500 Stafford Loan, and perhaps another $2,000 in state grant aid frequently does not add up to the total cost of attendance for students whose families do not have the resources to contribute to their support. In other words, many students face what has come to be known as "unmet need" and are forced to work to meet their tuition bills.[1]

In the absence of sufficient grant aid, students who do not have family financial support can enroll part time, diminishing the chances that they will complete their degrees; they can attempt to supplement their federal loans by borrowing large amounts of money through relatively expensive private lenders; or they can work excessive hours. Or, of course, they can give up on higher education altogether because it is not affordable.

As indicated in Table 1 and mentioned in the introduction to this volume, 46.5% of full-time, traditional-age college students were employed in

TABLE 1
Work Patterns of Full-Time College Students Ages 16 to 24

| | Full-Time College Students | | |
| | | Hours per Week Worked | |
	Employed (%)	= 20 (%)	= 35 (%)
1976	37.6	16.9	4.1
1986	43.1	21.9	4.3
1996	49.2	29.3	7.0
2006	46.5	30.1	8.1

Source: U.S. Department of Education (2008). *Condition of education* (Indicator 43–2008). Washington, DC: National Center for Education Statistics

2006. Thirty percent worked 20 or more hours per week, and 8% worked 35 or more hours per week. The proportion employed rose steadily through the 1970s, 1980s, and 1990s, peaking at 52% in 2000, and has declined slightly since then. However, the proportion working more than 20 hours per week and 35 hours or more per week has continued to increase (U.S. Department of Education, 2008). Whatever the merits of work and self-sufficiency, it is clear that spending so much time and energy in the labor force diminishes the time and energy these students can devote to their studies.

A more detailed look at patterns of work among students does not reveal consistent differences according to financial status. As indicated in Table 2,

TABLE 2
Work Patterns by Student Characteristics, 2003–2004
(Including Work-Study and Other Employment)

	Did Not Work (%)	Worked, by Average Hours per Week (%)			
		1 to 20 hours	21 to 34 Hours	35 or More Hours	Total
All Undergraduates	22	26	18	34	78
Dependent	25	36	22	18	75
Independent	20	16	13	50	80
Age					
22 or younger	25	35	21	19	75
23 to 24	18	24	21	38	82
25 to 29	18	17	15	51	82
30 or older	22	13	10	55	79
Dependent Students:					
Parental Income					
Less than $30,000	25	34	21	20	75
$30,000 to $59,999	21	36	23	19	79
$60,000 to $89,999	22	38	22	18	78
$90,000 or more	30	38	19	14	70
Attendance Status					
Exclusively full time	27	33	18	23	73
Mixed full time and part time	21	30	22	28	79
Exclusively part time	17	15	15	53	84

Source: American Council on Education (2006). *Working their way through college.* Washington, DC: Author

students older than age 22 are much more likely to work than younger students are, although a smaller proportion of those 30 or older than of those between the ages of 23 and 29 were employed in 2003–2004. Among dependent students, 70% of those with parent income $90,000 or higher worked, compared to 75% overall. The highest rates of employment, however, were among those from families with incomes between $30,000 and $90,000, rather than among those with incomes below $30,000 (American Council on Education, 2006).

Number of hours per week worked may actually be more relevant than the basic information about whether or not a student works in terms of the impact on the student experience. Notably, 50% of independent students reported working 35 hours per week or more in 2003–2004, while only 18% of dependent students were employed full time. About 23% of full-time undergraduates were employed full time compared to 53% of part-time students (American Council on Education, 2006).

Discussions of the distinction between work-study and student employment more generally can be put into better context when the proportion of working students whose employment comes through the financial aid system is clear. As reported in Table 3, in 2003–2004, 90% of all working students— and 86% of those who consider themselves primarily students—held jobs that did not come through the student aid system. Only 5% of all working students and 7% of those who considered themselves students relied on work-study as their sole employment. It is clear that if work-study makes an important contribution to students' college experiences, a much larger program would be required to make a meaningful difference. The vast majority of students who are employed work off campus for for-profit companies. Less than a third of those who consider themselves students first have jobs that are related to their majors. The findings in Table 3 are not surprising when viewed in the context of the information on the funding levels and numbers of participants in the Federal Work-Study (FWS) Program reported in the following section.

Federal Work-Study: Origins, Regulations, and Funding Levels

Federal Work-Study (FWS) has been part of the federal student aid system for as long as any of the current components have existed. FWS was created by the Economic Opportunity Act in 1964, along with Job Corps, VISTA, and other programs designed to increase employment opportunities and reduce poverty in the United States. Although it was soon integrated into the federal student aid system developed by the Higher Education Act that

TABLE 3
TYPES OF STUDENT WORK, 2003–2004

Characteristic	Employees Who Study (%)	Students Who Work (%)	All Working Students (%)
Type of Job			
Regular job	98	86	90
Work-study or assistantship	0	7	5
Both regular job and work-study/assistantship	2	7	5
Type of Employer			
College or university attended	3	10	7
For-profit company	55	68	63
Nonprofit organization	16	10	12
Government or military	21	7	12
Self-employed	5	6	6
Location of Job			
On campus	3	9	7
Off campus	97	88	91
Both on and off campus	1	3	2
Job Related to Major	54	31	39

Source: American Council on Education (2006). *Working their way through college.* Washington, DC: Author

was signed into law the following year, the initial intent of FWS was to generate employment opportunities for low-income students. This purpose contrasts with other financial aid programs, which are specifically designed to provide funds to supplement those that students and their families contribute from earnings and savings.

Some states have developed work-study programs to supplement the federal program. For example, in Washington, about $20 million in state money funds about 10,000 students in campus jobs, with awards ranging from about $2,000 to $5,000—much higher than individual federal work-study awards (Washington Higher Education Coordinating Board, 2008). The program is designed to pay wages similar to those of other workers and to provide jobs related to students' career interests. Other examples include Pennsylvania, where the work-study program offers financial aid recipients jobs in high-tech and community service fields, both during the academic term and during the summer (Pennsylvania Higher Education Assistance Agency, 2008). Minnesota's state work-study funds, packaged to help meet students' financial need, allowed about 12,000 students to earn an average of $1,200 in 2007 (Minnesota Office of Higher Education, 2008).

As is the case for the entire federal student aid system, FWS is subject to an elaborate set of government rules and regulations. One of these is the so-called over-award rule. According to federal directives, institutions must ensure that grant aid, education loans, and FWS earnings do not add up to more than the gap between Expected Family Contribution (EFC) and cost of attendance. Although from a student's perspective the earnings from a work-study job are the result of an effort indistinguishable from the effort involved in off-campus employment, these earnings are viewed by the government and the institution as an aid "award."

Federal Work-Study is part of the campus-based federal aid system. This set of programs, which includes Federal Supplemental Educational Opportunity Grants (FSEOG) and Perkins loans, in addition to FWS, requires that institutions provide matching funds. Institutions must provide at least 25% of the wages paid to students in on-campus and community services jobs, and at least 50% of the wages paid to students in jobs in the for-profit sector, which must be related to their academic pursuits. Another requirement is that at least 7% of each institution's FWS funds be used to support community service employment.

Table 4 shows the amounts of FWS awarded each academic year from 1970–1971 through 2007–2008, all in constant 2007 dollars. Notably, there has not been an increase in these funds over time. The 1971–1972 funding exceeded the 2007–2008 funding by 39%, after adjusting for inflation. The peak funding year was 1979–1980 and the lowest funding year was 1996–1997. As of 2007–2008, about 12% of these funds go to graduate students (College Board, 2008).

To the extent that FWS creates important opportunities for students, it does so for a very small number of students. With no real increase in funding, the FWS program has not been able to serve increasing numbers of students over time. As indicated in Table 5, 819,000 students received Federal Work-Study subsidies in 1980–1981. That number had declined to 687,000 a decade later and in 2007–2008 was still only 792,000.

The number of Pell Grant recipients increased from 2.7 million in 1980–1981 to 3.4 million a decade later and 5.4 million in 2007–2008 (College Board, 2008). Because the number of Pell Grant recipients has increased rapidly while the number of FWS recipients has been stagnant, FWS serves fewer and fewer of its core constituency. The number of FWS recipients declined from 30% of the number of Pell Grant recipients in 1980–1981 to 20% in 1990–1991 and 15% in 2007–2008. Many students are eligible for Federal Work-Study but not for Pell Grants, so the proportion of Pell Grant recipients receiving FWS is even smaller than these figures suggest. Overall, about 4% of all postsecondary students benefit from the

TABLE 4
Federal Work-Study Funds Awarded, 1970–1971 to 2007–2008
(in constant 2007 dollars)

Academic Year	FWS Funds in Millions of 2007 Dollars	Relative to 2007	Academic Year	FWS Funds in Millions of 2007 Dollars	Relative to 2007
70–71	$1,070	0.91	89–90	$1,111	0.95
71–72	$1,631	1.39	90–91	$1,163	0.99
72–73	$1,320	1.13	91–92	$1,162	0.99
73–74	$1,392	1.19	92–93	$1,156	0.99
74–75	$1,244	1.06	93–94	$1,113	0.95
75–76	$1,134	0.97	94–95	$1,063	0.91
76–77	$1,591	1.36	95–96	$1,043	0.89
77–78	$1,602	1.37	96–97	$1,030	0.88
78–79	$1,549	1.32	97–98	$1,176	1.00
79–80	$1,714	1.46	98–99	$1,166	1.00
80–81	$1,663	1.42	99–00	$1,146	0.98
81–82	$1,419	1.21	00–01	$1,132	0.97
82–83	$1,314	1.12	01–02	$1,211	1.03
83–84	$1,425	1.22	02–03	$1,269	1.08
84–85	$1,291	1.10	03–04	$1,253	1.07
85–86	$1,268	1.08	04–05	$1,190	1.02
86–87	$1,197	1.02	05–06	$1,120	0.96
87–88	$1,162	0.99	06–07	$1,067	0.91
88–89	$1,099	0.94	07–08	$1,171	1.00

Source: College Board (2008). *Trends in student aid.* Washington, DC: Author

FWS program. These numbers are critical for evaluating the effectiveness of the Federal Work-Study Program. The reality is that, although the funds may be very important to the institutions where they are concentrated and to individual recipients, the scale of the program makes it impossible for this program, as currently structured and funded, to make a major difference in how students finance their postsecondary education. As the figures in Table 3 confirm, FWS accounts for an extremely small proportion of college student employment.

The limited funding for Federal Work-Study has also prevented the relatively small number of participants from receiving higher earnings from the program. Average earnings per recipient declined from $2,030 in 2007 dollars in 1980–1981, to $1,691 in 1990–1991, $1,588 in 2000–2001, and $1,479 in 2007–2008. Given the rapid increase in tuition, fees, room, and board

TABLE 5
Federal Work-Study Recipients and Funds, 1980–1981 to 2007–2008

	1980–1981	1985–1986	1990–1991	1995–1996	2000–2001	2005–2006	2007–2008
FWS Recipients (000's)	819	728	687	702	713	711	792
Pell Grant Recipients (000's)	2,708	2,813	3,405	3,612	3,899	5,168	5,428
FWS Recipients / Pell Recipients (%)	30	26	20	19	18	14	15
Total Fall Enrollment (000's)	12,097	12,247	13,819	14,262	15,312	17,487	n/a
Total Dollars Awarded (millions of 2007 dollars)	$660	$656	$728	$764	$939	$1,050	$1,171
Aid per Recipient (current dollars)	$806	$901	$1,059	$1,087	$1,318	$1,478	$1,479
Aid per Recipient (constant 2007 dollar)	$2,030	$1,740	$1,691	$1,485	$1,588	$1,575	$1,479

Source: College Board (2008). *Trends in student aid.* Washington, DC: Author; U.S. Department of Education (2007). *Digest of education statistics.* Washington, DC: National Center for Education Statistics

over this period of time, it is clear that FWS plays a diminishing role in helping students finance their postsecondary education.

In addition to stagnant funding levels, the effectiveness of the Federal Work-Study Program is limited by the allocation formula that applies to all federal campus-based aid. Like Perkins loans and Supplemental Educational Opportunity Grants (FSEOG), FWS funds are distributed according to a complicated and controversial formula to campuses that apply for funds. The amount of funding available to an individual institution depends both on its historical levels of funding and the levels of financial need of enrolled students.

There is a base guarantee amount that depends on the share of funds an institution has received in the past. If additional funds are appropriated, this is supplemented by a "fair share" amount that depends on the amount of financial need the institution's students have (Smole, 2005). Need is influenced, but not directly determined, by financial circumstances. Defined as the difference between the cost of attendance and Expected Family Contribution (EFC), need may rise either because ability to pay declines or because the price of the institution increases. Students from families with relatively high incomes may have need at high-priced institutions, while those from much less affluent families have no measured need because they attend lower-priced institutions. The allocation formula directs more funds to higher-priced, longer-established institutions.

The current allocation formula is inequitable because growing schools cannot increase their funding and other institutions' funding levels are largely protected. The results of the allocation formula are starkly visible in the contrast between the distribution of campus-based funds—including FSEOG and Perkins loans as well as Federal Work-Study—and the distribution of total full-time equivalent enrollments, described in Table 6. Community colleges, which account for 28% of enrollments and disproportionately enroll low-income students, receive only 9% of campus-based funds. Not-for-profit private colleges account for 22% of total enrollments but receive 46% of campus-based funds. It seems clear that if work-study funds are the solution to employment opportunities for low-income students, the current system is not accomplishing its goals.

Student financial aid packages include FWS jobs as one component of the funding intended to meet financial need and make college enrollment possible. The Federal Methodology for determining financial need does not take these earnings into account. In contrast, earnings from other forms of employment, which are not part of the financial aid system, can diminish future eligibility for student aid.

Although work-study earnings have the advantage of not reducing eligibility for student aid the following year, considering earnings part of the student aid package has the problem of making it impossible for students to use

TABLE 6
Distribution of Campus-Based Aid and Enrollments by Sector, 2005–2006

Institutional Sector	*Percentage of Campus-Based Aid (%)*	*Percentage of Total FTEs (%)*
Public Two-Year	9	28
Public Four-year	39	43
Private Not-for-Profit	46	22
For-Profit	6	7

Note: Campus-based aid includes Federal Work-Study, Federal Supplemental Educational Opportunity Grants (FSEOG), and Perkins loans.
Source: College Board (2008). *Trends in student aid.* Washington, DC: Author

these funds to meet their expected contributions or to augment their budgets beyond the bare-bones amounts allowed in the cost of attendance. The following sections address the relationship between student work and student aid.

Impact of Student Earnings on Aid Eligibility

For students who depend on their earnings to supplement parent contributions and student aid, the existing need analysis system may create significant hardships. Congress requires that all federal student aid be allocated based on the Federal Methodology (FM), and most states and institutions follow similar approaches to distribute their own funds. Under FM, a dependent student with (non-work-study) earnings can subtract taxes paid and, in 2008–2009, a $3,080 allowance from total income. Students who earn more than this excluded amount see their expected contributions rise by 50 cents for every extra dollar of income. The logic behind this high "tax" rate on student earnings is that paying for education should be the primary claim on student earnings.

This approach is problematic for a number of reasons and federal policy would be more equitable and efficient if the work penalty were eliminated. Financial aid professionals on college campuses cannot change these rules themselves but should consider carefully how students may be affected by them. Undergraduate students whose earnings exceed $3,080 per year are generally students who have a compelling need to work.[2] Few of these dependent students (all of whom are under the age of 24) have the opportunity to earn high hourly wages. Child actors aside, these are young people who are dedicating many hours to the labor force to supplement family incomes or to accumulate savings because they cannot rely on their parents to support them while they are in school. The idea that these earnings may eliminate their eligibility for federal student aid means that they are fighting a losing battle. The more they work to meet expenses, the less financial aid they get.

High marginal tax rates change the payoff to work and therefore create disincentives. A student who is willing to give up an hour of study time or leisure time to earn $10 (after taxes) has to consider whether she is willing to give up that time to increase her disposable income by $5 because the student aid system takes $5 of the earnings in the form of decreased federal aid eligibility. Although most students may not be familiar with the details of the formula used to determine their financial need, many understand the basic approach. In any case, assuming that students will not realize that additional earnings decrease their aid is not a sound basis for policy.

Responses to this tax on earnings could potentially work in two opposing directions. On one hand, work may be much less appealing when it increases disposable income by only half of the wage rate. Some students may rationally decide to substitute leisure (or study time) for work because the price of that extra time has diminished. If this occurs, they will reduce their hours worked. On the other hand, those students most in need of funds—those whose families require their support or who have other obligations—may need to increase their work time to maintain their incomes in the face of the high tax rate imposed by the student aid system. Economists call this the *income effect*. This effect generates upward pressure on work hours when the hourly wage falls, while the *substitution effect* leads people to work less when the hourly wage falls because the price of alternative activities is lower.

It is the net effect of these two forces that determines whether students work more hours or fewer hours as a result of the 50% tax rate on student earnings in the need analysis methodology. These effects are likely to have different relative strengths in students with different characteristics. Although empirical evidence would be required to support this hypothesis, it is quite logical that the students for whom the income effect is strongest are likely to be those with the most meager financial resources. If they need extra money to eat or to buy books, they will work more. If earnings are devoted to extra pizzas or gas money, the work disincentive may be stronger. To understand the true significance of these differential effects, it is necessary to analyze the impact of extra work time on academic success. Other chapters in this volume examine the available evidence on this issue.

The idea that students who have higher earnings can afford to contribute more to their own education than those with lower earnings may sound equitable at first, but in fact, this provision quite clearly discriminates against students with more limited resources. Given the relatively low variation in the wage rates available to part-time undergraduates, the idea that the less affluent and/or more diligent should receive less financial aid than those for whom work is discretionary is difficult to justify.

The need analysis methodology separates dependent students, whose parents have primary responsibility for financing their education, from independent students, who are expected to support themselves. Independent students who have dependents (other than a spouse) are treated much more generously than those who do not. The incomes of independent students with dependents are treated similarly to the incomes of the parents of dependent students. In 2008–2009, an independent student with one dependent can earn $15,750 after taxes before being expected to contribute to the cost of education from earnings. A larger amount of earnings is protected for these students than for those without dependents, and tax rates on additional earnings are lower than 50%.

Independent students without dependents, on the other hand, face the same 50% tax rate on earnings that confronts dependent students. In 2008–2009, $6,220 of independent student earnings are protected before the 50% tax rate takes effect. In other words, a student who worked for a year and then applied for financial aid to begin full-time enrollment would be eligible for the maximum Pell Grants only if his or her earnings the previous year were below this protected amount. A student would become ineligible for Pell altogether with earnings of about $16,000 after tax. It is difficult to imagine that the student who earned $16,000 after taxes last year was able to set aside money in anticipation of enrolling in college. The expectation that he will maintain these earnings while in school without working full time is unrealistic.

The heavy reliance on past earnings in the need analysis system is quite problematic. The reality is that it is rare for students who have been working before they enroll to be able to maintain their earnings while in school without interfering with academic success. Moreover, many of those who have had minimal earnings have relied on family resources. It is frequently those with the least amount of family financial strength who have been most committed to the labor force. Those from the lowest-income backgrounds may, therefore, have the most to lose from this work penalty inherent in the need analysis methodology.

Some indication of the relationship between student work and grant eligibility can be seen by comparing the Pell Grant funds received by students with similar incomes but different work patterns. For independent students, this exercise is not feasible because student incomes are a direct function of student work. However, for dependent students, Pell Grant eligibility depends on parent income as well as student income. It is possible to compare the Pell Grants received by students who do not work to those received by students from families with similar incomes who do work. (See Table 7.)

TABLE 7
Pell Grant Awards by Family Income and Work Pattern (Excluding Work-Study) for Dependent Students, 2003–2004

Family Income	Percentage Receiving Pell			Pell per Student (including nonrecipients)		
	No Work	1–10 Hours	> 10 Hours	No Work	1–10 Hours	> 10 Hours
Dependent: Less than $10,000	74	73	68	$2,793	$2,802	$2,586
Dependent: $10,000–$19,999	76	61	74	$2,844	$2,207	$2,653
Dependent: $20,000–$29,999	77	68	70	$2,507	$2,159	$2,083
Dependent: $30,000–$39,999	61	50	46	$1,367	$1,069	$970
Dependent: $40,000–$49,999	36	32	24	$597	$515	$402
Dependent: $50,000–$59,999	15	12	9	$213	$197	$120

Source: U.S. Department of Education (2004). *National postsecondary student aid study, 2003–04.* Washington, DC: National Center for Education Statistics

At all income levels, students who did not work at all outside the work-study program were more likely to receive Pell Grants than those who did. Of course, some of the students who received Pell and are reported here as not working had work-study jobs. However, because a very small proportion of Pell Grant recipients receive work-study, this phenomenon is not likely to explain the entire difference. Average Pell Grant dollars per student were lower for students at every income level who worked more than 10 hours a week at standard employment than for those who did not work at all. The largest differences were for those from families with incomes between $20,000 and $40,000 per year, where Pell dollars per student (including both recipients and nonrecipients) were about $400 more for those who did not work than for those who worked more than 10 hours per week. These differences are at least partially attributable to the negative impact of student earnings on Pell eligibility.

With the exception of those facing unusual circumstances, all students should be expected to contribute to their educational costs with some contribution from term-time and summer earnings. An improved need analysis system would standardize expected contributions from student earnings during the years of enrollment and include no marginal assessment of additional earnings, at least for dependent students. Students might reasonably be expected to work 10 to 15 hours a week while in school, in addition to summer employment. But their financial aid should not be decreased if they are more successful in meeting this expectation.

Should Work-Study Funds Be Used to Meet Financial Need?

The common impression that some amount of term-time employment is good for students is consistent with the widespread sense among financial aid administrators at four-year institutions that Federal Work-Study funding is vital to the success of many of their lower-income students.[3] Although conclusions about the value of on-campus work are frequently stated in terms of the importance of work-study jobs, there have been few efforts to disentangle jobs awarded through the financial aid system from other on-campus jobs. As the data cited earlier confirm, FWS may appear very important for individual students, but it serves a remarkably small proportion of students and accounts for a tiny fraction of the employment that helps students pay for their college education.

One study that does separate work-study from other types of employment is Alon (2005). This analysis corrects for significant methodological problems inherent in many analyses of the impact of financial aid on students and points out the importance of considering not only work-study, but also other campus employment. Alon suggests that positive effects of work-study, as distinct from employment in general, on persistence are likely attributable to the fact that the number of hours a student can work during the year is strictly limited under work-study awards. The implication of this finding is that the benefits of providing on-campus employment would not be diminished by eliminating work-study jobs from financial aid packages.

In a synthesis of the literature on the impact of student aid on persistence, Hossler et al. (2008) write, "Even though more research is needed on college work-study, there is already sufficient evidence to indicate that it is a promising tool for enhancing persistence and that it deserves more institutional and public policy attention" (p. 102). Citing several studies with mixed results, the authors do not address the question of which characteristics of work-study—if any—are most likely to affect persistence, but they do suggest that any positive effect of college work-study is most likely associated with the role of campus jobs in helping students to integrate socially into the college community. They point out that little attention has been paid to the effects of on-campus employment not funded through FWS and speculate that the same positive effects would be present.

Under the existing financial aid system, grants, loans, and work-study are all packaged together as funds that can add up to allow students to pay for their education. According to federal regulations, federal work-study funds must be allocated to students who have measured financial need under the Federal Methodology (FM). As noted previously, total need-based aid, including FWS, cannot add up to more than the difference between the Expected Family Contribution and total cost of attendance. If an institution were to provide grant funds to meet the student's entire measured need, it would not be possible to also include a work-study job. That job could be provided only if grant aid were diminished and the FWS funds replaced those dollars to meet the student's need.

This role for work-study earnings is quite different from the role of earnings from other employment. As explained earlier, the previous year's non-work-study earnings are considered in the need analysis and, beyond the exclusion level, reduce measured need and eligibility for need-based aid. Each dollar of earnings reduces eligibility by 50 cents for dependent students and for independent student without dependents, and by a lower amount for dependent students with dependents.

Prior work-study earnings are excluded in the calculation of need. However, potential work-study earnings are included dollar for dollar in meeting need. In other words, for every dollar of work-study earnings a student is allowed, his eligibility for other forms of need-based aid is diminished by a dollar. The timing of the consideration of earnings is different, but in fact, FWS earnings diminish eligibility for institutional and other nonfederal grant aid and for federal subsidized loans even more than other earnings diminish that eligibility.

From the student's perspective, a work-study award is not really financial aid. It is a job that requires the same effort as any other job. The fact that the government is paying part of the wage is of considerable value to the institution or other employer but is irrelevant from the student's perspective. In essence, the packaging of work aid to meet need places a floor on the amount a student must work to finance even the basic expenditures allowed for in the institutionally defined student budget. If that budget proves inadequate to meet the student's expenses, which for low-income students may well include providing some level of support to parents or other family members not considered legal dependents, the student will either have to turn down the FWS or find a second job compatible with the demands of both the work-study job and academic coursework.

Obviously, eliminating FWS as an acceptable way of meeting financial need would not guarantee that the remaining gap would be met with grant aid. It would, however, make the very real gaps in financial need more obvious. From the student's perspective, a grant reduces the amount she has to pay for education. A loan allows her to postpone payment—and in the case of a government loan, may incorporate a significant subsidy. But earnings from jobs are simply one means of the student financing her own contribution. Certainly, ensuring that earnings opportunities will be available to students, and where possible that those opportunities will be on campus, is of great importance. Jobs that provide valuable labor market experience or that are related to the student's academic pursuits are particularly appealing. But this does not change the fact that earnings are compensation for services rendered, not a subsidy to students. Where finances permit, financial aid offices might do many students a favor by packaging funds other than work-study, leaving students free to supplement their financial aid with earnings from non-FWS employment.

Even affluent students whose parents pay the entire tuition, fees, room, and board for them are likely to find working for extra spending money appealing unless their parents also provide bottomless bank accounts. The difference is that students from families with more limited resources are more likely to be working to pay their tuition bills or to buy their books.

Giving priority for campus jobs to students with financial need is a reasonable approach to guaranteeing employment for those who are most dependent on term-time earnings. Both the convenience of working on campus rather than requiring transportation to another location and the possibility that an on-campus job will facilitate integration into the campus community and/or academic enrichment make this type of employment particularly critical for the students most likely to face barriers, financial or otherwise, to college success. To put these students on more equal footing, they should have priority for campus jobs, but their wages from these jobs should not be considered financial aid. Those on campus whose responsibility is to distribute available work-study funds may be inclined to take federal policies as a given. However, in addition to providing thoughtful advice to students, financial aid professionals have an important role in influencing federal policy by sharing the experiences of their students with representatives in Congress.

Conclusion

Many college students work to help finance their educations. Most of that work is in the form of off-campus jobs. Earnings from these jobs diminish financial aid eligibility. A small number of students have work-study jobs that do not diminish their future aid eligibility but are considered part of their current financial aid in the same way as grants and loans are. Understanding the distinction between work-study as a form of need-based financial aid and on-campus employment is critical both for government policymakers and for those with institutional responsibilities for student aid.

Many campus officials involved in helping students to finance their education think of FWS as a vital part of financial aid packages. Carefully sorting out both the differences between FWS and other campus employment and the pros and cons for students of relying on FWS earnings to meet their need can improve the way students are served. Positive and negative impacts of employment in general, of on-campus employment in particular, and specifically of employment closely related to academic pursuits may be quite distinct. In addition, these effects are separate from the questions of whose funds pay the wages and of how jobs should be allocated. A particularly neglected question is whether or not students are well served by the convention of considering wages earned for a subset of term-time jobs as a component of the aid package designed to make college financially accessible. The treatment of any wages earned in the determination of future eligibility for financial aid may also have very real implications for college access and success.

Unlike grants and loans, which subsidize students or allow them to postpone payment for their education, work allows students to earn the funds they need to help pay their own expenses. It is quite reasonable to consider a moderate amount of student earnings in estimating the amount of assistance needed to make college financially accessible. This reality does not, however, justify the work penalty that exists in the current financial aid system, diminishing aid eligibility for those students who, for whatever reason, participate most intensively in the labor force while they are in school.

Federal subsidy of student employment may make an important contribution to providing opportunities for campus employment, but this subsidy should be viewed as a subsidy to the employer and should not limit the amount of financial aid available to students. From the perspective of students, the source of funding of their wages bears no clear relationship to either the amount of grants and loans for which they are eligible in the year they are employed or to their financial aid the following year.

Endnotes

1. On one level, unmet need is a simple concept. Calculate a student's Expected Family Contribution (EFC) and add it to the financial aid awarded. Any difference between that total and the cost of attendance is unmet need. But we measure unmet need only for enrolled students. Presumably those students for whom the gap is largest are those who do not enroll for financial reasons. Anticipated earnings from FWS would be counted as aid and would diminish unmet need. However, the student has to work to receive these funds—just as she would at any other job.

2. Recent legislation will gradually increase the amount of income protected in the need analysis system through the year 2012.

3. Based on conversations with numerous financial aid professionals.

References

Alon, S. (2005). Model mis-specification in assessing the impact of financial aid on academic outcomes. *Research in Higher Education, 46,* 109–125.

American Council on Education. (2006). *Working their way through college.* Washington, DC: Author.

College Board. (2008). *Trends in student aid.* Washington, DC: Author.

Hossler, D., Ziskin, M., Kim, S., Cekic, O., & Gross, J. (2008). Student aid and its role in encouraging persistence. In S. Baum, M. McPherson, & P. Steele (Eds.), *The effectiveness of student aid policies: What the research tells us.* New York: College Board.

Minnesota Office of Higher Education. (2008). *State work study data.* Retrieved November 8, 2008, from www.ohe.state.mn.us/mPg.cfm?pageID = 535

Pennsylvania Higher Education Assistance Agency. (2008). PHEAA-administered work-study program. Retrieved November 8, 2008, from www.pheaa.org/work study/index.shtml#students

Smole, D. (2005). *The campus-based financial aid programs: A review and analysis of the allocation of funds to institutions and the distribution of aid to students.* Washington, DC: Congressional Research Service. RL32775.

U.S. Department of Education. (2004). *National postsecondary student aid study, 2003–04.* Washington, DC: National Center for Education Statistics.

U.S. Department of Education. (2007). *Digest of education statistics.* Washington, DC: National Center for Education Statistics.

U.S. Department of Education. (2008). *Condition of education.* Washington, DC: National Center for Education Statistics.

Washington Higher Education Coordinating Board. (2008). Washington State work study program. Retrieved November 9, 2008, from www.hecb.wa.gov/financial-aid/sws/swsindex.asp

SECTION TWO

WORK AS A COMPONENT OF STUDENT IDENTITY

2

ADULT WORKERS AS UNDERGRADUATE STUDENTS

Significant Challenges for Higher
Education Policy and Practice

Carol Kasworm

As noted in chapter 1, in American higher education, work is more common among undergraduate students who are adult learners—individuals who are 25 years of age and older—than among traditional-age students. Working adult students are a unique segment within the total undergraduate population, representing approximately 80% of all adult undergraduate students and approximately 60% of all working undergraduates (O'Donnell, 2006; National Center for Education Statistics [NCES], 2008).

Unlike younger undergraduates, adult students come to college at different stages in their lives and often are driven by broader forces such as global workforce turbulence, commitment to family survival and betterment, interest in developing personal competence, and the impact of a shrinking community economy (Kasworm, 2008). Their participation as part-time students and full-time workers, as well as their more complex and varied goals for engagement in higher education, challenge past paradigms of undergraduate participation.

Much past literature on collegiate participation suggests a *pipeline* metaphor for undergraduate education—a bridge between youth and future adulthood and career. However, as Ziskin and colleagues (chapter 4 in this volume) also note, these full-time working adults present more varied collegiate participation patterns. In addition, younger working adults who are part-time and/or intermittent students are increasingly represented.

Thus, as we consider adult workers and a growing subgroup of younger workers in higher education, we need to rethink the nature of participation. One alternative is the paradigmatic image of an airport. This notion of an airport reflects a different framework defining the new realities of undergraduate access and participation. This image of an airport suggests that higher education is a "terminal" with individuals entering and exiting to accomplish specific educational goals on a discontinuous basis. Thus, rather than a pipeline between youth and adulthood with a commitment to continuous involvement, higher education participation is now represented in segments across the life span of adulthood and based in learner-specific goals and needs. This paradigm of the airport also reflects the growing need for adult access to new advanced knowledge. Undergraduate education must also support the continuously evolving global knowledge economy and related adult learner needs for updated and often redefined knowledge and skills. As we consider participation of adult workers who are undergraduate students, we need to recognize that undergraduate education that is contiguous and complementary to the complex world of adult-life commitments is more appropriate than a pipeline solely focused on full-time, young student participation.

With a focus on the adult worker who is a student, this chapter presents four perspectives for future policy, research, and practice. The chapter first discusses the importance of a higher education system that is responsive to the global knowledge economy for a competitive knowledgeable workforce. The chapter then examines the demographic landscape of adult workers in undergraduate education. Given the lack of available conceptual models to guide theory, practice, and policy regarding adult workers as students, the third section presents a new framework, the Adult Undergraduate Student Identity (AUSI) model, which identifies the key psychological and cultural factors shaping the beliefs and actions of adults who are engaged in undergraduate studies. The chapter concludes by highlighting contemporary designs, delivery systems, and ideologies that have supported past access and successful engagement of working adults as students.

Global Knowledge Economy and the Adult Working Student

Over the past four decades, American employers have increasingly expected employees to have more advanced levels of knowledge and skills. Higher education and business leaders suggest that undergraduate education should provide cutting-edge knowledge, as well as cognitive complexity, instruction in abstract reasoning and decision making, opportunities for creativity, and innovation (Jones, 2002; Paul & Beach, 1995). Although directed to all participants in undergraduate education, this expectation has had a profound impact on adults who are currently in the workforce, especially those with more limited education, knowledge, and skills. Adult workers age 25 and older who lack an undergraduate credential often face an unstable work life and experience job changes, job dislocation, and difficulties in job advancement more often than younger students do (Kasworm & Blowers, 1994). In a study of adult undergraduates, Kasworm and Blowers found that approximately two thirds (approximately 60 of the 90 randomly selected adults in undergraduate studies) had faced major job or career issues because of the lack of an undergraduate credential, with 13%, or 12 of the 90 adults, experiencing job dislocation.

Recent unemployment figures have become a prominent catalyst for targeting national and state higher education agendas toward energizing policy and programs for workforce development and responsive undergraduate education. In this era of global economic transformation, an undergraduate education has become a desired component of educational and workforce policies designed to support a competitive economy and the viability of our communities and nation. As suggested by the World Bank, "Lifelong learning is crucial to preparing workers to compete in the global economy. But it is important for other reasons as well. By improving people's ability to function as members of their communities, education and training increase social cohesion, reduce crime, and improve income distribution" (n.d.).

This significant role of higher education in the knowledge economy is not just an American phenomenon. During the last two decades, a global imperative has emerged of the importance to the world economy of lifelong learning for workers. International policy and scholarly forums, including the United Nations Education, Scientific and Cultural Organization (UNESCO), OECD, European Union, and Pan-Asian forums such as the World Conference on Lifelong Learning in Korea, have noted the importance of lifelong learning as a policy tool for future higher education endeavors linked to economic vitality (Kasworm, 2007b).

Higher education has become interwoven with the broader lifelong-learning agenda. Higher education's role in lifelong learning is evidenced in part by the crumbling boundaries between the academic and business worlds, as represented by corporate colleges and contract on-site degree programs, as well as customized workforce training to attract industries to a particular locale. Higher education has experienced the merging of continuing education (e.g., evening colleges and summer school) with the growing use of distance outreach education, and evolving undergraduate on-campus education. In higher education, the traditional distinctions among teaching, research, and outreach/extension have blurred, resulting in adoption of a variety of change strategies, partnerships and stakeholder engagements, and creative financing intertwined with the broader agendas of lifelong learning

(Aspin, Chapman, Hatton, & Sawano, 2001; Kasworm, 2007b). Higher education has become an institution for lifelong learning directed to the diverse and complex population of adults in the workforce and in the global society, as well as serving the historic mission of preparing youth for future careers and world citizenship.

Within this mission of lifelong learning, societal policymakers also perceive higher education as vital for aiding undereducated and dislocated workers. There has been significant loss of human capital because of the millions of undergraduate dropouts and stop-outs who are now adult workers with limited advanced knowledge and skills and who have had difficulties in returning to undergraduate studies. These individuals represent approximately 32.3 million adults (Jones & Kelly, 2007), almost twice the current total U.S. undergraduate enrollment. In addition, there are untold numbers of other individuals who have previously completed a degree, but who do not view this degree as viable preparation for a career (Kohl & LaPidus, 2000). Many of these individuals seek out undergraduate studies as postbaccalaureate students to obtain credentials required to enter a preferred new career. Postbaccalaureate students were estimated to number approximately 1.5 million adults in 1999 (Kohl & LaPidus, 2000).

As suggested in a National Center for Higher Education Management Systems (NCHEMS) report (Jones et al., 2007), adult learners are the key force for the future of higher education and a competitive national economy. Reports by NCHEMS and the U.S. Secretary of Education's Commission on the Future of Higher Education (Stokes, 2006) suggest that a key challenge for responsive higher education is serving the adult worker. At the heart of this challenge is reconfiguring the policy and practice of undergraduate education to encourage and support adult learners who have complex life roles of worker, family member, spouse, and community leader alongside their student role.

Demographics of Adult Workers Who Are Undergraduate Students

To understand the complex worlds of adult workers who are undergraduate students, we first need to examine the broader landscape of adult participation in lifelong learning. In 2005, 54% of U.S. adults participated in formal educational activities, predominantly through credit or noncredit higher education, corporate universities, or related formal classroom and online training (NCES, 2008). This percentage represents a sizeable increase over time because earlier data show that 44% of U.S. adults (60 million) reported formal educational involvement in 2001. In both reports, the predominant involvement of adults was in work-related educational efforts. In 2005, more than 12 million adults age 25 and older participated specifically in credential or degree-granting programs in colleges and universities. An estimated 80% to 95% of these adults focused on achieving work-related educational goals (O'Donnell, 2006; NCES, 2008; Stokes, 2006).

Although adult workers who are also undergraduate students are a difficult population to track, data from the National Center for Educational Statistics provide selective understandings of the characteristics of undergraduates who work. In 1989–1990, 23% of young undergraduates and 46% of older undergraduates worked 40 or more hours a week. A more recent National Center for Education Statistics study (NCES, 2003), *Work first, study second: Adults who combine employment and postsecondary enrollment*, compared adults age 24 and older who viewed themselves as primarily *employees* who also study with those who view themselves as primarily *students who work* to pay for study. As noted in Table 1, a fundamental difference between these two groups is how students combine work and attendance. Most employees who study are enrolled part time (76%), while most students who work are enrolled full time (68%).

TABLE 1
Distribution of Students Who Work and Employees Who Study by Age and Enrollment Intensity: 2003–2004

	Enrollment Intensity (%)	
Characteristic	Full Time[a]	Part Time
Total	42.3	57.7
Students who work	67.9	32.1
Employees who study	24.1	75.9
All students 24–29	54.7	45.3
Students who work	71.1	28.9
Employees who study	32.0	68.1
All students 30–39	40.1	60.0
Students who work	67.7	32.4
Employees who study	24.2	75.8
All students 40 or older	27.4	72.6
Students who work	52.2	47.8
Employees who study	16.9	83.1

[a] Full-time attendance includes those with mixed full-time and part-time enrollment.
Source: National Center for Education Statistics (2003). *Work first, study second: Adult undergraduates who combine employment and postsecondary enrollment* (NCES 2003–167). Washington, DC: Author, p.vii

Employees who study are engaged in higher education to maintain or gain knowledge and skills and related certification to support their career advancement. Undergraduate credentials may help these individuals receive a raise or promotion and/or attain a new job or career with a new employer, as well as meet employer requirements to participate in advanced education (O'Donnell, 2006).

Adult workers who are students do not participate in equal numbers in the varied levels and types of higher education institutions. As noted in Table 2, working adults (i.e., employees who study) are more likely to participate in two-year than four-year colleges. This NCES (2003) report also suggests that differences in participation rates across different types of institutions may reflect differences in institutional mission for serving working students

TABLE 2
Distribution of Students by Type of Institution Attended, Student/Employee Role, and Attendance Intensity: 1999–2000

	Type of Institution Attended (%)				
Characteristic	Public Four-Year	Private Not-for-Profit Four-Year	Public Two-Year	Private For-Profit	More Than One Institution and Other
Total	22.5	10.3	53.9	6.5	6.9
Students who work	34.5	19.6	39.4	7.6	8.0
Employees who study	16.8	11.3	61.2	4.8	6.0
Enrolled Full-Time					
All full-time students	27.7	12.8	36.8	12.6	10.0
Students who work	37.6	12.0	31.9	9.9	8.6
Employees who study	16.4	17.7	39.4	14.5	12.0
Enrolled Part-Time					
All part-time students	18.6	8.5	66.4	2.0	4.5
Students who work	27.8	7.6	55.1	2.8	6.7
Employees who study	16.9	9.3	68.1	1.7	4.0

Note: Full-time attendance includes those who also had mixed full-time and part-time enrollment. Rows may not total 100% because of rounding. Total and "ALL" rows for each subgroup also include students who did not work while enrolled.
Source: National Center for Education Statistics (2003). *Work first, study second: Adult undergraduates who combine employment and postsecondary enrollment* (NCES 2003–167). Washington, DC: Author, p. iv

or differences in institutional orientation toward serving regional business and industry through offering educational programs targeted to workforce needs. The report notes that the lower percentages of workers as students in many four-year colleges and universities may reflect institutional requirements such as for full-time attendance. In addition, a number of these institutions schedule most classes during the day, a problematic design for full-time adult workers. Thus, four-year institutions often report lower enrollments of adult students, suggesting campus environments that are not accessible to adult students and that do not provide instruction and services that are responsive to adult workers.

These varied reports also show that workers who are also students have a number of characteristics that place them at risk for failing to complete college. These students take longer to gain a degree than other students. Adult working students are also more likely to have dependents as well as a spouse. Financial support for college studies is more problematic for them. Moreover, these individuals are more likely to be first-generation college students (NCES, 1995, 2003; O'Donnell, 2006). Reflecting these different characteristics and participation patterns, the following section presents an alternative framework for effectively serving this important undergraduate population.

Creating Responsive Undergraduate Education for Adult Workers Who Are Students: The Adult Undergraduate Student Identity (AUSI) Model

I propose the following model as an alternative perspective for responding to the unique needs of adult workers who are also undergraduate students. This proposed Adult Undergraduate Student Identity (AUSI) model offers a framework for identifying key factors that influence adult workers' participation in undergraduate education. Developed from a number of my prior research investigations, the AUSI model identifies key factors of adult identity that influence adult worker participation. This model suggests that adult workers who are undergraduates differ from younger adult undergraduates in the complexity of their age-related life roles as well as in their beliefs and life realities in regard to involvement in undergraduate education. This model presents a conceptual framework for delineating the complex and evolving world of decisions and actions of adult students in undergraduate education (Kasworm, 2007a; Kasworm, Polson, & Fishback, 2002).

Understanding adult workers who are students requires understanding their complex and competing adult identities—identities that include worker and student as well as others. As noted by Gee (2001), identity is "being recognized as a certain 'kind of person,' in a given context . . . all people have multiple identities connected not to their 'internal states' but to their performances in society" (p. 99). Individuals assume different identities in different social contexts and encounters. As individuals participate in knowledge construction and meaning making across their adult life roles, these varied identities and related efforts to assume agency influence the nature of their participation in higher education (Kasworm, 2003).

As noted in earlier research regarding adult students' sense of place, identity, and agency, these individuals place primary individual identity and energy in their significant worlds of work, family, and community responsibilities (Kasworm & Blowers, 1994; Kasworm et al., 2002). Collegiate participation for most adult students is important, but often it is one of four to six primary competing life investments—investments that are reflective of ego identity, life values, and resources. Although "time investment and involvement" may be a central definer for undergraduate student success and satisfaction, the AUSI framework and supporting research suggest that adult students participate in undergraduate studies through "identity anchor" commitments vis-à-vis their other life worlds. These committed worlds of self and action influence adult students' collegiate participation, engagement in learning, and sense of place within a student identity.

Overview of the Adult Undergraduate Student Identity Model

As mentioned, I developed the Adult Undergraduate Student Identity (AUSI) model based on my prior research conducted across a variety of collegiate institutions and adult students. The study includes interviews of 90 adult undergraduate students (age 30 years and older) who were purposefully selected to reflect the following characteristics: (a) had an interruption in their formal schooling with at least a 1-year absence from the collegiate environment; (b) had assumed financial independence; (c) had assumed a work role, predominantly in a full-time capacity (including the role of homemaker and dislocated worker); (d) often had assumed membership and participation in the civic community; and (e) often had assumed a life role of marriage and/or parenthood. These students were from six collegiate sites, representing two-year community colleges (focused on transfer program students), four-year liberal arts institutions (focused on specialized upper-level adult degree programs), and four-year research universities (predominantly focused on upper-level specialized curricula). Data were drawn from two regional sites, one a major metropolitan area (500,000+ population) and one in a smaller regional center (160,000+ population). Each site included a research university, an adult degree program offered by a private liberal arts college, and a community college.

Based in the social constructivism tradition, this qualitative research investigation identified the nature of multiple and competing identity roles of adult undergraduates and the complex perspectives of these identities vis-à-vis the student role. In particular, the study identified the adult student worker identity premised in situated learning and communities of practice as it influenced the adult's meaning making of knowledge and learning in the classroom (Lave & Wenger, 1991; Wenger, 1998). Because of the complex nature of adult identity and learning, the AUSI model also incorporates related works that reconcile epistemology and ontology regarding student identity (Packer & Goicoechea, 2000) and the perspectives of postmodern intersubjective self and its continually negotiated sense of self, agency, and place (Holland, Lachicotte, Skinner, & Cain, 1998). As part of this model, key factors of adult identity are further grounded in past theory and research of adult learning and development, as well as in related investigations and analyses of adult undergraduate student studies (Kasworm, 1990, 1995, 2003, 2005, 2007a, in press). Because this model has been discussed at length in earlier papers (Kasworm, 2007a), I describe its five key components only briefly in this chapter.

The Adult Undergraduate Student Identity model, as shown in Figure 1, is defined by the vectors of: (1) life world of the adult student; (2) epistemology and agency of knowledge of the adult student; (3) intersubjective coconstructed self as learner and student (identity anchors); and (4) intersubjective coconstructed self in other key adult roles of worker, family member, and community citizen (identity anchors). The fifth component of this model is the context-specific learning environments—the dynamic interrelationship of learning contexts in relation to the student identity. This background represents situated environments, particularly communities of academic practices that both attract and support, as well as deter and sabotage, learner engagement.

At the heart of this framework is the key assumption that the adult worker engages in choice and action through his adult worker identity, as well as through his student identity. The student identity reflects "coconstructed beliefs of student (identity) roles in decision positions and relationships of choice, privilege, and/or reciprocity" (Kasworm, 2005, p. 16). It suggests that monolithic images of undergraduate student and of adult worker, separated by geographic space, life stage, and total engagement in one role, are naïve conceptions. These two images of adult student and adult worker are interwoven within the individual. Individuals act through complex beliefs and understandings coconstructed through their lives, roles, identity anchors, and interactions with their worlds. Thus, the first component of this model is the adult student's life world. To understand the world of adult students who are workers is to understand their unique life world represented by their life biography of formal schooling, the trajectory of their work and career, their maturational stage of development, and their current

FIGURE 1
Adult undergraduate student identity model

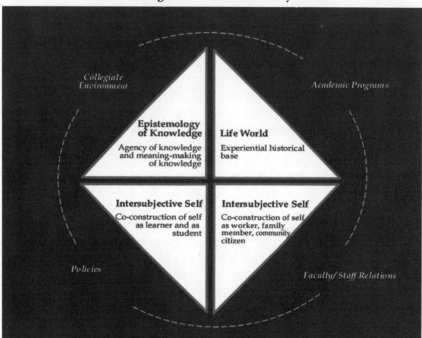

experiential learning engagements in their various key life roles (Hoare, 2006).

The AUSI framework has important implications for higher education leaders and researchers. It clearly defines the population of adult workers who are students as individuals who will never be undergraduates solely encapsulated in a student role at an undergraduate institution. As I and other researchers have previously noted, these undergraduates often engage in undergraduate work from their frame of career and work life. This life world fundamentally creates a *mirror universe* for adult participants in higher education, a world that is, in many respects, the reverse of current assumptions of undergraduate student engagement. Although these adult student workers want to achieve as undergraduates, their orientation and participation in the undergraduate learning process are different. They come with a different maturational level and world-view, identity anchors, and beliefs about the role of education in their future. They also come with past successful and unsuccessful experiences with formal schooling (high school and college);

these experiences influence their engagement: They might be open and interested learners or reluctant and resistant learners. As they participate in undergraduate studies from a life world based in work and career, this identity anchor shapes their external and internal motivational forces for participation, choice of academic major, and related supports or deterrents for participation. This *life world* shapes the factors affecting their selection of a specific institution, academic program, and potentially a particular delivery system (such as evening, weekend, e-learning, or accelerated degree).

The second component of the AUSI model, *epistemology and agency of knowledge*, suggests a figural component of adult participation in collegiate learning focused on adults' meaning making of engaged learning in the classroom. As noted in earlier research (Kasworm, 2003), adult students come with beliefs and value systems related to coconstructing knowledge in the classroom based on their engagement in other worlds and specifically in their work worlds of knowledge and truth. This epistemological orientation of knowledge and agency is based in adult students' cognitive world-view and postformal development. They make key choices for engagement based on their world-view of knowledge and learning that is embedded in their complex communities of practice. This also influences their selection of a specific academic program and/or institutional context.

In the Kasworm studies of adult students (who were predominantly workers), varied patterns of learning engagement were identified based on epistemological beliefs of learning specific knowledge and skills. These patterns, defined as voices embedded in views of knowledge and its utility, included: (a) work world applications as the key frame of learning engagement (Outside Voice), (b) belief of undergraduate studies as only a credential to validate current knowledge of their work role (Cynical Voice), and (c) undergraduate engagement through both cognitive growth in theory and concepts of academic knowledge while also seeking applications and understandings for their work world through "real, practical knowledge" (Straddling Voice). In addition to these three patterns of epistemological learning engagement, there was the Entry Voice, representing beginning development of knowledge and skills to be a successful student in the academic world, and an Immersion Voice focused on working with a world-view of theory and conceptual knowledge for undergraduate learning (Kasworm, 2003). Adult judgments of efficacy of learning specific classroom knowledge were based in adult beliefs of their identity worlds and the impact of that knowledge engagement on those identity worlds.

In addition, these adults ascribed differences in individual agency and in selection of a particular program orientation related to their epistemological beliefs. Some adults selected adult degree programs, a stylized context focused on practice and belief of instrumental acts directly connected with the worksite. Others in adult degree programs, as well as adult workers who were students in community colleges and universities, coconstructed more varied meanings based on past collegiate experiences, key goals for current collegiate engagement, and their beliefs of utility or efficacy of academic knowledge. Thus, adult students who were workers represented extremely varied beliefs and actions of learning; these beliefs were often linked with their expectations of specific institutional impacts, academic programs, instructional delivery designs, and expectations for work environment interactions with their student role.

Collegiate institutions are complex worlds; they represent competing cultural sites for adult students in relation to these students' life roles as students, workers, family members, and community citizens (Holland et al., 1998). The third component of the AUSI model, the *intersubjective coconstructed self as learner and student*, reflects the adult worker's sense of positionality and agency as a learner and student in a collegiate environment. Because adult student identity is coconstructed understandings in socially and culturally mediated engagements, the collegiate world validates or negates the adult as undergraduate and specifically the role of full-time worker in these learning contexts (Lave & Wenger, 1991; Twomey Fosnet, 1996).

As noted by Kasworm (2003), adult students value supportive interactions through *connected classrooms*, the social and psychological space for learning connecting one's adult life to one's academic studies. If the institutional environment is youth-oriented, the adult undergraduate worker often has difficulty gaining validation and locating connected classrooms for learning engagement. Thus, classrooms representing policies and an ethos directed to younger full-time undergraduates create disjunctures for the adult student. My past studies show that adult students report significant and varied negotiated engagements for their positionality and relationship to these dominant young adult cultural contexts. If specific classrooms and the ethos of a collegiate environment are not responsive to adult learners, these students face "a self-regulatory press of struggling with the conflict between personal models of the world and discrepant new insights, constructing new representations and models of reality as a human meaning-making venture" (Holland et al., 1998, p. ix).

These struggles reflect many adult students' concerns. Some concerns are presumed to be based in their beliefs of the physiological and sociological impacts of chronological age: They fear that college is only for the young and mentally agile. Other concerns are linked to their assumption that they are second-time students and need to prove themselves as academically worthy. Some fear discrimination because they are older students who work full time and can't or don't desire to participate in the undergraduate world of organizations and programs. Adults also express other concerns as they attempt to adapt and belong in the undergraduate world. Thus, most adult students have problematic fears at entry, often suggesting complex negotiations within themselves and between themselves and others in the institution (Kasworm, 2005, in press; Kasworm & Blowers, 1994).

In a recent thesis proposed by Packer and Goicoechea (2000), learning based within identity development involves becoming a member of a community, constructing knowledge in relation to expertise as a participant (legitimate peripheral participation), and taking into account the culture of one's community and adult roles as part of participation. Adult workers' engagement in higher education is influenced by both the ethos of the collegiate environment and by their own worker identity; some collegiate environments value and support adult workers, while others offer a tacit negative, if not conflictual, environment for adult learner involvement. Thus, the fourth component of the AUSI model, the *intersubjective coconstructed self as worker, family member, and community citizen,* also has a key influence on adult worker learning engagement. This component of the model is anchored in the understanding that adult student identity is an ongoing process of intersubjective meaning making based in other key referent identity anchors. Through these competing and complementary identities of worker, family member, or community citizen, adult undergraduate workers experience support or barriers to context-embedded resources and privileges. This sense of positionality and relationship enhances or denigrates their ability to draw on both intellectual and social resources.

These related assumptions of the identity anchors represent highly complex and evolving negotiated actions and beliefs in adult undergraduate workers. As noted by Twomey Fosnet (1996), "Since the process of construction is adaptive in nature and requires self-reorganization, cultural knowledge that is assumed to be held by members of the culture is in reality only a dynamically evolving, negotiated interaction of individual interpretations, transformation, and construction" (p. 24). Thus, to understand adult workers as undergraduate students, we need to understand the adult in the work expertise context; the adult as a responsible agent of family, marriage, and community; and the adult's sense of agency and motivation for learning in relation to these key identity anchors. In particular, Baxter Magolda (1999) notes that the work world "expects adults to be accomplished masters of their work rather than apprentices" (pp. 264–265). This perspective of the importance of adult work expertise is an influential referent frame. Adult students suggest that they do not always experience faculty who value their work world and their particular expertise in relation to the world of knowledge construction in the classroom (Kasworm, 2003; Kasworm & Blowers, 1994). Further, many adult workers who are students often view their student role, efficacy of knowledge, and learning outcomes as embedded in their work world rather than in a dominant focus on accretion of academic knowledge. Thus, these identity anchors influence adult learners' beliefs and actions.

The final component of the AUSI model, *dynamic interrelationship of learning contexts*, identifies students' differentiated experiences and expectations for their engagement or lack of engagement in different institutional undergraduate settings. Varied programs and institutional environments are viewed by adult students as representing different communities of practice and different values for individual choice, participation, and investment (Kasworm, 1995). My past research shows that different learning contexts attract and influence the participation and coconstruction of the adult worker's student identity in the world of collegiate learning. In essence, each of the three studied collegiate settings—community colleges, research universities, and adult degree programs in the liberal arts setting—appears to attract different types of adult students and different types of adult workers. In each of these settings, adult undergraduate workers also have different beliefs and expectations about their role as student, as well as for learning engagement and institutional support (Kasworm, 1995, 2005, in press; Wlodkowski & Kasworm, 2003).

In each of the three collegiate settings, adult students also held different coconstructed understandings of their role as student vis-à-vis their other key adult roles of work, family, and community; their relationships with faculty; and their actions in the classroom. As part of these negotiated identities and engagements, the social and human capital of adult students influences their selection of and participation at varied higher education institutions. For example, adult students often felt a social status press as well as a personal press to participate in college studies based in their work environments. My prior studies show that work settings that present a more dominant press to pursue collegiate studies also present a press to engage in a particular type of institutional setting, most often the research university or a particular adult degree program. Adult degree programs often attract adult students who come from worksites with employer reimbursement for tuition programs and/or a history of worker participation by that company in that specific adult degree program. Adults with limited financial resources and limited college education typically choose to attend a community college. They often have cycles of fragile and intermittent participation in collegiate coursework. These cycles reflect times of commitment to and resources for participating as well as lack of time and resources and therefore inability to participate.

In addition, adult undergraduate students from various work settings, resources supports, and collegiate and program environments held different beliefs about student involvement. Thus, adult workers who were students had complex, dynamic, and highly differentiated understandings of and actions across varied undergraduate settings, academic programs, and academic majors and delivery systems.

Last, a recent examination of adult undergraduates in research universities suggests that they experience a more difficult and turbulent environment, one that is often unsupportive of adults and particularly of adult workers. Students suggest that the research university environment is not as responsive to their life world given its restrictive academic structures, policies, and environment that privileges full-time young adults (Kasworm, in press). Further, adult workers who are undergraduates in research universities suggest they need a complex set of strategies, expectations, and beliefs to survive and persist in comparison to adult workers in community colleges and adult degree programs in liberal arts colleges.

This abbreviated presentation provides an overview of a complex model of adult undergraduate student identity in relation to adult students' worker and other life roles. The work identity anchor influences adults' selection and participation in specific academic programs, delivery systems, and related learning contexts, as well as their learning engagement patterns. Unlike simple statistics of adult undergraduate demographics and reasons for participating or dropping or stopping out, the AUSI model highlights the complex, dynamic, and multilayered understandings and actions of adult workers as students.

Supporting Access and Participation for Adult Workers Who Are Undergraduate Learners

Adult workers represent a complex and varied grouping of undergraduates because of their multiple identities and different patterns of participation. When accessing and participating in undergraduate institutions, these adults typically have difficulties with environments that reflect structures, policies, delivery systems, and support services focused more toward younger adults (17 to 24 years of age). To encourage a different reality that embraces the AUSI model, this section presents examples of policies, practices, and understandings that serve and accommodate adult workers who are undergraduate students. These examples emphasize institutional mission commitments, adult-oriented program designs and delivery systems, policies and practices targeted to working and part-time adult undergraduates, and the creation of a supportive community from the adult worker perspective.

Institutional Mission

Many collegiate institutions have institutional or program-based missions to serve adults, particularly working adults. These institutions include community colleges; evening and weekend schools and colleges; adult degree programs based in four-year public and private institutions; external degree programs; distance education programs; as well as specialized institutions for adult populations, such as SUNY Empire State College, Thomas Edison State University, Excelsior College, and such for-profit institutions as University of Phoenix (Hall, 1991; Maehl, 2000; Wlodkowski & Kasworm, 2003). Each of these organizations has stated a commitment, often imaged in the mission statement, that supports access, flexibility, and services directed to adult clientele.

Program Design and Delivery

Access to academic programs through various delivery modes is vitally important to adult students. Often adult learners are assumed to be best served through distance education. Many programs geared to adult learners offer online, teleconferenced, or DVD-based delivery or off-campus hybrid cohort programs at corporate sites, military bases, and other worker-oriented places. However, the vast majority of working adults seek regionally based programs and course schedules in classrooms that mesh with their work schedules.

One of the biggest concerns for adult students is gaining academic competence in specific academic majors and participating in learning environments that support their learning needs. Many adult learners purposefully seek out face-to-face courses for personal engagement with other minds and ideas in an interactive environment. Often these engagements are in fields with limited adult student program enrollments such as architecture, forestry, biotechnology, interior design, or chemistry. These specialized majors are typically in universities that have limited interest in serving adult workers. Thus, interviewed adults suggested that those who participated in these specialized majors experienced the realities of an uninviting environment and few student colleagues for support. Some adults value the convenience of asynchronous learning through online courses and programs aligned with their career interests. And some adults value hybrid offerings of both online and face-to-face instruction. However, these choices often rest on a clear commitment of the institution to offer the entire program in that mode and to offer all of the courses in an accessible sequence in relation to adult workers' limited time schedules. Often students praise adult degree programs for prescheduling all courses for the length of the students' involvement in the program, offering courses in shorter lengths (4 to 7 weeks per accelerated course) than the traditional semester, and committing to this set of course offerings and time schedule to facilitate timely student graduation.

Adult students report valuing program designs that integrate their mature engagement in the work world in terms of content, selection of faculty, course assignments, and adult-oriented instructional strategies and learning designs. Maehl (2000) suggests a variety of models for curricula, as well as key adult learning principles for adult-focused programs. For example, on its web site, the University of Phoenix indicates that students' experiences include:

> small, highly interactive classes, personalized attention and class times that fit your schedule. You can expect educational experiences that are focused, challenging and relevant. Our courses are taught by instructors with advanced degrees who also have substantial experience in the fields they teach. And the curriculum for our programs is regularly updated to meet the needs of today's workplace. (University of Phoenix, 2009)

Learning engagements that are adult experience based, challenging, and relevant, as well as focused on inquiry and that apply to adults' work worlds are often key themes of interest for adult working students.

Policies and Practices

Effective adult-focused programs and institutions are designed for access, responsiveness, and relevancy to adult workers who are students. Key personnel have a clear understanding and empathy for the adult worker, and services represent operating practices appropriate to the complex world of the adult worker. Institutionally required interactions, such as admissions, orientation, registration, and academic advising, are designed for, interact with, and send a targeted message to adult workers. Personnel, both university staff and faculty, are particularly sensitive to access issues and understand adult needs and desires (whether they are part-time, evening, weekend, or distance students).

These institutions may also have policies and practices that reflect reframed understandings of valued adult experiences in relation to reentry admissions standards and the nature of documented learning outcomes. These policies may include alternative credit options, such as DANTES (the U.S. Department of Defense's Defense Activity for Non-Traditional Education Support), CLEP (the College Board's College Level Examination Program), PLAR (Prior Learning Assessment for Recognition through portfolio review), and CREDIT (American Council on Education's college credit review service for workplace learning assessed for academic credit). These policies may also include revised admissions standards for adults (e.g., no required SAT or ACT scores), academic bankruptcy policies (e.g., eliminating ancient coursework GPAs from current GPAs), and military leave procedures (Kasworm et al., 2002). For many institutions, reoriented policies and services for adult students also include adult-oriented recruitment strategies and entry procedures, adult-supporting services and organizations, faculty instructional workshops on adult learning, and other unique ways to build community within programs or through services directed to specific types of part-time, evening, and/or distance learners.

Community of Learning From the Adult Worker Perspective

Adult undergraduate workers predominantly survive and thrive within the classroom, particularly the connected classroom (Kasworm et al., 2002). The "connected classroom" is a metaphor for a psychological and cultural community. It is a place where adult students can connect with others in friendship and collaborative learning. And it is the place for creating learning that is particularly meaningful for adult workers who are students. Adult-focused programs and/or institutions recognize that the adult worker's sense of collegiate community is orchestrated by each faculty instructor and related supportive policies and services. There are excellent examples of efforts to create adult learning communities through adult degree programs, evening or weekend programs, and required freshmen or sophomore courses for adult learners. However, these programmatic efforts are often not feasible for the vast majority of adult undergraduates who enter extremely varied academic programs based on past transcripts, time schedules, and personal needs. Thus, institutions that desire to serve adult workers must create faculty awareness, instructional program flexibility, and specific strategies to engage adult workers in connected classroom designs and instruction.

Adult workers as students value being part of an academic world—but they require an academic world that connects with their understandings and their lifestyles of limited access and participation. The challenge for higher education is to create new paradigms across institutions that establish relevant and responsive standards for engagement and support of adult workers. It is highly probable that when institutions establish a set of understandings, program and delivery designs, and services for the adult worker, they will create a responsive environment that also serves the younger (17- to 24-year old) adult worker. Suggesting the benefits of this strategy, University of Phoenix now admits younger students to its programs after determining that younger adult workers also value the access and delivery strategies that serve the adult student-worker population.

Conclusion

American higher education has a legacy of being highly responsive and adaptive to changing societal needs and learner clientele. Future policy and practice should focus on higher education's role in providing lifelong learning that serves the significant cadre of adult workers. These efforts will make a major contribution to developing innovative, cutting-edge knowledge and skills of adult workers, as well as the future of U.S. engagement in the global economy.

References

Aspin, D., Chapman, J., Hatton, M., & Sawano, Y. (Eds.). (2001). *International handbook on lifelong learning* (2 Volumes). Dordrecht, the Netherlands: Lower Press.

Baxter Magolda, M. B. (1999). *Creating contexts for learning and self-authorship: Constructive-developmental pedagogy.* Nashville, TN: Vanderbilt University Press.

Gee, J. (2001). Identity as an analytic lens for research in education. In W. Secada (Ed.), *Review of research in education. Volume 25.* Washington, DC: American Educational Research Association.

Hall, J. (1991). *Access through innovation: New colleges for new students.* New York: Maxwell Macmillan.

Hoare, C. (Ed.). (2006). *Handbook of adult development and learning.* London: Oxford University Press.

Holland, D., Lachicotte, W. J., Skinner, D., & Cain, C. (1998). *Identity and agency in cultural worlds.* Cambridge, MA: Harvard University Press.

Jones, D., & Kelly P. (2007). Mounting pressures facing the U.S. workforce and the increasing need for adult education and literacy. Retrieved November 10, 2007, from www.nationalcommissiononadultliteracy.org/content/nchemspresentation.pdf

Jones, R. (2002). Facing new challenges: The higher education community must take the lead in addressing the dramatic pace of external change. *National Cross-Talk, 10*(3), San Jose: National Center for Public Policy and Higher Education. Retrieved November 10, 2007, from www.highereducation.org/crosstalk/ct0302/voices0702-facing_new_challenges.shtml

Kasworm, C. (1990). Adult undergraduates in higher education: A review of past research perspectives. *Review of Educational Research, 60*(3), 345–372.

Kasworm, C. (1995). *Involvement from an adult undergraduate perspective.* Paper presented at the annual meeting of the American Educational Research Association, San Francisco, CA (ERIC Reproduction Document No. ED440275).

Kasworm, C. (2003). Adult meaning making in the undergraduate classroom. *Adult Education Quarterly, 53*(2), 81–98.

Kasworm, C. (2005). Adult student identity in an intergenerational community college classroom. *Adult Education Quarterly, 56*(1), 3–20.

Kasworm, C. (2007a). *Adult student identity: A proposed model.* Paper presented at the annual meeting of the American Educational Research Association, Chicago, IL.

Kasworm, C. (2007b). *Lifelong learning—the perspective of higher education serving adult learners.* Paper presented at the World Conference on Lifelong Learning, Chongwon, Korea.

Kasworm, C. (2008, November) *Looking Through a Mirror Darkly: Adult Workers as Undergraduate Students.* Paper presented at the Association for the Study of Higher Education, Jacksonville, Fl.

Kasworm, C. (in press). Adult learners in the research university: Negotiating an undergraduate student identity. *Adult Education Quarterly.*

Kasworm, C., & Blowers, S. (1994). *Adult undergraduate students: Patterns of learning involvement.* Report submitted to OERI, Department of Education, Washington, DC (ERIC Reproduction Document No. ED 376321).

Kasworm, C., Polson, C., & Fishback, S. (2002). *Responding to adult learners in higher education.* Malabar, FL: Krieger Publishing.

Kohl, K., & LaPidus, J. (Eds.). (2000). *Postbaccalaureate futures: New markets, resources, credentials.* Phoenix, AZ: American Council on Education and the Oryx Press.

Lave, J., & Wenger, E. (1991). *Situated learning: Legitimate peripheral participation.* New York: Cambridge University Press.

Maehl, W. (2000). *Lifelong learning at its best: Innovative practices in adult credit programs.* San Francisco: Jossey-Bass.

National Center for Education Statistics. (1995). *Profile of older undergraduates: 1989–90* (NCES 95–167). Washington, DC: U.S. Department of Education.

National Center for Education Statistics. (2003). *Work first, study second: Adult undergraduates who combine employment and postsecondary enrollment* (NCES 2003–167). Washington, DC: Author. Retrieved January 15, 2004, from http://nces.ed.gov/pubsearch/pubsinfo.asp?pubid = 2003167

National Center for Education Statistics. (2008). *Recent participation in formal learning among working-age adults with different levels of education* (NCES 2008–041). Washington, DC: Author. Retrieved July 6, 2008, from http://nces.ed.gov/pubs2008/2008041.pdf

O'Donnell, K. (2006). *Adult education participation in 2004–2005* (NCES 2006–077). Washington, DC: National Center for Education Statistics. Retrieved February 15, 2008, from http://nces.ed.gov/pubs2006/adulted/

Packer, M. J., & Goicoechea, J. (2000). Sociocultural and constructivist theories of learning: Ontology, not just epistemology. *Educational Psychologist, 35*(4), 227–241.

Paul, R., & Beach, D. (1995). Critical thinking: How to prepare students for a rapidly changing world. Paper presented at the Foundation for Critical Thinking. Retrieved January 5, 2009, from www.criticalthinking.org/articles/accelerating-change.cfm

Stokes, P. (2006). *Hidden in plain sight: Adult learners forge a new tradition in higher education.* Issue paper presented at A National Dialogue: The Secretary of Education's Commission on the Future of Higher Education. Retrieved August 3, 2008, from www.ed.gov/about/bdscomm/list/hiedfuture/reports/stokes.pdf

Twomey Fosnet, C. (Ed.). (1996). *Constructivism: Theory, perspectives, and practice.* New York: Teachers College Press.

University of Phoenix. (2009). Student experience. Retrieved October 1, 2008, from www.phoenix.edu/admissions/student_experience.aspx

Wenger, E. (1998). *Communities of practice: Learning, meaning, and identity.* New York: Cambridge University Press.

Wlodkowski, R., & Kasworm, C. (Eds.). (2003). *Accelerated learning for adults: The promise and practice of intensive educational formats* (Vol. 97). San Francisco: Jossey-Bass.

World Bank. (n.d.). Lifelong Learning in the Global Knowledge Economy. Retrieved October 6, 2009, from http://web.worldbank.org/WBSITE/EXTERNAL/TOPICS/EXTEDUCATION/0,,contentMDK:21723821~menuPK:540092~pagePK:14895

3

OVERCOMING ADVERSITY

Community College Students and Work

John S. Levin, Virginia Montero-Hernandez, and Christine Cerven

T his chapter addresses the topic of working students in the community college to identify gaps in the literature, present and analyze empirical data about working students at community colleges, and point out pathways for further research. The chapter describes some of the predominant conditions that characterize the educational experiences of students who work while enrolled at community colleges. Two broad questions guide the structure of this chapter:

1. How do students who work (i.e., full and part time) while studying navigate their college experiences?
2. What are the factors that enable community college students to face the challenges, conflicts, and opportunities that emerge as a result of their two-dimensional status as workers and students?

To answer these questions we integrate quantitative data from national and state sources as well as qualitative data from two community colleges in the states of California and New York. In so doing, we explain (a) the characteristics of the educational experiences of community college students who enact work and study as parallel activities in their daily lives, and (b) the factors, both organizational and personal, that influence the ways that the educational experiences of working students are constructed. Data interpretation is guided by the use of organizational and culture theory. We used this theoretical approach in our previous work to talk about the opportunities for development that students can achieve when community colleges offer sustained support as well as interactions that enable students to acquire new resources, skills, and perspectives (Levin & Montero-Hernandez, in press). In this chapter, we extend that framework to analyze the experiences of working students at community colleges. The interpretation of both quantitative and qualitative data aims to offer a more complex understanding of (a) what it takes to be a working student in a community college, and (b) how community colleges can construct structures (e.g., programs and student services) to respond to this critical sector of their student body. This chapter provides interpretations that enable us to advance our understanding of the relationship between work and persistence within the specific context of the community college.

The chapter has two parts. First, we review statistical data at the national level to identify the characteristics that define working students (i.e., the great majority—80%—of the community college student population). The quantitative data we present show a negative relationship between full-time work and persistence, defined as attending 9 or more months and/or attaining a credential. However, data also suggest a positive relationship between working part time and persistence. The nature of the quantitative data prevents us from offering a detailed explanation of the reasons behind this latter finding. Clearly, more comprehensive data sets and qualitative studies are needed to construct more complex representations of the issues facing working students in community colleges.

In the second part of the chapter, we analyze qualitative data from community colleges in two states, Bakersfield College in California and Borough Manhattan Community College in New York, to gain a more in-depth understanding of the challenges, conflicts, and potential opportunities that community college students face when they have to work and study simultaneously. We discuss the character of the work-study conflict and its effects on the ways that students experience college. We refer to two kinds of factors that moderate the impact of the work-study conflict on students. Initially, we talk about the ways that organizational structures and institutional personnel or agents in community colleges respond to working students' needs. Subsequently, we note the personal factors (e.g., motivation) that enable students to overcome the constraints that stem from having to perform two equally demanding roles: studying and working.

The Community College Context

The paradoxical condition for community colleges in the United States creates misunderstandings about the institution's organizational behaviors and students as well as confusion about its purposes (Bailey & Morest, 2004; Cohen & Brawer, 1996; Frye, 1994). Community colleges are unique organizations, dramatically distinct from four-year colleges and universities. On the one hand, the community college is a nonselective, open-access institution.

On the other hand, community colleges offer a host of programs that are subject to competitive entry for students. These institutions contain students who are as academically able as those at selective public universities and many who have specific occupational and vocational skills that exceed those of typical undergraduates. But the community college also enrolls students who lack high school completion; are intellectually and mentally challenged; are nonnative English speakers and virtually illiterate in their native language; and lack basic skills in mathematics, English, and computers. A large proportion of the student body at community colleges consists of nontraditional learners who are characterized by disadvantaged social class and ethnic backgrounds, academic deficiencies, and multiple roles (Astin, 1984; Baxter-Magolda, 2003; Cohen & Brawer, 1996; Heisserer & Parette, 2002; Hoachlander, Sikora, & Horn, 2003; Levin, 2007). Community college students are adults with competing priorities who have to make choices to maintain other significant adult life roles while simultaneously working and studying (Ashton & Elliott, 2007; Kasworm, 2005).

With more than 6 million students enrolled in credit-bearing courses and an estimated 3 to 5 million in non-credit-bearing courses including continuing education programs such as English as a second language, adult education, and skills upgrading and community education programs, community colleges contain an astounding variety and spectrum of learners (Levin, 2007). Both learners' goals and their needs are diverse and their use of the institution is highly variable (Adelman, 1992). These conditions alone suggest that organizational behaviors within the community college are multivariate.

Added to the multiple goals and needs of students are the expectations and requirements of the "community"—the businesses, higher education institutions, cities, regions, states, and national economy—that covets the products of community colleges. Taken together, this combination of students and community shapes the purposes and consequently the actions of the institution, which is arguably both postsecondary educational institution and some other entity—social service agency, community resource, workforce developer, feeder school, citizenship pathway, adult learning center, international relations agent, and even university and professional athlete preparation. Thus, it should be no surprise that the community college adapts to the conditions of its students. As well, students adjust to, take advantage of, and reject the patterns of organizational behaviors that characterize the community college. We refer to these combined behaviors as the coconstruction of student and organizational identity (Levin & Montero-Hernandez, in press). Although the literature on student performance in college frames student characteristics as preeminent in student academic attainment (Pascarella & Terenzini, 2005), institutional effects may play a larger role for different student groups, such as adult students, and for different student outcomes, such as goal identification, and at different types of institutions, such as community colleges (Levin, 2007; Levin, Hernandez-Montero, & Cerven, 2008).

Students' status as workers is one of the characteristics that students bring to this process of coconstruction. Unlike traditional conceptions of student behaviors, the actual behaviors of community college students involve work as much as college activities. Work is a defining characteristic of community college students. As noted in other chapters, the majority (80%) of community college students work, with 41% working full time (Horn & Neville, 2006). In addition, more than a third (34.9%) of community college students view themselves not as students first but primarily as employees or workers who attend college (Phillippe & Gonzalez Sullivan, 2005).

Community college students who work while studying are identified and defined in the literature in a variety of ways. They are defined in terms of their self-perceptions of their "primary role" in their working lives and are often identified as "students who work" or "employees who study" (Horn & Neville, 2006). They are also characterized more specifically in terms of the programs in which they are enrolled at the community college and are often identified as "worker retrainees" (Simmons, 1995) or "welfare-to-work" students (Brock, Matus-Grossman, & Hamilton, 2001; Pagenette & Kozell, 2001).

The literature that addresses the influences of work on persistence within the community college usually includes attention to such factors as family life circumstances, income, and transportation. However, this body of work offers neither consistent explanations about the nature of the working activities that students perform nor an in-depth examination of the many ways that work influences students' college experience and levels of persistence. Some studies have found that community college programs that allow work and academic activities to be combined easily and include employment on campus serve to aid students' management of their work and school schedules (Brock et al., 2001; Pagenette & Kozell, 2001). Other studies focusing on adult learners and reentry students often assume work as an element of these students' lives, but do not make work the primary topic of discussion. Still other scholarship finds flexible scheduling, understanding instructors, and counseling and guidance courses that help students "design realistic schedules" to be promising practices that help students who work while studying persist at community colleges (Woodlief, Thomas, & Orozco, 2003). But these studies provide only a superficial account of what it is about work (on or off campus) or the working students themselves that decreases their persistence within the community college.

Because of the diversity of ways that work relates to students' lives, it is understandable that the literature contains such a broad range of categories and discussions of working students. In general, the literature on working community college students is characterized by a lack of cohesion in that the manner that work is related to students varies in its conceptualization as well as its connection to other student characteristics.

Our interest in this chapter is with the association between work and persistence for students attending community colleges. We first present national statistics and statewide statistics from California and New York that depict the association between work and student persistence within the community college. Next, we draw on qualitative interview data with students at Bakersfield College in California to understand how work affects the lives of these students. Finally, we use data from interviews with administrators at Borough of Manhattan City College in New York to identify organizational structures and processes that help and hinder students' persistence in college.

Working Students at Community Colleges: The Numerical Picture

The quantitative data we analyze in this section were derived from two sources. First, we utilize data from the National Postsecondary Student Aid Study (NPSAS: 04) conducted by the National Center for Education Statistics (NCES). NCES issued a series of statistical reports focusing on particular topics using the NPSAS data; the report we use focuses on community college students (U.S. Department of Education, 2004). The NPSAS study is based on survey data collected from a sample of approximately 80,000 undergraduates including 25,000 community college students who were enrolled between July 1, 2003, and June 30, 2004. The second source is the American Association of Community Colleges' report entitled *National profile of community colleges: Trends and statistics* (4th edition), which also draws on survey data collected by NCES in 2005 (Phillippe & Gonzalez Sullivan, 2005). Each national survey collected data on a variety of subjects ranging from student characteristics, attendance, and work to tuition, financial aid, and degree attainment. We consider these two sources to be reliable because each draws on a large, nationally representative sample.

Working full time while enrolled is one "risk factor" known to reduce the likelihood of persisting to degree completion (Phillippe & Gonzalez Sullivan, 2005). Community college students average twice as many risk factors, including working full-time, as public four-year students (2.4 versus 1.1; Table 1). Of the entire community college student population, 41% work full time compared to only 23% of four-year college students. Because full-time work is considered a risk factor for all students in higher education and because a greater percentage of community college students work full time, the ways work may affect community college students' educational outcomes are noteworthy.

TABLE 1
Percentage of Undergraduates With Risk Factors Associated
With Decreased Persistence in College: 2003–2004

Risk Factor	Community College (%)	Public Four-Year (%)
Independent student	61.2	34.3
Delayed enrollment	50.3	23.3
Enrolled full-time	66.1	30.2
Has dependents	35.4	14.3
Single parent	17.2	6.3
Worked full time	40.8	22.9
Has GED or no HS diploma	11.6	3.6
Has at least one risk factor	85.7	51.4
Average number of risk factors	2.4	1.1

Source: Phillippe & Sullivan (2005, p. 53)

Community college students also work at different levels of intensity and duration than do four-year college students, as shown in Table 2. Table 2 represents the statistics for working students attending community colleges and public four-year colleges and universities. Nationally, a higher percentage of students in community colleges than in public four-year institutions work (79% versus 70%), and, among those who work, students at community colleges are more likely than students at public four-year institutions to work full time (about 50% versus 30%). These differences in the prevalence and intensity of working between students at community colleges and those at four-year colleges generally hold across student demographic characteristics.

With regard to the relationship between work and persistence, both community college and four-year college students who do not work are more likely to persist than students who do work. The measure of persistence we use was derived from an NPSAS survey that defined persistence as "attending college 9 or more months and/or attaining a credential" (U.S. Department of Education, 2004). Although this measure may appear to reflect a minor accomplishment, attending college for more than 9 months and/or attaining a credential for community college students is a considerable task given the multiple life circumstances facing these students. Working full time is detrimental for both community college and four-year college students' persistence. However, as Table 3 exhibits, working full time is more detrimental

TABLE 2

Characteristics of Working Students by Gender, Race, Dependency Status, Age, Income, and Type of Institution

	Community College Students			Public Four-Year Students		
	Did Not Work (%)	Worked Part Time (%)	Worked Full Time (%)	Did Not Work (%)	Worked Part Time (%)	Worked Full Time (%)
Gender						
Male	21.0	37.8	41.2	30.0	48.6	21.4
Female	21.6	37.9	40.5	27.5	50.7	21.8
Race/Ethnicity						
White, Non-Hisp.	20.6	39.1	40.3	27.3	51.7	21.0
Black, Non-Hisp.	22.7	33.5	43.9	31.5	41.8	26.7
Hispanic	19.7	38.2	42.1	26.9	46.3	26.8
Asian	30.7	36.9	32.4	40.8	47.9	11.3
Am. Indian/Alaskan	18.6	32.0	49.4	31.1	45.0	23.9
Pac. Islander/Hawaii	17.3	47.4	35.3	35.8	40.5	23.8
Other	24.8	35.5	39.7	24.1	47.7	28.3
More than one race	22.4	36.6	41.0	31.6	50.1	18.3
Dependency						
Dependent	19.9	54.4	25.7	32.0	57.0	11.0
Independent	22.3	27.4	50.3	22.1	35.9	42.0

TABLE 2 (Continued)

	Community College Students			Public Four-Year Students		
	Did Not Work (%)	Worked Part Time (%)	Worked Full Time (%)	Did Not Work (%)	Worked Part Time (%)	Worked Full Time (%)
Age 18 and under	26.3	56.7	17.0	47.9	45.3	6.8
19–23	18.5	50.3	31.2	28.4	58.3	13.4
24–29	19.5	31.6	48.9	20.2	40.9	38.9
30–39	24.1	24.3	51.6	23.4	27.3	49.3
40 and older	24.1	21.2	54.7	25.2	23.6	51.2
Income Levels						
Low	28.0	42.5	29.5	32.9	50.9	16.2
25–74 Middle	19.0	38.2	42.8	26.0	50.4	23.6
75–100 High	19.6	32.5	47.9	29.9	47.6	22.6
Type of Institution						
Public 2-year	21.4	37.9	40.8			
Public 4-year, non-doctoral-granting				25.8	46.5	27.6
Public doc-granting				30.2	51.6	18.2

Source: U.S. Department of Education, National Center for Education Statistics (2004). 2003–04 national profile of undergraduates in U.S. postsecondary education institutions (NPSAS: 2004 UG)

TABLE 3
Working Students' Persistence Rates Nationally and in California and New York

	N CC/4YR	Community College Students			Public Four-Year Students		
		Did Not Work %	Worked Part Time %	Worked Full Time %	Did Not Work %	Worked Part Time %	Worked Full Time %
Nationally	3,460/3,598	53.6	59.2	44.1	84.4	82.6	61.6
California	675/285	51.8	55.9	38.7	89.6	84.2	63.4
New York	157/188	63.0	61.3	49.1	84.3	84.4	63.8

Note: Persistence is defined as attending 9 or more months and/or attaining a credential (NPSAS: 2004 UG)

Source: U.S. Department of Education, National Center for Education Statistics (2004). 2003–04 national profile of undergraduates in U.S. postsecondary education institutions (NPSAS: 2004 UG)

for community college students. Only 44.1% of community college students who work full time persist compared to 61.6% of four-year college students working full time.

Working part time does not appear to have the same detrimental effects as full-time work on persistence for community college students. Table 3 shows that, among community college students who work part time, there is a higher level of college persistence (59.2%) than for those who did not work at all (53.6%).

The limited nature of the quantitative data available in major databases restricts our understanding of part-time work and its relation to persistence. Part-time work is defined in the NPSAS survey as working between 2 and 35 hours; however, other important intervening factors such as where students work (e.g., on or off campus), what kinds of work they do, and for what reasons students work also need to be considered to gain a comprehensive understanding of the nature of part-time work for students. We can speculate that having a part-time job enables students to enhance their personal circumstances that, in turn, encourage them to persist in college. First, students who work part time can earn money to satisfy their college-related expenses (e.g., books, course fees, and transportation). Second, students who have a job related to the program area in which they are enrolled may find their working activities as sources to apply to and contrast with what they learn in college. Finally, among adult students, working may be a source of motivation because these students can identify themselves as productive people.

Table 4 indicates the relationship between working and persistence rates for community college students by gender. Persistence rates at community colleges are two to three percentage points higher for women than for men regardless of work status. The reasons for these gender gaps in persistence are as yet undocumented, but perhaps women respond to the community college environment better than their male counterparts. National trends also

TABLE 4
Persistence Rates for Community College Students Nationwide by Gender and Working Status

Gender	Did Not Work (%)	Worked Part Time (%)	Worked Full Time (%)
Male	52.9	57.3	42.4
Female	54.0	60.6	45.4

Note: Persistence is defined as attending 9 or more months and/or attaining a credential (NPSAS: 2004 UG).

Source: U.S. Department of Education, National Center for Education Statistics (2004). 2003–04 national profile of undergraduates in U.S. postsecondary education institutions (NPSAS: 2004 UG)

suggest that working full time is detrimental for the persistence of both men and women in the community college: Both female and male students at community colleges suffer the same negative impact of working while studying. However, persistence rates are higher for students who work part time than for those who do not work and those who work full time, regardless of gender.

Table 5 displays the variations in the relationship between working and community college students' persistence rates by race/ethnicity. For all racial/ethnic categories, full-time work is associated with lower rates of persistence. However, there is some slight variation among some ethnic groups. For African American and Asian community college students, all kinds of work (part and full time) are associated with lower persistence rates than not working. For all other racial groups (Whites, Latinos, Hawaiian/Pacific Islander, and American Indian/Alaskan), part-time work is associated with greater persistence than not working. Even though part-time work does not decrease persistence dramatically for African American and Asian community college students, work, in general, does appear to hinder their chances of persisting in college. The racial/ethnic differences in persistence may be related to students' financial status. In addition, social and cultural capital theories may also inform this racial/ethnic variation in the relationship between work and persistence.

Finally, the persistence of working community college students grouped by income and dependency status shows several significant patterns, as displayed in Table 6. First, there is a marked distinction between dependent

TABLE 5
Persistence Rates for Community College Students Nationwide by Race and Working Status

Race/Ethnicity	Did Not Work (%)	Worked Part Time (%)	Worked Full Time (%)
African American	55.9	54.7	44.4
White	52.7	61.1	44.0
Latino	53.1	57.6	45.1
Asian	55.8	54.4	47.5
Am. Indian/Alaskan	46.8	60.5	40.1
Hawaiian/Pac. Islander	28.8	43.0	27.0

Note: Persistence is defined as attending 9 or more months and/or attaining a credential (NPSAS: 2004 UG).

Source: U.S. Department of Education, National Center for Education Statistics (2004). 2003–04 National Profile of Undergraduates in U.S. Postsecondary Education Institutions (NPSAS: 2004 UG)

TABLE 6
Persistence Rates for Community College Students Nationwide by Income and Dependency Status

Income	Independent Did Not Work %	Independent Worked Part Time %	Independent Worked Full Time %	Dependent Did Not Work %	Dependent Worked Part Time %	Dependent Worked Full Time %
$0–4,999	53.1	53.4	40.0			
$5,000–9,999	46.4	57.2	50.6			
<$10,000				70.4	63.7	51.9
$10,000–19,999	49.7	54.8	48.5	63.5	66.6	57.8
$20,000–29,999	48.8	54.4	48.1	66.1	64.0	49.8
$30,000–39,999				54.7	64.6	48.2
$30,000–49,999	53.0	43.6	43.1			
$40,000–49,999				65.6	69.8	43.6
$50,000 +	45.5	48.2	36.2			
$50,000–59,999				62.1	70.5	47.6
$60,000–69,999				59.5	45.8	45.2
$70,000–79,999				50.7	62.9	42.2
$80,000–99,999				56.4	58.5	49.1
$100,000 +				56.2	61.0	47.2

Note: Persistence is defined as attending 9 or more months and/or attaining a credential (NPSAS:2004 UG).

Source: U. S. Department of Education, National Center for Education Statistics (2004). 2003–04 National Profile of Undergraduates in U.S. Postsecondary Education Institutions (NPSAS:2004 UG).

and independent students. We can see that dependent students who do not work persist at higher rates than their independent counterparts. In addition, dependent students who work part time and full time persist at higher rates than their independent counterparts. This pattern suggests that dependency status plays a role in persistence and that this status may be an intervening variable in work and persistence. We could reasonably assume that dependency on one's family involves a stronger support system that these students may look to when distressed. Family members may also provide students with motivational and financial support when faced with the challenges inherent in postsecondary education. As well, independent students may have dependents and these responsibilities take time away from college work (Bowl, 2003).

In sum, full-time work is a characteristic that decreases community college students' persistence across social categories. Community college students who work full time may not allot enough time to devote to their studies, thus making it difficult to keep up with their college work. On the other hand, not working or working part time appears to be a general trend that facilitates persistence. Having an income at one's disposal allows students who work part time to pay for necessary college materials such as books and transportation, and because the work is not full time, students are able to devote adequate time to their college work. However, the nature of the quantitative data available makes it difficult to determine just how much part-time working students do work[1] and what the conditions of work were for these students (e.g., on or off campus).

Community College Working Students' Educational Experiences: The Qualitative Summary

The quantitative data we present show that working full time is detrimental for community college students. But working part time is related to increased levels of persistence. The databases we examine offer limited information to explain what it means for college students to be both students and workers (full or part time) or what enables students to persist at college when they have to work while studying. Although we know the detrimental effects of working full time while studying, we know little about those cases in which community college students are capable of achieving their educational goals despite their at-risk conditions. There is a lack of studies about working students' educational experiences, sources of support, and coping strategies (Pascarella & Terenzini, 1998).

Our qualitative summary considers the ways that working community college students live the process of working and studying and the kinds of organizational and personal conditions that can enable community college students to persist in the midst of their multiple roles, responsibilities, and challenges. We analyzed the narratives of working students and college personnel at Bakersfield College (Bakersfield) in California and college personnel at Borough of Manhattan Community College (BMCC) in New York to explain how work relates to students. We present qualitative data on California and New York because the patterns in these states largely mirror the national pattern.[2] We decided to analyze these two states on the basis of the availability of bistate databases as well as previous fieldwork conducted in these two sites and 11 other community colleges across seven other states in the nation. Student populations in these states reflect the national population both demographically and in terms of students' amount of work and persistence.

Bakersfield College in Kern County, California, is one of the state's oldest community colleges, originating in 1913. A major focus of the institution is underrepresented populations and students at risk of dropping out. The majority of students at Bakersfield were female; 60.4% of the students were between 19 and 24 years old. Borough of Manhattan Community College, located in downtown Manhattan, is acclaimed as the largest community college in the city university system (The City University of New York). Although from its origins BMCC provided liberal arts education to students who planned to transfer to four-year colleges, its primary focus was to enact a business/technical-oriented mission. The majority of the student population was female (63%). African American and Hispanic students were 68% of the student body, and the average age of students was 23.8 years old.

The Work–School Conflict Among Nontraditional Students

For students in higher education, work has been identified as a "situational constraint" that causes competing demands for time and attention (Keith, 2007). Working students continually have to decide which role to play in a demanding life context (Smith, 2006). Both at Bakersfield and BMCC, college personnel noted that the student body mainly consisted of nontraditional students (e.g., low socioeconomic status, abused lives, undocumented immigrant status, special education needs, minority groups, and the like) whose concerns revolved around work activities. Thus, we use the term *nontraditional* to identify the majority population of community college students who work and who possess at least one other characteristic that defines them as nontraditional college students (Levin, 2007). We argue that work has a more negative effect on nontraditional than traditional students in that work activities (on or off campus) aggravate the already present instability in their lives. Previous studies have shown that nontraditional students tend to have unsettled lives that hinder their opportunities to identify paths toward new forms of self-understanding, educational goals, and professional identities (Kim, 2002; Lange, 2004; Levin, 2007). Working excessive hours (i.e., more than 20 hours per week) becomes a negative influence on nontraditional students' process of development when job activities intensify the disorientation in their lives and become a source of anxiety, stress, isolation, and unhealthy behaviors (Ashton & Elliott, 2007; Miller, Danner, & Staten, 2008; Smith, 2006).

We argue that nontraditional students who face a role conflict (i.e., student versus worker) in the midst of distressed pasts and precarious futures are not only trying to achieve a sense of stability in their lives but are also trying to manage the transition to academic culture. Most working students in community colleges in their late 20s are unfamiliar with the academic environment and the accompanying expectations, including required academic skills (Horn & Nevill, 2006; McSwain & Davis, 2007). For all students, attending a community college is a constant experience of adaptation in which they have to learn how to maximize their time, efforts, and learning experiences to become integrated into the academic and social dynamics that characterize college life (Carney-Crompton & Tan, 2002; Chaves, 2006). Students who work while studying struggle to learn how to change their lack of understanding of higher education to become insiders of academic culture (Kasworm, 2005; O'Donnell & Tobbell, 2007). The amount of time that work-related activities require of nontraditional students, however, may reduce opportunities for students to acknowledge and access the personal and institutional resources they can use to understand academic culture and become insiders.

Successful Working Students and Their Support Structures

We understand that a successful student is someone who can understand academic culture and utilize it to participate in educational practices that enable that student to reach higher levels of personal, professional, and occupational development. At Bakersfield, college personnel acknowledged that to create successful students, they needed to organize academic experiences (i.e., forms of interaction and instructional techniques) that enabled nontraditional working students to manage the everyday routines that resulted from having to enact various roles. We found that overcoming the work–school conflict among nontraditional working students was directly associated with the support that college personnel can provide to these students.

> In my class [in the nursing program] we talk about time management, test taking, the pressure. . . . [I]t's difficult to work and go to school with what is demanded. So how do you prepare? . . . [I]t's something that we recognized as an issue and it directly impacts their ability to be successful. How

do you handle the stress, the anxiety, all those things? (Jennifer, faculty, Nursing, Bakersfield)

We use the concept of support structures to refer to those student programs, organizational spaces, and institutional agents' behaviors that enabled students to learn about the academic culture, improve their academic performance, identify future goals and pursue further education, obtain a credential, transfer to a university, develop self-confidence, and/or acquire a better job. Examples of support structures include counseling, peer mentoring, flexible scheduling, and tutoring programs.

> We provide three component areas of support [counseling, academic advising, and tutoring] to help students become mainstream, because the notion has been that a number of these inner city students were not initially able to go to college. . . . They [students] do have the distractions outside of the school. . . . [O]nce they buy into the [Discovery] program they [have to] come in and talk and try to get at whatever distractions are that might be affecting them, talk to their counselors or their advisors. (director, Discovery Program, BMCC)

Similar to the findings in other studies, we note that when social support and guidance are offered to nontraditional working students, despite their challenging conditions, they achieve personal and social development such as confidence (Baxter-Magolda, 2003; Baxter-Magolda & King, 2007; Kaufman & Feldman, 2004), group membership or social networks (Brewer, Klein, & Mann, 2003; Dutton, Dukerich, & Harquail, 1994), skills, knowledge (Ellermann, Kataoka-Yahiro, & Wong, 2006), and sociocultural awareness (Belgarde, Mitchell, & Arquero, 2002; Lange, 2004). Students' transition into higher education is facilitated when academic practices are designed to promote student engagement and a sense of belonging (Carney-Crompton & Tan, 2002; Chang, 2005; Hagedorn, Maxwell, Rodriguez, Hocevar, & Fillpot, 2000; McArthur, 2005; O'Donnell & Tobbell, 2007). The creation of positive educational experiences for nontraditional working students occurred when college personnel (1) acknowledged students' needs and opportunities, (2) managed to create "connected classrooms" in which learners' experiences are validated as reservoirs of knowledge and connected to academic studies, (3) created both sources of challenge and support for students to expand their capacities, and (4) facilitated learning experiences based on relational and caring ways (Carney-Crompton & Tan, 2002; Chaves, 2006; Kasworm, 2005; Keith, 2007; Keith, Byerly, Floerchinger, Pence, & Thornberg, 2006).

College personnel were interested not only in implementing strategies to facilitate educational experiences but also in ensuring the persistence of nontraditional working students. Nontraditional working students at

Bakersfield were capable of excelling in their formal educational experiences as a result of the combined work of college personnel and students:

> I've seen programs . . . integrating more real life learning examples into their curriculum, drawing upon students, student life learning experiences to illustrate teaching points or teaching objectives. I'm seeing in some areas the schedule shifts are late afternoon, evening. . . . We have had classes on Saturday in some of the areas that I have responsibility for, with those working adults here. (Nan, Dean of Student Learning, Bakersfield)

At BMCC, college personnel were interested not only in implementing strategies to facilitate educational experiences but also in ensuring the persistence of nontraditional working students:

> [Students] may move out of state with family, so they just discontinue school. Some will have just stopped attending because they found temporary jobs. . . . [W]e try to go after those students. . . . We do have structured programs for those academically challenged ones. [We] work closer with them prior to the point that we consider to be at-risk. (director, Discovery Program, BMCC)

Working students at Bakersfield emphasized their improved capacities to think about themselves and to define and manage their future plans when they received support from college personnel:

> I learned how to [manage] my studies better. . . . I learned a lot about life that I didn't know. . . . [Faculty] made me realize that I can get a degree; they made me believe in myself. (James, liberal arts student, Bakersfield)

> I learned how to find myself in [the speech class] actually. . . . I discovered I'm stronger than I thought. I discovered that I don't always have to say yes to everything. . . . I'm stronger in my goals. I can do this; I can just keep on, never give up, just keep going, keep going, keep going. (Nidia, pre-nursing student, Bakersfield)

Students going through a process of transition became incorporated into higher educational culture when they participated in academic practices as well as formal and informal social encounters with peers and college personnel (O'Donnell & Tobbell, 2007; Pascarella, 1980; Pascarella, Pierson, Wolniak, & Terenzini, 2004; Pascarella & Terenzini, 1976, 1978, 1998). At Bakersfield and BMCC, students noted repeatedly that most of their academic achievements resulted from the interaction and support they found among faculty and staff:

My best experiences here would probably be the networking that went on here with the instructors, with students. . . . They [college staff] have been extremely helpful. Mentors are almost like an open book of knowledge. . . . [A] lot of times when I find myself in a situation that I don't find any avenues or exits to get out of, I'll ask questions. So besides the supportive services, there's a group of individuals here at Bakersfield College that have helped me along, helped support me and kind of carry me on so that I may succeed in what I'm trying to accomplish. (José, student, Anthropology and Forestry, Bakersfield)

Faculty members and administrators acknowledged that students' active engagement was central for them to achieve social and academic integration at community colleges. Our analysis supports other studies that have confirmed that social support is central for higher education students to overcome the school–work conflict: The greater the quality and amount of support enjoyed by working students, the lesser the level of perceived strain (Adebayo, 2006). College personnel both at Bakersfield and BMCC were concerned with constructing well-organized educational experiences that provided comprehensive support to their students. Nontraditional students, who play both the role of worker and student, have greater opportunities to learn and achieve their goals when they are exposed to sources for support such as small group practice, personalized attention, flexible scheduling, and the integration of college and working (Brewer et al., 2003).

Personal Factors That Moderate the Work–Study Conflict

We argue that becoming a successful working student may depend not only on the existence of support structures and relational practices but also on students' agentic approach to their participation decisions. We understand one's agentic power as the capacity to coordinate thinking and actions to work on the definition and achievement of goals (Ortner, 2006). Agentic power can be constructed as part of a process of identity development and the construction of self-authorship (Baxter-Magolda & King, 2007; Pizzolato, 2005; Swidler, 2001). We found that students who excelled in college while working exhibited self-confidence and motivation to cope with multiple role demands. We suggest that nontraditional working students who persisted both at Bakersfield and BMCC were individuals who expressed their capacity of agency by developing personal projects or plans to gain academic knowledge, personal development, and working skills and qualifications. Students who persisted were motivated and developed a sense of self-confidence to define strategies of action to navigate their college experience. Working students at Bakersfield exhibited strong personal commitments:

They wanted to improve their lives by developing new attitudes and capacities to manage their everyday challenges and context demands.

> I'm 43. I'm a single mom of 6, first generation college student. Growing up I was never encouraged to go to college. Ended up in an abusive marriage; 2 years ago got out. And knew the only way we could stand on our own two feet was for me to come back to school. . . . I also work in addition to going to school and taking care of my family. . . . I had to fight to get here. . . . I fought and I got here. And I graduate in May. (Ellen, reentry student, Human Services program, Bakersfield)

Not all of the nontraditional working students were confident or had personal plans when they enrolled at Bakersfield or BMCC; however, the colleges' support structures enabled students to develop personal attributes (e.g., motivation and confidence) that moderated the negative effects of the work–study conflict. Students who worked while studying at Bakersfield were able to achieve their educational goals as a result of the personal development that they reached as part of their engagement in academic practices and their close interactions with college personnel.

Both at Bakersfield and BMCC, we found that nontraditional working students who were academic achievers expressed their agentic approach by developing coping styles that enabled them to respond to their multiple role demands. Morris, Brooks, and May (2003) suggest that a coping style is the typical manner in which an individual confronts a stressful situation. Working students have to develop specific styles of coping to be able to achieve their educational goals and perform proficiently in classrooms. Morris and colleagues found that nontraditional students tended to develop a "task-oriented coping style" that involved a student choosing to cope with stress by setting plans and mapping solutions. Nontraditional students' frequent use of task-oriented coping may be associated with the necessity of having to move across multiple roles and tasks. Students who persisted at college explained the strategies they developed to accomplish their academic demands in the midst of everyday life.

> I'm concentrating on one subject first. I want to go in and do writing classes, English classes; I want to do all my English at once. Then when I get in the science classes, I want to just do all science classes. That's why I'm not, I don't like to mix them all together, so that way I want to concentrate on one thing, know what I'm doing to get to the next step. . . . [A]fter I had my last child . . . he's three now, I decided I wanted to do something better than what I'm doing now and that's why I decided to come back to school. . . . I work full-time; I'm a mom and I come part-time to school. . . . I'm taking three courses, so mostly I study just all morning and afternoon until 3:00, from 8 to 3. (Nidia, pre-nursing student, Bakersfield)

These nontraditional working students who reached positive developmental outcomes (e.g., self-confidence, a certificate, an associate's degree) were supported by college structures designed to promote personal growth, future expectations, and acquisition of new skills. Support systems enabled students to develop confident selves and strategies of engagement (e.g., task-oriented coping style) to navigate their college experiences.

Conclusion

Work is certainly a central characteristic of community college students. Yet, as this and other chapters in this volume describe, research is scarce on the understanding of and theorizing about students who work and attend community colleges. Quantitative data sources do not classify types of work and whether the work is educationally related or not. Available databases offer limited information to gain a rich understanding about the relationships among: (1) the nature of the work activities that students perform, (2) the characteristics of community college students (e.g., varied roles, low incomes, and weak academic backgrounds), and (3) students' academic behaviors in college. Qualitative research can help to close the gaps in the literature and identify conceptual tools to make sense of the educational experiences of working students in community colleges. Scholars and researchers should review and renew previous research on community colleges and their students, particularly on student outcomes, incorporating student conditions such as work as major variables on the one hand and as a framework for understanding how college affects students and what students actually achieve. We suggest that research on community college students take a new direction in emphasizing the personal and life conditions (e.g., social and economic contexts) of students, the actions of institutions to accommodate these conditions, and the relationships between and among these conditions, institutional actions, and persistence.

Our findings emphasize that the work–study conflict is more detrimental for nontraditional working students than it is for other students. The vast majority (80%) of community college students can be viewed as nontraditional students. This population has to face conflicting roles in the midst of already strenuous conditions that demand both stability in their daily lives and their integration into academic life. Having to decide between the roles of student or worker is a source of stress and a constraint that may hamper attainment for those who do not have structures of support to navigate the varied responsibilities attached to multiple roles. Students who work and especially those who work full time have limited opportunities to engage socially and academically with other students, college personnel, or institutional life more generally. Both the positive and negative effects of engagement or its lack thereof are dependent on student characteristics (e.g., age, academic background, domestic status, financial status, native language, and physical condition). College programs that endeavor to support students would be wise to be adaptable to the populations that they serve. College services, such as counseling, day care, health, and library, would have greater saliency if they were adaptable to specific populations. For example, services that are available during nighttime or weekend classes would accommodate students who work in the day or during the week and attend classes only at night or on weekends.

Support structures may enable nontraditional working students to persist and even excel in college by strengthening personal and academic dimensions such as self-confidence, critical thinking, social networking, and decision making. Academic practices that emphasize interaction and dialogue among students and college personnel enable students not only to be integrated socially and academically into college life but also to develop personal goals, such as career pathways (Levin et al., 2008). Institutions have acted both formally and informally to offer support to ensure persistence. The actions of particular institutional agents in this regard can move beyond the norms or policies of institutions to provide appropriate service or help for students. More can be done to understand behaviors of both institutions, generally, and, specifically, institutional agents. We have begun to theorize "coconstruction" of student and organizational identity as a central and defining condition that explains the institution–student nexus that can advance student development, including persistence (Levin & Montero-Hernandez, in press).

We speculate that both practice and policy, at the state level and at the institutional level, can gain from attention to research and knowledge about students' conditions, specifically their lives as workers who are students or as students who work. Policymakers and state legislators need to be better informed about community college students, the overwhelming majority of whom work. The community college serves the least academically prepared and the least advantaged population of postsecondary students. These are the students with the greatest needs, and to fulfill their financial needs and attend college, they must work (Levin, 2007). Yet of all public educational institutions, community colleges are the least well state funded and the least financially endowed to help these students (Bailey & Morest, 2006). Students work to support themselves, or their families, or their college attendance, or any combination of these. Work, certainly at the level of full-time work, distracts students, takes time away from college and formal learning, and is associated with lack of persistence and potentially lower grades. Financial support from the state as well as from institutions may enable students to limit work hours and certainly refrain from full-time work.

Endnotes

1. Part-time work is defined by the Nation Center for Education Statistics (NCES) as any amount of hours worked under 35 hours per week (NPSAS: 2003 UG).

2. The demographic statistics for California and New York are available on request.

References

Adebayo, D. O. (2006). Workload, social support, and work-school conflict among Nigerian non-traditional students. *Journal of Career Development, 33*(2), 125–141.

Adelman, C. (1992). *The way we are: The American community college as thermometer.* Washington, DC: U.S. Department of Education.

Ashton, J., & Elliott, R. (2007). Study, work, rest and play: Juggling the priorities of students' lives. *Australian Journal of Early Childhood, 32*(2), 15–22.

Astin, A. W. (1984). Student involvement: A developmental theory for higher education. *Journal of College Student Personnel, 25*, 297–308.

Bailey, T., & Morest, V. S. (Eds.). (2006). *Defending the community college equity agenda.* Baltimore: The Johns Hopkins University Press.

Bailey, T. R., & Morest, V. S. (2004). *The organizational efficiency of multiple missions for community colleges.* New York: Teachers College, Columbia University.

Baxter-Magolda, M. (2003). Identity and learning: Student affairs' role in transforming higher education. *Journal of College Student Development, 44*(1), 231–247.

Baxter-Magolda, M., & King, P. M. (2007). Interview strategies for assessing self-authorship: Constructing conversations to assess meaning making. *Journal of College Student Development, 48*(5), 491–508.

Belgarde, M. J., Mitchell, R. D., & Arquero, A. (2002). What do we have to do to create culturally responsive programs? The challenge of transforming American Indian teacher education. *Action Teacher Education, 24*(2), 42–54.

Bowl, M. (2003). *Non-traditional entrants to higher education.* Stoke on Trent, England: Trentham Books.

Brewer, S. A., Klein, J. D., & Mann, K. (2003). Using small group learning strategies with adult re-entry students. *College Student Journal, 37*(2), 286–297.

Brock, T., Matus-Grossman, L., & Hamilton, G. (2001). Welfare reform and community colleges: A policy and research context. *New Directions in Community Colleges, 116*, 5–20.

Carney-Crompton, S., & Tan, J. (2002). Support systems, psychological functioning, and academic performance of non-traditional female students. *Adult Education Quarterly, 52*(2), 140–154.

Chang, J. C. (2005). Faculty–student interaction at the community college: A focus on students of color. *Research in Higher Education, 46*, 769–802.

Chaves, C. (2006). Involvement, development, and retention: Theoretical foundations and potential extensions for adult community college students. *Community College Review, 34*(2), 139–152.

Cohen, A., & Brawer, F. (1996). *The American community college* (3rd ed.). San Francisco: Jossey-Bass.

Dutton, J. E., Dukerich, J. M., & Harquail, C. V. (1994). Organizational images and member identification. *Administrative Science Quarterly, 39*(2), 239–263.

Ellermann, C. R., Kataoka-Yahiro, M. R., & Wong, L. C. (2006). Logic models used to enhance critical thinking. *Journal of Nursing Education, 45*(6), 220–227.

Frye, J. (1994). Educational paradigms in the professional literature of the community college. In J. Smart (Ed.), *Higher education: Handbook of theory and research* (Vol. X, pp. 181–224). New York: Agathon Press.

Hagedorn, L. S., Maxwell, W., Rodriguez, P., Hocevar, D., & Fillpot, J. (2000). Peer and student–faculty relations in community colleges. *Community College Journal of Research and Practice, 24*(7), 587–598.

Heisserer, D., & Parette, P. (2002). Advising-at-risk students in college and university settings. *College Student Journal, 36*, 69–84.

Hoachlander, G., Sikora, A. C., & Horn, L. (2003). *Community college students: Goals, academic preparation, and outcomes* (NCES 2003–164). Washington, DC: National Center for Education Statistics.

Horn, L., & Nevill, S. (2006). *Profile of undergraduates in U.S. postsecondary education institutions 2003–04, with a special analysis of community college students* (NCES 2006–184). Washington, DC: National Center for Education Statistics.

Kasworm, C. (2005). Adult student identity in an intergenerational community college classroom. *Adult Education Quarterly, 56*(1), 3–20.

Kaufman, P., & Feldman, K. A. (2004). Forming identities in college: A sociological approach. *Research in Higher Education, 45*(5), 463–496.

Keith, P. M. (2007). Barriers and non-traditional students' use of academic and social services. *College Student Journal, 41*(4), 1123–1127.

Keith, P. M., Byerly, C., Floerchinger, H., Pence, E., & Thornberg, E. (2006). Deficit and resilience perspectives on performance and campus comfort of adult students. *College Student Journal, 40*(3), 546–556.

Kim, K. A. (2002). Exploring the meaning of "non-traditional" at the community college. *Community College Review, 30*(1), 74–89.

Lange, E. A. (2004). Transformative and restorative learning: A vital dialectic for sustainable societies. *Adult Education Quarterly, 54*(2), 121–139.

Levin, J. S. (2007). *Non-traditional students and community colleges: The conflict of justice and neoliberalism.* New York: Palgrave Macmillan.

Levin, J. S., & Montero-Hernandez, V. (in press). *Community colleges and their students: Co-construction and organizational identity.* New York: Palgrave Macmillan.

Levin, J. S., Montero-Hernandez, V., & Cerven, C. (2008, May). *Co-construction, constraint, and self-expression.* Paper presented at the Association for Institutional Research, Seattle, WA.

McArthur, R. C. (2005). Faculty-based advising: An important factor in community college retention. *Community College Review, 32*(4), 1–18.

McSwain, C., & Davis, R. (2007). *College access for the working poor: Overcoming burdens to succeed in higher education.* Washington, DC: Institute for Higher Education Policy.

Miller, K., Danner, F., & Staten, R. (2008). Relationship of work hours with selected health behaviors and academic progress among a college student cohort. *Journal of American College Health, 56,* 675–679.

Morris, E. A., Brooks, P. R., & May, J. L. (2003). The relationship between achievement goal orientation and coping style: Traditional vs. non-traditional college students. *College Student Journal, 37*(1), 3–8.

O'Donnell, V. L., & Tobbell, J. (2007). The transition of adult students to higher education: Legitimate peripheral participation in a community of practice? *Adult Education Quarterly, 57*(4), 312–328.

Ortner, S. (2006). *Anthropology and social theory. Culture, power, and the acting subject.* London: Duke University Press.

Pagenette, K., & Kozell, C. (2001). The advanced technology program: A welfare-to-work *success* story. *New Directions in Community Colleges, 116,* 5–20.

Pascarella, E. T. (1980). Student–faculty informal contact and college outcomes. *Review of Educational Research, 50,* 545–595.

Pascarella, E. T., Pierson, C. T., Wolniak, G. C., & Terenzini, P. T. (2004). First-generation college students: Additional evidence on college experiences and outcomes. *Journal of Higher Education, 75,* 249–284.

Pascarella, E. T., & Terenzini, P. T. (1976). Informal interaction with faculty and freshman ratings of academic and nonacademic experience of college. *Journal of Educational Research, 70,* 35–41.

Pascarella, E. T., & Terenzini, P. T. (1978). Student–faculty informal relationships and freshman year educational outcomes. *Journal of Educational Research, 71,* 183–189.

Pascarella, E. T., & Terenzini, P. T. (1998). Studying college students in the 21st century: Meeting new challenges. *Review of Higher Education, 21,* 151–165.

Pascarella, E. T., & Terenzini, P. (2005). *How college affects students: A third decade of research.* San Francisco: Jossey-Bass.

Phillippe, K. A., & Gonzalez Sullivan, L. (2005). *National profile of community colleges: Trends and statistics* (4th ed.). Washington, DC: American Association of Community Colleges.

Pizzolato, J. E. (2005). Creating crossroads for self-authorship: Investigating the provocative moment. *Journal of College Student Development, 46*(6), 624–641.

Simmons, D. L. (1995). Retraining dislocated workers in the community college: Identifying factors for persistence. *Community College Review, 23*(2), 47–59.

Smith, J. S. (2006). Exploring the challenges for non-traditional male students transitioning into a nursing program. *Journal of Nursing Education, 45*(7), 263–269.

Swidler, A. (2001). *Talk of love. How culture matters.* Chicago: University of Chicago Press.

U.S. Department of Education (2004). *2003–04 national profile of undergraduates in U.S. postsecondary education institutions* (NPSAS: 2004 UG). Washington, DC: National Center for Educational Statistics.

Woodlief, B., Thomas, C., & Orozco, G. (2003). *California's gold: Claiming the promise of diversity in our community colleges.* Oakland, CA: California Tomorrow.

4

MOBILE WORKING STUDENTS

A Delicate Balance of College, Family, and Work

Mary Ziskin, Vasti Torres, Don Hossler, and Jacob P. K. Gross

Increasingly, education policymakers are turning attention to the access and persistence of the new college majority—a group that may be described as *mobile working students* (Ewell, Schild, & Paulson, 2003). Traditionally, much research on college students has focused on students who graduate from high school and move on to attend a four-year college on a full-time basis, graduating in four to six years. However, as Adelman (2006) and others show, even among traditional-age college students this pattern of linear enrollment is less and less common. Thus, as Kasworm (chapter 2) also argues, metaphors such as the education *pipeline* no longer fit. Instead, students are more accurately represented as moving along *pathways* or even *swirling* toward postsecondary success.

The experience of the mobile working student as conceived in this chapter encompasses multiple aspects of mobility and the varied, nonlinear, and evolving patterns of college going increasingly characteristic of students nationwide. One aspect of mobility in this complex and emerging picture centers on students' experiences at commuter institutions, *moving onto and off of* campuses. In addition, students enroll in multiple institutions, moving *between* them. Finally, because they move *into and out of* institutions as well, the concomitant issues of attrition, stop-out, and degree attainment are also important to this project.

The role of paid work in these evolving patterns of enrollment, college experience, and student success is central. As others in this volume also note, about 80% of American undergraduates worked while attending college in 1999–2000 (King, 2003). This rate represents an 8 percentage point increase over undergraduates less than a decade earlier, when 72% worked (Cuccaro-Alamin & Choy, 1998). Moreover, the percentage of *full-time* college students who are employed has risen steadily over the past three decades, from

36% in 1973 to 48% in 2003 (Fox, Connolly, & Snyder, 2005). The share of full-time college students who work at least 20 hours a week has also been growing, rising from 17% in 1973 to 30% in 2003. Perna, Cooper, and Li (2006) note the prevalence of work for pay among college students and argue that we must examine student employment patterns, reduce the financial need to work, improve the quality of students' employment experiences, and adapt educational services to better enable working students to achieve, persist, and graduate.

Many current education policies at the campus, state, and federal levels are based on the stereotype of the "traditional student"—one who moves through the educational system in a linear and predictable manner. In this context, many campus and state policies—on issues ranging from financial aid to academic probation—are not designed to serve mobile working students. Policymakers wishing to reformulate relevant policies for mobile working students, however, face a dearth of state- and campus-oriented policy research on working students.

The purpose of the chapter is to illuminate students' experiences balancing work, family, and college. Reporting on the analysis of focus groups and interviews with more than 90 working students attending three commuter institutions in a Midwestern metropolitan area, we explore working students' descriptions and meaning making, with the goal of developing theory and practice that support equity and success for these students.

The chapter serves the central questions of this volume in a number of ways. The chapter first highlights and differentiates the diversity of experiences typically included under the broad label "working college student." This discussion improves our understanding of how students make meaning of school, work, and academic success, thus illuminating how working students' strategies, decisions, and behaviors are conditioned by varying circumstances and structures. This kind of inquiry does not lead to causal explanation. Rather, this research contributes direct and nuanced expression from students and a contextualized critical analysis of how structures—which include socioeconomic conditions and previous educational experience, as well as education policy, institutional culture, and praxis on campus—shape students' experiences and ultimate success in college.

Students' daily lives and the obligations they strive to balance reflect the changing landscape of culture, economy, history, and college going. Hearing students' direct and detailed descriptions of these obligations and the reasoning used to balance them is essential to moving higher education research and institutional practice into areas and orientations that are consonant and supportive of students' lives.

In this research, we draw on previous work regarding working students (Bradley, 2006; Choy & Berker, 2003; Hughes & Mallette, 2003; Pascarella & Terenzini, 2005; Perna et al., 2006), academic success and degree attainment (Berger & Milem, 2000; Braxton & McClendon, 2001–2002; Calcagno, Crosta, Bailey, & Jenkins, 2006; Tinto & Pusser, 2006), and the role of financial aid in postsecondary access and success (Paulsen & St. John, 1997; St. John, Paulsen, & Starkey, 1996; Stage & Hossler, 2000). Taking these threads as a point of departure, we define the relevant questions surrounding working students as a convergence of these three problems. The nexus studies of St. John and colleagues (e.g., St. John et al., 1996) highlight the need to contextualize models of academic success within a nexus of social, academic, and financial pressures. Our study broadens this focus with the use of relevant qualitative data.

We also draw on a social reproduction perspective to expand the frame for understanding students' college-going behaviors beyond local processes and encompass the contexts and complexity of the broader social world. In adopting this perspective, we hold that educational institutions—and the structures that define and shape their practices—contribute to the replication and legitimation of existing social power structures from one generation to the next. The result of this replication is that students are channeled toward roles that reflect their class origins, defined in the United States by race/ethnicity as well as by economic class.

Whereas Bourdieu's (1973) original critiques sought to emphasize the replicative role of schooling in the face of contemporaneous emphases on the transformative potential of schools, this chapter builds on the understanding, also implicit in his work, that educational institutions simultaneously accomplish both transformative and replicative roles (Bourdieu & Wacquant, 1992). Focusing the chapter this way provides us with important advantages. For example, taking this approach allows us to acknowledge the dedication and resistance that faculty, advisors, and students practice in these institutions. Dedication and resistance of this kind are rooted in a belief not only in social mobility, but also in the potentially transformational roles of these institutions in that mobility. At the same time, it is important to see and understand the replicative workings of educational institutions and to broaden the view on improving equity and educational opportunity beyond the discourse of institutional improvement. Engaging in research to understand these workings is not to attribute purposeful or deterministic direction of students into roles defined in part by racial and economic power. Rather it is to see how these structures inform all of our actions as educators and students, as individuals and institutions. In addition it is to understand how these structures and dynamics shape what we are able to perceive as possibilities, as the bounds of our actions. Thus, to approach the research of student experiences in this way is also to deepen our understanding of praxis through and within institutions.

Within this social reproduction perspective, Berger's (2000) framework is particularly relevant because it posits that both institutions and individuals seek to optimize economic and cultural capital. Berger sees this as one central mechanism shaping students' enrollment decisions and ultimately their success in college. Incorporating this view into new research holds potential for understanding how colleges and universities work within the broader social, economic, and political structures that define and shape educational opportunity.

Drawing on extensive qualitative data, this chapter sharpens the focus of higher education research on working students. The findings contribute to the development of research and theory surrounding the academic success of commuting, working, and independent students. In addition, this chapter lays a foundation for education policy and practices based on real experiences and actual enrollment patterns increasingly characteristic of students across the country. Where professional development and expectations on campus are based on misaligned conceptions of student experience, faculty members, institutional policymakers, and student services professionals will struggle to skillfully communicate with and support students. The resulting social distance can undermine students' efforts to develop a viable path toward completing college, especially for those students balancing complex interdependent goals. In all, this situation exacerbates the replicative potential of educational institutions and weakens the transformative contributions and orientations that administrators, faculty, practitioners, and students bring to these campuses. Exploring the tensions described in social reproduction theory in this way provides a more direct and nuanced sense of the obligations and understandings that shape students' experiences balancing family, work, and college at these institutions. As a result, this chapter contributes improved tools and frameworks that institutional leaders in particular may use to shape practice.

Previous Research on Working College Students

Higher education research based on the traditional college student experience has focused on linkages between academic and social integration, and on the resulting positive impact on student persistence (Bean, 1985; Kuh, 1995; Pascarella & Staver, 1985; Pascarella & Terenzini, 1983; Tinto, 1975). Not surprisingly, studies of working students have found that as students devote more time to employment they are less likely to be as engaged in academic and social activities (Fjortoft, 1995; Lundberg, 2004). Several studies report a negative relationship between working more than 15 hours a week and social and academic integration (King, 2003; Pascarella & Terenzini, 1991; Perna et al., 2006), as well as persistence (Cuccaro-Alamin & Choy, 1998; Kulm & Cramer, 2006).

Other studies have found paid work to have a positive effect on student persistence (Choy, 2000; Horn & Berktold, 1998; King, 2002). Students who worked 1 to 15 hours per week had a higher rate of degree attainment than did students who did not work and students who worked more than 15 hours per week (Choy & Berker, 2003). Other research demonstrates that the number of hours worked per week is unrelated to academic achievement as measured by standardized tests (Pascarella & Terenzini, 2005) or grade point average (Bradley, 2006; Furr & Elling, 2000). As other authors in this volume contend, the seeming contradictions in research examining the relationship between working and student engagement, academic achievement, and persistence warrant further investigation.

Bradley (2006) notes that the literature in this area is defined mainly by four threads, each separately testing an underlying proposition regarding the relationship between work and college going: (a) that work is detrimental to students' academic success, (b) that there is a negative correlation between the number of hours worked and grades, (c) that work in excess of 15 to 20 hours per week is detrimental to academic performance, and (d) that the quality or relevance of the work moderates the effects of work on academic success. Citing less widely pursued conclusions within the literature, Bradley notes a few studies with findings that support a fifth proposition: (e) that "there may be no reliable relationship between paid work and academic performance" (p. 484). Clearly, more research is necessary to resolve the contradictions that characterize the literature and to develop our understanding of how paid work influences academic success and degree completion.

The extent to which these threads of research adequately consider institutional context is unclear. Whereas Levin and colleagues (chapter 3) observe that few studies look at working students at community colleges, we also note that little research has examined working students attending four-year commuter institutions. Hughes and Mallette (2003) recommend that future research focus on students at commuter institutions separate from students in residential institutions.

This chapter considers working students in the context of commuter institutions in a metropolitan area where work for pay outside of the college environment is considered the norm. Our focus on urban commuter institutions is supported by data from recent studies. In 2003, for example, 59% of undergraduate students attended college on less than a full-time basis, and 40% of undergraduates attended community colleges (American Council on Education [ACE], 2005). Urban institutions in particular tend to attract more working students, a trend that is likely to increase considering that 37% of undergraduate students at four-year institutions were financially independent in 2000 (Choy, 2002). Moreover, urban universities tend to serve commuter, first-generation, and minority students (Elliott, 1994). These attendance patterns make research on urban commuter institutions critical to understanding the changing picture of student success. Carol Kasworm (chapter 2) offers further support for the focus on commuter institutions.

As also noted by other chapters in this volume, studies on the effects of work on academic success seldom examine the effects of working on older and nontraditional students, who, given commitments to supporting a family, may not have a choice whether to work (Baum, 2006). The literature considering community college students, as described by Levin et al. (chapter 3) and other researchers, sheds light on the experiences of this group of students. In a large-scale qualitative study of working students at community colleges in several states, Matus-Grossman and Gooden (2002) found that juggling work, family, and school was a major reason many students reported for not completing their degree. Lapovsky (2008) offers the following observations regarding adult learners and independent students:

> The group we define as independent students based on our current financial aid definitions makes up about half of all undergraduate college students in the United States today. The students in this group are extremely diverse; they are characterized by factors that lead them to have a lower probability of graduating from college than dependent students. (pp. 154–155)

Consistent with these recommendations, Tom Bailey and his colleagues at the Community College Resource Center are shedding light on the variegated and complex world of students enrolled at community colleges. Calcagno and colleagues (2006) found that older working community college students enrolled in remedial courses showed greater levels of academic intensity than younger students did. Nevertheless, Bailey, Calcagno, Jenkins, Kienzl, and Leinbach (2005) also report that adult community college students are more likely to enroll in certificate than associate's degree programs; these two types of programs may be affected in different ways by policy and practice.

These working students—nontraditional students and students enrolled at commuter institutions and at community colleges—share experiences that are both underexamined and central to understanding how to ensure their genuine opportunity and academic success. Because regional, urban institutions and community colleges are more likely to enroll part-time, nontraditional, and working adults (Elliott, 1994), the context for this study is an important contribution; this intersection of students represents a large proportion of students at the three site institutions for this study. Consequently, this research contributes empirical knowledge on little-understood student experiences that are relevant to the assessment and improvement of education policies and practices.

Research Methods

Structured to expand the focus beyond what one institution can do for "its" students, this study explores and describes college going, working, family demands, and academic success among students attending institutions in a single metropolitan region in the deindustrialized Midwest. The chapter relies on extensive qualitative data and situated description to examine these phenomena. Our research questions and methods focus on students, student experiences, and the potential influence institutions and the context of the region as a whole can bring to students' experiences. More specifically, the chapter explores the following research questions:

1. What are the characteristics, perceptions, and experiences of mobile working students who enroll in postsecondary education in this region?
2. What roles do the demands of college, work, and family life play in the academic success of mobile working students?

A regional focus is necessary because, as we note earlier, a traditional model of linear college attendance at a single institution does not provide an accurate framework through which to understand the complex postsecondary patterns of nontraditional students and students who attend commuter institutions. Moreover, the region of interest in this study offers an opportunity to understand how economic trends intersect and interact with education. Like much of the United States, this region has seen a marked decrease in manufacturing jobs over the past few decades. Job growth in the region has occurred in healthcare-related industries, which often require postsecondary credentialing. The region's demographic trends also parallel broader national trends. African Americans and Latinos make up a growing portion of the overall population, including students enrolled in K–12 education. In the next 10 to 20 years, the face of postsecondary education in the region will literally and figuratively look much different from how it has historically looked, and will change in ways that are similar to what much of the country will experience. Taken together, these trends suggest that, although this chapter does not produce broadly generalizable results, many of the findings may be applicable to higher education throughout the United States.

The students in the Midwestern metropolitan region we study epitomize mobile working students. In 2003–2004, approximately 15,000 undergraduates were enrolled at the three institutions that participated in the study (regional campuses of two public universities and one multicampus community college). Few of these students fit into the category of *traditional* student; they instead have the following characteristics:

- Nearly 26% were age 30 or older, whereas only 25% were under age 21.
- Just 44% were enrolled full time.

- More than 50% neither received nor applied for any form of financial aid.
- Nearly 30% reported incomes below $30,000.

Students enrolled in these schools are also likely to be working. A recent survey conducted by the participating institutions showed that more than 80% of students were employed part or full time, more than 35% were employed full time, and 20% reported working more than 40 hours a week (Hossler, Gross, Pellicciotti, Fischer, & Excell, 2005).

Study Design

The primary research design for the larger study combines an applied ethnographic approach (Chambers, 2000) with a range of descriptive and inferential analyses using a statewide longitudinal student unit record database. In this chapter, we share findings from the qualitative portion of the larger project. Applied ethnographic research and robust qualitative data are used to understand the experiences and identify ways to foster the success of mobile working students.

The academic success of college students revolves around an interaction between institutions and students. Culture is often an operative part of complex social interactions such as the ones that occur as institutions of higher education adapt to evolving student realities. Previous research on student success has been criticized for its limitations in understanding the processes and experiences relevant to the persistence of many students: students at nonresidential institutions (Braxton, Hirschy, & McClendon, 2004), low-income students, students of color (Bensimon, 2007; Guiffrida, 2006; Rendón, Jalomo, & Nora, 2000; Tierney, 1992), part-time students (Adelman, 2007), working students (Perna et al., 2006), and students who attend multiple institutions over time (Adelman, 2007). This study seeks to illuminate the underexamined aspects of these interactions in ways that are currently not possible with existing data sets and the limitations associated with quantitative survey research methods. It is difficult for surveys to capture the critical or less socially desirable understandings of students and institutions (Chambers, 2000; Converse & Presser, 1986; Groves et al., 2004), but it is possible to capture these understandings through qualitative data and the approaches adopted in this study.

Data Collection Procedures

In the first year of this study, we conducted a set of focus groups and interviews centered on students' experiences with work. Specific interview questions probed: (1) how students' educational goals and the demands of their programs play into decisions related to family and work, (2) how students understand their work lives as affecting their educational decisions, and (3) how students pay for their education. We also conducted focus groups and interviews with institutional practitioners and faculty on each partner campus. Although not the focus of this chapter, faculty and practitioner data have enabled us to derive a complete picture of the interactions at the center of student success.

To ensure the representation of a broad range of student experiences and perspectives, student focus group participants were recruited through required introductory general education courses and ad hoc recruitment in areas visited by a high volume of students on each campus. The 92 first-round student focus group participants ranged from age 18 to older than 55, were representative of the region's racial and ethnic diversity, and included students with and without children.

Data Analysis Procedures

Data analysis began with low-inference coding and, through a collaborative process, built toward more focused and theoretically defined coding and categorization (Carspecken, 1996). Early analyses of focus groups and interview transcriptions revolved mainly around an iterative coding process whereby multiple rounds of open coding and discussions among the research team led to an initial list of low-inference codes to be applied in subsequent rounds of thematic coding. We used a qualitative data analysis software package *Atlas.ti* to store and organize the data and analyses.

To understand the role of norms and expectations in more extended exchanges with students, we used pragmatic horizon analysis (Carspecken, 1996) and focused alternately on "discourses-in-practice" and "discursive practice" as outlined by Gubrium and Holstein (2000). Consistent with the recommendations of these approaches, we examined interview data in context and by theme in alternation. These processes and the resulting documents provided material for peer debriefing sessions in which we discussed analyses with outside and collaborating researchers to probe the inferences folded into our emerging analyses.

Quotes included as examples in the results section below represent prominent patterns from the analyses. Although we chose one excerpt over other examples because of its particular features—a succinctness in some cases or an additional, contextual point brought to the fore—each quote is drawn from within groupings of similar examples in the focus group data. In presenting each point, we also include information about the prevalence of the pattern within the focus group data. We also employ a reflexive process in selecting examples, probing our own reasoning and perceptions in the analysis, and probing counterexamples for further nuance.

Trustworthiness, or the quality of the research process, was supported not only through these reflexive practices but also through the use of a research team to collect and analyze data. Each person on the research team represented different life experiences and each had some experience as student, researcher, or employee at commuter institutions like those considered in this study. Peer debriefing further allowed multiple perspectives to be considered when the codes were examined.

Results

In this chapter, we focus on how students make sense of their roles, actions, and conditions with regard to work, family, and college. Our analyses led us to highlight two areas of students' descriptions: (1) the range of obligations shaping their daily lives, and (2) their college experiences and perceptions of connection and disconnection on campus.

Delicate Balances: Students Describe Obligations and Daily Lives

To answer one of the most basic questions at the heart of this research—What are the daily obligations of working students, commuting students, and adult learners?—we explored in depth how participating students described their daily lives and routines. In preliminary focus groups (Hernandez, Ziskin, Gross, & Fashola, 2007), we found that working students often described heavy, highly structured daily and weekly schedules. In the full round of student focus groups conducted in 2008, we asked students to tell us about the events, obligations, and contours of their daily lives.

The nature and scope of these patterns varied greatly across students with different financial and family situations, as illustrated in a brief exchange among five regional university students:

> P2: I schedule work around my classes. Work is just not even that important. It's not my career. So, I really don't care about it.
>
> P3: . . . Working [until late], and closing—like I like to go [out] after work too sometimes, or study—I have to give myself at least a later class. So ten's about a good time, because then you, there's a lot more classes around ten and one, so that's how I pick my classes. And then . . . I did one day longer and one day earlier, so on those days that I get out earlier from school I can get more hours in at work. So I did schedule at the beginning and after work pretty much.
>
> P1: I just like going [to class] two days a week. . . . [It allows] just more time to study too. I have Wednesday and Monday to finish what I need. So I can do a class for each day if I wanted to.
>
> P5: I usually do the opposite of that. I usually go to school Monday through the Thursday because I know if I have those two extra days

off I'll end up working those two days and then I won't have any—
I'll lose time that I'd be either studying or doing homework, or
something like that.

P4: I just go around the time I think somebody can watch the baby.

Although all the students in this exchange appeared to be traditional-age
students, the conversation highlights important differences in their personal
situations as well as in their approaches to balancing work and family obligations along with college study. One participant (P4) was a mother in her
early 20s with two part-time jobs. Another, a full-time student in her mid-
20s (P2), worked about half time. A third young woman, a dependent student in her late teens (P3), carried a full-time course load while holding down
two part-time jobs totaling nearly 40 hours per week. The remaining two
participants were young men—a father with a part-time job (P5) and a late
teen dependent-status student (P1) working about 35 hours per week. This
passage provides a particularly concentrated example of the variations in
approaches and personal context that emerged in nearly all the student focus
groups.

Of course this variation reflects variations in life circumstances—of having children or having parental financial support in some way. We saw some
variation among older students as well, again reflecting different underlying
circumstances. Some lived in multigenerational settings, while others shared
a combined family income either with partners or other relatives. Just as with
the traditional-age students in this example, family obligations differed for
parents and nonparents and with the ages of participants' children.

Dividing the Week

Participating students described how they structured time as a basic strategy
in balancing work, family, and college. The most common time-structuring
pattern divided the week in varying schedules day-by-day in regular patterns.
This might take the form of planning for classes on Tuesdays and Thursdays
only, for example, to reserve Monday, Wednesday, and Friday for work and
other responsibilities. Perhaps because of its advantages in consolidating
transportation runs and general compatibility with the flexible hourly scheduling characteristic of many retail and service-industry jobs, this pattern was
described by financially dependent students as well as by students who relied
principally on their earnings to support themselves and their families. This
strategy is illustrated by P2's preceding quote. In many instances, participants presented the resulting routines as stable and manageable. One participant, for example, described a familiar pattern of weekdays focused on
school work and a part-time job scheduled primarily for the weekend:

It's not really that hard to balance it. I always have like the week would be,
I'd be up from 7:00 to 10:00 every day doing homework and school and

work. Like I'll have, I'll do all my [school]work during the week and on the weekend I'll just work and have some time off. So I just have five long days and two days where I can just work and relax. It's not that hard to juggle.

This dependent-status student, in his early 20s, was carrying 16 credit hours per term and working a flexible part-time job. In addition to characterizing his routine as not very difficult to manage, the participant stipulated through added detail that he was both completing his course assignments and regularly sleeping 8 hours per night.

Others' descriptions of time structuring were characterized by intensive multitasking, stressful episodes, and very long weeks. Weeks with major portions of each day predesignated for either work or school were typical of this second group of week-dividers:

> I only work on the weekends. So I do 12-hour shifts . . . Friday, Saturday, and Sunday. . . . I go to work at six o'clock in the morning. I don't get home until 6 pm. So if there was homework that I needed to get done, a lot of teachers give you homework Thursday or Wednesday, because I had two separate classes each day [last term]. And it had to get done by that weekend, so it was—I didn't have the time to do it. . . . I was always stressed doing homework, and there was never no family time. It was either homework, or work, or that was basically it.

This participant described her week as completely full. Because she worked long shifts through the weekend, she noted that it was particularly stressful trying to fit in enough time to complete assignments between weeks. In a similar way, another participant—a mother working full time and enrolled in a community college nursing program—described a week characterized by an intensive 7-day schedule and long hours:

> Well, I get up every day at 6:00. I have classes four days a week. . . . Mondays and Wednesdays I have one class and I'm done by 11:15, but then I go straight to work and then I work until 7:00 or 8:00. Then the good thing about my daycare is that she stays open to 11:30. So she has a home daycare. . . . She's a real Christian lady and she takes care of my daughter really well. So if I need to stay late she'll keep her for me. I just have to call her and let her know. And she's there five days a week. Then Tuesdays and Thursdays are my long days. I'm in school from 8:30 to 5:00. . . . Tuesdays and Thursdays I don't work but every other day I do work. And then Saturday and Sunday [my daughter]'s with my mom. . . . She's off on the weekends so she keeps my daughter.

This student drew extensively on multiple sources for childcare. With reliable and flexible childcare in place, this student was able to push the limits of her weeks and meet obligations for family, work, and her degree program. Later in the discussion, this student expressed a sense of missing her daughter. Despite the intensity and sacrifice, however, the student's strong determination to graduate was reflected in her confidence and in her detailed description of the remaining steps for completing her degree.

Dividing Days

Another prominent pattern described by participants incorporated both work and school into multiple days. In this pattern, a student might work in the morning most days, and then attend classes three or four afternoons in the week. This pattern was most often associated with work situations that did not offer flexible scheduling, but regular and predictable hours. Students describing this pattern generally performed shift work or held long-term jobs in industry, business, or healthcare. Although a small number of dependent-status students described this pattern, for the most part independent students described their days this way. As is apparent in the following quote, participants who divided time like this often referred to fatigue and long, difficult days:

> Well, during the period that I was working it was, it was a little difficult at times. I would be a full-time student, be here during the mornings and afternoons and then have maybe an hour or two to rest or get something to eat and then go straight to work and work at night from 5:00 to 10:00 or sometimes a little bit later, come home, eat and be too sleepy to want to do any homework and then have to wake up in the morning and do it pretty early before I would go to school again and do the schedule all over again.

This excerpt shows a student recalling a recent arrangement that she found untenable. Likewise, in the following brief exchange among three women enrolled in community college, one participant encapsulates the dynamic of long days and sleep deprivation in her current situation, while two others comment:

> P3: I just work straight midnights so my days are free [for classes].
> P2/P1: That's hard. You get tired though.
> P3: My eyes are crooked, but at least I'm available.

This is a particularly concise example of a pattern described by several students—a pattern they typically characterized as resulting in diminished alertness while sitting in class or completing course work.

Improvisatory Combinations

A less prominent but still notable pattern of how students structure time may be characterized as "improvisatory." Routines in this category were often but not always presented as unmanageable and driven by intensive multitasking. In many cases, this pattern coincided with a particularly flexible work schedule. In some of those cases, students nested their descriptions within the broader goal of prioritizing school. In one example, a full-time community college student described the parameters of her week:

> Well, with me I usually get up at about 5:00 in the morning with my husband and make him a lunch because that's about the only thing I can do for him. He has to make dinner every night and he does everything. I have a flexible [work] schedule. I'm lucky. So whatever my school classes are I just work my job around it. I just need to get my 40 hours in. Then, like I said, I play sports some nights but I also work another job of bingo on Monday nights. Monday through Wednesday I'm not usually home until about between 10:00 and 11:00. And then if I have to work late on Thursdays I do, or some Fridays because I work for [a community organization] and we have different programs. And I work Saturdays. So I work usually six days a week. Most of my homework gets done when I'm taking my kids to their soccer games. So while they're playing or practicing or whatever that's when I usually have the most time to do homework. Some I do at work and then some of it I do here.

In other instances, this kind of routine focused on students' need to fit school around work and family obligations that were either very demanding or not entirely predictable. Nearly all parents participating in the study described a pattern of studying only late at night, after their children were asleep. One student, for example, described this pattern, detailing the childcare and transportation considerations shaping her daytime hours:

> P4: You maybe study at nighttime when the kids are asleep. I have a teenage daughter who is a freshman at [a local high school] and I have to be on her like hot water. So I have to make sure that she's taken care of first. Then I go down to my [younger children]. I make sure that they have their things together. . . . Then when Monday comes I'm just blessed to have a babysitter. She's able to pick them up and drop them off. Then I don't have transportation, so I catch the bus and come to school. By the time I get home my 10-year-old beats me home. So then I've already decided and planned out what we're going to have for dinner and get that ready and prepared by the time they get home. "Eat and do your homework, take a bath, get ready for bed," and start it all over the next day. . . . I don't go to bed until like 12:30 or 1:00, sometimes later than that. Sometimes I may get like three or four hours of sleep.

> Interviewer: So you're getting up early too. . . .

P4: . . . I wake my 10-year-old up at 6:00 because she has to catch the bus by 7:00. I get the kids up at 7:00 and then get them dressed. We're all ready by 8:15. By 8:30 [the sitter] picks them up and by 8:35 I'm at the bus stop. I get to school anywhere between 9:30 and quarter to 10:00. Then when I leave my last hour about 2:45, I wait for that bus to come out, or if my mother is off she'll pick me up. Then I'll call the babysitter and tell her I'm at home. By that time it's about 3:30 or 4:00 and I'm preparing dinner, getting them ready for bed by 7:30 or 8:00. By 9:00 they're in the bed.

Two things to note in this description are that schoolwork is fit in mainly at the expense of sleep, and that each day's schedule is predesignated in fairly tight intervals for school and family obligations. These intervals are stipulated nearly down to the minute in the morning, as she gets her children out the door and herself ready in time to make the bus. If the sitter or a bus is late, or if a child is sick, much of the whole routine is affected.

Many students juggling school, family, and work naturally raised questions about how to manage competing priorities. The following example, from a community college student and mother in her early 30s, illustrates this complexity.

They were telling us that when we start clinicals that we can't work . . . because they can't guarantee that we have either day clinical or night clinical. But it's hard because I can't just work weekends. It's just really stressful because it's like I barely see my daughter as is and then it's . . . almost two years of this between—. . . . It's like, "Okay I have to quit the job that I have, or just work Saturday and Sunday, and then do the clinical." But then I'm not getting paid . . . at the clinical. . . . I mean in the long run its good, but then it's a sacrifice in between.

Numerous concerns and questions are raised in this example. The student describes needing to balance multiple pressing goals. These demands include not only fulfilling the requirements for the degree program, but also seeing her 2-year-old daughter more, working enough hours on Saturdays and Sundays, and managing the consequent personal and financial sacrifices for her family. In concluding, she places all of these aims within the context of a final goal: arriving at a better financial situation by obtaining the degree. A majority of students who spoke with us exhibited an orientation—somewhat surprising to us in its prevalence among student comments—toward an understanding of college principally as a vehicle of social mobility. In many cases participants' explanations implied that this was the understood purpose of pursuing college. This excerpt is one of the many examples in which students from all participating institutions puzzled through worries about finances and family life juxtaposed against the belief that graduation will improve the family's financial situation.

Taken together, these time-structuring strategies illustrate that, with few exceptions, working students scheduled specific, limited time periods for school work, rather than taking the time necessary to complete assignments. Most participants made the homework fit their work schedule instead of fitting their schedule around the amount of homework assigned.

Connection and Disconnection on Campus

To explore students' college experiences, we cast a broad net for stories and descriptions that included statements about students' direct and indirect experiences at their current institutions. Because students often introduced their direct and indirect experiences at other colleges as a referent for their current college experiences, we examined these descriptions as well. We analyzed these statements with a particular eye to the norms, pressures, understandings, and strategies embedded in what the students shared.

Students' comments in this area predominantly focused on the possibility of being negatively or positively judged in their programs. Although other topics were raised in these excerpts, this theme was the most prominent. Not surprisingly, statements about being accepted or judged often tied to discussions of academic success or struggles, but examples of more generally personal descriptions are also present. The following passage focuses on the theme of feeling accepted—and therefore supported to succeed—regardless of nontraditional status:

> I am past my plan for where I was supposed to be at this age of my life, but being here has made me feel like, it's okay. It's "you were supposed to be here, you're supposed to finish and graduate, you're an undergraduate here. We have the resources, and we have the reputation, and we'll get you to the places where you're supposed to be."

This student, who originally attended a residential college out of state right after graduating high school, characterized herself as behind where she thought she would be by her late 20s. She noted, however, that her more recent experiences in college have offset that feeling: "It's okay." Citing her perceptions of the institution's particular strengths—and possibly also implicitly referring to the affirming presence of other older students on campus—she feels that this perceived delay will not prevent her from achieving her goals (i.e., arriving at where she is "supposed to be").

Many focus group participants recounted experiences at these institutions in highly positive ways, as demonstrated in the preceding quote. It is both affirming and important to witness students relating these rewarding experiences. What is of even more interest to this study, however, is how and in what contexts participants introduced these positive descriptions. Positive feelings regarding campus life stemmed, in example after example, from the perceived availability of one-on-one interpersonal connections in interactions on campus. In one excerpt, an adult learner community college student recounted a course experience that fostered a sense of connection for her:

> I actually had a professor that had a buddy list which she gave us—copies of . . . everybody's numbers and everybody's name. This is how we developed our relationship. If I didn't have a homework assignment and she didn't have a homework assignment we went to that buddy list. . . . And that was agreed upon . . . every student had to agree with that. So that opened this up. Our class that we had, well we're in English right now together, but our business class we were just like a big family. And my teacher was like I've never had a class like you all. So that was beautiful.

According to this participant, the buddy list not only provided a way for students to contact each other for missed assignments. Rather, the arrangement—and the group's collective agreement to it—facilitated a sense of connection and exchange among students (e.g., "So that opened this up"; "We were just like a big family"). In addition to the student-to-student connection, this participant also remembered the instructor expressing a personal connection with the group. The student found these exchanges not only rewarding but also personally meaningful; she characterizes the experience as "beautiful."

A third example from another institution similarly illustrates the central role that one-on-one connection—or, in contrast, an impersonal setting—plays in students' understandings of campus environments.

> The reading lab, last semester, I had to go to all the time. And the girls knew me by face, "Oh, just sign in, [Tina]." . . . It's kind of nice to know that they remember who you are. It's more person-to-person . . . here. Your class settings aren't as big. You get that one-on-one, or the attention that you kind of need. I couldn't imagine myself in a classroom with 700 people or 1,000 people, kind of just like a number I guess. To me, here, it's just more personal.

In expressing her preference for the type of campus she was attending and attributing the amount of personal attention to the institution's small size, this student implies that one-on-one interaction was important to her ability to succeed in college.

Often presented in less directly personal terms, negative experiences were described in conjunction with feeling either helpless or judged. One student, for example, began an explanation speaking about nontraditional students in general, without including herself in the category until a few sentences later, and then only implicitly by referring to "when we were in high school."

> P5: We have nontraditional students and we have traditional students. Our traditional students are coming out of high school. Our nontraditionals have been out of school for 10 or 20 years and they're coming back. They're not catching the stuff like that. The math that they taught in high school now is nothing like what we had when we were in high school and [faculty] don't understand that.
>
> P3: Well, there are some that understand and they just don't care.
>
> P6: Yeah, they don't care.

As we suggested earlier, this quote is somewhat unusual—although not unique—among the student focus groups because it includes some negative description of the institution. More relevant to this discussion, however, the exchange is typical of how the community college participants made sense of the dynamics of academic success for older students on campus. The student asserted first that nontraditional students at this community college were having academic difficulties. She then theorized that the difficulties stemmed from years of being away from school and, in particular, from how the material, in math, for example, had changed in the intervening years. According to this explanation, courses are built on the current high school math curriculum and do not match what older students learned in high school. Finally, in this scenario, the faculty do not realize this situation and therefore fail to adjust the course or offer a way for nontraditional students to bridge the gap. The alternative explanation, offered by another participant, is that instructors understand the trouble but either do not think it matters if nontraditional students struggle or fail to identify it as their responsibility to help. This description not only centers on curriculum and faculty practice, but also suggests a distance in communication between students and faculty.

A second example brings out further complexity in college experiences. Students' perceptions about connecting with institutions most often implicated academic difficulty, as in the following story:

> But when you go . . . to financial aid they feel like it's coming out of their pocket to give you money to pay for your classes. They're worse than working with the folks at the aid office. They talk to you like you don't know nothing, like you're dumb. To me that just makes me really teed off. So I have to excuse myself because, see, I have a very potty mouth. I say things that ain't right. So I excuse myself and leave until I'm in a better frame of mind. This is my second go around here. I graduated from [community college] with an associate's degree in early childhood education. So now I'm back for nursing. The [entrance exam for the nursing program]! Like

these ladies over here, my worst subject is that math. And that's probably everybody else's too. I have just decided that I'll just take one class during the summer and practice the [exam] . . . so that when I do decide to pay my $30 maybe I'll pass. But I'm like them. I work part time and I have three kids at home and I'm trying to pay rent. I'm the only person working in my household. So between trying to juggle rent, car note, [electricity], cable, and whatever else I may want to do, I have to do it out of my income. And $30 to give to somebody that I know that I'm not going to pass a test is stupid. I'm not going to do that.

This student first recounted some sensitive exchanges surrounding financial aid. We cannot know the real course of events in these interactions but can conclude from this description that the student perceived resistance from the financial aid staff. The student related specifically the feeling of being talked down to, suggesting once again the consequentiality of perceived social distance in how students experience college. Moreover, the student saw this behavior as normatively incorrect and believed that she responded in ways that worsened the exchange ("I say things that ain't right"). The frustrating quality of her financial aid example was then linked immediately to more global frustration with the college experience.

The second half of this excerpt focuses on academic difficulties described within the context of the student's stretched financial situation. Whereas the final sentences focus on the decision not to pay an exam fee—and therefore not to take the entrance exam—the repeated references to her own expectation that she would not pass the test despite having completed prerequisite coursework clearly reflect an important part of her frustration.

Although positive descriptions far outnumbered negative descriptions of campus experiences, both exemplify two sides of the same perception from students. This perception centers on the belief that they are at risk of being judged out of place in college—whether they attribute it to age, race, financial situation, academic performance, or work and family obligations—and they link this risk to their ability to succeed. Throughout the many positive and negative descriptions offered in these focus group discussions, students' comments hinged on the perceived possibilities of interpersonal connection and the perceived acts of judgment or affirmation from faculty, staff, and fellow students.

Discussion

This chapter focuses on how students in one metropolitan area balance obligations related to work, family, and college. The range of experiences represented in the focus groups is wide and complex, encompassing multiple dimensions of balancing these combined demands. By examining how the study participants make sense of their experiences, we begin to see how structures, norms, and implicit theories shape their strategies and ultimately condition their academic success. Moreover, we begin to see how questions regarding the academic success of working students, commuting students, and adult learners can be understood not only in light of previous research on student success, but also with an eye to understanding the workings of social reproduction through the educational context. With this type of analysis, findings can be extended to illuminate ways to improve practice to enhance equity and academic success for these college students.

Prior to this volume, much higher education research on working students has narrowly focused on traditional images of college going. The increased prevalence of employment during college makes it plain that working students are neither exceptions nor a monolithic group. This chapter illuminates the central dimensions along which mobile working students' experiences are differentiated. For example, whether participants described college going while balancing family and work obligations as manageable or unmanageable seemed to depend primarily on the reliability of income for basic needs (in some cases associated with dependent financial status) and, for parents of young children, the availability of reliable childcare.

This finding shows the workings of social reproduction in multiple ways. It shows that the stability needed to make this delicate balance *work* is more easily accessible to students from higher socioeconomic backgrounds and less accessible to students whose financial and social situations do not provide the necessary resources to troubleshoot and recover when disruptions inevitably occur (e.g., a car breaks down; a child with a fever cannot go to childcare). On a concrete level, the necessary resources include accessible, reliable, and flexible transportation and support for family obligations (most predominantly childcare). Neither financial aid policy nor broader public investment in social supports (e.g., childcare, public transportation, student aid, healthcare) provide the level of support necessary to maintain and succeed in the situations described by participants. Those students who have private access to these resources are more likely not only to sustain their efforts and recover from inevitable disruptions, but also to be seen as stable, serious, and capable in college contexts. In this way, social reproduction is clearly under way.

It is against this backdrop that students, practitioners, and institutions work to resist these replicative pressures and create transformative spaces and experiences within education. Highlighting these two dimensions in the variation of student experience provides an important direction for future research. It also points to implications for practice, confirming, for example, the continued centrality of financial aid, transportation, and childcare in institutional efforts to support the academic success of students as they balance work, family, and school.

Students with different obligations follow different paths and obviously face different pressures. Nevertheless, this chapter suggests some commonalities across situations as well. With only a few exceptions, participants organized their days around tightly packed intervals of structured activity. Open-ended time for studying and course assignments—only rarely mentioned by study participants—may be a casualty of tight financial circumstances, but perhaps also of a societal orientation legitimating work for pay and structured activity over other types of endeavor. Material needs and conditions clearly inform students' time-structuring decisions, but cultural norms about work and money may play into the pattern as well. If students with tightly structured schedules are driven by both economic factors and the predominant norms at institutions where most students pursue work and college simultaneously, and if more privileged students are subject to norms that allow for less tightly structured schedules, the potential for social reproduction is plain. These complexities show how subtle and entrenched patterns of social reproduction through schooling can become (Bourdieu & Passeron, 1979). Institutions and researchers need to understand more about how culturally situated pressures exist and shift across time and between regional and economic contexts. Moreover, as McDonough and Calderone (2006) suggest, inquiry should focus on how cultural norms around work and money inform the expectations and experiences of both students and practitioners. A nuanced and empirically grounded understanding of both conditions *and* norms can help higher education researchers break loose from models for student success that presuppose continuous enrollment and 6-year graduation rates and can inform practitioners in ways to advise and connect with working students.

This chapter also identifies academic difficulty as a pivotal matter to many students. Moreover, results underscore the relevance of the sorting function of education in students' implicit theories regarding college. Together, academic difficulty and the consequentiality of interpersonal connection form a crux for the positive and negative college experiences our participants described.

There is a component of education that is itself discursive. Students, faculty, practitioners, and policymakers (and researchers) all attend to the discourses of selectivity, merit, and the sorting function in college. These arguably comprise an important part of what we write about and experience as the workings of capital in research on student academic success. Understanding that you belong on campus—and that an institution believes in that belonging and your potential—are important assets in succeeding as a student. Privileged students most likely take this acceptance for granted and trust implicitly in its truth. Our findings suggest, in contrast, that these questions remain open and salient for participants in this study. Students' comments suggest that combating the expectation of being judged saps their energy, complicates their interactions on campus, and undermines their academic success. In this way, the norms and structures of educational institutions, including the institution of higher education research, channel students toward class- and race-defined roles that reflect their current positions, thus undermining the potential for social mobility and the transformative purposes students often cite as the reason for going to college. Stigma-resistant forms of academic support and broad-based efforts to foster one-on-one interaction between students and others on campus are bound to increase the affirming experiences that so many students described. The same strategies may also decrease the kind of negative distancing experiences students also described.

Students' positive comments also reflect the workings of social reproduction and resistance. While suggesting the likelihood of continued student success, participants' assertions that they prefer the environments at these institutions may also point to troubling implications with respect to college choice and the cultural capital of institutions (Berger, 2000). In these appreciative statements, students implicitly contrasted the regional campuses and community college with institutions they characterized as higher status. Statements about preferring how things are in these institutions (implicitly designated as lower status) suggest that forms of *habitus* may be at work in students' college choice process.

Conclusion

In summary, this chapter highlights important dimensions of the experiences of working students. Exploring time-structuring strategies suggests how students are able to sustain their efforts. The central dimensions marking the tenable from the untenable included basic financial resources (including transportation, and money for books, childcare) and support for family obligations. The focus group results also show how personal interaction and the discourse of being judged come together as a crux around which students experienced connection and disconnection on campus. This dynamic comes into particularly strong relief in students' experiences with academic difficulties.

Building on implications forwarded by McDonough and Calderone (2006), we recommend further study of cultural norms pertaining to work, money, academic merit, and institutional prestige among students, college counselors, financial aid professionals, and college faculty. Continued inquiry in this vein can provide differentiated and contextualized descriptions of the structures and norms within which working students operate. This kind of finding is necessary for researchers, practitioners, and policymakers to see the complexities and varied experiences often conflated under the single category "working student." Moreover, by exploring how the norms adopted by practitioners come together with working students' norms and expectations in educational contexts, this kind of research will prepare institutions and practitioners to offer the kinds of interactions, advice, and academic support that will connect working students to campuses and support their success.

References

Adelman, C. (2006). *The tool box revisited: Paths to degree completion from high school through college.* Washington, DC: U.S. Department of Education, Office of Vocational and Adult Education.

Adelman, C. (2007, March 12). Making graduation rates matter. *Inside Higher Ed.* Retrieved June 6, 2007, from http://insidehighered.com/views/2007/03/12/adelman.

American Council on Education. (2005). *College students today: A national portrait.* Washington, DC: Author.

Bailey, T., Calcagno, J. C., Jenkins, D., Kienzl, G., & Leinbach, T. (2005). *The effects of institutional factors on the success of community college students.* New York: Columbia University, Teachers College, Community College Research Center.

Baum, S. (2006). Lowering work and loan burden: The current status of student reliance on grants, loans, and work. In *Reflections on college access and persistence* (pp. 62–74). Proceedings and papers from a symposium held in Washington, DC, September 8, 2005. Washington, DC: Advisory Committee on Student Financial Assistance.

Bean, J. P. (1985). Interaction effects based on class level in an explanatory model of college student dropout syndrome. *American Educational Research Journal, 22,* 35–64.

Bensimon, E. M. (2007). Presidential address: The underestimated significance of practitioner knowledge in the scholarship on student success. *Review of Higher Education, 30,* 441–469.

Berger, J. B. (2000). Optimizing capital, social reproduction, and undergraduate persistence: A sociological perspective. In J. M. Braxton (Ed.), *Reworking the student departure puzzle* (pp. 95–124). Nashville, TN: Vanderbilt University Press.

Berger, J. B., & Milem, J. F. (2000). Organizational behavior in higher education and student outcomes. In J. C. Smart (Ed.), *Higher education: Handbook of theory and research* (Vol. 15, pp. 268–338). New York: Agathon Press.

Bourdieu, P. (1973). Cultural reproduction and social reproduction. In R. Brown (Ed.), *Knowledge, education, and cultural change* (pp. 71–112). London: Tavistock.

Bourdieu, P., & Passeron, J. C. (1979). *The inheritors: French students and their relation to culture.* Chicago: University of Chicago Press.

Bourdieu, P., & Wacquant, L. (1992). *Invitation to reflexive sociology.* Chicago: University of Chicago Press.

Bradley, G. (2006). Work participation and academic performance: A test of alternative propositions. *Journal of Education and Work, 19*(5), 481–501.

Braxton, J. M., Hirschy, A. S., & McClendon, S. A. (2004). *Understanding and reducing college student departure.* San Francisco: Jossey-Bass.

Braxton, J. M., & McClendon, S. A. (2001–2002). The fostering of social integration through institutional practice. *Journal of College Student Retention, 3*(1), 57–71.

Calcagno, J. C., Crosta, P., Bailey, T., & Jenkins, D. (2006). *Stepping stones to a degree: The impact of enrollment pathways and milestones on older community college student outcomes.* Community College Research Brief, No. 32. Retrieved June 28, 2007, from http://www.inpathways.net/SteppingStonestoaDegree.pdf

Carspecken, P. F. (1996). *Critical ethnography in educational research: A theoretical and practical guide.* New York: Routledge.

Chambers, E. (2000). Applied ethnography. In N. K. Denzin & Y. S. Lincoln (Eds.), *Handbook of qualitative research* (pp. 851–869). Thousand Oaks, CA: Sage.

Choy, S. P. (2000). *Low-income students: Who they are and how they pay for their education* (NCES 2000–169). Washington, DC: U.S. Department of Education, National Center for Education Statistics.

Choy, S. P. (2002). *Access and persistence: Findings from 10 years of longitudinal research on students.* Washington, DC: American Council on Education.

Choy, S., & Berker, A. (2003). *How families of low- and middle-income undergraduates pay for college: Full-time dependent students in 1999–00* (NCES 2003–162). Washington, DC: U.S. Department of Education, National Center for Education Statistics.

Converse, J., & Presser, S. (1986). *Survey questions: Handcrafting the standardized questionnaire.* Newbury Park, CA: Sage Publications.

Cuccaro-Alamin, S., & Choy, S. P. (1998). *Postsecondary financing strategies: How undergraduates combine work, borrowing, and attendance.* Washington, DC: Department of Education, National Center for Education Statistics.

Elliot, P. G. (1994). *The urban campus: Educating the new majority for the new century* (American Council on Education Series on Higher Education). Phoenix, AZ: Oryx Press.

Ewell, P. T., Schild, P. R., & Paulson, K. (2003). *Following the mobile student: Can we develop the capacity for a comprehensive database to assess student progression?* Indianapolis, IN: Lumina Foundation for Education.

Fjortoft, N. F. (1995, April). *College student employment: Opportunity or deterrent?* Paper presented at the annual meeting of the American Education Research Association, San Francisco, CA.

Fox, M. A., Connolly, B. A., & Snyder, T. D. (2005). *Youth indicators, 2005: Trends in the well-being of American youth* (NCES 2005–050). Jessup, MD: National Center for Education Statistics.

Furr, S. R., & Elling, T. W. (2000). The influence of work on college student development. *NASPA Journal, 37*(2), 454–470.

Groves, R. M., Fowler, F. J., Couper, M. P., Lepkowski, J. M., Singer, E., & Tourangeau, R. (2004). *Survey methodology.* New York: Wiley.

Gubrium, J. F., & Holstein, J. A. (2000). Analyzing interpretive practice. In N. K. Denzin & Y. S. Lincoln (Eds.), *Handbook of qualitative research* (2nd ed., pp. 487–508). Thousand Oaks, CA: Sage.

Guiffrida, D. A. (2006). Toward a cultural advancement of Tinto's theory. *Review of Higher Education, 29,* 451–472.

Hernandez, E., Ziskin, M., Gross, J. P. K., & Fashola, O. R. (2007). *Making meaning of work for undergraduate students who are employed.* Paper presented at the annual meeting of the Association for the Study of Higher Education, Louisville, KY.

Horn, L. J., & Berktold, A. (1998). *Profile of undergraduates in U.S. postsecondary institutions: 1995–96, with an essay on undergraduates who work* (NCES 98–084). Washington, DC: U.S. Department of Education, National Center for Education Statistics.

Hossler, D., Gross, J. P. K., Pellicciotti, M. B., Fischer, M. A., & Excell, D. (2005). [Northwest Collaborative on Working Students—2005 survey of students]. Unpublished raw data.

Hughes, P., & Mallette, B. I. (2003). A survey of student term-time employment: Choosing subpopulations for further study. *Journal of Student Financial Aid, 33*(3), 41–62.

King, J. (2002). *Crucial choices: How students' financial decisions affect their academic success.* Washington, DC: American Council on Education, Center for Policy Analysis.

King, J. E. (2003). Nontraditional attendance and persistence: The cost of students' choices. In J. E. King, E. L. Anderson, & M. E. Corrigan (Eds.), *Changing student attendance patterns: Challenges for policy and practice* (Vol. 121, pp. 69–83). San Francisco: Jossey-Bass.

Kuh, G. (1995). The other curriculum: Out-of-class experiences associated with student learning and personal development. *Journal of Higher Education, 66,* 123–155.

Kulm, T. L., & Cramer, S. (2006). The relationship of student employment to student role: Family relationships, social interactions and persistence. *College Student Journal, 40,* 927–938.

Lapovsky, L. (2008). Rethinking student aid: Nontraditional students. In S. Baum, M. McPherson, & P. Steele (Eds.), *The effectiveness of student aid policies: What the research tells us* (pp. 141–157). New York: College Board. Retrieved February 20, 2009, from http://professionals.collegeboard.com/profdownload/rethinking -stu-aid-effectiveness-of-stu-aid-policies.pdf

Lundberg, C. A. (2004). Working and learning: The role of involvement for employed students. *NASPA Journal, 41,* 201–215.

Matus-Grossman, L., & Gooden, S. (2002). *Opening doors: Students' perspectives on juggling work, family, and college.* (ERIC Document Reproduction Service No. ED 471815). New York: Manpower Demonstration Research Corporation.

McDonough, P. M., & Calderone, S. (2006). The meaning of money: Perceptual difference between college counselors and low-income families about college costs and financial aid. *American Behavioral Scientist, 49,* 1703–1718.

Pascarella, E., & Terenzini, P. (1983). Predicting voluntary freshman year persistence/withdrawal behavior in a residential university: A path analytic validation of Tinto's model. *Journal of Educational Psychology, 75*(2), 215–226.

Pascarella, E. T., & Staver, J. (1985). The influence of on-campus work in science on science choice during college: A causal modeling approach. *Review of Higher Education, 8,* 229–245.

Pascarella, E. T., & Terenzini, P. T. (1991). *How college affects students: Vol. 1. Findings and insights from twenty years of research.* San Francisco: Jossey-Bass.

Pascarella, E. T., & Terenzini, P. T. (2005). *How college affects students: Vol. 2. A third decade of research.* San Francisco: Jossey-Bass.

Paulsen, M. B., & St. John, E. P. (1997). The financial nexus between college choice and persistence. In R. A. Voorhees (Ed.), *Researching student aid: Creating an action agenda* (pp. 65–82, New Directions for Institutional Research, No. 95). San Francisco: Jossey-Bass.

Perna, L. W., Cooper, M. A., & Li, C. (2006). *Improving educational opportunities for college students who work.* Bloomington: Indiana Project on Academic Success. Retrieved July 10, 2007, from www.indiana.edu/~ipas1/Perna%20Improving%20Educational%20Opportunities.pdf

Rendón, L. I., Jalomo, R. E., & Nora, A. (2000). Theoretical considerations in the study of minority student retention in higher education. In J. M. Braxton (Ed.), *Reworking the student departure puzzle* (pp. 127–156). Nashville, TN: Vanderbilt University Press.

St. John, E. P., Paulsen, M. B., & Starkey, J. B. (1996). The nexus between college choice and persistence. *Research in Higher Education, 37,* 175–220.

Stage, F. K., & Hossler, D. (2000). Where is the student? Linking student behaviors, college choice, and college persistence. In J. M. Braxton (Ed.), *Reworking the student departure puzzle* (pp. 170–194). Nashville, TN: Vanderbilt University Press.

Tierney, W. G. (1992). An anthropological analysis of student participation in college. *Journal of Higher Education, 63,* 603–618.

Tinto, V. (1975). Dropout from higher education: A theoretical synthesis of recent research. *Journal of Higher Education, 45,* 89–125.

Tinto, V., & Pusser, B. (2006, June). *Moving from theory to action: Building a model for institutional action for student success.* Washington, DC: National Postsecondary Education Cooperative.

5

ACADEMIC SUCCESS FOR WORKING ADULT STUDENTS

Heather T. Rowan-Kenyon, Amy K. Swan,
Nancy L. Deutsch, and Bruce Gansneder

With rising college prices, it is increasingly necessary for college students to work while enrolled. Research (Astin, 1993; Berkner, Cuccaro-Alamin, & McCormick 1996; Horn & Carroll, 1996) has found that the more a college student works, the less likely she or he is to persist in college. Astin found that traditional-age college students who work off campus more than 20 hours a week tend to be less successful than students who work fewer hours in an on-campus position.

Little has been written, however, about the academic outcomes of nontraditional students, defined as those who are older than age 25 and/or who have children, who work. This is an important population to focus on because, in 1999, about 39% of students enrolled in postsecondary education were older than the age of 25 (Choy, 2002) and the National Center for Education Statistics (2008) expects the enrollment of adult students to increase by 21% from 2005 to 2016, surpassing the growth of traditionally aged undergraduate enrollment. Because most of these older undergraduate students work while enrolled in school (Horn, Peter, & Rooney, 2002), their experiences of academic success in the context of balancing work and school is an important area of study.

More likely to be financially independent (Horn & Carroll, 1996) and have children than their traditional-age counterparts (Kasworm, Polson, & Fishback, 2002; Matus-Grossman & Gooden, 2002), many adult students have to work to support their families while they attend school. Unfortunately, many of these students are not successful in attaining a degree, as Pusser et al. (2007) concluded that adult students who work 20 hours or more a week are at "high risk" of failure. Berker, Horn, and Carroll (2003) found that adult students who work full time and are part-time students are less likely than other students to complete a postsecondary credential within a 6-year period. However, they do not explore the academic progress of students after enrollment other than to measure degree completion. Degree completion is a narrow measure of academic success because it does not consider factors influencing academic progress and achievement. More research is needed to explore the factors that influence the academic success of adult students, such as their course grades, because academic success is an important step toward degree completion.

Using a conceptual model of nontraditional undergraduate student attrition (Bean & Metzner, 1985), the study in this chapter employs a mixed-method design to learn more about the academic experiences and achievement of adult working students. Drawing on quantitative methods, the chapter identifies the predictors of one measure of academic success, grade point average (GPA), for adult students who work full time, part time, and not at all. Then, drawing on qualitative methods, the chapter uses focus group data to explore the barriers and supports that influence academic success for adult working students. The chapter concludes by offering recommendations for institutional policy, practice, and future research.

Literature Review and Theoretical Framework

This study tests a conceptual framework that was developed based on Bean and Metzner's (1985) model of nontraditional undergraduate student attrition. Compared with models that focus on traditional undergraduates, this model places less emphasis on the concept of social integration and the socializing importance of college environments. Instead, Bean and Metzner stress personal background, academic and environmental factors, and psychological indicators as major influences on student dropout and persistence decisions. Environmental factors are presumed to be particularly important to nontraditional students' attrition and persistence. For example, if a student cannot adjust his or her work schedule, arrange for childcare, or obtain adequate financial support for college, then the student will be less likely to persist regardless of academic support (Johnson, 1991). Likewise, if students are encouraged by family members, they will likely persist despite academic uncertainties (Johnson, 1991). Chartrand's (1992) empirical work supports the Bean and Metzner model, finding that academic and external factors predict institutional commitment, which in turn influences intent to continue.

Literature Review

Based on analyses of the National Postsecondary Student Aid Study (NPSAS) and the Beginning Postsecondary Students Longitudinal Study,

Horn and Carroll (1996) identify nontraditional students by the presence of one or more of seven characteristics, including part-time enrollment and full-time employment. Horn and Carroll classify those students with one such characteristic as "minimally non-traditional," and students with four or more characteristics as "highly non-traditional" (p. i). Among highly nontraditional students—28% of the undergraduate population in 1999–2000— 67% considered themselves primarily employees (Choy, 2002). Similarly, Berker et al. (2003) found that, among a national sample of working adult undergraduates, two thirds considered employment their main activity.

Although there is a dearth of research on the relationship between adult students' employment status and academic performance, many studies have examined this relationship for traditional students. In a review of these studies, Pascarella and Terenzini (2005) note that as the number of work hours increased, students reported more problems with academic performance. One recent study found that each additional weekly work hour reduced academic year GPA by 0.011 points (DeSimone, 2008). However, Pascarella and Terenzini also found several studies indicating that on-campus part-time employment had positive net effects on factors related to academic performance. One study found that "reasonable amounts" of part-time work, either on or off campus, may facilitate students' cognitive development (Pascarella, Edison, Nora, Hagedorn, & Terenzini, 1998). Among nontraditional students, those in the highly and moderately nontraditional categories were more likely than minimally nontraditional students to report that working had a negative effect on their academic performance (Choy, 2002). Cleveland-Innes (1994) found that academic integration, including current college GPA, had a direct positive effect on nontraditional students' institutional and goal commitments, which in turn increased their likelihood of persisting.

Just as work responsibilities can affect the academic performance of adult students, so too can family responsibilities (Bean & Metzner, 1985; Chartrand, 1992; Teachman & Polonko, 1988). Nontraditional students who consider work their primary activity are more likely than other nontraditional students to be married and to have children and other dependents (Berker et al., 2003). Indeed, 52% of nontraditional students have one or more dependent children, a responsibility that adds to what is already a complicated balancing act (Kasworm et al., 2002; Matus-Grossman & Gooden, 2002). Although having young children has been found to have a negative effect on degree completion for all students (Jacobs & Berkowitz-King, 2002; Taniguchi & Kaufman, 2005), Scott, Burns, and Cooney (1996) wrote that this is a primary challenge for mothers. They noted that mothers' reasons for dropping out were strongly influenced by socioeconomic class, a finding the researchers associated with a complex combination of reasons including lack of family support, domestic responsibilities, lack of money, and lack of knowledge or skills expected in college. Approximately 21% of female non-traditional students are single parents (Kasworm et al., 2002), and low-income women are more likely than higher-income women to experience lack of family support and financial difficulties (Home, 1997, 1998; Sands & Richardson, 1984; Scott et al., 1996).

In no small part because so many are supporting families, adult students cite finances as their highest-priority issue and most stressful concern (Kasworm et al., 2002; Kirk & Dorfman, 1983). Some higher education leaders have suggested that adult students require less financial aid because they work and therefore have higher incomes than their traditional-age counterparts (Kasworm, 2003). Although likely true for some adult students, analysis of data from the 1999–2000 NPSAS revealed that one quarter of working adult parents who were enrolled less than half time earned less than 200% of the federal poverty level for a family of four, and only 7.7% of these students received any federal, state, or institutional aid. Among working students who received aid, the average award of $1,800 fell short of the estimated student budget required at the nation's most affordable institutions (Bosworth & Choitz, 2002). Thus, for many working adult students, college costs are beyond financial reach after paying for expenses associated with raising a family (Bosworth & Choitz, 2002; Heller & Bjorklund, 2004).

Outside encouragement is an important factor in the persistence of adult students (Carney-Crompton & Tan, 2002). Employer support, in the form of tuition reimbursement and flexible work schedules, helps some adult students manage the demands of college education (Adebayo, 2006; Kasworm, 2002). Berker et al. (2003) found that about one quarter of students who consider themselves primarily employees received aid from their employers, with bachelor's degree enrollees most likely to receive employer financial support. These benefits are often available only to full-time workers, however, placing students in a catch-22 position (Matus-Grossman & Gooden, 2002). Social support from friends, family, and faculty minimizes the depression and anxiety that can result from the increase in roles, demands, and time conflicts faced by adult students (Kirk & Dorfman, 1983; Mallinckrodt & Leong, 1992; Roehl & Okun, 1984). For adult students in particular, perceived level of support from family members and friends also predicts positive psychological outcomes such as reduced vulnerability to stress (Home, 1997; Mallinckrodt & Leong, 1992) and higher levels of self-esteem (Quimby & O'Brien, 2006).

High school performance also influences nontraditional student attrition (Bean & Metzner, 1985; Chartrand, 1992). Betts and Morrell (1999) found that, although high school grades and test scores were strongly linked to college academic performance, so too were contextual influences including sex, ethnicity, and family income. For nontraditional students, such contextual influences have been shown to be predictive of persistence (Jacobs & Berkowitz-King, 2002; Johnson, 1991), as well as college grades (Farabaugh-Dorkins, 1991; Sandler, 1998; Wlodkowski, Mauldin, & Gahn, 2001).

Bean and Metzner (1985) and Chartrand (1992) identify academic advising, course availability, and major selection as other academic variables that play a role in nontraditional student attrition. In a mixed-method study of nontraditional student attrition at two schools, students expressed a desire for better advising and emphasized that "inflexible scheduling of courses posed an intolerable burden on their personal and professional lives" (Wlodkowski, Mauldin, & Campbell, 2002, p. 7). Other researchers have also found that the complexity of nontraditional students' lives outside the classroom limits their class schedule, number of classes they can take, and class choice (Choy, 2002; Kazis et al., 2007).

Although many studies have examined the characteristics of adult students, as well as the challenges facing these students as they pursue postsecondary degrees, few of these studies have been based on national samples. Little research on adult students has focused specifically on the relationship between employment status and academic performance. This study addresses both of these issues, drawing on quantitative and qualitative data from a national sample of adult students, with a focus on variations in employment status and the impact of these variations on academic outcomes.

Methods

This study addresses the following three research questions:

1. How do characteristics of adult students who work full time compare to the characteristics of nontraditional students who work part time as well as those who do not work at all?
2. How do the variables that are related to academic performance vary among adult students who work full time, part time, or not at all?
3. What are the barriers to academic success faced by adult students who work full time and part time, and what supports do they draw on in completing their education?

Quantitative Methodology

To address the first two research questions, this chapter uses data from the 2007 National Study on Non-traditional Students, conducted as part of Phase II of the Emerging Pathways project that surveyed 1,857 students attending more than 50 institutions across the nation (Parker, 2008). The sample for this chapter was limited to students who were enrolled in associate's or bachelor's degree programs ($n = 1,179$), excluding students taking one or a few classes for job training or personal enrichment.

To examine differences in students' characteristics based on work status, chi-square distributions and ANOVAs were conducted. Three blocked-entry multiple regression analyses were subsequently conducted: one for the entire sample, one for all employed students, and one for students who were employed full time.

Instrument and Variables

The 2007 National Study on Non-traditional Students Survey consisted of 52 items. Items pertained to demographic characteristics as well as personal, social, and institutional measures (Parker, 2008). The dependent variable for this study is current grade point average (GPA), a measure self-reported by students. All of the collected data come from students' self-reports, so students answered the questions based on their own knowledge and perceptions. One limitation is that we do not have transcript data for variables such as GPA or number of credits earned. Also, GPA is measured at a single point in time, which differs across study participants based on their year in school (e.g., first year, second year).

The independent variables in the model were chosen based on a review of the literature and what is known about student success, as well as research on attrition for nontraditional students (Bean & Metzner, 1985). Tables 1 and 2 describe the variables used in the analyses. The first block of variables entered into the regression analyses measures background characteristics: race, gender, age, income, high school grades, whether the student delayed enrollment after high school, and if the student had dependents. The second block of variables measures institutional and enrollment characteristics such as enrollment status, type of degree program in which the student was enrolled, and the type of financial aid that a student received. In the third block, social barriers and supports were added to measure work support, work stress, family and friend support, and family stress. Each was a factor-based scale computed after principal axis factoring with Varimax rotation. Cronbach alphas for factor-based scales were 0.91, 0.72, 0.90, and 0.70, respectively (see Table 2). Work status was in the fifth and final block of the model.

Qualitative Methodology

We used qualitative methods to build on the quantitative analyses and to better understand the variety of issues surrounding the academic experiences of adult learners. Data were collected using focus groups, with the goal of eliciting more detailed and complete understandings of the barriers adult students face and supports they draw on in completing their education.

Sites and Sample

Focus groups were conducted at 10 institutions across the United States, with 3 in the Northeast, 3 in the mid-Atlantic/Southeast, 2 in the Midwest,

TABLE 1
Model of Academic Success for Nontraditional Students

Variable	Definition
Dependent variable	
Current grades	Standardized measure of current grades
Background characteristics	
Race	African American = 1, White = 2, Other Race/ Ethnicity = 3
Gender	Male = 0, Female = 1
Age	Standardized measure of student age
Income quartiles	Income of the students broken into quartiles. Quartile 1 = 0–19k, Quartile 2 = 20–49k, Quartile 3 = 50–79k, Quartile 4 = over 80k
High school grades	Bs and Cs or below = 1, Mostly Bs and Above = 2
Delayed enrollment after high school	No = 0, Yes = 1
Dependents	No = 0, Yes = 1
Institutional and enrollment characteristics	
Current enrollment status	Less than full time = 1, Full time = 2
Degree type	Associate's = 1, Bachelor's = 2
Type of financial aid received	Loans = 1, Scholarships/Grants = 2, Both loans and scholarships/grants = 3, None = 4
Social supports	
Family and friend support network	Factor composite of 4 variables shown in Table 2
Work stress	Factor composite of 4 variables shown in Table 2
Family stress	Factor composite of 5 variables shown in Table 2
Work support	Factor composite of 4 variables shown in Table 2
Employment status	No employment = 1, Part-time employment = 2, Full-time employment = 3

Note: All categorical variables used were recoded to be 0/1 dummy variables for the purpose of the regression analysis.

and 2 in the West/Southwest. Institutions were purposefully selected to represent a range of Carnegie Classifications from within and across geographic areas and types of communities. Selected institutions included public urban two-year colleges, a private urban two-year college, a private four-year rural college, private four-year urban colleges, and public four-year urban universities. Researchers coordinated times and spaces for the groups with the administrators of the adult-student programs at each college.

TABLE 2
Factors Used in Model of Nontraditional Student Success

Factor and Survey Items	Loadings	Alpha Reliability Coefficient
Family and Friend Support Network		0.899
Friends—very supportive returning to school	0.760	
Relatives—very supportive returning to school	0.784	
Friends—very supportive to continue	0.763	
Relatives—very supportive to continue	0.796	
Work Support Network		0.908
Coworkers—very supportive returning to school	0.770	
Supervisor/employer—very supportive returning to school	0.805	
Coworkers—very supportive to continue	0.783	
Supervisor/employer—very supportive to continue	0.811	
Work Stress		0.717
Inability to give 100% to job when school intervenes	0.512	
Inability to give 100% to school when job intervenes	0.569	
Conflicts with job commitments	0.437	
Conflicts between work and school—difficult to stay in school	0.503	
Family Stress		0.700
Family financial obligations—challenge	0.389	
Inability to give 100% to school when family intervenes	0.510	
Less time with significant other	0.423	
Inability to make or participate in family commitments	0.463	
Conflict with family life	0.494	

Source: Analyses of 2007 National Study on Non-traditional Students Survey

Administrators at each institution assisted researchers in recruiting students by sending out e-mail messages and posting flyers announcing the focus groups. The groups were targeted to nontraditional students as defined by age (older than age 25) and/or employment or parental status. Researchers scheduled between one and three focus groups per institution, depending on student interest. Participation in the groups varied from 2 to 11 students, with most groups including 5 to 8 people. In rare cases, individual interviews were conducted. The total number of students participating in the focus groups across schools was 124. Four schools had fewer than five participants each, three schools had 10 to 20, and three schools had more than 20 students participate. The demographics of focus groups varied from school to school. At most schools the gender of focus groups was mixed, with an overall breakdown of 89 women and 35 men. We did not ask participants to identify their race/ethnicity, but researcher notes indicated that students from a variety of racial, ethnic, and national backgrounds were represented. The vast majority of participants were older than the age of 25.

Data Collection and Analysis

The principal investigator (PI) of the qualitative portion of the study conducted interviews with the assistance of a doctoral or postdoctoral research assistant at 8 of the 10 schools. At one institution, the PI conducted the focus groups without an assistant and at another institution two postdoctoral researchers who had assisted the PI in previous focus groups conducted the groups without the PI present. Focus groups typically lasted from 45 to 60 minutes. All groups were audio-recorded and transcribed and researchers also took notes during the groups.

Focus group questions were developed from the framework guiding the project. Questions centered on understanding barriers and supports to adult students' completing their education. Follow-up probes were designed to encourage focus group participants to expand on data collected through the surveys.

All focus group transcripts were uploaded into NVivo. A start-list of codes was developed from the themes identified through the literature review (Miles & Huberman, 1994). A postdoctoral researcher on the project coded the data from all the focus groups based on these initial start codes and added codes that emerged through the coding process. The PI also coded data by focus group question to allow for easy comparison across schools and as a tool for initially separating data by the larger themes of interest in the study. The second author of this chapter then reviewed the data for information specifically related to issues surrounding student work and employment. Start codes within these themes were developed based on the conceptual framework laid out at the beginning of the chapter. In addition, codes related to specific survey data and emergent themes that were not previously identified were developed during the process. Themes presented here represent codes that were prevalent across focus groups. The findings describe common experiences as well as unique issues.

Results

Characteristics of Adult Students by Employment Status

More than half of survey respondents were White (56.5%), a little less than one third were African American (30%), and 13% were of other races/ethnicities. The average age was 37.5 years, more than three quarters of the participants were women (77%), and more than half of the students had

dependents (56%). About half of the sample (47%) delayed college enrollment after graduating from high school, and 59% reported having high
school grades of mostly Bs or better. With respect to enrollment, more than
55% of students were enrolled in college half time or less. More than 60% of
the students were enrolled in a bachelor's degree program, and 35% did not
receive any financial aid.

When breaking down the sample by work status, 17% of the participants
were not employed, 18% were employed part time, and the remaining 65%
of the sample worked full time. The descriptive analyses reveal differences in
many characteristics of nontraditional students based on employment status,
with the exception of gender, age, delayed enrollment, and having dependents (Table 3). Whites were better represented among students who did not
work (63%) than among students who worked part time (59%) or worked
full time (54%). Students in the lower two income quartiles were better represented among students who worked part time (70%) than among students
who did not work (56%) or worked full time (55%). A higher share of students who worked full time reported earning "mostly B's or above" in high
school (62%), than students who worked part time (55%) or not at all (51%).

For institutional and enrollment characteristics, more full-time employees were enrolled in bachelor's degree programs (66%) than were students in
other groups. As for financial aid (i.e., scholarships, grants, loans), a higher
percentage of students who were employed full time received no financial
aid (41%) compared to the other two groups (33% not employed, 28%
employed part time). More students who were employed part time received
financial aid (72%) than students who were not employed (67%) or
employed full time (58.6%) (Table 3).

There were also descriptive differences in the current college grades of
students depending on employment status, with higher percentages of students who worked full time receiving "mostly A's and B's or above" (72%)
compared to students who work part time (67%), and those not working at
all (63%) (Table 3). Students who were not employed reported higher levels
of family stress and lower levels of family and friend support than their working peers. Students who worked full time reported higher levels of work
stress and work support than their peers.

Differences in Academic Performance for Adult Students Based on Work Status

Results from the multiple regression analyses indicated that the model's predictive ability was not strong, explaining only 13% of the variance in participants' self-reported GPA (Table 4). Several background characteristics were
related to GPA in the final model. Controlling for other variables, age was a

TABLE 3
Characteristics of Sample by Work Status

Student Characteristics	Not Employed	Employed Part Time	Employed Full Time	Total
Race***				
African American	16.9	28.8	33.7	30.1
White	63.1	58.5	54.4	56.5
Other Race/Ethnicity	20.0	12.7	11.9	13.3
Gender				
Male	26.2	18.9	23.3	23.0
Female	73.8	81.1	76.7	77.0
Age				
Mean	38.0	36.8	37.5	37.5
Standard Deviation	11.1	11.2	9.7	10.2
Income (Quartiles)***				
Quartile 1 (0–19k)	25.2	40.0	13.1	20.0
Quartile 2 (20–49k)	30.7	30.2	36.6	34.5
Quartile 3 (50–79k)	22.3	16.9	24.0	22.4
Quartile 4 (over 80k)	21.8	12.9	26.2	23.0
High School Grades**				
Bs and Cs or below	48.9	44.7	37.6	40.7
Mostly Bs or above	51.1	55.3	62.4	59.3
Delayed Enrollment After HS				
No	47.5	53.9	53.7	52.8
Yes	52.5	46.1	46.3	47.2
Dependents				
No	37.6	46.9	45.4	44.5
Yes	62.4	53.1	54.6	55.5
Current Enrollment Status***				
Less than full time	58.2	55.8	75.2	69.0
Full time	41.8	44.2	24.8	31.0
Degree Program***				
Associate's	51.3	47.3	34.1	39.2
Bachelor's	48.7	52.7	65.9	60.8
Type of Financial Aid Received***				
Loans	16.8	13.4	16.6	16.0
Scholarships/Grants	20.8	19.5	10.9	14.0
Both of the above	29.2	38.9	31.1	32.2
None	33.2	28.2	41.4	37.7

TABLE 3 (Continued)

Student Characteristics	Not Employed	Employed Part Time	Employed Full Time	Total
Family and Friend Support**c,d				
Mean	−0.1	0.2	0.0	0.0
Standard Deviation	1.2	0.8	1.0	1.0
Work Support***a,b				
Mean	−0.7	−0.3	0.1	0.0
Standard Deviation	1.07	0.9	0.9	1.0
Family Stress**e,f				
Mean	0.2	0.0	0.0	0.0
Standard Deviation	1.0	1.0	1.0	1.0
Work Stress***a,b,c				
Mean	−0.7	−0.2	0.2	0.0
Standard Deviation	0.7	0.9	1.0	1.0
Current Grades*				
Mostly Bs or below	37.5	32.8	28.1	30.5
As and Bs or above	62.5	67.2	71.9	69.5

Note: Number of cases in the analysis: 1,188.

[a] Significant difference between Column 1 (Not Employed) and Column 2 (Employed Part Time), $p < .001$.

[b] Significant difference between Column 1 (Not Employed) and Column 3 (Employed Full Time), $p < .001$.

[c] Significant difference between Column 2 (Employed Part Time) and Column 3 (Employed Full Time), $p < .001$.

[d] Significant difference between Column 1 (Not Employed) and Column 2 (Employed Part Time), $p < .01$.

[e] Significant difference between Column 1 (Not Employed) and Column 2 (Employed Part Time), $p < .05$.

[f] Significant difference between Column 1 (Not Employed) and Column 3 (Employed Full Time), $p < .01$.

*$p < .05$, **$p < .01$, ***$p < .001$.

Source: Analyses of 2007 National Study on Non-traditional Students Survey

positive predictor, whereas being male, being in the lower two income quartiles, and having high school grades that were Bs or below were negative predictors of college grades.

In terms of the relationship between employment and academic performance, the regression analyses revealed that students who were not employed had lower grades than students who worked full time. With only a few exceptions, the predictors of grades did not vary based on students'

TABLE 4
Predictors of Current Grades of Nontraditional Students by Work Status
(last block only)

	Total Sample β	FT and PT Employment β	FT Employment β
Student Background Characteristics			
African American	−.06	−.05	−.02
White	.05	.10	.12
Gender (male)	−.18***	−.11**	−.04
Age	.12***	.12**	.11**
Income quartile 1 (0–19k)	−.18***	−.18***	−.17***
Income quartile 2 (20–49k)	−.18***	−.19***	−.20***
Income quartile 3 (50–79k)	−.08	−.06	−.03
HS grades B or below	−.14***	−.11**	−.08*
Delayed enrollment	.02	.03	.02
Dependents	−.02	−.05	−.02
R² change	*.13*	*.14*	*.14*
College/Structural Characteristics			
Enrolled less than full time	−.01	.01	.02
Loans	−.06	−.07	−.07
Scholarships/grants	.00	−.03	−.04
Both loans and scholarships/grants	−.07	−.10*	−.09
Associate's	.02	−.04	−.07
R² change	*.01*	*.01*	*.01*
Social Supports			
Work support	N/A	.05	.11*
Family and friend support	.03	.01	−.02
Family and friend stress	−.01	.00	−.04
Work stress	N/A	−.02	−.02
R² change	*.00*	.00	.01
Work Status			
Not employed	−.09**	N/A	N/A
Work part time	−.03	−.01	N/A
R² change	*.01*	*.00*	
Adjusted *R²*	.13	.12	.14
F	8.07***	6.31***	5.97***

Note: FT = full time; PT = part time.
*$p \leq 0.5$; **$p \leq .01$; ***$p \leq .001$.
Source: Analyses of 2007 National Study on Non-traditional Students Survey

employment status. One unexpected result is that, among students who were employed, those who received both scholarships/grants and loans had lower grades than students who did not receive financial aid (Table 4, column 2). One other difference in the predictors of grades by employment status is the role of work support: Students who worked full time and reported having a supportive supervisor and coworkers reported higher grades than other students who worked full time (Table 4, column 3).

Barriers and Supports

The qualitative analyses shed additional light on the forces that limit and promote the academic success of adult students who work. As described by participants, these forces revolve around two central themes: time and money. In terms of time, participants discussed the challenges of balancing the competing demands of school, work, and family. In terms of money, participants cited the prospect of promotion and a higher salary as motivation for attending school, as well as the role of employer tuition reimbursement in reducing the costs of attending.

For the working adult students in this study, time management is particularly complex. Describing their lives as a "stamina marathon" and a "horserace," participants talked about being constantly tired. Students gave detailed accounts of their daily routines to explain the difficulties they faced in meeting the demands of both school and work. For example, one participant said:

> I mean, I go to work at 5 o'clock in the morning. Sometimes I leave around 4:30 or 5:00. I work through lunch . . . [I] come down here several nights a week, but I do try to take some online classes so that I can stay home once in a while, but even this quarter I'm—Wednesday and Thursday nights I am—from 4 o'clock in the morning until 10 o'clock at night I'm not home. . . . Then it's Friday, you know, the weekend, and then, you know, there's your class again right on your shoulders and they give us plenty of homework, so finding the time to—Time management is a big factor. It's difficult. It's not impossible, but it's difficult.

To simultaneously meet work and school demands, students must either find classes that complement their work schedule or negotiate a work schedule that enables them to attend classes that meet their degree requirements. One student said that she found online discussion boards helpful in managing her time because if she missed a class, she could still "log on and see what other students were talking about in the class" and give her own input. Some participants expressed frustration that schools did not offer more evening and weekend classes or offer more classes during the summer. As one student said,

It's like the school is not taking responsibility for the people who need to take the classes, like they're at wrong times for people that work. Like, if you work night shift and you're getting off work to come to school, how many 8 o'clock [a.m.] classes are there available for so many students or if you have to wait till 10:40 after you've just got off of work at 7:30 and you have to wait until 10:40 to take the class you want to take, you know, and then they'll have two classes at the same time. . . .

Because students' schedules are so structured, unexpected changes are problematic. The introduction of one new element—a sick child, or a new work project—can mean that students must at least temporarily allow other demands to take precedence over school. One student explained that, if something happened to take away from time set aside to study, then a domino effect occurred: She had less time to study for an exam, which resulted in a lower exam grade, so she had to spend even more time studying for the next exam to make up for the low grade, all while maintaining work and family obligations.

Some participants discussed the role that employers played in accommodating classes and school work. Not all participants had supervisors who supported their decision to attend school. As one participant said, some bosses "just don't get it." Nonetheless, many participants gave examples of supervisors who encouraged them and who permitted them to study on the job if they had completed their required work. Some participants said their supervisors were willing to help them develop flexible work schedules that accommodated day classes. In the words of one participant,

Actually, my employer has been really good. This semester he like allowed me to condense my work week working three days. I work Friday, Saturday, Sunday but I do three 14-hour days and then I'm done so it makes it easier for me to be able to schedule whereas before I was working a traditional 7:00 to 4:00 Monday through Friday. It kind of messes up my weekends, but . . . life goes on. I figure another year or so and I'll be done with it.

Employer tuition reimbursement provided a motivation for some participants to attend school because this financial support enabled them to progress toward a degree. Many participants expressed gratitude for the financial support offered through their place of work. As one student explained, tuition reimbursement is "a big consideration" for adult students who have life expenses such as car payments and mortgages: "trying to pick up an extra two or three thousand dollars a semester or even if you space it out and it's only for the year, that still sometimes can be lot of money."

Several participants, however, noted that tuition reimbursement can have strings attached. As one student explained, "they're paying 100% of it as long as I can maintain my grades. . . . every time I had a review, it was like so how's school coming, you know, so it's a big, big, big issue there." Whereas some participants' tuition reimbursement was contingent on grades, others' was also limited to a certain number of credit hours. One participant's employer would only pay if his degree was related to his job. Other participants decided not to use tuition reimbursement because they did not want to "owe" their employer anything or because they wanted to avoid the stress of keeping certain grades. One participant shared,

> . . . the tuition here, in order for me to get reimbursed, I'd have to get a certain grade that I would have to present to my manager so I would like be horrified if I have to give her a bad grade for a couple of hundred of dollars for tuition, so that would be . . . That's a reason why I don't seek the reimbursement. . . .

Finally, those students who worked part time as a condition of financial aid, or to better accommodate class schedules, expressed frustration that part-time employment did not cover their cost of living. As one participant explained, the prospect of supporting herself on a part-time salary had deterred her from returning to school for many years: "That's why I've been away for so long. . . . I knew I wouldn't be able to necessarily work full time." Another student with a part-time on-campus job explained that she was limited to working 20 hours per week on campus, so she was looking for a second job off campus to generate additional income. Other students were already working two part-time jobs to pay college costs. And a student who wanted to shift from full-time to part-time work said she was having a diffi-cult time finding a part-time position that both paid enough and accommo-dated her class schedule.

Conclusion

The descriptive analyses in this chapter demonstrate differences among adult college students who are enrolled in associate's or bachelor's degree programs based on their work status. The focus group data show that full-time workers experienced stress related to balancing the demands of work and school. However, the focus group data also revealed that students who opt to return to school while working full time may benefit from the encouragement and support of supervisors and coworkers, and that they may be motivated to maintain higher grades by employer incentives. Although work stress and support networks were unrelated to grades in the regression analyses, the analyses did show that full-time workers who reported greater levels of work support reported receiving higher grades than other full-time workers. None-theless, the complexity of this relationship is further indicated by the focus group data, which show that requiring certain grades for tuition reimbursement may motivate some students toward academic success while deterring other students from seeking financial support. Although the survey and focus groups explored general employer or coworker support, future research should give more in-depth consideration to the specific issue of employer tuition reimbursement.

Our analyses support the conclusions by Bean and Metzner (1985) and Chartrand (1992) that high school performance may influence nontraditional students' success in college. Full-time workers reported having higher grades in high school than students who worked part time or not at all, which may mean that full-time workers had higher levels of academic preparation for college. Students who work full time also reported having higher college grades than those who work part time or not at all, a finding that differs from research on traditional-age undergraduate students (e.g., Astin, 1993; Berkner et al., 1996; Horn & Carroll, 1996). Although some focus group participants briefly touched on their high school experiences in the context of discussing other issues, further qualitative research focusing on the high school experiences of nontraditional students, as well as their decision to initially leave school or delay enrollment, would be useful in explaining the influence of high school performance.

In terms of institutional practice, our qualitative findings support Bean and Metzner's (1985) hypothesis that the academic factors of academic advising and course availability are important considerations for nontraditional undergraduate students. Some students did not utilize academic advising services because they found the advising process too confusing, because they did not have time as a result of their busy school/work schedules, or because advising services were not available in the evenings or on weekends when full-time workers are typically on campus. Although students in the focus groups did not specifically discuss their grades, it may be inferred that, when studying is necessarily limited to late night or early morning hours, extra supports may be needed to ensure academic success. Simply providing the usual tutoring or advisement services may not suffice. Students expressed frustration with the limited availability of required courses during evening and weekend hours and with last-minute course cancellations at the beginning of the semester. These findings suggest that academic services administrators should be cognizant of the advising and scheduling needs of all students, not just those who are on campus from 9 a.m. to 5 p.m. Monday through Friday, particularly given the fact that more than 90% of institutions offer evening and weekend degree options (Cook & King, 2005). In addition, academic services administrators should make it easier for adult students to receive virtual advising. Convenient spaces for students to study in between work and school or between classes is important, especially given that so many students were juggling their work and class schedules and these may be the only times they can devote to homework.

Clearly, adult working students face a multitude of challenges in balancing work and school and draw upon a variety of resources to navigate these challenges. With the numbers of adult students increasing on college campuses, future researchers and administrators may want to reconsider use of the term *nontraditional* because it implies that adult students are somehow nonnormative. Working adult students are becoming the norm and institutions must adapt accordingly. Organizational structures that predominantly cater to residential students ages 18 to 22 must change to engage and support adult learners who are earning their degrees at night, on the weekends, and online.

References

Adebayo, D. O. (2006). Workload, social support, and work-school conflict among Nigerian nontraditional students. *Journal of Career Development, 33*(2), 125–141.

Astin, A. (1993). *What matters in college?* San Francisco: Jossey-Bass.

Bean, J. P., & Metzner, B. S. (1985). A conceptual model of nontraditional undergraduate student attrition. *Review of Educational Research, 55*, 485–540.

Berker, A., Horn, L., and Carroll, C. D. (2003). *Work first, study second: Adult undergraduates who combine employment and postsecondary enrollment.* (NCES 2003–167). Washington, DC: U.S. Department of Education, National Center for Education Statistics.

Berkner, L. K., Cuccaro-Alamin, S., & McCormick, A. C. (1996). *Descriptive summary of 1989–90 beginning postsecondary students: Five years later* (NCES 96–155). Washington, DC: U.S. Department of Education, National Center for Education Statistics.

Betts, J. R., & Morrell, D. (1999). The determinants of undergraduate grade point average: The relative importance of family background, high school resources, and peer group effects. *Journal of Human Resources, 34*, 268–293.

Bosworth, B., & Choitz, V. (2002, April). *Held back: How student aid programs fail working adults.* FutureWorks. Retrieved September 23, 2008, from www.future works-web.com/pdf/Held%20Back%20report.pdf

Carney-Crompton, S., & Tan, J. (2002). Support systems, psychological functioning, and academic performance of nontraditional female students. *Adult Education Quarterly, 52*, 140–154.

Chartrand, J. M. (1992). An empirical test of a model of nontraditional student adjustment. *Journal of Counseling Psychology, 39*, 193–202.

Choy, S. P. (2002). *Condition of education 2000: Nontraditional undergraduates.* Washington, DC: U.S. Department of Education, National Center for Education Statistics.

Cleveland-Innes, M. (1994). Adult student drop-out at post-secondary institutions. *Review of Higher Education, 17*, 423–445.

Cook, B., & King, J. E. (2005, May). *Improving lives through higher education: Campus programs and policies for low-income adults.* Retrieved September 20, 2008, from www.acenet.edu/bookstore/pdf/2005CampusPP4Adults.pdf

DeSimone, J. S. (2008, May). *The impact of employment during school on college student academic performance* (NBER Working Paper 14006). Cambridge, MA: NBER. Retrieved September 2, 2008, from www.nber.org/papers/w14006

Farabaugh-Dorkins, C. (1991). *Beginning to understand why older students drop out of college: A path analytic test of the Bean/Metzner model of nontraditional student attrition.* Tallahassee, FL: Association for Institutional Research.

Heller, D. E., & Bjorklund, S. A. (2004). Student financial aid and low income mothers. In V. Polakow, S. S. Butler, L. S. Deprez, & P. Kahn (Eds.), *Shut out: Low income mothers and higher education in post-welfare America* (pp. 129–148). Albany, NY: SUNY Press.

Home, A. (1997). Learning the hard way: Role strain, stress, role demands, and support in multiple role women students. *Journal of Social Work Education, 33,* 335–347.

Home, A. (1998). Predicting role conflict, overload and contagion in adult women university students with families and jobs. *Adult Education Quarterly, 48,* 85–98.

Horn, L., & Carroll, D. (1996). *Nontraditional undergraduates, trends in enrollment from 1986 to 1992 and persistence and attainment among 1989–90 beginning postsecondary students* (NCES 97–578). Washington, DC: U.S. Department of Education, National Center for Education Statistics.

Horn, L., Peter, K., & Rooney, K. (2002). *Profile of undergraduates in U.S. postsecondary institutions: 1999–2000* (NCES 2002–168). Washington, DC: U.S. Department of Education, National Center for Education Statistics.

Jacobs, J. A., & Berkowitz-King, R. (2002). Age and college completion: A life-history analysis of women aged 15–44. *Sociology of Education, 75,* 211–230.

Johnson, D. R. (1991). *Formulating a conceptual model of nontraditional student attrition and persistence in postsecondary vocational education programs.* Berkeley, CA: National Center for Research in Vocational Education.

Kasworm, C. (2002). African American adult undergraduates: Differing cultural realities. *Journal of Continuing Higher Education, 50*(1), 10–20.

Kasworm, C. E. (2003). Setting the stage: Adults in higher education. *New Directions for Student Services, 102,* 3–10.

Kasworm, C. E., Polson, C. J., & Fishback, S. J. (2002). *Responding to adult learners in higher education.* Malabar, FL: Krieger.

Kazis, R., Callahan, A., Davidson, C., McLeod, A., Bosworth, B., Choitz, V., & Hoops, J. (2007, March). *Adult learners in higher education: Barriers to success and strategies to improve results.* U.S. Department of Labor, Office of Policy Development and Research. Retrieved September 23, 2008, from http://www.jff.org/sites/default/files/adultlearners.dol_.pdf

Kirk, C. F., & Dorfman, L. T. (1983). Satisfaction and role strain among middle-age and older reentry women students. *Educational Gerontology, 9*(9), 15–29.

Mallinckrodt, B., & Leong, F. T. L. (1992). Social support in academic programs and family environments: Sex differences and role conflicts for graduate students. *Journal of Counseling & Development, 70,* 716–723.

Matus-Grossman, L., & Gooden, S. (2002, July). *Opening doors: Students' perspectives on juggling work, family, and college.* Retrieved September 23, 2008, from www.mdrc.org/publications/260/full.pdf

Miles, M. B., & Huberman, A. M. (1994). *Qualitative data analysis: An expanded sourcebook.* Thousand Oaks, CA: Sage.

National Center for Education Statistics, U.S. Department of Education. (2008). Postsecondary education. In *Digest of Education Statistics 2007* (chapter 3). Retrieved November 20, 2008, from http://nces.ed.gov/programs/digest/d07/ch_3.asp

Parker, M. (2008). *The relationship between personal, social, and institutional factors and the academic outcomes of non-traditional students.* Unpublished doctoral dissertation, University of Virginia.

Pascarella, E. T., Edison, M. I., Nora, A., Hagedorn, L. S., & Terenzini, P. T. (1998). Does work inhibit cognitive development during college? *Educational Evaluation and Policy Analysis, 20*(2), 75–93.

Pascarella, E. T., & Terenzini, P. T. (2005). *How college affects students: A third decade of research.* San Francisco: Jossey-Bass.

Pusser, B., Breneman, D. W., Gansneder, B. M., Kohl, K. J., Levin, J. S., Milam, J. H., & Turner, S. E. (2007). *Returning to learning: Adults' success in college is key to America's future.* Indianapolis, IN: Lumina Foundation for Education.

Quimby, J. L., & O'Brien, K. M. (2006). Predictors of well-being among nontraditional female students with children. *Journal of Counseling Development, 84,* 451–460.

Roehl, J. E., & Okun, M. A. (1984). Depression symptoms among women reentering college: The role of negative life events and family social support. *Journal of College Student Personnel, 25,* 251–254.

Sandler, M. E. (1998, April). *Career decision-making self-efficacy and an integrated model of student persistence.* Paper presented at the annual meeting of the American Educational Research Association, San Diego, CA.

Sands, R. G., & Richardson, V. (1984). Educational and mental health factors associated with the return of mid-life women to school. *Educational Gerontology, 10,* 155–170.

Scott, C., Burns, A., Cooney, G. (1996). Reasons for discontinuing study: The case of mature age female students with children. *Higher Education, 31,* 233–253.

Taniguchi, H., & Kaufman, G. (2005). Degree completion among nontraditional college students. *Social Science Quarterly, 86,* 912–927.

Teachman, J. D., & Polonko, K. A. (1988). Marriage, parenthood, and the college enrollment of men and women. *Social Forces, 67,* 512–523.

Wlodkowski, R. J., Mauldin, J. E., & Campbell, S. (2002). *Early exit: Understanding adult attrition in accelerated and traditional postsecondary programs.* Indianapolis, IN: Lumina Foundation for Education.

Wlodkowski, R. J., Mauldin, J. E., & Gahn, S. W. (2001). *Learning in the fast lane: Adult learners' persistence and success in accelerated college programs.* Indianapolis, IN: Lumina Foundation for Education.

SECTION THREE

WORK AS A VEHICLE FOR PROMOTING COGNITIVE DEVELOPMENT AND LEARNING

6

USING ECONOMICS TO ILLUMINATE THE DYNAMIC HIGHER EDUCATION LANDSCAPE

Doug Lynch, Michael Gottfried, Wendy Green, and Chris Allen Thomas

For many decades, researchers have investigated the social and economic stratification of higher education, arguing that significant barriers to educational access and success exist for the working class (Laing, Chao, & Robinson, 2005; Lynch & O'Riordan, 1998; Sewell, 1971; Winston, 2004). Other researchers, such as Ogbu (1992), argue that cultural barriers are most significant in limiting educational access. These arguments frame educational access as a problem and characterize issues of access to higher education in terms of a deficit. Such a framing—particularly one that makes a priori assumptions about students, institutions, and the purposes of attending higher education—may provide an inaccurate picture and lead to poor public and institutional policy. A deficit perspective assumes that all students have the same needs and bring to college the same endowments, leading to a belief that prevailing structures and policies are best for all students.

In this chapter, we explore whether the widely accepted traditional model of higher education (i.e., student enters higher education immediately upon high school graduation, is financially dependent on parents, has little work experience, is enrolled full time) (Choy, 2002) applies to all students. If student characteristics and needs are homogeneous and have not changed over time, then the current model is appropriate. However, if students' endowments and needs are heterogeneous, we may need to consider whether the widely accepted model effectively addresses students' needs, given their changed characteristics and unchanged institutional characteristics, such as cost or pedagogy. If students' characteristics have changed, there may be a misalignment among public policy, institutional goals and characteristics, and student needs. The "traditional" model is assumed to apply to the entire student population, with an expectation that a more diverse student body must conform to its standards rather than that the institution needs to rethink the model. Lack of conformity to the traditional pattern of enrollment is viewed problematically and as a student deficit. This chapter explores the validity of the current model.

We begin our exploration by positing that students are making informed decisions regarding their college enrollment. From this perspective, developing institutional accommodations to meet the needs of nontraditional students and expanding "nontraditional" institutions (e.g., for-profit institutions) are appropriate responses to the growth in nontraditional students. This heterogeneous group of learners may have a different set of needs and different, even positive, attributes, such as work experience, life experience, and the ability to make informed decisions regarding their educational choices based on concrete ideas of where they would like to progress (Bash, 2003; Jarvis, 2001; Lane, 2003). If higher education values these attributes, then educational programming could be reflective of and possibly leverage these needs. In such models, the Carnegie Classification scheme would be less of an ordinal map than a categorical one, and nontraditional institutions would be as valued as other institutions. On campuses, distance learning and continuing or executive education would be perceived less as profit centers and more as equal siblings to traditional programs.

As a conceptual frame for this exploration, we draw on an analytical tool derived from the economics of education literature. The education production function is a common economic framework for understanding how student outcomes are realized. The primary goal of the education production function is to understand the relationship between student inputs and academic outputs. Essentially, through learning, various inputs are transformed into educational outcomes. These inputs may include student, faculty, and institutional characteristics. This approach allows researchers to evaluate what would happen to educational outcomes if inputs were manipulated. Learning, from this perspective, is analogous to the materials and machinery involved in a manufacturing production process.

Studies on production functions began in what is commonly referred to as the "Coleman Report" (Coleman, 1966).[1] This landmark study employed statistical methods to evaluate how differential levels of academic achievement (i.e., one output of the education production function) can be attributed to racial and geographic backgrounds (i.e., inputs to the education production function). Coleman's work concluded that peer effects, and not schools, are the most important determinants of academic achievement. The report, which was delivered to Congress, resulted in a research movement to identify and examine variables that affected the learning process. Since the Coleman Report, many researchers have used the education production function to evaluate student inputs and academic achievement. The most noteworthy studies date back to Henderson, Mieszkowski, and Sauvageau (1978), Summers and Wolfe (1977), and Hanushek (1979). Although presenting mixed results regarding the influence of inputs (e.g., classroom ability) on achievement, these studies provide a basis for rigorously investigating the relationship between classroom effects (another input) and subsequent academic achievement.

The education production function has become a popular methodology to evaluate educational outcomes. However, since the seminal works of the late 1970s, not much has changed in terms of the structure of the education production function. Moreover, nearly identical production functions are used to evaluate outcomes for primary and secondary students and schools and traditional students and colleges. The outcome has consistently been specified as academic achievement or income, and inputs typically include student endowments, family background, classroom peer inputs, faculty characteristics, class size, and institutional and community factors (Hanushek, 1989). To specify the standard education production function more precisely, outputs are generally defined as a vector:

$$Y = (y_1, y_2, y_3, \ldots, y_n)$$

There is also an analogous vector of inputs:

$$X = (x_1, x_2, x_3, \ldots, x_n)$$

The education production process, then, becomes a function in which a given y from Y is a function of inputs x from all possible choices in X:

$$y = f(x_1, \ldots, x_n)$$

Although these formulations represent potentially important tools for evaluating the input–output relationship in education, a production function derived empirically for K–12 or traditional college students in the 1970s may not accurately depict the learning process or learning outcomes for a heterogeneous student populace given changes in student characteristics and experiences (i.e., student inputs) as students enter adulthood. This chapter disaggregates this heterogeneity of students by comparing the characteristics of traditional and nontraditional students.

Who Are the Traditional and Nontraditional Students?

In many contexts, *traditional* has become a pejorative term, standing in contrast to *modern, progressive,* or *innovative.* However, with regard to educational access, the opposite holds true. Nontraditional students are those who, for many possible reasons, have either not been afforded the opportunity or consciously elected not to follow a streamlined path to higher education. At traditional institutions, these nontraditional students have been classified as different, in one form or another, from the prototypical and ideal student.

The classification of a student as nontraditional is far from precise (National Center for Education Statistics [NCES], 2002). Age and enrollment status are main themes in most characterizations (Bean & Metzner, 1985). NCES conducted a study to determine the 1999–2000 college enrollment and persistence patterns of students who lacked traditional status. Following Horn and Carroll (1996), NCES defines a nontraditional student as having one or more of the following characteristics:

- Delayed enrollment (i.e., not entering postsecondary education in the same calendar year of high school completion)
- Attends part time for at least part of the academic year
- Works full time (35 hours or more per week) concomitant with enrollment
- Is financially independent for purposes of determining eligibility for financial aid
- Has dependents other than a spouse
- Is a single parent (unmarried, divorced, or separated)
- Has not completed high school or received a GED or high school equivalency certificate

These criteria for nontraditional students imply that a fully traditional student is a person with little or no work experience, is financially dependent on parents, and has continued full-time education from high school to a two- or four-year college without interruption. Given these differences, it is not unreasonable to suggest that traditional and nontraditional students have divergent endowments, learning needs, and goals.

Updating the Education Production Function

From the perspective of an education production function, these differences in the characteristics of traditional and nontraditional students suggest substantial differences in the inputs that these two groups bring to the educational process. A traditional education production function emphasizes only the characteristics of traditional students. Identifying variables that are characteristic of nontraditional students produces a new function that more appropriately captures this group's experiences.

The basic education production function is consistent for both traditional and nontraditional students: A series of inputs will influence outputs.

But some inputs to the education production function are more relevant to traditional students, while others are more relevant to nontraditional students. Although inputs are related to outputs for both groups, the types of inputs and outputs and the relative import of various student inputs in the production function vary.

Inputs to the education production function are typically defined as follows, where X is a vector of inputs:

$$X_{\text{Historical}} = f(G, F, S, T, C, P, N)$$

G is a host of student-level demographic characteristics, F is family background, S is school environment, T is faculty characteristics, C is classroom environment, P is peer effects, and N is neighborhood/environmental characteristics. This historical form of the education production is ubiquitous within the economics of education literature (e.g., Hanushek, Kain, Markman, & Rivkin, 2003; Lamdin, 1996; Lazear, 2001) and has seen little change over time.

We argue that these historical inputs do not provide a complete picture of students in contemporary higher education, a fact that becomes clear when comparing the socioeconomic and developmental characteristics of traditional and nontraditional students. Many of the inputs from the original education production function are still relevant. For example, because traditional students continue their education uninterrupted from K–12 into higher education, the inputs to the education production function of traditional students may replicate those from K–12 education. For students who may be only one year older than their high school counterparts, teacher, classroom, and school inputs may still hold a dominant influence on college achievement outcomes simply because these inputs align with the learning framework with which these students are most accustomed and because the students are not yet developmentally or socioeconomically classifiable as adult learners. In other words, additional variables have not yet come into play.

For some traditional students and many nontraditional students, however, additional inputs influence the education production function beyond the inputs considered in the historical function. This addition reflects the observation that nontraditional students are, to some degree, in more advanced stages of developmental maturity and financial independence. To account for these differences, an education production function for higher education must incorporate not only historical inputs to education but also a new vector of characteristics unique to nontraditional students. These additional inputs to the education production function may be defined as follows:

$$X_{\text{Updated}} = f(FS, LE, WE, WS, SS, G)$$

These variables include *FS*, representing financial status (whether the student is wholly independent, partially independent, or wholly dependent); *LE* are life experience characteristics (marriage and parenthood, cognitive development, social awareness, and time management skills); *WE* is a vector of work experience indicators (such as having acquired skills-based knowledge or management skills); *WS* is work status (full time, part time, unemployed, or in a phase of pre-employment); *SS* is student status (full time, part time, occasional, degree, or certificate); and *G* is a set of goals (such as academic, career, and personal interests).

With a set of inputs relevant to the historical production function and the updated inputs, it is possible to create a single education production function to evaluate the academic outcomes of traditional and nontraditional students in aggregate. Here, output is *Y*, derived from a set of inputs from both historical and updated inputs:

$$Y = X_{Historical} + X_{Updated}$$

Fleshing out the inputs of *Y* with specific inputs from traditional and nontraditional students would provide the following, single education production function for college students:

$$Y = f(G, F, S, T, C, P, FS, LE, WE, WS, SS, G)$$

The updated education production function not only incorporates historical inputs to education production, but also recognizes inputs previously unexamined in the role of higher educational outcomes. This model does not bias the relationship between learning inputs and academic achievement to those factors strictly defined by the original education production function. This updated model assumes that academic achievement is influenced by a host of factors that are relevant to both traditional and nontraditional students. This model also provides a more complete picture of how education is attained, recognizing that students in higher education are a heterogeneous and complex group representing a variety of socioeconomic and developmental backgrounds.

The updated model also suggests there will be changes in educational outputs. For statistical and conceptual reasons, the original education production function for K–12 schooling focused on student achievement as the sole output (Hanushek, 1989). Statistically, metrics of student achievement, such as standardized test scores, provide a so-called unbiased measure of the outcomes of the learning process. In higher education, some outcomes are analogous with outcomes in K–12 education. For example, the GPA for a particular cohort of students in a given year in a given major or course may provide a standard metric for evaluating the effectiveness of inputs, such as course attendance. Another higher education outcome is bachelor's degree attainment. A consideration of the characteristics of nontraditional students suggests that potential outputs of the higher education production function also include attainment of a degree or certificate, job placement, job or career enhancement, income, and quality of life improvements.

Accounting for Students' Needs and Educational Choices

To illustrate in terms of the education production function why a student selects a particular path of learning within higher education over another (e.g., online vs. physical classrooms; early entry vs. delayed entry), we provide three scenarios. The first scenario considers the implications of the financial constraints that often face nontraditional rather than traditional students. The second scenario considers differences in the preferences of traditional and nontraditional students. The third scenario considers differences in the mix of educational inputs that traditional and nontraditional students bring to the educational process.

Scenario 1: Different Access

Traditional and nontraditional students often have distinct college experiences because of differences in their cost constraints. A traditional student may be able to enter college full time and complete a degree in 4 years, whereas a nontraditional student may enroll on a part-time or intermittent basis to meet other financial responsibilities. As a result, traditional and nontraditional students in the scenario differ by access.

Assume that student A is a traditional student who matriculates immediately into a four-year private or public college after high school. Based on data from 1999–2000, the average cost is approximately $20,277 for a private college and $7,302 for a public college (Riggert, Boyle, Petrosko, Ash, & Rude-Parkins, 2006). Students can pay this cost using four options: (1) personal and family endowment; (2) loans such as Stafford, which require repayment; (3) grants, such as the National Merit Scholarship, which do not require repayment; and (4) employment.

After 4 contiguous years of college, student A graduates at age 22 and works for an average of 40 years. Under a combination of financing options (1) and (3), student A would have no financial debt after college. Option (2) would yield debt. A student would repay the loan at regular intervals over a standard 10-year period using one of a variety of repayment methods. By 32, these loans have been repaid. Holding all else constant, this scenario provides student A with a minimum of 30 career-years free of educational debt.

Student B is a nontraditional student who attends college over an 8-year period. The first 4 years are spent attending a community college part time, culminating in an associate's degree. The final 4 years are spent attending a public university part time, after which time a bachelor's degree is earned.

The student is 26 when she has completed college and then continues to work for 36 years, for a total of 44 years of work.

The financial constraints of the nontraditional student differ from those of the traditional student. For the first 4 years of college, the nontraditional student (i.e., student B) works part time, earning a salary equivalent to not having earned a college degree. During the second 4 years, the student continues to be enrolled part time and earns a salary based on having a two-year degree. Student B pays for access to college education through a variety of means, including earnings from her own employment, employee tuition reimbursement, loans, and grants.

Reflecting their differing cost constraints, students A and B also differ in their educational experiences. Student B has access to work experience to inform decisions regarding major and course of study and thus uses college to advance her career. College for student B, although it may not provide a liberal arts education, enables her to hone skills that will satisfy workplace needs and propel her career. Student A spends the first 1 or 2 years fulfilling liberal arts requirements at a four-year institution before delving into her major. Student B attends a different type of university with different costs from those of student A. Many nontraditional students initially enter two-year community college programs prior to moving on to four-year universities. Many of these students enter community colleges to complete prerequisites, decide on majors, save money, or increase employability through upgrading skills, obtaining certificates, or receiving diplomas (Lane, 2003).

The educational outcomes of the two students are similar. Student A works approximately 40 years with a bachelor's degree, while student B works 36 years with the same degree. The two students have similar preferences—both enter the postcollege workplace with the same degree and have similar career lengths. What differs between these students is not the inputs or outputs of the education production function, but rather the educational pathways that result from the differential financial resources and constraints faced by today's traditional and nontraditional students. Both pathways are viable strategies because both ultimately result in a bachelor's degree.

Scenario 2: Different Preferences

This scenario assumes that traditional and nontraditional college students differ in terms of their preferences regarding the time value of money (i.e., in economics terms, the net present value of money). Assume that the output of the education production function is the cumulative salary earned over 10 years, when a student is between ages 18 and 28. Further assume that an average-achieving student, with financial need, can decide how to invest in education and employment over a 10-year period. What education path does the student choose? At age 18, the student has two choices: attend a traditional two- or four-year college immediately after graduating from high school and delay salary earnings, or earn a salary immediately by delaying college attendance and earning a bachelor's degree later or part time over subsequent years.

Because this hypothetical student is an average achiever, the likelihood is high that the student will be admitted into a traditional four-year, state-run university; he is unlikely to gain acceptance to a top college that meets 100% of a student's financial need. This student would pay the upfront costs of college and complete his degree in 4 years at age 22. In this case, the student follows the traditional educational path and receives salary in years 5 through 10. In these final 6 years of the 10-year range, assume that the student earns $50,000 for each of the first 3 years and receives a promotion to $60,000 for each of the following 3 years. The aggregate salary for this student is then $330,000 over the 10-year span. The cost for college over this span is $15,000 per year, leaving the student with a "profit" of $270,000.

This same student also has the option of working for several years, acquiring income for the first 2 years, and then enrolling part time in college for 6 years. By the eighth year, the student has attained a bachelor's degree and acquired 8 years of work experience. This pattern delays degree completion until age 25. However, the student gains salary in all 10 years. Assume the student receives a salary of $25,000 per year for each of the first 4 years, and then receives a raise to $30,000 per year for the latter 4 years. However, after graduation, the student's salary increases to $50,000 for the last 2 years of this model. Over the 10-year span, the student earns a total of $320,000. College for this student is $5,000 a year, leaving a net profit of $290,000.

This hypothetical comparison suggests that students choose educational paths based on their discount rate. In economics, discounting is the process by which the value of future income is reduced to reflect an individual's preference for having the money now rather than at some future time. In other words, the discounted value reflects how much money an individual would exchange today for some greater amount at a future date. A student who chooses the traditional path of education has a high discount rate because the student is willing to forgo current earnings in exchange for higher future earnings. A student who chooses the nontraditional educational path has a low discount rate because the student values current earnings more than future earnings.

Thus, although both paths in this scenario lead to similar outputs, that is, similar 10-year cumulative salaries, the paths differ based on a student's preferences for present versus future income. A student with sufficient financial resources and a high discounted value of future earnings is likely to pursue a traditional educational pathway. However, a student who needs immediate income and values a dollar today more than a dollar tomorrow is likely to choose a nontraditional educational path.

Scenario 3: Different Inputs

The first two scenarios demonstrated that similar educational outcomes can be achieved even when students have different financial access and/or preferences for present versus future earnings. The third scenario assumes that nontraditional and traditional students differ in terms of the inputs that they contribute to the education production process. Recall that, in the education production function, learning is the technology that transforms inputs into educational outputs. In this third scenario, the nontraditional student beneficially alters the learning technology. In economic terms, this is known as *innovation to the education production function*. The nontraditional student may contribute four new inputs to the classical education production function.

One new input may be the nontraditional student's workplace experience. Work experience may enhance the educational production process by focusing students' attention on experiences that will improve their current or future career outcomes and by improving students' administrative and time-management skills.

A second new input to the education production function that nontraditional students may bring is life experience. Nontraditional students may possess practical know-how that is still relatively unknown to the 18- to 22-year-old traditional student. As such, nontraditional students may bring to their college experience a broader foundation of ideas and frameworks than a traditional student does.

Third, reflecting the value of work and life experiences, peer effects (Zimmerman & Winston, 2004) may be stronger in classrooms with nontraditional rather than traditional students. In other words, the classroom experience itself becomes a more pertinent input to the learning process simply because of the different experiences that nontraditional students bring to the classroom. Gleaned from both the workplace and private life, these experiences spill over to benefit other students, both traditional and nontraditional.

Finally, for nontraditional students, the workplace becomes a kind of laboratory to test new knowledge. Higher education institutions may benefit from this "laboratory" and include this laboratory as an input in the education production function, without having to pay for the cost of this laboratory.

Therefore, in Scenario 3, nontraditional students differ from their traditional counterparts not with regard to their financial constraints or preferences but with regard to the inputs that they contribute to the learning process. Rather than detracting from the learning process, these new inputs may actually enhance learning. The next section examines how this innovation in learning is situated in the current higher education climate.

Are These Scenarios Plausible?

The traditional student has been a minority in two- and four-year colleges and universities at least since 1986. According to NCES data, in fall 1986, 64.6% of undergraduates had at least one nontraditional characteristic, with the primary nontraditional characteristics being age (i.e., delayed entry) and financial independence (Horn & Carroll, 1996).

Data from the 2000 National Postsecondary Student Aid Study (Choy, 2002) suggest that the number of nontraditional students is on the rise. Students who fit one or more of the nontraditional criteria during the 1999–2000 academic year represented 73% of all students at public, not-for-profit private, and for-profit private colleges. The most common reason for being classified as nontraditional was financial independence (51%), closely followed by part-time attendance (48%) and delayed enrollment (46%). The numbers of working students and students with dependents have increased since the 1992–1993 academic year (Choy, 2002).

Clearly, both students and colleges look vastly different from how they did a generation ago—traditional schools and traditional students are now no longer the norm. Although the growth in nontraditional students has been a huge boon for schools that serve these students, traditional schools have been closing (e.g., Antioch College, Mary Holmes College, Uppsala College).

The increased enrollment of nontraditional students should encourage an examination of how attitudes and educational policies and practices preference traditional students (Bash, 2003; Lane, 2003; Pusser, Gansneder, Gallaway, & Pope, 2005). This reexamination is particularly appropriate given the innovations to learning that nontraditional students may contribute (as highlighted earlier by Scenario 3). As seen in the NCES criteria (Choy, 2002), "adults" are labeled by the biological aging process, where age is used to identify the nontraditional population. Other lenses (e.g., Bash, 2003; Clark & Caffarella, 1999; Knowles, 1990; Merriam, Caffarella, & Baumgartner, 2007) approach nontraditional students functionally as adult learners with regard to their development, experiences, and roles. Research in adult learning may provide insight into how to better serve students with differing experiences and expectations. In addition, and as described in other chapters in this volume, alternative certification programs may assist in translating work and life experience into college credit (CAEL, Council for Adult and Experiential Learning; ACE, American Council of Education). Research on adult learning may also help identify institutional offerings and pedagogical stances that more effectively meet the needs of nontraditional students.

Why Might These Scenarios Be Emerging?

In the 1970s and 1980s, the purpose of educational programming in higher education and adult continuing education was shaped by larger societal trends—in particular, the development of a knowledge-based economy, which has been propelled forward in part because of significant technological advances. Jarvis (2001) argues that changes in technology, communication, and knowledge structures have usurped industrialism as the underlying societal structure, echoing Machlup's (1962) argument that knowledge is an economic resource, Drucker's (1968) contention that modern society has transitioned away from industrialism toward knowledge, and Bell's (1973) proclamation of the emergent postindustrial society focused on technical innovation and information. By the 1980s, the advent of computer technology further shifted the economy from manufacturing to knowledge production, or from a manufacturing-based to an information-based society (Cooper, Basson, & Schapp, 2006; Jarvis, 2001; Tharenou, Saks, & Moore, 2007). As noted by others (e.g., Jarvis, 2001; Kasworm, chapter 2), societies in a knowledge economy are dependent on the skills of knowledge workers, including investment bankers, lawyers, professors, research scientists, and engineers. Because of these changes, increasing numbers of employees require some type of postsecondary education to keep their skills current (Pusser et al., 2005). Employees who choose higher education settings to improve their skills are classed as nontraditional students.

As argued by other authors in this volume, this shift toward a knowledge economy manifests in higher education systems through an increase in nontraditional students and resultant calls for alternative programming and services. Nontraditional students often have different goals than traditional students do because nontraditional students may be more interested in learning content knowledge, process knowledge, and skills to adjust to a rapidly changing workplace. As a result, institutions of higher education are challenged to respond to and value multiple student goals.

Are Institutions Responding to These Perceived Preferences?

The concept of a nontraditional student may be a red herring that higher education leaders use to avoid a more crucial issue—namely, the need to respond to shifting social and economic landscapes by modifying educational processes, including course offerings, course scheduling, financial aid, and pedagogical strategies. In this chapter, we argue that, compared with traditional students, nontraditional students have different preferences, access to financial resources, and opportunity costs. Perhaps most radically, we have hypothesized that work itself may make a significant positive contribution to individual and peer learning.

Like others (e.g., Bash, 2003), we have argued that work experience informs a nontraditional student's educational choices, experiences, and future employment needs. At a minimum, experienced workers may be more discerning in terms of the subjects they choose to study. Nontraditional students may also contribute to and utilize the existing pedagogical systems in a manner that is substantially different from what was intended when those systems were designed (i.e., the needs and goals of traditional students). Individuals who are looking to increase employability through higher education often want opportunities that accommodate their work life (Bash, 2003). This may mean taking classes in the evening or choosing classes that are immediately applicable to employment situations. The demand for part-time undergraduate programs has also increased tremendously because such programs fit more easily into busy work schedules and are easier to pay for through tuition reimbursements offered by employers (Pusser et al., 2005). Furthermore, many adult learners are interested in occupational placement. Employability and occupational placements are issues that traditional institutions of higher education have tended to avoid.

Shifts in the university student population also call for greater recognition of the value of work and prior experience that students bring to their educational endeavors. At least 80% of today's undergraduates are employed (Baum, chapter 1, this volume; Riggert et al., 2006). One consequence of the increasing prevalence of working is the growing demand by students for formal credit for prior work experience relevant to the educational goals of a particular degree or certificate. In the United States, university credits are offered through organizations such as the Council for Adult and Experiential Learning (CAEL), College Level Examination Program (CLEP), and American Council on Education (ACE). By granting academic credit for prior knowledge and experience, these alternative certifications promote the educational attainment of nontraditional students by promoting timely degree completion and reducing the costs of enrollment.

Discussion

Ramifications of a Changing Student Body

The fastest growing population in higher education is individuals pursuing part-time study and classified by NCES as adult learners (National Center for Education Statistics, 2007). These students are typically engaged in some form of employment—most commonly, full time—while enrolled in coursework (Bash, 2003). These learners may be characterized as students who work or as employees who study (Riggert et al., 2006). With increasing numbers of delayed enrollment, full-time working, and single-parent students, colleges and universities are challenged to reformulate how to offer educational opportunities (Bash, 2003; Jarvis, 2001).

Yet most of the literature that purports to be advocating for students may be interpreted as being quite paternalistic; it starts with the assumption that adult learners are operating at a deficit because of their educational choices. Laing and associates (2005) examine the changing participation policies that encourage access to higher education for working-class adults in the United Kingdom. Following the House of Commons (2001), they define nontraditional students as those who are disproportionately underrepresented because of ethnicity or social class. This definition is roughly the same as Choy's (2002) definition of nontraditional students. Like others (e.g., Cook & Leckey, 1999; Ozga & Sukhnandan, 1998; Yorke, 1999), Laing and colleagues argue that students who do not follow the traditional path to higher education lack a foundation to build adequate expectations of college life. They propose that institutions of higher education implement "negotiation systems" to encourage nontraditional students to meet the institution's expectations of a decreased work schedule and a high academic load. They suggest that the negotiation system can eliminate students' "unrealistic expectations" (Laing et al., 2005, p. 177) and enable the institution to retain its ideal of the traditional, dependent, nonworking and nonadult student.

In contrast, like Bye, Pushkar, and Conway (2007), we argue that academic status is a continuum, ranging from fully traditional to fully nontraditional. In their study of 300 university undergraduates, they operationalize traditional and nontraditional students in the following way:

> Traditional students were defined as those most likely to have followed an unbroken linear path from high school into a university undergraduate program and to belong to an age group for whom attending school is a relatively normative experience. Non-traditional students were defined as those who re-entered school after experiencing nonacademic life events or those for whom the undergraduate experience is non-normative for their age group in that they may be combining it with other major life tasks. (pp. 148–149)

By not assuming a deficit perspective of older or working students, one arrives at a vastly different picture of the nontraditional student.

Implications for Policy and Practice

As a society, we often become deeply concerned that young people who do not enter college immediately after graduating from high school are giving up a cherished competitive advantage. However, this chapter argues that students, traditional and nontraditional alike, make choices about their educational pathways that reflect their financial needs and preferences. The three hypothetical scenarios suggest plausible explanations for why some students choose paths that diverge from the traditional, prevailing notions.

If we accept that these educational decisions reflect sound economic decision-making principles, then we must also consider how public and institutional policymakers can support these decisions. The answers, of course, depend on which of the three scenarios best explains a student's decision.

The first scenario suggests that higher education institutions and policymakers should take a fresh look at financial assistance for nontraditional students. As Baum (chapter 1, this volume) and others note, such federal, state, and institutional support is designed with only traditional students in mind. For example, college students are not considered financially independent of their parents until the age of 25, thus restricting access to an important source of funding for many nontraditional students. Tuition reimbursement policies should also be reconsidered. Cappelli (2004) suggests that the vast majority of large employers have tuition reimbursement programs in effect—a seemingly promising resource for nontraditional students. Yet on average only about 6.5% of employees use the tuition reimbursement benefit. This low rate of usage may be because current policy treats tuition reimbursement as a taxable benefit.

The second scenario suggests that educational decisions are merely a matter of preferences. Nontraditional students have different needs, which reveal themselves in the selected path of college education. As suggested by other chapters in this volume (Kasworm, chapter 2; Levin, Montero-Hernandez, & Cerven, chapter 3; Ziskin, Torres, Hossler, & Gross, chapter 4; Rowan-Kenyon, Swan, Deutsch, & Gansneder, chapter 5), many nontraditional students divide their energies between work and family responsibilities in addition to being enrolled in classes. In this scenario, higher education institutions must recognize that nontraditional students are the majority of higher education consumers in the United States and adapt institutional policies and practices to accommodate their multiple roles and responsibilities (see Kasworm and other chapters in this volume).

The third scenario suggests that adult learners may have workplace and life experiences that benefit both their own and their peers' educational experiences. This scenario suggests the value of programs that offer credit for students' prior experience, such as CAEL's Prior Learning Assessment and CLEP.

All three scenarios suggest the benefits of adapting course offerings and pedagogical styles to address the needs of nontraditional students, as noted in research by adult-education scholars (e.g., Bash; 2003; Jarvis, 2001; Merriam & Brockett, 1997). Group work facilitated through online learning environments may facilitate the participation of working students in higher education. Jacobs (2006) suggests that "the field of adult education generally professes to serve the broad purposes of social justice, individual self-development, and workforce preparation and advancement for individuals and organizations" (p. 21). Nontraditional, adult students may be more interested than traditional-aged college students in taking classes that will enable them to move forward in their adult roles and occupations, to find substance in learning that offers direct applicability to work, such as just-in-time learning or task-based learning (Levine, 2001). These choices may be informed by work or life experience as well as a sense of immediacy in the applicability of the learning.

From a pedagogical standpoint, higher education institutions should consider that adult learners may engage with curricular materials in a way that is different from traditional students. Acknowledging and integrating the knowledge and skill levels that many nontraditional students bring to the classroom may create a rich learning environment. For example, through appropriate pedagogical styles, the life and work experience that nontraditional adult students bring to a classroom setting may be utilized to further the educational goals of all students. Situating activities in workplace scenarios and providing real-world applicability may also provide a more salient learning experience.

Conclusion

Although these implications for policy and practice may seem quite broad, they are happening in real time. Some progressive institutions have offered a rubric of how institutions might better recognize students' preferences. For example, Maricopa Community College system has worked to remove barriers to registration, payment, enrollment, and attendance for nontraditional students. This institution offers many support mechanisms for adult learners, such as web-based registration, daycare, and evening and weekend classes. In addition, it does not penalize students for not remaining continuously matriculated. By allowing longer periods for students to finish coursework, the institution allows students the opportunity to finish their degree on their own schedules rather than on an institutionally defined time frame. Recognizing that a large number of its students meet nontraditional criteria, the institution has also put support systems in place to facilitate a student's eventual success. Alternative course scheduling allows working students to engage in learning outside of the 9 to 5 work schedule, and childcare support may facilitate increased attendance for students who are also parents. This approach is in contrast to support systems that focus solely on academic or social programming to assist a more traditional student body. This model of education, although small in scale, may provide a framework for other higher education institutions.

We must wonder whether the scenarios presented in this chapter are just the tip of the iceberg. The chasm between what students—acting rationally—want and what institutions offer may get worse. If we consider the hypothesis that degrees are projected to lose currency within a few years of graduation and workers need to change careers several times, it may be rational for adult learners to parse out learning in chunks and return to the educational front periodically to develop skills as needed to meet the demands of a changing workplace or to increase employability. In this situation, many students may be expected to enter college later and take longer to complete degrees, but require educational experiences that more fully support developmental and lifelong learning needs. Nontraditional patterns of enrollment also may be the financially logical approach, given the cost of tuition, the burden of student loans, and the availability of tax credits and tuition reimbursement programs from many employers. In such a scenario, assessing institutional performance based on criteria such as graduation rates in six years may be a moot point.

Endnote

1. The original report uses *et al.* to refer to many unnamed coauthors. We simply refer to Coleman as the author.

References

Bash, L. (2003). *Adult learners in the academy.* Bolton, MA: Anker Publishing Company.

Bean, J. P., & Metzner, B. S. (1985). A conceptual model of non-traditional undergraduate student attrition. *Review of Educational Research, 55,* 485–540.

Bell, D. (1973). *The coming of post-industrial society.* New York: Basic Books.

Bye, D., Pushkar, D., & Conway, M. (2007). Motivation, interests, and positive affect in traditional and nontraditional undergraduate students, *Adult Education Quarterly, 57*(2), 141–158.

Cappelli, P. (2004). Why do employers pay for college? *Journal of Econometrics, 121,* 213–241.

Choy, S. (2002). *Nontraditional undergraduates.* Washington, DC: U.S. Department of Education, National Center for Education Statistics. Retrieved October 12, 2008, from http://nces.ed.gov/pubs2002/2002012.pdf

Clark, C., & Caffarella, R. (1999). Theorizing adult education. In C. Clark and R. Caffarella (Eds.) *An update on adult development theory: New ways of thinking about the life course* (pp. 3–8). San Francisco: Jossey-Bass.

Coleman, J. S. (1966). *Equality of educational opportunity.* Washington, DC: U.S. Department of Education, National Center for Education Statistics. Retrieved October 12, 2008, from http://eric.ed.gov/ERICDocs/data/ericdocs2sql/content_storage_01/0000019b/80/33/42/82.pdf

Cook, A., & Leckey, J. (1999). Do expectations meet reality? A survey of changes in first year student opinion. *Journal of Further and Higher Education, 23*(2), 157–171.

Cooper, J., Basson, J., & Schapp, P. (2006). A training programme based on the principles of social constructivism and focused on developing people for the future world of work: An evaluation. *Human Resource Development International,* *9*(4), 467–483.

Drucker, P. (1968). *The age of discontinuity.* New York: Harper & Row.

Hanushek, E. A. (1979). Conceptual and empirical issues in the estimation of education production functions. *Journal of Human Resources, 14*(3), 351–388.

Hanushek, E. A. (1989). The impact of differential expenditures on school performance. *Educational Researcher, 18*, 45–62.

Hanushek, E. A., Kain, J. F., Markman, J. M, & Rivkin, S. G. (2003). Does peer ability affect student achievement? *Journal of Applied Econometrics, 18*(5), 527–544.

Henderson, V., Mieszkowski, P., & Sauvageau, Y. (1978). Peer group effects and educational production functions. *Journal of Public Economics, 10*, 97–106.

Horn, L. J., & Carroll, C. D. (1996). *Non-traditional undergraduates: Trends in enrollment from 1986 to 1992 and persistence and attainment among 1989–90 beginning postsecondary students* (NCES 97–578). Washington, DC: U.S. Department of Education.

House of Commons. (2001). *Government's response to the fourth report from the Education and Employment Committee, session 2000–01.* Select Committee on Education and Employment, 6th special report. Retrieved January 23, 2008, from www.publications.parliament.uk/pa/cm200001/cmselect/cmeduemp/384/38403 .htm

Jacobs, R. L. (2006). Perspectives on adult education, human resource development, and the emergence of workplace development. *New Horizons in Adult Education and Human Resource Development, 20*(1), 21–31.

Jarvis, P. (2001). *Universities and corporate universities.* London: Kogan Page.

Knowles, M. (1990). *The adult learner, a neglected species* (4th ed.). Houston, TX: Gulf Publishing Company.

Laing, C., Chao, K.-M., & Robinson, A. (2005). Managing the expectations of non-traditional students: A process of negotiation. *Journal of Further and Higher Education, 29*(2), 169–179.

Lamdin, D. J. (1996). Evidence of student attendance as an independent variable in education production functions. *Journal of Educational Research, 89*, 155–162.

Lane, J. (2003). Studying community colleges and their students: Context and research issues. *New Directions for Institutional Research, 2003*(118), 51–68.

Lazear, E. P. (2001). Educational production. *Quarterly Journal of Economics, 116*(3), 777–803.

Levine, A. (2001). The remaking of the American university. *Innovative Higher Education, 25*(4), 253–267.

Lynch, K., & O'Riordan, C. (1998). Inequality in higher education: A study of class barriers. *British Journal of Sociology of Education, 19*(4), 445–478.

Machlup, F. (1962). *The production and distribution of knowledge in the United States.* Princeton, NJ: Princeton University Press.

Merriam, S., & Brockett, R. (1997). *The profession and practice of adult education.* San Francisco: Jossey-Bass.

Merriam, S., Caffarella, R., & Baumgartner, L. (2007). *Learning in adulthood* (3rd ed.). San Francisco: Jossey-Bass.

National Center for Education Statistics. (2002). *Special analysis 2002: Non-traditional undergraduates.* Retrieved October 8, 2008, from http://nces.ed.gov/pro grams/coe/2002/analyses/nontraditional/index.asp

National Center for Education Statistics. (2007). *The condition of education 2007.* Retrieved February 1, 2009, from http://nces.ed.gov/programs/coe/2007/pdf/ 10_2007.pdf

Ogbu, J. U. (1992). Understanding cultural diversity and learning. *Educational Researcher, 21*(8), 5–14.

Ozga, J., & Sukhnandan, L. (1998). Undergraduate non-completion: Developing an explanatory model. *Higher Education Quarterly, 52*(3), 316–333.

Pusser, B., Gansneder, B, Gallaway, N., & Pope, N. (2005). Entrepreneurial activity in non-profit institutions: A portrait of continuing education. *New Direction for Higher Education, 129,* 27–43.

Riggert, S. C., Boyle, M., Petrosko, J. M., Ash, D., & Rude-Parkins, C. (2006). Student employment and higher education: Empiricism and contradiction, *Review of Educational Research, 76*(1), 63–92.

Sewell, W. H. (1971). Inequality of opportunity for higher education. *American Sociological Review, 36*(5), 793–809.

Summers, A. A., & Wolfe, B. L. (1977). Do schools make a difference? *American Economic Review, 67,* 639–652.

Tharenou, P., Saks, A., & Moore, C. (2007). A review and critique of research on training and organizational-level outcomes. *Human Resource Management Review, 17*(3), 251–273.

U.S. Department of Education, National Center for Education Statistics. (2008). *Digest of education statistics, 2007* (NCES 2008–022). Retrieved October 27, 2008, from http://nces.ed.gov/fastFacts/display.asp?id = 98

Winston, G. C. (2004). Differentiation among US colleges and universities. *Review of Industrial Organization, 24*(4), 331–354.

Yorke, M. (1999). *Leaving early: Undergraduate non-completion in higher education.* London: Falmer Press.

Zimmerman, D. J., & Winston, G. (2004). Peer effects in higher education. In C. Hoxby (Ed.), *College choices: The economics of where to go, when to go, and how to pay for it.* Chicago: University of Chicago Press.

7

OF A MIND TO LABOR

Reconceptualizing Student Work and Higher Education

Brian Pusser

Human beings reach out, gather the materials of nature, and fashion them into objects of one kind or another. We collect an armload of wood, pick up a piece of flint, extract a stone from a quarry—or for that matter, capture a sight or sound that moves us. The true character of humankind is reflected in the objects we produce as a result of that process: a campfire, an axe, a cathedral, a sonnet. Work of that kind is necessary for humans to fulfill their true nature. That is how, Marx said, they "develop" their slumbering powers.

—K. Erikson, "On Work and Alienation"

This passage from Kai Erikson points to one of the most powerful purposes of the contemporary university: its role as a center for intellectual work. At its best, the university is a place for students and faculty to labor together in the creation and sharing of knowledge, a place where, through teaching and learning, we may awaken our "slumbering powers" of creativity and reason. Given that intellectual labor entails challenging entrenched beliefs and extending the boundaries of social thought, the university is also a site of contest and dissonance, two fundamental elements of cognitive growth. As some of the most powerful symbols in global society, universities also serve as instruments in broader contests over social, political, and cultural values. A number of scholars have argued that for the university to serve as a site of knowledge creation, contest, and critique, it needs to be constituted as a public sphere, a public space beyond the control of private interests, state influence, or the institutions themselves, where students, faculty, and others can engage in critical intellectual work (Ambrozas, 1998; Fraser, 1992; Marginson, 2006; Pusser, 2006, 2008). While in reality intellectual work is surely more constrained than in the concept of the university as a public sphere, the ideal type is nonetheless conceptually powerful for modeling and analysis (Marginson, 2007).

As constrained as it may be, intellectual work in the academy stands in stark contrast to another type of labor in higher education, the efforts of undergraduate students as employees. Although undergraduate employment for wages is an honorable and in most cases necessary pursuit, it can be argued that developing the capacity for intellectual work is of paramount importance to student success on campus and beyond. Student intellectual development requires that a number of essential conditions prevail: the presence of intellectual autonomy for students and teachers; the existence of a space for unfettered critique; the ability to challenge fundamental political, social, cultural, and institutional premises; and so forth.

Seen from this perspective, certain types of student employment may not only be unproductive in the process of developing the capacity for student intellectual work, but they may also be counterproductive. Furthermore, as the number of students who are employed grows, sociocultural expectations for the balance of public and private goods produced through higher education may shift further in the direction of a private benefit model and reduce the efficacy of the university as a public sphere. This chapter draws on social theories of work, prior research on students who work, and data collected from a longitudinal study of adult learners to reconceptualize our understanding of the many ways that employment increasingly shapes the lives of undergraduate learners.

What We Talk About When We Talk About Students Who Are Employed

As noted in other chapters in this volume, one of the remarkable aspects of a review of the contemporary research on postsecondary students and employment is the number of inconclusive or counterintuitive findings. Working for wages while enrolled matters somewhat in some cases, but not much in others. In a review of 20 years of research on the impact of student employment on postsecondary student achievement, Stinebrickner and Stinebrickner (2003) found "no consensus exists" (p. 473). Their review includes studies that found negative effects on academic performance from employment (Paul, 1982), positive effects for on-campus work but not for off-campus employment (Ehrenberg & Sherman, 1987), and high grade point averages for those who were employed a moderate number of hours (Hood, Craig, & Ferguson, 1992). In their overview, Pascarella and Terenzini (2005) also found few educational benefits to students from employment, other than some evidence that students developed workplace competencies, particularly through internships, and that students with work experience were more attractive to employers upon graduation. A number of studies have endeavored to find relationships between student employment and various measures of academic success, with mixed results. Furthermore, because prior research generally does not measure such student characteristics as motivation and commitment, we should be cautious about attributing causal effects, whether positive or negative, to student employment. In their exceptional summary of research on postsecondary students who work, Perna, Cooper, and Li (2007) note, "Working has been shown to be unrelated to academic achievement, even though research consistently shows that working is negatively related to academic involvement and time spent studying" (p. 132).

Again as other chapter authors observe, the effect of work on student retention is also puzzling, with lower retention rates for students who do not work at all than for those who work between 1 and 15 hours a week. Those who did not work at all had higher retention rates than did those who worked 16 to 20 hours per week (Perna et al., 2007). Similarly mixed signals emerge for the effect of work on other key variables in the postsecondary literature, such as future earnings. Pascarella and Terenzini (2005) conclude, on the basis of studies indicating either mixed or negative career earnings based on type and duration of student employment (e.g., Fuller & Schoenberger, 1991), that there is little to indicate a positive relationship between student employment and future earnings.

It appears from prior research that the impacts of working while enrolled in postsecondary education vary for different age and racial/ethnic cohorts. It is also possible to infer different impacts for students in different socioeconomic cohorts and in different institutional settings. The difficulty in drawing meaningful conclusions from the existing research literature on postsecondary students who work is compounded by a more significant liability: the lack of conceptual models or theoretical frameworks for understanding students who labor, or student labor itself, in higher education. Perna, Cooper, and Li's (2007) four perspectives on student work (public policy, sociocultural, human capital, and demographic) are a useful starting point, but much more needs to be done. Generally speaking, when the findings of research on a given topic are consistently inconclusive or contradictory, it is time to revisit the premises at the heart of the research. We know that the majority of students work for wages and that employment rates are growing. However, we neither know whether working has a positive or negative effect on student success, nor have a conceptual model to account for the phenomenon.

Modeling Education and Work

Developing a conceptual model for understanding students who work requires three dimensions: an understanding of postsecondary education, an understanding of work, and an understanding of the role of work in postsecondary education.

Higher Education

Let's begin with premises about higher education. What do the various stakeholders of public and private higher education expect for and from the process of higher education? How do students, families, communities, commercial interests, the state, and postsecondary institutions themselves conceptualize the purposes of higher education?

At the most basic level, postsecondary schools are institutions of the state because they are regulated, subsidized, chartered, and legitimated by state action (Marginson, 2006; Ordorika, 2003; Pusser, 2008). As such, they are expected to produce some mix of public and private goods, including new forms of knowledge and understanding, democratic citizens, and economic development, to preserve institutional and systemic legitimacy. This role suggests that, during the process of acquiring a postsecondary education, students should be treated equitably, and that no particular interests dominate the allocation of costs and benefits from higher education. As such, all constituents have a compelling interest to preserve the university as a public sphere, a site for the production and transmission of knowledge and for deliberation over the broader society, capital, and labor, the public good, and private interests (Marginson, 2006; Pusser, 2006).

Work

Although many analyses of work begin by noting that delineating the concept is a complex and contextually mediated task (Anderson, 1974; Morgan, 2006; Pahl, 1988), Charles Mueller (2000) offers a succinct definition: "Work thus is defined as the mental or physical activity of an individual directed toward the production of goods or services that are valued by that individual or others" (p. 3269). Mueller's definition emphasizes productivity, the concept that separates work from leisure. Work is further differentiated as a practice that produces both exchange value (work for remuneration) and use value (work for personal development). This definition points to a key distinction between student work and student employment. Employment is defined as work for which remuneration is offered (Pahl, 1988). Pahl writes, "It is not the nature of the task that matters most in determining whether or not it is to be financially rewarded and whether it is to count as 'work' but rather the social relations in which the task is embedded" (p. 2). In a similar manner, Hannah Arendt (1958) differentiates *labor*, the reproduction of employment relations that is done out of economic need, from *work*, a creative process. This definition suggests that the ways in which one turns one's hands to employment also shape the ways in which one turns one's hands to labor. For students, the challenge in separating the conditions of work for wages from intellectual work raises the possibility that the conditions and processes of student employment will shape the conditions and processes of a student's intellectual work.

The Distinction Between Intellectual Work and Student Employment

Social theory suggests that what is generally characterized as student work in research in higher education is actually student employment, or "work for wages." It is important to distinguish the different types of employment that students engage in and to develop a clear conceptual distinction to maximize the intellectual and developmental potential of students who are employed. Although work is treated in a variety of ways in social theory, given the neo-liberal principles that have dominated the past two decades of social thought, economic theories of work that stress exchange values of work, the relationship between capital and labor, and the role of human capital have been dominant (Becker, 1993; Friedman, 2002; Marginson, 1997). Social theorists have also long treated work as a social and individual phenomenon, with particular attention to work in relation to culture, gender, and social class (Dahrendorf, 1979; Willis, 1977). Freidson (1990) draws on several strands of this research to suggest a useful continuum for thinking about work that ranges from a pure form of work for wages, where work is done for its maximum exchange value, to work that is done for its maximum use value, what he terms "labors of love" (p. 154).

Intellectual work on campuses, whether by students or faculty, falls somewhere in between. Although constrained by historical norms and power relations within colleges and universities, intellectual work offers far more autonomy, allows for considerably more criticality, and is more often oriented to the production of public goods than are conventional employment relations. Student employment, whether campus based or off campus, is more often embedded in the norms of authority relations, conformity, and private benefits. Studies of student employment indicate that, with the exception of some graduate student workers, relatively few students are employed on projects that are closely related to their postsecondary intellectual work (Perna et al., 2007).

Why Does Student Employment Matter?

Understanding why undergraduate students work for wages is central to understanding the impact of employment on their intellectual development. Prior research and authors of other chapters in this volume suggest that the primary reason students work for wages while enrolled is to subsidize the cost of education. The increasing number of students subsidizing their college educations through employment is attributed to such factors as rising tuitions, a desire to limit overall indebtedness, and shifts in the allocation of student financial aid (Ehrenberg, 2000; Gladieux & Perna, 2005).

One conclusion that might be drawn from prior research is that student employment does not matter. That is, if employment does not affect students' academic outcomes, and the income generated through employment makes access and persistence possible or offsets loan indebtedness, why shouldn't students work? The answer is that it matters very much whether students are employed, but not just for the reasons generally addressed in existing research. Understanding the full impact of student employment, for all types of students, requires attention to a more nuanced conceptualization of the nature of intellectual work and student employment, a conceptualization that goes beyond the student to the role of the broader political economy in supporting the postsecondary educational development of students and society. Five key factors shape a conceptual model for understanding and transforming student employment: (1) enabling students to develop critical, intellectual identities; (2) understanding student intellectual development as a public good; (3) recognizing the centrality of intellectual work in maximizing students' life chances; (4) understanding the impact of intellectual work as powerfully shaping the norms of authority and subordination that characterize work for wages; and (5) understanding the role of student intellectual and personal development in reducing stratification and inequality in higher education and the broader society.

Developing a Critical, Intellectual Identity

To construct and implement a transformative model of student work, it is essential to note that much of the energy students devote to employment for wages does little to promote one of higher education's central goals, the development of critical, intellectual thought. This is because of, in part, the fundamental nature of low-wage employment, where critical thought is not always privileged (Willis, 1977). Hannah Arendt (1958), in her work on the human condition, had this to say about the impact on creativity and intellectual work of the expansion of employment relations over time:

> The point is not that for the first time in history laborers were admitted and given equal rights in the public realm, but that we have almost succeeded in leveling all human activities to the common denominator of securing the necessities of life and providing for their abundance. Whatever we do, we are supposed to do for the sake of "making a living"; such is the verdict of society, and the number of people, especially in the professions who might challenge it, has decreased rapidly. (pp. 126–127)

Arendt points to an essential tension for scholars and practitioners in higher education: the need to preserve colleges and universities as spaces for critical intellectual and personal development in a political economy increasingly devoted to training for global economic production (Schugurensky, 2006).

Over the past four decades, education has increasingly been promoted and financed on the basis of its exchange value, a trend particularly prevalent in the political economy of colleges and universities (Marginson, 1997). A number of contemporary scholars of higher education have noted, and in many cases critiqued, the changing relationship between the academy and the market (Kirp, 2003; Slaughter & Leslie, 1997), the university as a center of knowledge and the university as a center of commerce (Bok, 2003; Geiger, 2004), and the university as a fundamentally public sphere and the university as a space for the reification of private sector values (Aronowitz, 2000; Engell & Dangerfield, 2005).

Jane Rhinehardt (2002) argues that the contemporary university has come under considerable pressure to restructure itself as a site for the transfer of the norms and values of private sector employment into the public arena. She argues this has particularly detrimental effects for feminist education and the development of student consciousness: "In the current emphasis on the importance of the acquisition of 'transferable skills' in higher education, what we can see at work is the transformation to the public sphere of skills once associated with the private world" (p. 164).

Student Work and the Public Good

Over the past three decades the rise of neoliberal policies at the federal and state levels in the United States has created enormous pressure to reduce public financial contributions to higher education and to increase students' financial contributions to their own educations. Neoliberalism, which emerged from theoretical propositions advanced by Fredrich Hayek, has been defined as "a theory of political economic practices that proposes that human well-being can best be advanced by liberating individual entrepreneurial freedoms and skills within an institutional framework characterized by strong private property rights, free markets and free trade" (Harvey, 2005, p. 2). Contemporary neoliberalism draws heavily on human capital theory (HCT), which suggests that the benefits of investment in higher education are essentially private (Becker, 1962). Under HCT, such outcomes of education as higher levels of national literacy, reduced rates of crime and greater social mobility are generated by the investment decisions of individuals, largely independent of government action.[1] One of the most influential proponents of neoliberalism, Milton Friedman, argued for individual—not governmental—responsibility for the finance of higher education this way:

"Adam Smith's invisible hand makes their private interest serve the social interest. It is against the social interest to change their private interest by subsidizing schooling" (Friedman & Friedman, 1980, p. 179).

Translated from theory into policies, neoliberalism is manifest in reduced subsidies for public higher education at state levels, leading to a rapid increase in tuition, student loans, and expected family contributions (Pusser, 2008; Slaughter & Rhoades, 2004). Perhaps most important, it has privileged private action and private benefits over collaborative effort and the public good. The neoliberal emphasis on private benefits suggests that, without a conscious commitment of resources to promote such student contributions to the public good as individual intellectual work, community service, and public benefit research, the need for student employment to defray the costs of education will continue to increase. As a result, students' abilities to participate in the production of public goods through higher education will diminish. A key challenge faced by postsecondary practitioners is how to conceptualize and implement a public goods approach to student employment.

Maximizing Life Chances

The social theorist Ralf Dahrendorf (1979), following Max Weber's work on class and stratification, advanced the concept of "life chances," the possibility of individual transformation through "patterns of social organization, at once social and structural" (p. 29). Life chances, according to Dahrendorf, are not fundamentally a function of individual attributes. "Individuals have life chances in society; their life chances may make or break them; but their lives are responses to these chances" (p. 29). Life chances are shaped by options (possibilities or choices) and constraints (bonds or obligations) that shape the ability to maximize opportunities. Both options and constraints are shaped by social structures and processes, history, culture, and social status. Life chances arise from the interaction of options and constraints. Following Dahrendorf, access to higher education can be seen as an essential life chance, an option facilitated or diminished by a range of constraints. In turn, one's understanding of two crucial social structures, education and employment, powerfully shapes one's success in higher education.

In a system constructed to maximize the widest range of life chances, postsecondary students would not trade labor for wages to subsidize attendance. The intellectual work of each student would be seen as both a public and a private good and an opportunity to maximize student development and public benefit. Going forward, practitioners and others in higher education must consider ways to ensure that, wherever possible, student employment maximizes positive life chances.

Student Work and the Norms of Authority Relations

The reproduction of social, political, and economic norms through higher education is not a new topic, although it is rarely applied to student employment. Theories of social reproduction have traditionally been applied to the role of colleges and universities in the broader process of social and economic stratification (Karabel, 2005; Kingston & Lewis, 1990; Lemann, 1999). Although much of the research on student employment suggests that a very high percentage of students are employed while enrolled, it is worth noting that the students least likely to be employed are dependent students enrolled at the institutions with the highest average tuition, private four-year institutions (Perna et al., 2007).

Our understanding of the essential structures of the employment relationship has been shaped by classic theoretical work on the interplay of the social, economic, legal, and intellectual structures of society (Durkheim, 1933; Marx, 1867/1906; Weber, 1947). As Carnoy and Levin (1985) put it, "Both capitalist (business) and labor consciousness are shaped by their relationship in the process of production that sustains the society" (p. 34). Bowles and Gintis (1976) argue that education is a key site of social conflict because it serves as both a site for the reproduction of authority relations and an essential source of social mobility. These analyses can be extended to argue that postsecondary student employment is also a site of contest between the reproduction of norms of the workplace and higher education as a site for emancipatory student intellectual work.

Student Work, Stratification, and Inequality

Just as it plays a key role in the contest over norms of authority, so too does higher education stand as a force for the transformation of structures and processes of stratification and inequality on campuses and in the broader society. Carnoy and Levin (1985) have argued, "Utilitarian and pluralist views of education and society emphasize the role that education plays in altering the characteristics of individuals and the position of those individuals in the economy, social structure and polity" (p. 33). Thus, postsecondary institutions can be sites for both reinforcing and transforming inequities. There is a long tradition of contest in the wider political economy of higher education over social and economic stratification in colleges and universities and over the role of colleges and universities in social mobility (Astin & Oseguera, 2004; Kingston & Smart, 1990). Depending on whether they raise or constrain consciousness, and the degree to which they empower students to make personal and collective choices about social justice, both student intellectual work and employment for wages have the potential to shape stratification and inequality.

Adult Students and the Reconceptualization of
Student Employment

A useful perspective on reconceptualizing student employment emerges from research on adult learners in higher education. Students who work and workers who study exist at the intersection of various contemporary, historical, political, cultural, social, and economic trajectories. To conceptualize the distinctions in the role of employment in the intellectual lives of adult learners and traditional-aged learners, it is helpful to think in terms of "the flow of life courses" (Abbott, 2006). From a life courses perspective, individuals move in and out of various "spells" of activity: employment, unemployment, education, caring for dependents, retirement, and so forth. Some of these spells overlap, as when an employed individual enrolls in postsecondary education.

Social structures, culture, resources, and path dependence shape an individual's sense of possibility during the life course, as do deeply embedded social norms. As one example, over the past two decades a number of scholars have remarked on the difficulty adult students face endeavoring to enroll in colleges and universities designed to accommodate traditional-aged undergraduate students (Levin, 2007). These difficulties are also described in other chapters in this volume (e.g., Kasworm, chapter 2; Levin, Montero-Hernandez, & Cerven, chapter 3; Ziskin, Torres, Hossler, & Gross, chapter 4; Rowan-Kenyon, Swan, Deutsch, & Gansneder, chapter 5). Put simply, traditional-aged students who are employed and adult workers who are enrolled may attend the same institutions at the same time, but they coexist at the intersection of quite different life courses. Traditional-aged students, particularly those who work full time, are for the most part adding employment to a life course that has been most recently and significantly shaped by formal education. Adult learners, those older than 25 years who are enrolled in the postsecondary system, are adding the role of postsecondary student to a life course most recently and significantly shaped by employment. Turning attention to the narratives of adult and nontraditional learners offers useful insights for understanding the relationship between postsecondary enrollment and employment.

As part of a national study conducted by the Emerging Pathways project at the University of Virginia, data were gathered from focus groups of nontraditional postsecondary learners (primarily students 25 and older in degree-granting programs) at 10 institutions across the United States, purposely selected to represent a range of Carnegie Classifications (two-year and four-year, public and private) and institutional locations. Participants were not asked to identify their race/ethnicity, but researcher notes indicate that students from a variety of racial, ethnic, and national backgrounds were represented. The gender of focus groups was mixed, with a total sample breakdown of 89 women and 35 men (Deutsch & Schmertz, 2009; Rowan-Kenyon et al., chapter 5). A substantial percentage of the students in the focus groups were employed, which is consistent with national data on adult learners (Council for Adult and Experiential Learning & National Center for Higher Education Management Systems, 2008). The student narratives offer interesting perspectives on the five key issues shaping the reconceptualized model of student employment: critical intellectual development, postsecondary education as a public good, the maximization of positive life chances, the challenge to norms of authority in employment, and the reduction of stratification and inequality.

Critical Intellectual Development

A number of participants in the focus groups pointed to the contrast between their work lives and their experiences as students. One consistent theme was the validation of workers as intellectuals through postsecondary attainment. One student described it this way:

> Your point of getting up in the morning is completely different. I mean, I used to get up in the morning and say, okay, I have to go type all these letters so I can make whatever I was making, not that much, in order to pay my rent and do all this and do all that, but now you feel like—I feel like I have such a greater purpose. I'm like getting up, I'm learning all these hard things and it feels so much better to actually be learning something that you want to learn instead of settling and doing something that you're just doing because you feel you have to.

Participants also indicated that their sense of themselves was changed by participating and succeeding in the intellectual life of higher education. The following comment represented the common theme:

> I thought that I wasn't college material until I got into this program and started doing well. I thought I wasn't very smart which is just silly because I am, I mean, I don't mean to sound like, but I was like "I can do this" and "I can think and I can learn and I can—I love to learn," but I really felt like before I took the initiative to see what I could achieve, I felt really stunted and being in the program has really helped me to just grow so much as a person.

An additional benefit of critical intellectual work was that it opened up possibilities in ways that students had not experienced as workers. As one student explained,

> And it's really inspired me to not only look at, wow, I could've done this 15 years ago. Actually, I couldn't have done this 15 years ago, but it looks like if I can finish the program at the level that I'm at, I have many more

opportunities to—I may go look at a liberal arts degree from the University of Chicago and I think that's amazing.

Postsecondary Education as a Public Good

Some of the most powerful narratives from the focus groups came from parents who sought to improve the lives of their children by increasing their own levels of education. Although some of the benefits they hoped to extend to their children were private, they also expressed a more generalized and altruistic sense of embodying the importance of education for its own sake. One student put it this way:

> I have three children, two daughters and a son, and I'm always promoting how important school is and to get a college education and all that wonderful stuff and my oldest daughter said to me, "Well, why should I go to college, you didn't," and that was a wake-up call that I needed. Oh, boy, I need to do something about this. She's absolutely right. I've been talking about it forever. I really need to do something, so here I am.

Other students in the focus groups noted the importance of knowledge for its own sake, disconnected from its commodity value, as expressed in these remarks:

> I just returned back to school last semester and the reason why I think I returned back to school, I had a lot of—I just wanted to really improve my way of thinking, being informed of like the basics and then from there making my choice, so it wasn't really to like further an education or excuse me, not—scratch that one. Not education but it's not to further like a career or anything like that, but it was just to get the basics so I can make up my mind, you know, whether if I needed school to validate my way of life.

Some students pointed to the value of work that improved the world, independent of maximizing material gain for themselves. One woman described why she returned to school to conduct research after working with at-risk children:

> I couldn't go back anywhere near my other life, so I decided to go to school because I always kind of thought of it and here I was at that point, 51. Fifty-one, yeah, and I thought, well, this is kind of a nice break and I also decided I needed to change careers. I needed a new career and I was always interested in death and dying, end of life care, stuff like that, so I thought—And I wanted to write some books about these kids and what their lives were like, what the reality was of losing your parents as little kids and what they'd been through before I got them.

Life Chances

Several students expressed concern over how employment constrained their ability to maximize their life chances through education. One student expressed her frustration this way:

> Well, I work part-time in retail and I have my full-time school schedule and I have kind of managed work around that schedule, but when I'm not working, you know, they constantly call me to come in to fill in, but it's like, you know, I have studying to do and I can't, you know, I want to work those set hours and that's it. You know, as much as I'd like the money, the studying is more important to me.

Another student described the intense pressures associated with balancing employment and educational obligations:

> I did everything I could, but just the time, putting the energy and effort and everything in, it just made it so hard that I ended up having to withdraw at the last minute and that's something that it—it really affected my emotions and my self-esteem for a long time and knowing that that's a possibility ahead of time, knowing that you're not going to have the time to really put in the time for studying, for getting tutoring, for going about talking to the teachers, especially because the teachers have their own schedule as well, it's a little discouraging. Actually, it's not a little, it's a lot discouraging.

Restructuring Authority Relations in the Workplace

A number of participants in the focus groups cited the desire to use postsecondary attendance as a way to break out of the subordinate position they felt in the workplace. One student was willing to maintain that stance even though it meant giving up a job that had provided an educational subsidy:

> They have tuition reimbursement, but I didn't pursue it for multiple reasons. I didn't want to feel like I owed them anything back like if they paid for my education, then they would expect me to take this promotion or take this responsibility and I kinda wanted to be free to do what I want with my education.

Another student described his pride when he was able to present evidence of his success in school to an authority figure at his place of employment:

> Where I worked, they had a program where it was tuition reimbursement if you got a certain grade and it gave me real personal satisfaction that every time he had to sign off on my A and that I showed him that, yeah, you

know, I was smart and that I was worth something more than what he said
I was.

The Reduction of Stratification and Inequality

Another refrain from students was the desire to improve their standard of
living by escaping low-wage jobs that limited their opportunities. One
woman described the challenge this way:

> I'm 46. This is [my son] who is five. I'm single parenting him, going to
> school full-time. I work because [I can't quit] my job but I certainly would,
> but I came back to school 2¹/₂ years ago after I realized that, I was catering
> before, you know, I can't work 17-hour shifts at a time and have—at the
> time he was an infant and so here I am back and trying to keep up with
> him and keep my GPA respectable. That's my story.

Another student related frustration at working and being dependent on a
parent:

> No matter what, the world still goes on. The bills still show up in the mail.
> People still got to eat and it's just—you know, what do you do so you can
> meet all those expenses and right now, I'm—Even though my mom says
> I'm not taxing her, I'm sure I am to a certain extent. Well, I know I am
> and at 44, it's not—It doesn't feel good, first of all, and then, you know,
> so it's just—that's about the biggest struggle I've got or I had to think
> about when I had to come back.

Summary

The narratives of these students affirm the key themes that delineate the distinction between postsecondary education as intellectual work and student
employment as the pursuit of economic subsidies for education through
labor. These narratives also add a novel perspective to the economic construct of opportunity cost. That is, in economic theory, enrollment in college
without working is understood to entail a significant loss of earnings. Yet a
number of the students also saw being employed while enrolled as a lost
opportunity to test themselves academically, learn, and fully participate in
intellectual work. They understood the loss of income from not being
employed, but they also saw employment as a key constraint on maximizing
their life chances through education. As one student described the duality,

> For me, it was I had to realize that you couldn't serve like two gods. You
> had to either do this (return to school) or keep doing whatever it is you
> were doing. If you were satisfied with it, fine; if not, you had to like cut
> everything off.

Although many students who are employed understand the constraints of employment and the value of intellectual work, many have no other choice than to do both, at considerable cost to themselves and, in a number of cases, their families. One focus group participant summed it up this way:

> Like I said before, my first year I didn't work at all and I went full-time but I got this job in June and I was also going to summer school so I was working three days a week 21 hours and—but it was tough and I'm still working three days a week and I'm only taking two classes. It's tough. I could never do a full—work full-time and take a full load or even a part-time load. It's just—it's tough. Very tough. I'm exhausted right now.

From Theory to Practice: Promoting the Transformative Forms of Student Work

The tensions faced by adult and nontraditional learners who are employed offer a window into the challenge faced by all postsecondary students who are employed and by postsecondary practitioners who are charged with developing and implementing student employment programs, service-learning projects, internships, and other programs where intellectual work, student employment, and institutional missions intersect. Practitioners and other advocates for students in various arenas of higher education can make a significant contribution to the transformation of student employment by remaining mindful of the distinction in higher education between employment and intellectual work. Transformation will also require reducing the overall commitment to student employment as well as reimagining the role of employment in student development. It is essential to acknowledge that broader patterns of resource allocation to higher education will need to be significantly altered to find new forms of subsidy for student attendance. While the idea of providing a meaningful stipend for student living expenses that is not connected to student employment is not entirely utopian—it has been implemented in some western European higher education systems—before such a transformation can take place in the broader political economy it needs first to be conceptualized and then made manifest by changes in practice.

What might a model of student employment that contributes to a broader project of transformative student intellectual development look like? A number of essential conditions for transforming student employment emerge from social theory and research in higher education: the terms of employment should maximize intellectual creativity, diversity of thought, and action. A transformative model will enable students to make significant contributions to the public good generated by higher education. It should, at best, restructure the relations of authority and subordination that characterize much of contemporary student employment for wages, and at least not reproduce those relations. It should maximize the options inherent in positive life chances and minimize the constraints on those chances. As is the case for the higher education project writ large, student employment should be constructed in such a way that its own characteristics and intended outcomes serve as a force to reduce inequality and stratification.

Practitioners need to begin by assessing the potential of the extracurricular programs based in their institutions for maximizing transformative benefits from student labor. Table 1 serves as a template for conceptualizing the transformative potential of a few of the key arenas of student work: on-campus employment for wages, on-campus volunteer activities, off-campus employment for wages, off-campus volunteer activities, and service-learning programs. Each of these activities, as with many other aspects of higher education, can be seen as offering varying degrees of transformative potential on five key dimensions: critical intellectual development, contribution to the public good, maximization of life chances, the nature of authority relations, and reducing stratification and inequality. Although such forms of employment as off-campus work for wages generally offer less potential for transformation given the considerable variation between student cohorts and institutional employment arrangements, the potential exists for meaningful exceptions in every arena. Institutional actors need to maximize the benefits of their systems in place, while looking forward to new opportunities to reduce student employment and provide meaningful financial subsidies for student intellectual work. One key to changing the system in place is to develop interventions designed to increase student employees' awareness of the meaning of employment for wages and to encourage students to use their workplaces as cases for studying authority relations, stratification, and public and private goods. Workshops, focus groups, and learning communities can be devoted to helping student employees make sense of the tension between intellectual work and employment.

Given the varied demographics and life circumstances of postsecondary learners, there is no single prescription for transforming student employment. Moreover, institutional missions, histories, structures, and resources vary widely. Practitioners and other institutional change agents should consider positive transformations for students who are employed in ways that address the lives of their students in context. A common challenge will be to work with institutional development and political liaisons to increase financial support for those student activities most closely linked to intellectual work and transformation. Undergraduate student internships and other initiatives that place students in positions of greater authority offer considerable

TABLE 1
The Potential for Transformative Outcomes in Various Forms of Undergraduate Student Work

	On Campus for Wages[a]	On Campus, Volunteer[b]	Off-Campus for Wages[c]	Off-Campus Volunteer	Service-Learning[d]
Maximizes critical intellectual development	Some potential	High potential	Low potential	High potential	High potential
Promotes the public good characteristics of higher education	High potential	Some potential	Low potential	High potential	High potential
Maximizes the development of positive life chances	Some potential	Some potential	Low potential	High potential	High potential
Restructures authority relations	Low potential	Some potential	Low potential	High potential	Some potential
Contributes to the reduction of stratification and inequality	Some potential	Some potential	Low potential	Some potential	Some potential

[a] This category refers primarily to students covered by federal work-study funding or institutional work-study programs.
[b] Volunteer work may be institutionally mediated, but is uncompensated and not for academic credit.
[c] This category refers primarily to employment other than that provided by federal work-study funding.
[d] Here service-learning is understood as off-campus student work that produces public benefits and provides students with academic credit.

promise for increasing student autonomy and critical intellectual development. Such opportunities may also effectively contribute to student employees' awareness of the challenges institutions face in reducing inequality and maximizing student life chances.

Conclusion

If scholars of higher education and practitioners are to make a difference in the arena of student labor, we need to further deconstruct the basic premises through which we understand higher education and the nature of student employment. The current set of mixed results from empirical research and shifting signals from institutional leaders and policymakers requires that we continually reconceptualize student employment as part of broader social, political, and economic currents.

Several essential questions may guide future research and policymaking in this arena. First, given increasing postsecondary institutional commitments to "student-centered" programs, why do student employment models that offer uncertain benefits persist? In an era of heightened accountability with increasing attention to student success, further analysis is required to understand the constraints on reconstructing existing systems of student employment.

Second, in what ways can the contemporary global economic crisis open space for a critical conversation at the institutional, state, and national levels about the limitations of neoliberal market models for subsidizing student participation in higher education? Whereas in the short term, many practitioners and scholars will be challenged to restructure programs with fewer resources, before long attention must also be turned to new ways of financing student attendance.

Finally, future research should address why those institutional programs that combine student intellectual work with service or leadership development are generally decoupled from remuneration. What is it about the historical evolution of intellectual work, student employment, and student development that results in students receiving a direct subsidy for the least rewarding of their investments of time and energy? Understanding student work requires attention to a broad range of social, economic, political, and institutional arrangements. Yet the most essential transformations may well emerge from listening to the voices of students who are employed, as they struggle to turn their hands to the work of transforming their own lives and the world in which they live.

Endnote

1. Human capital theory does suggest a role for government action to ensure the smooth functioning of markets, and, through making such instruments as student

loans available, to prevent capital constraints from limiting optimal individual investments in education.

References

Abbott, A. (2006). Mobility: What? When? How? In S. L. Morgan, D. B. Grusky, & G. S. Fields (Eds.), *Mobility and inequality: Frontiers of research in sociology and economics* (pp. 137–161). Stanford, CA: Stanford University Press.

Ambrozas, D. (1998). The university as a public sphere. *Canadian Journal of Communication, 23*(1). www.cjc-online.ca/viewarticle.php?id = 447

Anderson, N. (1974). *Man's work and leisure.* Leiden, Netherlands: E. J. Brill.

Arendt, H. (1958). *The human condition.* Chicago: University of Chicago Press.

Aronowitz, S. (2000). *The knowledge factory: Dismantling the corporate university and creating true higher learning.* Boston: Beacon Press.

Astin, A. W., & Oseguera, L. (2004, Spring). The declining "equity" of American higher education. *Review of Higher Education, 27*(3), 321–341.

Becker, G. S. (1962). Investment in human capital: A theoretical analysis. *Journal of Political Economy, 70*(5), 9–49.

Becker, G. S. (1993). Nobel lecture: The economic way of looking at behavior. *Journal of Political Economy, 101*(3), 385–409.

Bok, D. (2003). *Universities in the marketplace.* Princeton, NJ: Princeton University Press.

Bowles, S., & Gintis, H. (1976). *Schooling in capitalist America.* New York: Basic Books.

Carnoy, M., & Levin, H. M. (1985). *Schooling and work in the democratic state.* Palo Alto, CA: Stanford University Press.

Council for Adult and Experiential Learning & National Center for Higher Education Management Systems. (2008). *Adult learning in focus: National state-by-state data* [Electronic version]. Chicago: CAEL.

Dahrendorf, R. (1979). *Life changes: Approaches to social and political theory.* Chicago: University of Chicago Press.

Deutsch, N., & Schmertz, B. (2009, January). *"I was starting from ground zero": Constraints and experiences of adult women returning to college.* Working paper. Center for the Study of Higher Education. University of Virginia. Charlottesville, VA.

Durkheim, E. (1933). *The division of labor in society.* New York: Macmillan.

Ehrenberg, R., & Sherman, D. (1987). Employment while in college, academic achievement and postcollege outcomes. *Journal of Human Resources, 22*(1), 1–24.

Ehrenberg, R. G. (2000). *Tuition rising: Why college costs so much.* Cambridge, MA: Harvard University Press.

Engell, J. E., & Dangerfield, A. (2005). *Saving higher education in the age of money.* Charlottesville: University of Virginia Press.

Erikson, K. (1990). On work and alienation. In K. Erikson & S. P. Vallas (Eds.), *The nature of work: Sociological perspectives* (pp. 19–35). New Haven, CT: Yale University Press.

Fraser, N. (1992). Rethinking the public sphere: A contribution to the critique of actually existing democracy. In Bruce Robbins (Ed.), *The phantom public sphere* (pp. 1–32). Minneapolis: University of Minnesota Press.

Freidson, E. (1990). Labors of love in theory and practice: A prospectus. In K. Erikson & S. P. Vallas (Eds.), *The nature of work: Sociological perspectives* (pp. 149–161). New Haven, CT: Yale University Press.

Friedman, M. F. (2002). *Capitalism and freedom* (40th anniversary ed.). Chicago: University of Chicago Press.

Friedman, M. F., & Friedman, R. (1980). *Free to choose: A personal statement.* New York: Harcourt.

Fuller, R., & Schoenberger, R. (1991). The gender salary gap: Do academic achievement, internship experience, and college major make a difference? *Social Science Quarterly, 72,* 715–726.

Geiger, R. L. (2004). *Knowledge and money.* Palo Alto, CA: Stanford University Press.

Gladieux, L., & Perna, L. (2005). *Borrowers who drop out: A neglected aspect of the college student loan trend.* San Jose, CA: National Center for Public Policy and Higher Education.

Harvey, D. (2005). *A brief history of neoliberalism.* Oxford, England: Oxford University Press.

Hood, A. B., Craig, A., & Ferguson, B. (1992). The impact of athletics, part-time employment, and other academic activities on academic achievement. *Journal of College Student Development, 33,* 441–462.

Karabel, J. (2005). *The chosen: The hidden history of admission and exclusion at Harvard, Yale, and Princeton.* Boston: Houghton Mifflin.

Kingston, P. W., & Lewis, L. (1990). Undergraduates at elite institutions: The best, the brightest and the richest. In P. Kingston & L. Lewis (Eds.), *The high-status track: Studies of elite schools and stratification* (pp. 105–120). Albany: State University of New York Press.

Kingston, P. W., & Smart, J. C. (1990). The economic pay-off of prestigious colleges. In P. Kingston & L. Lewis (Eds.), *The high-status track: Studies of elite schools and stratification* (pp. 147–174). Albany: State University of New York Press.

Kirp, D. L. (2003). *Shakespeare, Einstein and the bottom line.* Cambridge, MA: Harvard University Press.

Lemann, N. (1999). *The big test: The secret history of American meritocracy.* New York: Farrar, Straus and Giroux.

Levin, J. S. (2007). *Nontraditional students and community colleges: The conflict of justice and neoliberalism.* New York: Palgrave Macmillan.

Marginson, S. (1997). *Markets in education.* St Leonards, Australia: Allen and Unwin.

Marginson, S. (2006). Putting "public" back in the public university. *Thesis Eleven, 84,* 44–59.

Marginson, S. (2007). The new higher education landscape: Public and private goods, in global/national/local settings. In S. Marginson (Ed.), *Prospects of higher education: Globalization, market competition, public goods and the future of the university* (pp. 29–77). Rotterdam: Sense Publishers.

Marx, K. (1906). *Capital, Volume 1.* (F. Engels, Ed.). (S. Moore & E. Aveling, Trans.). London: Charles H. Kerr. (Original work published 1867)

Morgan, S. L. (2006). Past themes and future prospects for research on social and economic mobility. In S. L. Morgan, D. B. Grusky, & G. S. Fields (Eds.), *Mobility and inequality: Frontiers of research in sociology and economics* (pp. 3–20). Stanford, CA: Stanford University Press.

Mueller, C. W. (2000). Work motivation. In E. Borgatta & R. Montgomery (Eds.), *Encyclopedia of sociology* (2nd ed., pp. 3261–3279). New York: Macmillan Academic Publishers.

Ordorika, I. (2003). *Power and politics in university governance: Organization and change at the Universidad Nacional Autonoma de Mexico.* New York: RoutledgeFalmer.

Pahl, R. E. (Ed.). (1988). *On work: Historical, comparative and theoretical approaches.* Oxford, England: Basil Blackwell.

Pascarella, E. T., & Terenzini, P. T. (2005). *How college affects students, Volume 2. A third decade of research.* San Francisco: Jossey-Bass.

Paul, H. (1982). The impact of outside employment in student achievement in macroeconomic principles. *Journal of Economic Education, 13,* 51–56.

Perna, L. W., Cooper, M. A., & Li, C. (2007). Improving educational opportunities for college students who work. In E. St. John (Ed.), *Confronting educational inequality: Reframing, building understanding, and making change, Readings on Equal Education* (Vol. 22, pp. 109–160). Brooklyn, NY: AMS Press.

Pusser, B. (2006). Reconsidering higher education and the public good: The role of public spheres. In W. Tierney (Ed.), *Governance and the public good* (pp. 11–28). Albany: State University of New York Press.

Pusser, B. (2008). The state, the market and the institutional estate: Revisiting contemporary authority relations in higher education. In J. Smart (Ed.), *Higher Education: Handbook of Theory and Research: Vol. XXIII* (pp. 105–139). New York: Agathon Press.

Rhinehardt, J. A. (2002). Feminist education: Rebellion within McUniversity. In D. Hayes & R. Wynward (Eds.), *The McDonaldization of higher education* (pp. 167–179). Westport, CT: Bergin & Garvey.

Rowan-Kenyon, H. T., Swan, A. K., Deutsch, N., & Gansneder, B. M. (2010). Academic success for working adult students. In L. Perna (Ed.), *Understanding the working college student: New research and its implications for policy and practice.* Sterling, VA: Stylus Publishing.

Schugurensky, D. (2006). The political economy of higher education in the time of global markets: Whither the social responsibility of the university? In R. Rhoads & C. Torres (Eds.), *The university, state and market: The political economy of globalization in the Americas* (pp. 301–320). Palo Alto, CA: Stanford University Press.

Slaughter, S., & Leslie, L. L. (1997). *Academic capitalism.* Baltimore: Johns Hopkins University Press.

Slaughter, S., & Rhoades, G. (2004). *Academic capitalism and the new economy: Markets, state, and higher education.* Baltimore: Johns Hopkins University Press.

Stinebrickner, R., & Stinebrickner, T. R. (2003). Working during school and academic performance. *Journal of Labor Economics, 21*(2), 473–491.

Weber, M. (1947). *The theory of social and economic organization.* Glencoe, IL: Free Press.

Willis, P. (1977). *Learning to labor: How working class kids get working class jobs.* New York: Columbia University Press.

8

JOB FARE

Workplace Experiences That Help Students Learn

Jonathan S. Lewis

There is little doubt that the learning outcomes of student employees matter a great deal. Whether one looks to external stakeholders—parents, legislators, accrediting bodies, or state and federal departments of education—or those internal to a college or university—faculty, administrators, trustees, students, or alumni—the expectation is clear: All campus activities must add measurable value to a student's education. A full-time student's on-campus employment setting is no less a part of this mandate. Nonetheless, many administrators and professionals in higher education who supervise student employees may neglect their role as educators, preferring instead to limit their oversight merely to job performance. Regardless of the reason—disinterest, lack of awareness, resistance to change, inability to conduct research—student employees lose when their workplace neglects its potential as a laboratory for learning.

This chapter offers administrators and supervisors concrete recommendations for enhancing learning among student employees. Utilizing data gathered from a 2007 study of student employees and staff supervisors at Northwestern University's college union, the chapter argues that enriching student employee engagement with key workplace experiences or activities can foster growth in the primary learning outcomes that have been established by researchers and leaders in the field of student development. The chapter concludes with recommendations on how to utilize such tools as job descriptions, evaluations, unit mission or vision, professional organizations, and empirical research to assist in the creation of a comprehensive, learning-centered student employment program.

Learning Domains and Research Methods for 2007 Study of Student Employees

In 2007, I conducted a study at Northwestern University's college union, the Norris University Center, to learn students' and supervisors' perceptions of workplace learning. The study was designed to identify the extent to which student employees and their staff supervisors believed learning was occurring on the job, as well as the specific workplace experiences that are related strongly to higher reported levels of learning. The college union was an ideal study site, given its role as campus community center and a work site that includes a wide variety of positions, such as audiovisual technician, retail clerk, building manager, setup crew, marketing, and maintenance assistants (Peters, 1997).

Learning is defined as a composite measure that reflects constituent knowledge or content areas, also known as domains. Example domains, such as career development and leadership, are discussed in greater detail later. We assume that on-campus employment is one type of college experience that can promote engagement in one or more learning domain areas. Employment may provide an opportunity for a student to engage with certain learning domains more frequently, or more meaningfully, than with others.

Drawing on an extensive literature review, I selected five learning domains that referenced knowledge or skills that could plausibly be affected by a student's employment at the college union. These domains were pulled from longer lists of desired learning outcomes recommended by the Council for the Advancement of Standards in Higher Education (CAS, 2003); Northwestern University's Division of Student Affairs (2005); and *Learning Reconsidered* (Keeling, 2004), a publication on student learning coauthored by five higher education professional organizations, led by the American College Personnel Association (ACPA) and the National Association of Student Personnel Administrators (NASPA). (See Table 1.) The specific learning domains included in this study were career development, civic and community engagement, leadership, ethics and values, and responsible independence. The survey instrument defined each learning domain as follows:

- *Career development* entails establishing an understanding of oneself in relation to one's professional life choices. It includes gaining knowledge and experience related to preparing for the emerging career path.
- *Civic and community engagement* involves active participation in campus life and the broader society. It includes one's connectedness to others, involvement in groups, and commitment to socially responsible action.

TABLE 1
Learning Domains Used in the 2007 Study

Northwestern University	Council for the Advancement of Standards in Higher Education	Learning Reconsidered
Career development	Intellectual growth	Cognitive complexity
Civic and community engagement	Effective communication	Knowledge acquisition, integration, and application
Intra- and interpersonal competence	Enhanced self-esteem	Humanitarianism
	Realistic self-appraisal	
Ethics and values	Clarified values	Civic engagement
Healthy living	Career choices	Interpersonal and intrapersonal competence
Intercultural competence/ maturity	Leadership development	Practical competence
	Healthy behavior	Persistence and academic achievement
Leadership	Meaningful interpersonal relationships	
Responsible independence	Independence	
	Collaboration	
	Social responsibility	
	Satisfying and productive lifestyle	
	Appreciating diversity	
	Spiritual awareness	
	Personal and educational goals	

Source: Northwestern University Division of Student Affairs (2005). *Student learning outcomes project.* Unpublished: Author; Council for the Advancement of Standards in Higher Education (2003). Relevant and desirable student learning and development outcomes. In *The book of professional standards for higher education 2003.* Washington, DC: Author; and Keeling, R. P. (Ed.) (2004). *Learning reconsidered: A campus-wide focus on the student experience.* Washington, DC: American College Personnel Association & National Association of Student Personnel Administrators.

- *Leadership* involves creating and demonstrating a philosophy and style that will guide one in leadership roles. It includes visualizing a common goal, communicating effectively, enlisting others in a vision, and implementing a strategy for meeting the desired outcomes.
- *Ethics and values* encompass the ability to develop, articulate, and live within a personally meaningful value system. It includes differentiating between contrasting ethical principles and being willing to question and revise one's beliefs.
- *Responsible independence* involves being self-reliant and managing one's life effectively. It includes developing a balance among education, work, and leisure time; demonstrating economic self-sufficiency; and maintaining health and wellness.

Utilizing survey instruments, 164 student employees were asked to evaluate their relative strength or capability in each domain area. Most of these students' positions were funded through the federal work-study program, although that was not a restriction to participate; the purpose and implications of this study focused more broadly on all full-time students working part time at the college union. Ninety-seven students completed the survey, a 59% response rate. Likewise, 15 professional staff were asked to rate each individual student employee they supervised in these learning domains in a separate survey. All invited staff participants completed the survey, a 100% response rate. These two perspectives on the same data provide a more comprehensive and accurate picture of student employee learning. (See Table 2 for descriptive data.) After the data were collected, student and staff responses were averaged into a composite measure for use in correlation and partial-correlation analyses; this decision reflected the belief that the most accurate findings were more likely to be found somewhere in between the two viewpoints. Most of the data gathered by this study were quantitative,

TABLE 2
Descriptive Statistics of Learning Composite and Five Learning Domain Composites

Learning Measure	Mean	SD	Range
Learning	4.76	0.77	2.60–6.60
Career development	4.40	1.09	1.50–6.50
Civic and community engagement	4.43	1.00	2.00–7.00
Leadership	4.72	1.04	2.00–7.00
Ethics and values	5.20	0.87	2.50–7.00
Responsible independence	5.11	0.91	2.50–7.00

although the survey instruments included a qualitative, free-response section as well. Both quantitative and qualitative results are included in the discussion of workplace experiences that follows.

Workplace Experiences

Perhaps the most important aspect of studying how people learn is in understanding what components (setting, content, delivery of information, etc.) must come together to produce the most positive outcomes. A wide body of literature—from primary, secondary, and higher education, as well as in workplace settings—has identified the best learning as that which occurs within a meaningful context; as part of a cycle of experience, observation, and reflection; and in stages of progressive difficulty (Association of American Colleges and Universities [AAC&U], 2007; Brown, Collins, & Duguid, 1989; Jarvis, 1987; Kolb, 1984; Vygotsky, 1978). In higher education specifically, research encourages students to engage actively with their learning and obliges administrators to create compelling situations to catalyze student growth and development (American Association for Higher Education [AAHE], American College Personnel Association [ACPA], & National Association of Student Personnel Administrators [NASPA], 1998; ACPA, 1996b; Keeling, 2004).

For supervisors of student employees, this body of literature suggests the importance of identifying compelling situations that are present in everyday workplace activities, studying the impact of these situations on student learning, and using those results to amplify or modify the situations, in the same way that other educators shape and adapt curriculum. During the literature review, I gathered a list of experiences, activities, or tasks that could potentially lead to learning, and later narrowed that list to include only those that could reasonably be assessed as part of the survey instrument. To be measurable, the workplace experiences had to be specific, concrete, and realistic within the student's responsibilities. In the end, students and their supervisors were asked to consider 13 experiences: formal training, informal training, observation of coworkers, collaboration and teamwork, feedback from peers, supervisor feedback, informal interactions with the supervisor, task repetition, problem solving, idea experimentation, reflection, intuitive decision making, and congruence between one's job and coursework or academic study. Table 3 provides descriptive statistics for these measures. What follows is a description of each workplace experience, including a definition, examples of where the experience may be found in a workplace setting, and data on the experience gathered from the study at Northwestern's college union (Lewis, 2007). Table 4 summarizes the correlations among the learning domains and workplace experiences.

TABLE 3
Descriptive Statistics of 13 Composite Workplace Experiences

Workplace Experiences	Mean	SD	Range
Formal training	3.21	0.90	1.00–6.00
Informal training	4.37	1.05	1.50–6.50
Observation	4.14	1.35	2.00–7.00
Collaboration	5.07	1.25	2.50–7.00
Feedback from peers	3.89	1.18	1.50–7.00
Feedback from supervisor	4.59	1.12	1.50–7.00
Informal interaction with supervisor	4.66	1.23	2.00–7.00
Task repetition	5.40	1.01	3.00–7.00
Problem solving	4.84	1.16	2.00–7.00
Idea experimentation	4.37	1.27	1.50–7.00
Reflection	4.05	1.18	1.50–6.50
Intuition	4.45	1.28	2.00–7.00
Congruence	2.98	1.08	1.00–5.50

Formal Training

Formal training appears most frequently as a classroom-like situation, with a designated teacher/trainer distinct from the students or attendees, a clear time frame and structure, and a deliberative framework of material the students are expected to learn over the course of the program (Eraut, 2000). In a student employment setting, formal training may appear as the first official gathering between a student and professional staff supervisor, when the goal is explicitly for the student to learn how to perform the job he or she has been hired for (Ekleberry & Hoddy, 1997). Formal training may also occur in larger groups, for example, in the form of a retreat, and may extend over the course of several days. In the 2007 study, neither students nor staff reported high instances of formal training—a mean of 3.21 on a 7-point scale—and formal training was the only one of all 13 measured experiences that did not produce a significant positive correlation with any of the five learning domains.

Informal Training

Informal training differs from formal training in its lower level of intention and much shorter time frame. Additionally, informal training differs in location, usually right when a situation occurs that requires additional guidance; this almost always takes place outside a classroom or formalized training environment. Eraut (2000) describes informal or "reactive" learning as

TABLE 4
Correlation Between Learning Composite and 5 Learning Domain Composites and 13 Workplace Experiences

	Learning	Career Development	Civic and Community Engagement	Leadership	Ethics and Values	Responsible Independence
Formal training	.09	.05	.00	.16	.06	.05
Informal training	.26*	.33**	.16	.27*	.14	.08
Observation	.25*	.15	.06	.28**	.13	.20
Collaboration	.46**	.45**	.32**	.37**	.23*	.38**
Feedback from peers	.38**	.41**	.22*	.33**	.19	.15
Feedback from supervisor	.42**	.36**	.25*	.35**	.32**	.27**
Informal interaction with supervisor	.27*	.26*	.27**	.15	.18	.20
Task repetition	.23*	.20	.23*	.12	.17	.24*
Problem solving	.68**	.53**	.43**	.51**	.51**	.46**
Idea experimentation	.48**	.45**	.34**	.44**	.36**	.06
Reflection	.41**	.26*	.30**	.32**	.33**	.24*
Intuition	.61**	.39**	.46**	.51**	.40**	.51**
Congruence	.44**	.45**	.32*	.42**	.18	.16

$* p < .05$, $** p < .01$.

"brief, near-spontaneous reflection on past episodes, communications, events, experiences" (p. 116). Examples of informal training in the workplace include a quick reminder during a shift of a policy or procedure and rapid feedback about a situation that only just occurred. In the 2007 study, informal training was positively correlated with two learning domains—career development and leadership—indicating the importance of informal training in developing the skills needed to be an employee in an organization.

Observation of Coworkers

Observation is cited by Collins, Brown, and Newman (1990) as the first step in an apprenticeship-like model of learning that includes coaching and eventually approximating the desired behavior. In this model, a student observes and notes actions over time in an attempt to socialize with the dominant culture (Eraut, 2000). In an employment setting, students have the opportunity to observe their more experienced (and often older) peers as they carry out job tasks, noting qualities such as the relative pace and attitude with which a task is approached, the interaction style used when conversing with clients or other coworkers, and the ratio of time spent on work tasks as compared with schoolwork or personal tasks. The newer (and often younger) student employee then can decide to what extent he will mimic the observed behavior or choose to behave differently. Likewise, observation from the perspective of the more experienced student worker is a key component of those who have supervisory responsibilities over their peers and can contribute to that student's management competencies. In the 2007 study, observation was positively correlated with the leadership learning domain.

Collaboration and Teamwork

Adults must be able to learn and work in teams to function in society (Gardner, 1993). Therefore, a stronger focus on independent as opposed to group work (as is emphasized in much of primary and secondary education) leaves students unprepared for the collaborative work environment that they will face after graduation (Resnick, 1987). Collaborative learning while in college allows students to practice such skills as collective problem solving; deliberative thinking and the ability to rapidly respond in conversation; displaying multiple roles, which may vary depending on a group's dynamics or needs; and confronting ineffective strategies and misconceptions regarding the project at hand (Brown et al., 1989; Eraut, 2000; Wenger, 2004). Finally, collaboration encourages students to interact with peers who have diverse backgrounds and experience a connectedness that may contribute to an inclusive campus climate (AAHE et al., 1998; Sandeen et al., 1987).

In a student employment setting, collaboration and teamwork may occur when several members of the same working group discuss how to attack a project together; ultimately someone assigns roles to each person involved in the process and the project moves toward completion as a result of everyone's combined efforts. In the 2007 study, one student called teamwork "crucial" to learning, while another wrote that "work[ing] in a team environment, doing things such as planning and problem solving . . . has also given me leadership experience and made me realize how much I enjoy working in a team" (Lewis, 2007). A comment from another student demonstrates how teamwork can help student employees become more efficient on the job: "Sometimes everybody on the shift has an exam the next day—we all come together to get the work done so that we can study later if there is free [time]" (Lewis, 2007). Collaboration and teamwork was positively correlated with all five learning outcomes assessed.

Feedback From Peers or Supervisor

Feedback is a critical component of learning; without effective feedback there may be little to no improvement in performance (Chickering & Reisser, 1993). When given appropriately, feedback should be both feasible and produce a net positive effect on future employee behavior (Eraut, 2000). Feedback should communicate an expectation of "high but achievable standards," a commitment to improvement, and support for responsible risk taking (AAHE et al., 1998, pp. 7–8). Feedback from peers is especially important in communities where participants actively seek a dynamic, growth-oriented environment (Wenger, 2004). In a student employment setting, feedback may take the form of midyear and end-of-year performance assessments; informal "check-in" meetings; or other communication that establishes, changes, or reiterates policies in light of a current or recent situation.

In response to a free-write survey question, several participants in the 2007 study described opportunities to receive or provide feedback as a catalyst for personal growth. One in particular described a connection between offering feedback to a newer employee and growth in important leadership skills:

> I feel like I have gained valuable leadership experience when dealing with new-hires and even just interacting on the everyday job. . . . Both at the beginning of the school year and throughout the entire year, I have been actively involved with teaching and helping new employees to better their on-the-job performance.

Feedback from a supervisor was positively correlated with all five learning domains, while feedback from peers was positively correlated with three domains: career development, civic and community engagement, and leadership.

Informal Interactions With a Supervisor

"Much learning takes place informally and incidentally, beyond explicit teaching or the classroom, in casual contacts with faculty and staff, peers, campus life, active social and community involvements, and unplanned by fertile and complex situations" (AAHE et al., 1998, p. 8). Informal interactions with a supervisor have the potential to create mentoring relationships between students and the (older) adults on campus. In addition to fostering friendships, these interactions can further enhance the integration of a student's social and academic worlds (ACPA, 1996b; Pascarella & Terenzini, 2005).

In a student-employment setting, informal interactions may occur during working hours, outside the workplace at office receptions or parties, or at community or sporting events that attract attendees from all over campus. In the 2007 study, one student remarked that "the quarterly dinners and long training session are the great ways to bond that I have experienced. It's easy to see the effects coming back from summer and getting to meet everyone again." Informal interactions were positively correlated with two learning domains: career development and civic and community engagement.

Task Repetition

Repeating tasks is an important component of the learning process. On the road to skill development, task repetition helps students move beyond a checklist of daily procedures on the way toward developing an intuitive or tacit understanding of how to carry out a job's requirements (Eraut, 2000). Additionally, task repetition is often the first step taken after receiving constructive feedback on how to improve performance; as the old saying goes: "practice makes perfect."

Student-employment settings are ripe with task repetition, whether it's answering the phone with a specific script, providing consistent information to a wide variety of clients, processing paperwork and filing, or assembling a sound system before a musical performance. One student in the 2007 study referred to the helpfulness of "day to day answering of questions, and taking initiative to maintain the smoothness of building operations." Task repetition also can teach college students how to become accustomed to certain "human resources" expectations of an employee (e.g., filling out paperwork accurately, arriving on time for work, or dressing a certain way for work). In the survey, task repetition was positively correlated with two learning domains: civic and community engagement and responsible independence.

Problem Solving

Problem-solving opportunities allow students to take charge of their learning, utilizing their experiences and perspective to overcome conflicts or other roadblocks (AAHE et al., 1998). Likewise, problem-solving skills help students thrive in collaborative settings, where problems can derail the work of the entire group (Brown et al., 1989) or where the entire group cannot move the practice forward until the issue is overcome (Wenger, 2004). Resnick (1987) points out that the most successful students after graduation will be those who are adaptive learners—flexible and able to respond to whatever unexpected situation might arise. In other words, every problem that a student encounters and overcomes will make him or her better prepared to handle whatever comes next.

Opportunities for problem solving in student employment settings likely vary wildly depending on job content or level of responsibility. For example, a student with supervisory responsibilities almost certainly must solve more complex problems (e.g., scheduling issues, personality conflicts, and competing demands for time) than does a student employee with fewer responsibilities. In the 2007 study, many students commented specifically on workplace situations that called for problem solving. "We work with difficult situations and people every day. People demand the impossible and we get to deal with them," wrote one student. Another wrote: "I have learned how to think on my feet and how to be patient." Both student workers and staff supervisors identified strong connections between problem solving and learning while on the job. All five learning domains were positively correlated with problem solving.

Idea Experimentation

The opportunity to experiment with new ideas is a unique skill, one that encourages growth in appropriate risk assessment. Idea experimentation requires time to put theories into practice and requires students to be active participants in the task at hand (AAHE et al., 1998; ACPA, 1996a). In a student-employment setting, idea experimentation can be tested behind the scenes (e.g., managing styles), with clients or patrons (e.g., an innovative solution to a complex problem), and with a supervisor (e.g., testing different styles of interaction). In the 2007 study, idea experimentation was positively correlated with four out of five learning domains: career development, civic and community engagement, leadership, and ethics and values. The following comment from one student sheds additional light on the role of idea experimentation in the workplace:

> I have learned how to find creative solutions to unforeseen problems that arise . . . what helped me learn that was just being put in the position where it was my responsibility to create solutions, and practicing doing that as things came up.

Reflection

Eraut (2000) describes two cognitive components of deliberative reflection: reflective deliberation and prospective deliberation. The former exists to "make sense of and/or evaluate one's experience, including what one has heard and read," whereas the latter "is directed towards a future course of action and includes decision-making and resolving contentious issues" (p. 127). In other words, reflection consists of the ability to assess one's current experiences as well as analyze future issues that might arise.

For a student employee, reflecting on what aspects of her job she likes or dislikes is a key step in thinking about what comes next—whether a summer job, internship, or budding career track—and ensuring that the next job she has best fits her inclinations (Little & Chin, 1993). In a student-employment setting, reflection may take the form of many questions each student poses to him- or herself. Examples might include: How do I feel about working so much with paperwork? Am I more productive when I work in the afternoon as opposed to the morning? My supervisor is extraordinarily hands-off in her management style; would I prefer a supervisor who is more engaged?

In the 2007 study, reflection was positively correlated with all five learning domains. Many student responses to open-ended questions commented on opportunities to reflect through their jobs. One student discussed a self-knowledge of reacting under pressure, as well as a greater understanding of how effective teamwork can lead to a more productive work environment:

> I have learned a lot about myself. I know how to respond to certain situations, ones that include being under a lot of pressure, and ones that involve competing priorities that I have to decide between. I've learned work can be a great way to bond people, and that people work better if they have time to get to know each other in a cooperative, non-competitive setting.

Another wrote about understanding his role as one key player in a larger organization:

> I have learned to be more of a self-starter . . . take the initiative to take a step back and understand the function of our department and how we can be more creative in conveying more benefits to the entire team. . . . I have also learned how to work with people of various working styles—it is interesting to learn how to adapt to all different types of people.

Others echoed this theme, describing a more full understanding of themselves in relation to their coworkers. "I have learned to recognize my own boundaries," wrote one participant, "[this job] has taught me a reliance upon others that I previously had not developed as well. It has taught me that I cannot do everything for myself and that it is okay to ask for and receive help." Reflecting on workplace lessons likely helps students succeed in life.

Intuitive Decision Making

Intuitive decision making reflects a fundamental, deep understanding of the many, varied, and sometimes conflicting responsibilities in the work environment. It also implies a comprehensive awareness of the past and a vision for the future. The result of such intuition is the ability to depart from routine or standard operating procedures and appropriately justify one's actions to others (Eraut, 2000). In a student-employment setting, intuitive decision making is demonstrated when employees are able to handle more difficult or complex situations without needing to consult a training manual or a supervisor before taking action. One student wrote about the perceived value of an experience to make decisions in this vein:

> At all my previous jobs I was working under direct supervision a lot of the time so if something came up that I didn't know how to handle it was not my responsibility to find a solution; I was to refer the problem to my supervisor. But at [this job] I am personally in charge of many things and I am the one who finds the solutions and that has been a great learning experience.

In the 2007 study, intuitive decision making was positively correlated with all five learning domains.

Congruence Between One's Job and Coursework or Academics

Connections between experiences inside and outside the classroom are at the heart of a successful program of cocurricular involvement (Braskamp, Trautvetter, & Ward, 2006). Research on student employment overwhelmingly indicates that greater learning outcomes appear when students' jobs are congruent (overlapping) with their academic coursework or future career interests (AAHE et al., 1998; Luzzo, 1993; Pascarella & Terenzini, 2005). In addition to enhanced career outcomes, greater job congruence may address students' developmental needs more holistically by merging aspects of their academic and extracurricular worlds (Keeling, 2004). Examples of student employment settings that might provide high levels of congruence include lab settings, where a student studying chemistry assists a professor of chemistry in a research project; the student newspaper, where a journalism student can practice his skills in writing and editing; or a marketing office, where a design student can create materials that could later be used in a portfolio. In the 2007 study, congruence between a student's job and coursework was positively correlated with three learning domains: career development, civic and community engagement, and leadership. It is important to note, however, that students reported low levels of congruence on the job overall: a mean of 2.98 on a 7-point scale.

Control Experiences

Recognizing that there are many other significant major experiences shared by a majority of undergraduates, this study included six as control experiences to gauge their impact on student learning. These control experiences were employment outside the Norris Center, extracurricular involvement (including student organizations and sports teams), residence hall or residential college activities, fraternity or sorority involvement, experiences in classroom settings, and experiences prior to enrolling at Northwestern. After controlling for these activities, most of the workplace experiences retained their significant relationships with career development, civic and community engagement, and leadership, while a smaller number retained their significance with ethics and values and responsible independence. (See Table 5 for correlation statistics.) These findings remained unchanged when job satisfaction was also included as a seventh control variable.

Five of the six control variables—all except residence hall/residential college activities—were significantly correlated with the learning domains. These correlations suggest that—as Braskamp et al. (2006) describe—students make concrete gains in learning through many varied cocurricular "places" of learning and involvement with related "activities" or organizations (p. 130). In this case, the control places and activities may be separate and unrelated to employment at the college union, but they are no less powerful in sparking undergraduate learning. Nonetheless, even after controlling for these other experiences, students engaging in certain workplace experiences demonstrated overall learning in key domain areas.

Summary

Results from the 2007 study of student employees at Northwestern University's union show that workplace experiences have at least a limited impact—and in some cases, a major impact—on student and staff perceptions of learning. Twelve of the 13 examined experiences (all except formal training) were positively correlated with a composite measure of learning (representing five learning domains). Both student employees and staff supervisors reported these experiences as occurring on the job, and students drew connections between engaging in these experiences while working and gains in key learning domains. These findings validate some of the literature on student learning and workplace learning, the two primary areas of research that guided this study.

TABLE 5
Partial Correlations Between 5 Learning Domain Composites and 13 Workplace Experiences Controlling for 6 Control Variables and Job Satisfaction

	Career Development	Civic and Community Engagement	Leadership	Ethics and Values	Responsible Independence
Formal training	.01	−.09	.06	−.05	−.07
Informal training	.35**	.17	.24*	.03	.07
Observation	.17	.03	.13	.07	.17
Collaboration	.42**	.31**	.35**	.19	.45**
Feedback from peers	.37**	.16	.21	.06	.07
Feedback from supervisor	.32**	.17	.27*	.19	.18
Informal interaction with supervisor	.27*	.24*	.05	.12	.17
Task repetition	.10	.23*	.06	.12	.23*
Problem solving	.49**	.40**	.49**	.49**	.44**
Idea experimentation	.43**	.26*	.36**	.27*	.00
Reflection	.25*	.27*	.27*	.22	.20
Intuition	.40**	.44**	.52**	.41**	.53**
Congruence	.50**	.28*	.36**	.08	.15

* $p < .05$, ** $p < .01$.

169

Implications and Additional Methods for Improving Workplace Learning

Integrating the workplace experiences described earlier more thoroughly into a student employee's responsibilities can be a pivotal first step for administrators attempting to heighten learning in specific domains. For example, Table 5 suggests that, if the goal is to focus student employee growth in leadership, staff should expand concrete opportunities for informal training or supervisor feedback. If the focus is on students developing a personally meaningful system of ethics and values, staff members should ensure that students have opportunities to meet challenges on their own by experimenting with new ideas or making judgments intuitively. And if the goal is to spark learning across all domains, staff should give their student employees opportunities to problem solve as much as possible. In other words, learning may be targeted to certain domain areas by providing opportunities for particular workplace experiences that have been shown to be empirically and qualitatively significant.

At this point a question arises: What other actions can administrators take to refocus a student employment program on learning? After all, staff who supervise student employees have many tools at their disposal that can affect a student's learning. A review of the study's findings, relevant literature, and recommendations from higher education researchers and advocacy organizations suggests that, in addition to focusing students on the workplace experiences described previously, supervisors and administrators can improve learning outcomes by effectively utilizing job descriptions, evaluation and assessment, mission and vision statements, professional organizations, and findings from empirical research. Each is discussed in greater detail in the following subsections.

Revise Job Descriptions

Accurate and thorough job descriptions can be effective tools in setting the stage for a student employee's potential learning (CAS, 2003). Utilizing explicit references to the workplace experiences and learning domains suggested earlier, potential student employees will understand prior to accepting a job offer the opportunities and expectations for their learning (Lewis & Contreras, 2008). Job descriptions are also an effective means of communicating the "situated" context in which learning will take place—that is, the learning that is embedded within the job tasks and the problems or challenges that comprise their daily responsibilities (AAC&U, 2007; Brown et al., 1989). At the time of the 2007 study of the college union at Northwestern, job descriptions did not explicitly reference many learning opportunities or tasks that may lead to learning, although since then they have been revised (Lewis & Contreras, 2008).

Refocus Student Evaluations

Students, like all learners, want to know what is expected of them and how they can improve their performance (Toohey, 1999). Just as supervisors complete performance evaluations, a learning-focused employment program requires a learning-based evaluation as well. According to Fried (2006), a learning-focused assessment can serve as a necessary "feedback loop" to help students document growth in the learning outcome areas described earlier.

Evaluations are often either summative or formative. Summative assessment is conclusive and judgmental in nature and is often used to measure proficiency in a specific area of expertise (Light & Cox, 2001). Summative evaluations, such as the SAT or GRE, are also effective in comparing individual learning against some sort of public standard. However, because they are often given after some period of formal teaching has concluded, the feedback provided is often too late for the learner to use. An example of summative assessment in an employment setting would be an end-of-the-year performance evaluation. Formative assessment, on the other hand, is developmental in nature and focuses on learning as it happens (Light & Cox, 2001). Formative assessments tend to be more collaborative and can help the learner understand where adjustments need to be made before the period of learning concludes. An example of formative assessment in an employment setting would be a midyear performance evaluation.

Supervisors of student employees should institute a regular assessment program that combines both summative and formative elements. Obtaining multiple perspectives throughout the process—by encouraging student workers to self-assess, collecting feedback from a student's coworkers, or referencing evaluations from clients or the student's academic advisor, for example—ensures that the evaluation remains as focused on learning as on performance. The evaluation should also be aligned with the learning-focused job descriptions discussed previously. A well-crafted assessment series is integral to the success of a student employment program; it engages students in reflection, provides necessary feedback to a student in the process of learning, and informs supervisors about needed changes that can better address organizational goals (Lewis & Contreras, 2009).

Look to Mission and Vision

An institution's mission and vision set the course and parameters for its actions and choices (Barr, 2000; Kramer, 2007). It is therefore vitally important to identify desired outcomes and develop programs that fulfill that vision. Learning goals vary based on institutional type (e.g., research, religiously affiliated, community college) and the values espoused at different levels (e.g., college-wide, divisional, unit-level) (Komives & Schoper, 2006). For example, student affairs leaders at Longwood University (Longwood

University Office of Student Affairs, 2008), in Virginia, have identified learning opportunities in partnership with academic units that serve the broader institutional mission of "develop[ing] citizen leaders prepared to make positive contributions to the common good." Elsewhere, administrators at Bridgewater State College (Bridgewater State College Student Affairs Division, 2008), in Massachusetts, developed learning outcomes by drawing on the core curriculum as well as ACPA and NASPA's 2004 publication *Learning Reconsidered*. Regardless of which internal sources are utilized for this purpose, administrators must ensure that a student employee's workplace focuses growth in those outcome areas that, in turn, realize components of the broader mission (Kramer, 2007).

Incorporate Goals Established by Professional Organizations

The 2007 study conducted at Northwestern University measured perceptions of growth in learning outcome areas that were informed not only by its own student affairs division, but also by the Council for the Advancement of Standards in Higher Education (2003) and seven professional organizations that contributed jointly to the *Learning Reconsidered* series (Keeling, 2004, 2006; Lewis, 2007). Much research continues to be done on student learning. Since the Northwestern study was conducted, the Association of American Colleges and Universities published a set of "essential learning outcomes" in a report entitled *College Learning for the New Global Century* (AAC&U, 2007). Each of these professional organizations has attempted to provide a framework within which administrators can better structure learning on their individual campus. Collectively, it appears these groups also attempt a delicate balancing act: on the one hand, identifying key areas of knowledge in which all college students should demonstrate proficiency and, on the other hand, opposing the codification of a nationwide college-level curriculum that limits its focus to a few critical areas (e.g., nursing, teaching, and the STEM fields: science, technology, engineering, and mathematics), as has been proposed by the Spellings Commission on the Future of Higher Education (U.S. Department of Education, 2006). Although the resolution of such large questions will undoubtedly be debated at the highest levels of education policy development, it is essential for administrators to begin integrating learning outcomes recommended by professional organizations into their student employment programs, so long as the outcomes themselves stay within the institutional and unit-level mission and vision. It will be difficult for administrators to justify the expansion—and in some cases the existence—of their student services and programs without intentional promotion and measurement of specific student learning outcomes (Kramer, 2007; Schuh, 2007).

Conduct More Research

For administrators who see themselves more as practitioners than as research-ers, the prospect of conducting research on their student employment pro-gram can seem at best daunting or at worst pointless. Nevertheless, few would deny the present climate of accountability, where all types of stake-holders—parents, legislators, accrediting bodies, the media, and so forth—look to administrators to justify skyrocketing tuition amid a tough economy; delineate the value added by a college education; and demonstrate student growth and development in subjects where Americans have failed to remain competitive, such as science and math. Looming questions remain unan-swered: What exactly are college students learning? How do we know these students are learning? In what ways are today's students being prepared for the jobs of tomorrow's economy?

The only way to respond to these serious concerns is with reliable data collected through rigorous and empirical research. Supervisors of student employees can play a vital role by researching the learning produced in stu-dent-employment settings. Some questions this research could address include: In what areas are student employees learning? How exactly does the employment experience catalyze student growth and development? In what ways does learning vary based on a student's demographics (e.g., year in school, position, major, GPA)? And how does workplace learning change over time? Some administrators may be able to call on research faculty at their institution to assist with study design; others will have to rely on pub-lished research or their own instincts as a primary guide. For supervisors without a research background, conducting research likely will be more art than science at first, and will necessarily improve over time.

Conclusion

As Devaney (1997) wrote, "We must teach ourselves to see our service areas as learning environments rather than as work places. We must see ourselves as teachers rather than as managers or taskmasters focused on getting the work done right" (p. 1). For supervisors of student employees, many tools are available to build a learning-centered student employment program. The process should start with a determination of specific learning outcomes (e.g., leadership, career development) that are valued within the particular unit. Institutional or unit mission and vision statements, as well as outcomes sug-gested by professional organizations in higher education, may be helpful in this determination. Supervisors must then identify and implement experi-ences, activities, processes, or tasks that students can engage on the job that encourages development in the desired learning domains. Examples of such experiences include collaboration, problem solving, reflection, and congruence with academic interests. Job descriptions must be revised to illustrate anticipated learning opportunities, and thoughtful assessments must be conducted periodically that focus on the developmental aspects of learning in the workplace. Finally, administrators must begin conducting empirical research on student employment programs to identify successes and shortcomings, communicate progress to stakeholders, and retool for future performance.

The challenges for higher education administrators in the months and years ahead will be difficult, although not insurmountable. Administrators must recognize that, "in this global century, every student—not just the fortunate few—will need wide-ranging and cross-disciplinary knowledge, higher-level skills, an active sense of personal and social responsibility, and a demonstrated ability to apply knowledge to complex problems" (AAC&U, 2007, p. 11). Supervisors of student employees play a vital role in our students' achievement; the work has only just begun.

References

American Association for Higher Education, American College Personnel Association, & National Association of Student Personnel Administrators. (1998). *Powerful partnerships: A shared responsibility for learning.* Washington, DC: Author.

American College Personnel Association. (1996a). *Principles of good practice for student affairs.* Washington, DC: Author.

American College Personnel Association. (1996b). *The student learning imperative: Implications for student affairs.* Washington, DC: Author.

Association of American Colleges and Universities. (2007). *College learning for the new global century.* Washington, DC: Author.

Barr, M. J. (2000). The importance of the institutional mission. In M. Barr & M. Desler (Eds.), *The handbook of student affairs administration* (pp. 25–49). San Francisco: Jossey-Bass.

Braskamp, L. A., Trautvetter, L. C., & Ward, K. (2006). *Putting students first: How colleges develop students purposefully.* Bolton, MA: Anker Publishing.

Bridgewater State College Student Affairs Division. (2008). Student learning outcomes. Retrieved December 22, 2008, from www.bridgew.edu/StudentAffairs/ SLOutcomes2008.doc

Brown, J. S., Collins, A., & Duguid, P. (1989, January–February). Situated cognition and the culture of learning. *Educational Researcher.* Washington, DC: American Educational Research Association.

Chickering, A. W., & Reisser, L. (1993). *Education and identity* (2nd ed.). San Francisco: Jossey-Bass.

Collins, A., Brown, J. S., & Newman, S. E. (1990). Cognitive apprenticeship: Teaching the crafts of reading, writing, and mathematics. In L. B. Resnick (Ed.), *Knowing, learning, and instruction: Essays in honor of Robert Glaser* (pp. 563–577). Hillsdale, NJ: Erlbaum.

Council for the Advancement of Standards in Higher Education. (2003). Relevant and desirable student learning and development outcomes. In *The book of professional standards for higher education 2003.* Washington, DC: Author.

Devaney, A. (Ed.). (1997). *Developing leadership through student employment* Bloomington, IN: Association of College Unions International.

Ekleberry, J., & Hoddy, M. (1997). Creating dialogue in training. In A. C. Devaney (Ed.), *Developing leadership through student employment* (pp. 114–135). Bloomington, IN: Association of College Unions International.

Eraut, M. (2000). Non-formal learning and tacit knowledge in professional work. *British Journal of Educational Psychology, 70,* 113–136.

Fried, J. (2006). Rethinking learning. In R. P. Keeling (Ed.), *Learning reconsidered 2: A practical guide to implementing a campus-wide focus on the student experiences* (pp. 3–9). Washington, DC: American College Personnel Association & National Association of Student Personnel Administrators.

Gardner, J. N. (1993). Conclusion. In R. Kincaid (Ed.), *Student employment: Linking college and the workplace* (pp. 131–136). Columbia, SC: National Resource Center for the Freshman Year Experience & Students in Transition.

Jarvis, P. (1987). *Adult learning in the social context.* London: Croom Helm.

Keeling, R. P. (Ed.). (2004). *Learning reconsidered: A campus-wide focus on the student experience.* Washington, DC: American College Personnel Association & National Association of Student Personnel Administrators.

Keeling, R. P. (Ed.). (2006). *Learning reconsidered 2: A practical guide to implementing a campus-wide focus on the student experience.* Washington, DC: American College Personnel Association & National Association of Student Personnel Administrators.

Kolb, D. A. (1984). *Experiential learning: Experience as the source of learning and development.* Upper Saddle River, NJ: Prentice Hall.

Komives, S. R., & Schoper, S. (2006). Developing learning outcomes. In R. P. Keeling (Ed.), *Learning reconsidered 2: A practical guide to implementing a campus-wide focus on the student experience* (pp. 17–41). Washington, DC: American College Personnel Association & National Association of Student Personnel Administrators.

Kramer, G. L. (Ed.) (2007). *Fostering student success in the campus community.* San Francisco: Wiley.

Lewis, J. S. (2007). *Learning while earning: Student employment and learning outcomes.* Unpublished master's thesis, Northwestern University, Evanston, IL.

Lewis, J. S., & Contreras, S. (2008, January). Research and practice: Connecting student employment and learning. *Bulletin of the Association of College Unions International, 76*(1), 30–38.

Lewis, J. S., & Contreras, S. (2009). Student learning outcomes: Empirical research as the bridge between theory and practice. In B. Perozzi (Ed.), *Enhancing student learning through college employment.* Bloomington, IN: Association of College Unions International.

Light, G., & Cox, R. (2001). *Learning and teaching in higher education: The reflective professional.* London: Sage.

Little, T., & Chin, N. (1993). The context of student employment. In R. Kincaid (Ed.), *Student employment: Linking college and the workplace* (pp. 105–121).

Columbia, SC: National Resource Center for the Freshman Year Experience & Students in Transition.

Longwood University Office of Student Affairs. (2008). Website. Retrieved December 22, 2008, from www.longwood.edu/studentaffairs/

Luzzo, D. A. (1993). Career decision-making benefits of college student employment. In R. Kincaid (Ed.), *Student employment: Linking college and the workplace* (pp. 25–30). Columbia, SC: National Resource Center for the Freshman Year Experience & Students in Transition.

Northwestern University Division of Student Affairs. (2005). *Student learning outcomes project.* Unpublished data. Evanston, IL.: Northwestern University.

Pascarella, E. T., & Terenzini, P. T. (2005). *How college affects students: A third decade of research.* (Vol. 2). San Francisco: Jossey-Bass.

Peters, T. J. (1997). The role of the union, student development, and student employment. In A. C. Devaney (Ed.), *Developing leadership through student employment* (pp. 17–28). Bloomington, IN: Association of College Unions International.

Resnick, L. R. (1987). The 1987 presidential address: Learning in school and out. *Educational Researcher, 16*(9), 13–20.

Sandeen, A., Albright, R. L., Barr, M. J., Golseth, A. E., Kuh, G. D., Lyons, W., & Rhatigan, J. J. (1987). *A perspective on student affairs: A statement issued on the fiftieth anniversary of the Student Personnel Point of View.* Washington, DC: National Association of Student Personnel Administrators.

Schuh, J. H. (2007). Changing student services through assessment. In G. L. Kramer & Associates (Eds.), *Fostering student success in the campus community* (pp. 61–80). San Francisco: Wiley.

Toohey, S. (1999). *Designing courses for higher education.* Philadelphia: Open University Press.

U.S. Department of Education. (2006). *A test of leadership: Charting the future of U.S. higher education.* Washington, DC: Author.

Vygotsky, L. S. (1978). *Mind in society: The development of higher psychological processes.* Cambridge, MA: Harvard University Press.

Wenger, E. (2006). Communities of practice: A brief introduction. Retrieved October 6, 2009, from http://www.ewenger.com/theory/

SECTION FOUR

WORK AS A VEHICLE FOR IMPROVING STUDENT ENGAGEMENT

9

WORKING DURING COLLEGE

Its Relationship to Student Engagement and Education Outcomes

Alexander C. McCormick, John V. Moore III, and George D. Kuh

ollege students have combined work and schooling since the earliest colleges were established in the United States (Lucas, 1994; Rudolph, 1977). As described in other chapters in this volume, fully two thirds of undergraduates at four-year institutions are employed, as are about four out of five community college students. Nearly one quarter of four-year students and 41% of those at community colleges work at least 35 hours per week. Nearly half of undergraduates describe themselves as students working to meet their expenses, while about one quarter describe themselves as employees who are taking classes (Horn & Nevill, 2006). With so many students working, and large numbers devoting a considerable amount of time to work, it is no wonder that scholars, institutional researchers, policymakers, and others are keenly interested in how employment affects the undergraduate experience (Tuttle, McKinney, & Rago, 2005).

As also noted in other chapters in this volume, the literature shows a mixed picture of the relationship between work and college success. Some observers fear that the number of hours students work may have deleterious effects on persistence, time to degree, and other qualitative dimensions of the student experience (King, 2003; Stern & Nakata, 1991; Tuttle et al., 2005). Some students elect to work long hours, perhaps combined with part-time enrollment, to reduce or avoid debt. But such a strategy can reduce the likelihood of degree completion by reducing the time available for academic work and prolonging the amount of time needed to complete requirements (Cuccaro-Alamin & Choy, 1998; Cunningham & Santiago, 2008; King, 2002). Working—particularly full time or off campus—is thought to negatively affect students' ability to participate in a range of activities that are related to positive learning outcomes (Fjortoft, 1995; Lundberg, 2004), such as service-learning, out-of-class work with faculty members, and cocurricular activities.[1]

Whereas other chapter authors note that working may benefit students by helping them finance their education, working may also have other benefits. Working may provide a venue to apply classroom learning in an applied setting. Working on campus may strengthen students' bonds with fellow student workers as well as with faculty or staff supervisors because they are spending more time engaged in campus life (Astin, 1999). Campus employment may broaden and deepen a student's support network—people who can help with academic or personal challenges. In addition, work commitments obligate students to budget their time effectively (Curtis & Shani, 2002). Finally, students who have concrete workplace experience may be preferred by employers because it is in those settings that students have opportunities to apply what they have learned in class and demonstrate—for better or worse—their ability to perform in messy, unstructured situations and work effectively with others.

Many studies of working students are based either implicitly or explicitly on a framework outlined by Tinto (1975), who postulated that student success is in large part a function of their ability to form strong academic and social connections at their college. Activities that take students away from the academic and cultural campus milieu risk weakening their connection to the campus and important agents of socialization and support—faculty and peers. As a result, the likelihood of persisting is reduced. As Pusser (chapter 7) contends, working, especially off campus, competes with what many argue should be a student's primary role orientation, that of focusing exclusively on academic matters. Working off campus forces students to split their commitments between work and study, devoting less time and attention to either (Hodgson & Spours, 2001) or to potentially enriching academic and social activities (Fjortoft, 1995; Lundberg, 2004). The demands of the dual commitments of study and work may also lead to higher levels of stress (Hey, Calderon, & Seabert, 2003; Levin, Montero-Hernandez, & Cerven, chapter 3).

Despite these findings, the impact of student employment on educational outcomes such as grades, time to degree, and retention remains equivocal, a conclusion noted by other authors in this volume (e.g., Levin et al., chapter 3; Pusser, chapter 7). Some studies have found that working students have lower GPAs than those who do not work (Hunt, Lincoln, & Walker, 2004), while others have found that working students actually had higher persistence and graduation rates than their nonworking peers (Beeson & Wessel, 2002). Working above a certain threshold number of hours (typically between 15 and 20) has been found to negatively affect desired educational outcomes (Harding & Harmon, 1999; King, 2002; Pascarella & Terenzini, 1991; Perna, Cooper, & Li, 2006; Stinebrickner & Stinebrickner, 2003). Work below the threshold has either no effect (Bradley, 2006; Furr & Elling,

2000, Harding & Harmon, 1999; High, 1999; Nonis & Hudson, 2006; Pascarella & Terenzini, 2005) or beneficial effects (Choy & Berker, 2003; Dundes & Marx, 2006–2007; Hood, Craig, & Ferguson, 1992; Moore & Rago, 2007; Rago, Moore, & Herreid, 2005).These seemingly contradictory findings may be caused in part by methodological factors. For example, some studies operationalize work as a dichotomous variable (i.e., students either work or they do not). Other studies consider the amount of time spent working. Some researchers combine on- and off-campus work, while others attend to only one of the two. Some studies fail to control for important student variables such as age, class year, and enrollment status. Many studies are based on students at a single institution, limiting their analytical power and inferential relevance. Student experiences across multiple institutions are rarely examined. Rarer still are studies that utilize advanced modeling techniques to properly account for the nesting of students within institutions. Given the changing demographics of the undergraduate population (more older and part-time students), the increase in student employment, and the number of hours students work (Stern & Nakata, 1991; King, 2003), it is important to account for these factors to understand more fully how employment affects student success.

This chapter examines college student employment by analyzing data from a large survey of undergraduates attending bachelor's degree–granting colleges and universities in the United States. Students at such institutions constitute 57% of total fall undergraduate enrollment nationwide (Snyder, Dillow, & Hoffman, 2008, calculated from table 184). We begin by describing the broad contours of work patterns: who works on and off campus, how much they work in each setting, and the relationships between various configurations of work and both student engagement and educational outcomes. We then employ multivariate hierarchical modeling to estimate the relationships between work and important process and outcome measures net of other student and institutional characteristics.

Student engagement represents the degree to which students are exposed to and take part in effective educational practices—practices that have been empirically linked to learning outcomes (Kuh, 2001, 2003; Kuh, Kinzie, Schuh, & Whitt, 2005). Outcome variables include students' own assessments of their growth and development in cognitive and noncognitive domains while in college, as well as their self-reported college grades. We estimate separate models for full- and part-time students in the first and senior years of college.

Data and Methods

Data for the study are from the 2008 administration of the National Survey of Student Engagement (NSSE). Every spring, NSSE surveys random samples of first-year and senior students attending participating institutions to determine the extent to which they are exposed to and participate in practices that research has shown to be positively related to desirable educational outcomes. NSSE also asks students how they spend their time (including hours worked on and off campus), how they rate their relationships with others on campus, how they judge their development in college along a range of cognitive and noncognitive dimensions, what their grades are, what cocurricular and other out-of-class activities they participate in, and other background and contextual factors. The NSSE survey was developed with input from a variety of higher education scholars and is grounded in best practices in undergraduate education (Kuh, 2001; National Survey of Student Engagement [NSSE], 2003).

The 2008 NSSE data include nearly 380,000 randomly sampled first-year and senior students attending 722 U.S. colleges and universities.[2] Although institutions elect to participate in NSSE, the group of participating institutions is broadly representative of the diversity of U.S. colleges and universities. When compared with the 2005 Basic Carnegie Classification, the list of 2008 NSSE institutions contains a slight overrepresentation of Master's Colleges and Universities (larger programs) and Baccalaureate Colleges–Arts & Sciences, and a concomitant underrepresentation of Research Universities (very high research activity) and Baccalaureate Colleges–Diverse Fields. Public institutions are also somewhat overrepresented in NSSE 2008 (42% of NSSE institutions compared with 35% nationally). The average institution-level response rate was 37%. Although respondent characteristics generally matched the underlying student population, women and full-time students were overrepresented among respondents. Women accounted for 56% of eligible students but 64% of respondents, and full-time students constituted 86% of eligibles but 90% of respondents. Descriptive statistics reported here are weighted to account for response bias according to gender, enrollment status, and institution size.

The analyses reported in this chapter were limited to U.S. institutions classified among the three major Carnegie types: doctorate-granting, master's, and baccalaureate institutions. Special-focus institutions in NSSE 2008 were not included because of their small number and distinctive educational character—which may extend to a special role for work (for example, at institutions specializing in business or health professions).

Examining Work Among Both First-Year and Senior Students

We conducted separate analyses of first-year and senior students (the two populations surveyed in NSSE). This permits us to examine the effects of work at two distinct points in the educational career, when students have different needs and experience different parts of the undergraduate curriculum. Examining first-year students allows us to assess work in the context of the all-important transition to college, while looking at seniors lets us assess participation in certain enriching educational experiences that are typically not available to first-years, such as study abroad, research with faculty members, and participation in internship and co-op programs. This approach also addresses the risk of selection bias that could result from an exclusive focus on seniors, who are survivors by definition, having succeeded in college. Some risk of selection effects remains, however. The spring NSSE administration is limited to enrolled students, which restricts the sample to those who have made it to the spring of the first or senior year. We return to the issue of sample selection when discussing our results and note when the results for first-year students suggest a different interpretation from those for seniors.

Educational Process and Outcome Measures

Student engagement was measured by the five NSSE benchmarks of effective educational practice, defined later with examples of survey elements that make them up (for more information, see National Survey of Student Engagement, 2008):

- *Academic challenge*: The extent to which a student is challenged by in- and out-of-class course work (for example, the amount of reading and writing, time spent on academic work, complexity of mental tasks required, and high faculty expectations)
- *Active and collaborative learning*: The extent to which a student actively engages with and applies academic work (for example, classroom participation, presentations, group work, and service-learning)
- *Student–faculty interaction*: The amount of a student's reported contact with faculty members (for example, discussing class topics with faculty outside class, working with faculty on research projects or other activities outside class, and receiving prompt feedback on assignments)
- *Enriching educational experiences*: A student's involvement in a range of beneficial educational and cocurricular activities (for example, learning communities, internships, community service, study abroad, and culminating senior experiences, as well as meaningful experiences with diverse others)
- *Supportive campus environment*: A student's assessment of institutional support for students and the quality of relationships with peers, faculty, and staff

We also examine three scales that portray how students characterize their collegiate growth in knowledge, skills, and development in three domains:

- *General education*: General education, writing, speaking, thinking critically
- *Personal and social development*: Developing values, understanding self and others, civic and community affairs, ethics, spirituality, learning independently
- *Practical competence*: Job skills, working with others, using technology, quantitative skills, real-world problem solving

Finally, grade point average (GPA) was based on a NSSE item that asks, "What have most of your grades been up to now at this institution?" with response options ranging from "A" to "C−" or lower." The responses were recoded to their equivalent grade point value (e.g., an "A−" was coded as 3.7).

Characterizing Work

As suggested earlier, work on campus and off campus can affect students in different ways. The NSSE survey section on students' time allocation asks respondents how many hours they spend in a "typical 7-day week" on various activities, including work on and off campus (asked separately), with a categorical response set made up of discrete spans of time. We collapsed the responses as follows:

- Zero hours
- 1–10 hours
- 11–20 hours
- 21–30 hours
- More than 30 hours

For descriptive analyses, we computed total hours worked by combining the two responses.[3] Multivariate models included a series of dichotomous variables representing the total number of hours worked on campus, off campus, or in both settings (those working zero hours serve as the reference category). This strategy permits us to examine the unique effects of the amount of work in each setting. The NSSE survey only asks about students' *current* time commitments. We do not know whether a student's work commitments at the time of the survey (spring of the first or senior year) represent a steady pattern of employment over prior periods.[4] Our interpretations assume such continuity. This assumption affects inferences about engagement and outcomes equally for first-year students, but for seniors our inferences about the relationship between work and the engagement variables—which refer to the current year—may have stronger warrant than inferences about longer-term outcomes because of unknown continuity in the pattern of work over the undergraduate career.

Other Variables Included in Analyses

Other student-level variables used in multivariate analyses are age, gender, race/ethnicity, first-generation status,[5] transfer status,[6] on-campus residence,[7] and the highest degree attained by either parent. For models examining educational outcomes, the five student-level benchmarks of effective educational practice were added as independent variables.

Institutional variables include Carnegie Classification; admissions selectivity (as designated by Barron's); urbanicity (a 7-point scale ranging from "rural" to "large city"); control (public or private); and a set of contextual characteristics such as percent female, percent transfer, percent full time, percent residential, and percent first generation. The first set of variables captures differences in institutional mission, setting, and financing that can affect who attends and what kinds of employment opportunities may be available to students, as well as the process and outcome variables that we examined. The contextual variables similarly capture institution-level differences in the student population that can be related to the services available to students, which in turn can influence processes and outcomes. Controlling for these institutional differences allows us to isolate the unique impact of different amounts of on- and off-campus work, independent of the particular institutional setting.

Multivariate Analyses

For the multivariate analyses, we estimated a separate series of models for each of the five engagement and four outcome variables, with separate models for full- and part-time first-year and senior students. Because of the nesting of students within institutions, we implemented a multilevel modeling approach using the HLM software package (Raudenbush, Bryk, Cheong, & Congdon, 2004). With HLM, we can control for unique institution-level effects to focus attention on the student-level results. Both the level 1 (student) and level 2 (institution) samples were sufficiently large to accommodate the number of variables included in the models. Because multilevel models are particularly sensitive to outliers, we excluded cases with extreme or improbable values (for example, student ages of 14 or 99). We also limited the analysis to cases with full information (i.e., we did not impute missing values). As a result of these procedures, the analyses are based on a final sample consisting of 127,938 first-year students and 142,337 seniors at 719 institutions.[8] Because of the large sample size, we adopted a conservative standard for statistical significance for student-level results (alpha = .001 for full-time student models, 124,087 first-years and 125,766 seniors; .01 for part-time student models, 3,851 first-years and 16,571 seniors).

Table 1 summarizes demographic characteristics of the analysis sample, depicting the four populations under study (full- and part-time first-year and senior students). Of particular note in Table 1 is that, compared with full-time students, part-time students include higher percentages of African American, Latino, and transfer students. Part-time students are also about 9 years older than full-time students, on average.

Who Works, Where Do They Work, and How Much Do They Work?

Employment was common among all groups, both first-year and senior students, whether full or part time. Nearly half of full-time first-year students (46%) and 3 out of 4 full-time seniors reported working for pay during a typical week (Table 2).[9] More than three quarters of part-time students were employed (76% of first-years and 84% of seniors). Off-campus employment

TABLE 1
Demographic Characteristics of the Analytic Sample

Characteristic	Full Time		Part Time	
	First-Year	*Senior*	*First-Year*	*Senior*
Percent female	55.6	57.0	60.1	58.4
Race/ethnicity distribution				
American Indian or other Native American	0.8	0.7	1.0	1.0
Asian, Asian American, Pacific Islander	5.6	5.1	4.3	5.5
Black or African American	8.1	6.1	13.8	10.0
Latino	6.4	5.7	11.2	10.2
White	69.3	71.8	59.3	62.5
Multiracial	2.8	2.4	3.0	2.0
Other/Missing	7.1	8.1	7.4	8.8
Percent first-generation[a]	38.2	40.9	59.6	59.1
Percent transfer[b]	7.1	37.4	34.9	67.3
Percent living off campus[c]	24.1	47.3	79.9	87.5
Average age	18.9	23.8	27.5	32.5
	(10.3)	(2.9)	(5.7)	(11.3)
N	124,087	125,766	3,851	16,571

Note: Data weighted for gender, enrollment status, and institution size. For averages, standard deviations are shown in parentheses.
[a]Defined as those for whom neither parent holds a bachelor's degree.
[b]Defined as those indicating they began college elsewhere.
[c]Defined as those living in a residence within driving distance of campus.

TABLE 2
Percentage Distribution of Hours Worked by Class Year, Enrollment Status, and Employment Location

	Zero	1–10	11–20	21–30	31 or more
Full-time first-years					
On-campus employment	79.3	11.7	7.6	1.0	0.5
Off-campus employment	69.1	9.3	11.1	6.8	3.7
All employment	53.5	16.4	16.1	8.7	5.3
Full-time seniors					
On-campus employment	69.6	14.6	12.6	2.2	1.0
Off-campus employment	46.2	12.3	17.9	13.2	10.3
All employment	26.1	17.7	25.6	16.9	13.8
Part-time first-years					
On-campus employment	88.5	3.4	3.5	0.5	4.1
Off-campus employment	30.5	7.9	11.2	13.4	36.9
All employment	23.7	7.6	13.2	13.8	41.8
Part-time seniors					
On-campus employment	86.8	3.7	4.3	1.1	4.1
Off-campus employment	23.2	6.5	11.1	12.6	46.6
All employment	15.8	5.9	12.2	14.2	51.9

Note: Data weighted for gender, enrollment status, and institution size.

was more common than work on campus. About one third of full-time first-years worked off campus, compared with 1 in 5 who worked on campus. More than half of full-time seniors worked off campus, while roughly 1 in 3 worked on campus. Only 11–13% of part-time students worked on campus; 69–77% worked off campus.

Considering hours worked across job locations, comparable shares of full-time first-years worked 1–10, 11–20, or more than 20 hours per week (16% in each of the first two groups and 14% in the third). Full-time seniors were more concentrated in the higher categories, with about one third working more than 20 hours per week. Part-time students did not necessarily work full time, however. Only about 2 out of 5 part-time first-years and half of part-time seniors worked more than 30 hours per week.[10]

Relatively few students (2–5%) worked on campus for more than 20 hours per week. The small group working more than 30 hours per week on campus may be full-time college employees. About 1 in 10 full-time seniors reported at least 30 hours per week of off-campus employment, a significant time commitment.

Next, we consider the relationships between work and selected institutional and student characteristics (Tables 3a and 3b). Unless otherwise noted,

TABLE 3a

Among Full-Time Students, Percentage Distribution of Hours Worked by Location of Work and Selected Student and Institution Characteristics

	Full-Time First-Years					Full-Time Seniors				
	Zero	1–10	11–20	21–30	31 or more	Zero	1–10	11–20	21–30	31 or more
On-campus employment										
Public institution	83.1	8.1	7.2	1.0	0.6	73.4	11.1	12.1	2.4	1.1
Private institution	69.3	20.9	8.7	0.9	0.3	59.2	24.0	14.1	1.9	0.8
First-generation	78.1	11.5	8.7	1.2	0.5	73.5	11.5	11.7	2.3	1.0
Not first-generation	80.1	11.8	6.8	0.8	0.5	66.9	16.7	13.3	2.2	1.0
Residence on/near campus	76.6	13.7	8.3	0.9	0.5	56.8	22.1	17.0	2.8	1.3
Residence off campus	87.8	5.1	5.6	1.1	0.4	81.1	7.8	8.6	1.7	0.7
Off-campus employment										
Public institution	67.4	9.0	11.9	7.7	4.0	45.1	11.7	18.3	14.3	10.6
Private institution	73.4	9.9	9.2	4.5	3.0	49.3	13.9	16.8	10.4	9.5
First-generation	61.0	9.5	14.1	9.5	5.9	38.7	10.8	18.8	16.3	6.9
Not first-generation	74.6	9.1	9.1	5.0	2.2	51.4	13.4	17.3	11.1	15.3
Residence on/near campus	79.8	8.5	7.6	3.0	1.1	60.4	13.5	15.4	7.7	3.0
Residence off campus	35.3	11.7	22.4	18.7	11.9	33.4	11.3	20.2	18.2	16.9
All employment										
Public institution	55.3	13.3	16.2	9.6	5.6	27.5	15.3	25.4	17.7	14.1
Private institution	49.0	24.6	15.7	6.4	4.3	22.0	24.4	26.0	14.6	13.0
First-generation	45.3	15.6	19.4	11.8	7.8	22.5	13.9	24.8	19.6	19.1
Not first-generation	59.1	17.0	13.8	6.6	3.5	28.5	20.4	26.1	15.0	10.1
Residence on/near campus	61.2	17.9	13.4	4.9	2.5	29.4	23.9	27.3	12.6	6.8
Residence off campus	29.3	11.8	24.4	20.6	13.9	23.1	12.1	24.0	20.7	20.0

TABLE 3b
Among Part-Time Students, Percentage Distribution of Hours Worked by Location of Work and Selected Student and Institution Characteristics

	Part-Time First-Years					Part-Time Seniors				
	Zero	1–10	11–20	21–30	31 or more	Zero	1–10	11–20	21–30	31 or more
On-campus employment										
Public institution	88.9	3.3	3.6	0.5	3.7	86.5	3.7	4.4	1.2	4.1
Private institution	86.5	3.9	3.1	0.3	6.2	87.9	3.4	3.8	0.9	4.0
First-generation	88.3	2.4	3.4	0.5	5.4	88.5	3.1	3.3	0.9	4.2
Not first-generation	88.8	5.1	3.6	0.5	2.0	84.3	4.5	5.8	1.5	3.9
Residence on/near campus	80.4	8.3	8.5	0.8	2.1	70.2	10.0	12.2	3.4	4.3
Residence off campus	90.5	2.2	2.2	0.4	4.6	89.1	2.7	3.2	0.8	4.1
Off-campus employment										
Public institution	30.5	8.1	11.7	14.7	34.9	24.3	6.8	11.5	13.3	44.1
Private institution	30.6	6.9	8.2	5.9	48.5	18.3	5.5	8.8	9.2	58.3
First-generation	27.1	7.0	9.7	12.6	43.5	20.6	5.5	9.4	11.8	52.6
Not first-generation	36.0	9.4	13.5	14.8	26.3	27.0	8.0	13.5	13.7	37.8
Residence on/near campus	55.4	10.7	10.3	11.9	11.7	43.2	9.6	15.9	13.7	17.5
Residence off campus	24.3	7.2	11.4	13.8	43.3	20.4	6.1	10.4	12.4	50.7
All employment										
Public institution	24.6	7.5	12.9	14.5	40.4	16.7	6.1	12.7	15.1	49.4
Private institution	21.2	7.0	8.3	7.2	56.4	11.9	4.8	9.6	10.1	63.5
First-generation	20.0	6.2	11.5	12.5	49.9	14.4	4.7	9.8	13.2	57.9
Not first-generation	29.7	9.8	15.9	16.0	28.6	17.9	7.6	15.6	15.7	43.3
Residence on/near campus	43.4	11.7	16.5	13.7	14.6	25.5	9.6	21.1	19.2	24.7
Residence off campus	18.8	6.5	12.3	13.8	48.5	14.5	5.3	10.9	13.5	55.8

Note: Data weighted for gender, enrollment status, and institution size.

all references are to full-time students who make up more than 90% of the respondent group. Work was common among full-time students at both public and private institutions, and slightly more common at privates, where 51% of first-years and 78% of seniors worked for pay. But students at public institutions worked more hours. Fifteen percent of first-years and 32% of seniors at public institutions worked more than 20 hours per week, compared with 11% and 28%, respectively, at private institutions.

The differences in the number of hours worked reflect, in part, a substantial difference in on-campus work between public and private institutions. Full-time first-year students at private institutions were nearly twice as likely as their counterparts at public institutions to be working on campus, 31% versus 17%. Fourteen percentage points also separate full-time seniors employed on campus at the two types of institutions (41% versus 27%). This suggests that private institutions are more successful at providing employment opportunities for their undergraduates, which may reflect in part their differential access to employment subsidies through the Federal Work-Study (FWS) Program, as described by Baum earlier in this volume.[11]

Working was somewhat more common among first-generation students, although the difference is more pronounced for first-year students (55% versus 41% working). First-generation students were also more likely to work more hours and to work off campus. Relative to students with at least one parent who holds a bachelor's degree, a larger share of first-generation students worked more than 20 hours per week (20% versus 10% of first-years and 39% versus 25% of seniors). First-generation seniors were twice as likely as their peers with college-educated parents to work at least 30 hours per week (20% versus 10%).

Residence is another factor that differentiates students with respect to work location and hours. Our analysis distinguished commuting students from those living on or near campus.[12] Work was far more common among first-year commuters: 71% of full-time first-year students who lived away from campus were employed, compared with 39% of campus residents. The difference was less pronounced among seniors, but work was still more common among commuters. Although first-year students worked less than seniors across all subgroups, the gap was notably smaller among commuting students (Figure 1).

A larger share of commuting students also worked long hours. One in five full-time commuting seniors worked more than 30 hours per week, contrasted with only 7% of those living on or near campus. Not surprisingly, full-time students who lived away from campus were also much more likely to work off campus: about 2 out of 3 first-year or senior commuters held off-campus jobs, while 12% and 19%, respectively, worked on campus. By contrast, those who lived on or near campus were about twice as likely as commuters to hold on-campus jobs.

FIGURE 1
Percentage of Full-time Students Who Work

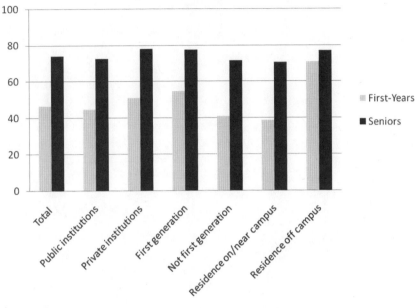

Living away from campus, working off campus, and having substantial work commitments while enrolled full time raise concerns about the ability of students to derive maximum benefit from the college experience. Of particular concern is the effect of these constraints on interacting with faculty outside class, participating in cultural and cocurricular activities, and using campus academic and support resources. Because student characteristics, institutional characteristics, and the location and intensity of employment are interrelated, we conducted multivariate analyses to investigate the independent impact of work after controlling for these other factors.

Multivariate Results: Engagement

The first set of models examines the relationship between work and each of NSSE's five benchmarks of effective educational practice. Because of the possible selection bias that could result from analyzing only seniors that we discussed earlier, we estimated separate models for first-year and senior students. Also, because of substantial differences in the levels of engagement and the nature of work for full- and part-time students, we estimated each model separately for full- and part-time students.[13] Our findings are presented in abbreviated form in Tables 4a through 5b.[14] To test for differences

TABLE 4a

Engagement Models for Full-Time Students: Selected Parameter Estimates

	Dependent Variable				
	Academic Challenge	Active and Collaborative Learning	Student–Faculty Interaction	Enriching Educational Experiences	Supportive Campus Environment
Full-time first-years					
Hours worked on campus					
1–10	0.01	0.12***	0.13***	0.08***	0.06***
11–20	0.07***	0.17***	0.20***	0.16***	0.06***
More than 20	0.20***	0.25***	0.32***	0.24***	0.09**
Hours worked off campus					
1–10	0.05***	0.13***	0.11***	0.07***	−0.01
11–20	0.02*	0.08***	0.09***	0.05***	−0.09***
21–30	0.08***	0.11***	0.11***	0.08***	−0.13***
More than 30	0.11***	0.17***	0.11***	0.11***	−0.14***
Hours worked both					
1–20	0.03	0.39***	0.40***	0.19***	0.00
21–30	0.04*	0.44***	0.51***	0.27***	−0.09***
More than 30	0.33***	0.67***	0.69***	0.45***	0.03

| | Dependent Variable | | | | |
	Academic Challenge	Active and Collaborative Learning	Student–Faculty Interaction	Enriching Educational Experiences	Supportive Campus Environment
Full-time seniors					
Hours worked on campus					
1–10	0.00	0.16***	0.28***	0.16***	0.11***
11–20	0.02	0.15***	0.30***	0.19***	0.08***
More than 20	0.09***	0.22***	0.36***	0.27***	0.11***
Hours worked off campus					
1–10	0.00	0.10***	0.07***	0.07***	0.02
11–20	−0.03**	0.08***	0.04***	0.06***	−0.03**
21–30	−0.01	0.07***	−0.01	0.02	−0.10***
More than 30	−0.03	0.04**	−0.06***	−0.02	−0.13***
Hours worked both					
1–20	0.03*	0.34***	0.42***	0.28***	0.13***
21–30	0.05**	0.32***	0.41***	0.26***	0.07***
More than 30	0.20***	0.44***	0.53***	0.43***	0.12***

Note: Selected results from hierarchical linear models estimating student-level benchmark scores (in columns), run separately for first-year and senior full-time students. Only parameters corresponding to work are reported. Dependent variables were standardized, so coefficients indicate effects in standard deviation units. Other level 1 (student) independent variables include age, gender, race/ethnicity, parents' highest level of education, first-generation status, transfer status, and off-campus residence. Level 2 (institution) independent variables included: control, size, basic Carnegie Classification, selectivity, percent female, percent full time, percent transfers, percent living off campus, and urbanicity.

TABLE 4b
Engagement Models for Part-Time Students: Selected Parameter Estimates

	Dependent Variable				
	Academic Challenge	Active and Collaborative Learning	Student–Faculty Interaction	Enriching Educational Experiences	Supportive Campus Environment
Part-time first years					
Hours worked on campus					
1–10	−0.07	−0.04	0.16	0.06	−0.13
11–20	−0.06	0.13	0.19	0.08	−0.01
More than 20	−0.28**	−0.15	0.08	0.02	0.06
Hours worked off campus					
1–10	−0.07	0.07	0.03	0.15*	−0.11
11–20	−0.01	0.08	0.02	0.10*	−0.02
21–30	−0.02	0.03	0.02	0.08*	−0.17**
More than 30	−0.07	−0.02	−0.10*	0.01	−0.20***
Hours worked both					
1–20	−0.30	0.24	0.36*	0.27	−0.36*
21–30	0.16	0.49**	0.41*	0.30*	0.10
More than 30	0.37**	0.36**	0.50***	0.52***	0.27

	Dependent Variable				
	Academic Challenge	Active and Collaborative Learning	Student–Faculty Interaction	Enriching Educational Experiences	Supportive Campus Environment
Part-time seniors					
Hours worked on campus					
1–10	−0.04	0.10	0.25**	0.21**	0.09
11–20	−0.01	0.19**	0.33***	0.26***	0.09
More than 20	−0.47***	−0.22***	−0.03	−0.04	0.09*
Hours worked off campus					
1–10	−0.03	0.05	0.06	0.10**	0.01
11–20	−0.05	0.02	0.01	0.10**	−0.01
21–30	−0.05	0.01	−0.01	0.06**	−0.06*
More than 30	−0.22***	−0.09***	−0.19*	−0.12***	−0.12***
Hours worked both					
1–20	0.02	0.47***	0.47*	0.32***	0.18**
21–30	0.07	0.31***	0.39*	0.34***	0.13**
More than 30	0.06	0.31***	0.41***	0.36***	0.18**

Note: Selected results from hierarchical linear models estimating student–level benchmark scores (in columns), run separately for first-year and senior part-time students. Only parameters corresponding to work are reported. Dependent variables were standardized, so coefficients indicate effects in standard deviation units. Other level 1 (student) independent variables include age, gender, race/ethnicity, parents' highest level of education, first-generation status, transfer status, and off-campus residence. Level 2 (institution) independent variables include control, size, basic Carnegie Classification, selectivity, percent female, percent full time, percent transfers, percent living off-campus, and urbanicity.

* $p < .05$, ** $p < .01$, *** $p < .001$

in the role of on- and off-campus work as well as the number of hours worked, the models include separate variables for the number of hours worked exclusively in each setting, plus an additional set of variables for the total number of hours worked by students with on- *and* off-campus jobs.[15] The reference (excluded) category in these analyses consists of students who were not working. Thus, the coefficients for hours worked in a given setting are relative to not working, net of the other variables in the model. For example, a significant positive coefficient for working 1–10 hours per week on campus would indicate that, relative to not working at all, working 1–10 hours on campus is positively related to the outcome in question.

In looking at the relationship between work and NSSE's five benchmarks of effective educational practice, it is again important to be clear about how the results should be interpreted. The NSSE benchmarks vary in the extent to which they reflect relatively objective features of the educational experience (such as the amount of reading and writing, the frequency of group work, and prompt feedback from faculty); student perceptions (such as perceived institutional emphasis on academics or quality of relations with peers and faculty); and activities that reflect students' preferences and choices (such as out-of-class interaction with faculty or students, research with a faculty member, participation in cocurricular activities, or study abroad). Some benchmark elements (for example, community-based projects or culminating senior experiences) may be required on some campuses but optional elsewhere. Clearly, employment does not cause the amount of coursework that is required or the frequency of prompt feedback by faculty. But it may well play a role in students' choices about which educational opportunities to pursue, it can affect relationships with peers and faculty, and it affects the amount of time available for academic and nonacademic pursuits. The point is that these models investigate *relationships* between work and the benchmarks, without implying causation.

For full-time first-year and senior students, the results of on-campus work are quite consistent. In almost every case (26 out of 30 coefficients across all models), relative to not working and after controlling for other student and institution characteristics, work on campus shows a significant positive relationship with all five benchmarks of effective educational practice (Table 4a).[16] The magnitude of these relationships varies, to be sure, with some relatively weak and others stronger. Student–faculty interaction showed the strongest relationship, followed by active and collaborative learning and enriching educational experiences. Of these, the strongest effects were for working more than 20 hours per week. Relative to not working, working more than 20 hours per week on campus was associated with an increase on these benchmarks of about one quarter to one third of a standard deviation.

TABLE 5a
Educational Outcomes Models for Full-Time Students: Selected Parameter Estimates

		Dependent Variable		
	Gains: *General* *Education*	*Gains:* *Personal and* *Social* *Development*	*Gains:* *Practical* *Competence*	*GPA*
Full-time first years				
Hours worked on campus				
1–10	−0.01	−0.03***	0.02**	0.11***
11–20	−0.01	−0.01	0.06***	0.03*
More than 20	−0.02	−0.03	0.07**	−0.13***
Hours worked off campus				
1–10	−0.01	0.00	0.01	0.00
11–20	0.03***	0.03**	0.05***	−0.13***
21–30	0.04**	0.05***	0.06***	−0.26***
More than 30	0.03	0.04*	0.05**	−0.29***
Hours worked both				
1–20	−0.05**	0.07***	0.04*	−0.03
21–30	−0.11***	0.10***	0.00	−0.14***
More than 30	−0.20***	0.10***	−0.08***	−0.28***

TABLE 5a (Continued)

	Dependent Variable			
	Gains: General Education	Gains: Personal and Social Development	Gains: Practical Competence	GPA
Full-time seniors				
Hours worked on campus				
1–10	−0.04***	−0.06***	−0.07***	0.15***
11–20	−0.03***	−0.04***	−0.06***	−0.05***
More than 20	−0.02	0.00	−0.03	−0.09***
Hours worked off campus				
1–10	−0.02*	0.00	0.00	−0.02
11–20	0.03**	0.02**	0.02**	−0.10***
21–30	0.05***	0.05***	0.03**	−0.21***
More than 30	0.05***	0.07***	0.03**	−0.17***
Hours worked both				
1–20	−0.09**	−0.03*	−0.09***	0.08***
21–30	−0.08***	−0.01	−0.09***	−0.07***
More than 30	−0.13***	0.00	−0.10***	−0.19***

Note: Selected results from hierarchical linear models estimating self-reported gain scales and GPA (in columns), run separately for first-year and senior full-time students. Only parameters corresponding to work are reported. Dependent variables were standardized, so coefficients indicate effects in standard deviation units. Other level 1 (student) independent variables included: age, gender, race/ethnicity, parents' highest level of education, first-generation status, transfer status, off-campus residence, and student-level benchmark scores. Level 2 (institution) independent variables included: control, size, basic Carnegie Classification, selectivity, percent female, percent full-time, percent transfers, percent living off-campus, and urbanicity.

* $p \leq .05$ ** $p \leq .01$ *** $p \leq .001$

198

TABLE 5b
Educational Outcomes Models for Part-Time Students: Selected Parameter Estimates

	Dependent Variable			
	Gains: General Education	Gains: Personal and Social Development	Gains: Practical Competence	GPA
Part-time first years				
Hours worked on campus				
1–10	−0.10	−0.10	−0.06	−0.08
11–20	0.09	−0.01	0.06	0.01
More than 20	0.04	0.15	0.21**	0.14
Hours worked off campus				
1–10	0.01	0.11	0.04	−0.02
11–20	0.07	0.03	0.05	−0.18**
21–30	0.05	0.13*	0.14*	−0.19**
More than 30	0.06	−0.02	0.07	0.06
Hours worked both				
1–20	−0.20	0.27*	0.05	−0.54**
21–30	−0.14	0.24	−0.03	−0.07
More than 30	−0.27*	−0.06	−0.17	−0.11

TABLE 5b (Continued)

	Dependent Variable			
	Gains: General Education	Gains: Personal and Social Development	Gains: Practical Competence	GPA
Part-time seniors				
Hours worked on campus				
1–10	0.00	−0.12*	−0.01	0.17**
11–20	0.01	−0.07	−0.02	0.05
More than 20	−0.02	−0.02	0.00	0.04
Hours worked off campus				
1–10	−0.04	0.02	−0.02	−0.03
11–20	0.02	0.04	0.06*	−0.07*
21–30	0.07**	0.01	0.04*	−0.13***
More than 30	0.09***	0.03	0.07***	−0.01
Hours worked both				
1–20	−0.06	0.07	−0.06	−0.05
21–30	−0.09	0.01	−0.13*	−0.03
More than 30	−0.11**	0.05	−0.10*	−0.12*

Note: Selected results from hierarchical linear models estimating self-reported gain scales and GPA (in columns), run separately for first-year and senior part-time students. Only parameters corresponding to work are reported. Dependent variables were standardized, so coefficients indicate effects in standard deviation units. Other level 1 (student) independent variables included: age, gender, race/ethnicity, parents' highest level of education, first-generation status, transfer status, off-campus residence, and student-level benchmark scores. Level 2 (institution) independent variables included: control, size, basic Carnegie Classification, selectivity, percent female, percent full-time, percent transfers, percent living off-campus, and urbanicity.

In one sense, these results confirm prior findings: Work on campus is educationally beneficial. But contrary to previous research, we did not find an attenuation or reversal of the positive effect for students working more than 20 hours per week. Indeed, we found a fairly robust positive effect for this group. One account for this counterintuitive finding may be that having substantial work commitments forces students to manage their time well so as to maximize the benefit of their "student time," and those with the heaviest commitments are those who can most effectively manage these multiple obligations.[17] Another possibility is that some students working long hours on campus are spending at least some of their work time in educationally productive ways. Unfortunately, this intriguing proposition is not directly testable in the NSSE data. It is appropriate in this context to return to the sample selection issue raised earlier. The consistency of results for first-year and senior students shows no evidence of selection effects (that is, attrition prior to senior year of students for whom work has negative effects). Still, it is possible that some students with unmanageable work commitments in the fall left school or curtailed their obligations before the spring term, or equivalently that some successful students increased their commitments in the spring, but we have no way to test these possibilities.

Although the results for off-campus work by full-time students are not as uniform, they show similar patterns of significant, positive relationships between off-campus work and several benchmarks, relative to not working. Regardless of the number of hours worked (with a single exception), off-campus employment shows a positive relationship with four of the five benchmarks for first-year students, and a negative relationship between working off-campus more than 10 hours and the last benchmark, supportive campus environment. However, the magnitude of all of these effects is generally modest. For seniors, positive effects of working off campus were limited to active and collaborative learning (up to 30 hours per week), student–faculty interaction, and enriching educational experiences (with the last two showing small positive effects only for work up to 20 hours per week). For seniors, working off campus more than 20 hours per week was negatively associated with supportive campus environment, and more than 30 hours a week of off-campus work was negatively related to interaction with faculty, but the magnitude of these effects is small.

Though small, the positive benefits of off-campus work contradict conventional wisdom, which holds that involvements away from campus undermine a student's connection to the campus and substantial engagement with educationally purposeful activities. The negative relationship with supportive campus environment is more consistent with this reasoning, suggesting three possibilities. One is that students who work off campus find their institutions and the people in them generally insensitive or unresponsive to their needs. Such students may have turned to off-campus work because of insufficient financial aid; some students may feel that college personnel are inflexible when it comes to their needs and off-campus commitments. Also, it is possible that perceiving the campus environment or faculty, staff, and peers to be unsupportive may lead students to spend more of their time in non-campus-based activities, including work. Finally, it may be that students who work many hours off campus do not spend enough time on campus to develop supportive relationships with faculty, staff, and peers.

Few full-time students—5% of first-years and 10% of seniors—reported having both on- and off-campus jobs. But for these students, work showed a moderate to fairly strong positive relationship with active and collaborative learning, student–faculty interaction, and enriching educational experiences, relative to students who did not work. This surprising result is difficult to interpret. It suggests that there may be something distinctive—and educationally beneficial—about these students, the jobs they hold, or both. Another possibility that cannot be discounted is that these students may simply interpret some survey items (for example, those asking about behavioral frequency) differently from how other students do.

The results were less consistent for part-time students, with more significant effects found for seniors than for first-years (Table 4b). Among part-time first-year students who worked on campus, the only significant result was a negative relationship between working more than 20 hours per week on campus and academic challenge, compared to those not working. A similar negative effect was found for seniors, for both academic challenge—the largest of the negative effects, associated with nearly one half of a standard deviation decrease—and active and collaborative learning. Unlike first-years, however, the results showed a positive effect of lesser amounts of on-campus work on student–faculty interaction, enriching educational experiences, and active and collaborative learning.[18] These effects were generally of moderate size, with the strongest positive effects observed for student–faculty interaction.

Off-campus work had little effect on engagement for part-time first-year students. A small negative relationship between off-campus work and supportive campus environment exists for more than 20 hours per week of such work. For part-time seniors, we found that working off campus for more than 30 hours per week was negatively related to four of five benchmarks. In the case of academic challenge, the negative effect was slightly larger and manifested at 21–30 hours per week.

As with full-time students, the strongest positive effects of working were found for the small percentage (5–6%) of part-time students who reported both on- and off-campus employment.

For part-time seniors, the consequences of work more closely match previous empirical findings and theoretical expectations than they do for full-time seniors. That is, there are benefits for moderate levels of work on campus, and negative effects for higher work commitments on and off campus.

Multivariate Results: Outcomes

Now we turn to the analysis of self-reported gains in three domains and self-reported college grades.[19] Work experience can be expected to contribute positively to some outcomes, especially the noncognitive—practical competence as well as personal and social development. In the models that follow, the student-level benchmarks discussed in the previous section were included among the independent variables. Thus, the effects of work discussed in this section are net of any relationships between work and engagement, and between engagement and these outcomes.

For full-time students, there is little evidence of a meaningful relationship between work and self-reported gains relative to students who do not work, net of engagement and other student and institutional characteristics (Table 5a). Although several coefficients are statistically significant, the effects tend to be extremely small. This suggests that any meaningful effect of work on self-reported gains is mediated by student engagement. An exception is for full-time first-year students with both on- and off-campus jobs totaling 30 hours per week. Self-reported gains in general education are somewhat lower for these students (one fifth of a standard deviation). A comparable but smaller negative effect appears for full-time seniors with an equivalent mix of on- and off-campus employment.

The results for GPA comport with prior research for both first-years and seniors: a slight GPA benefit associated with up to 10 hours per week of on-campus work, and lower GPAs for students working more than 20 hours per week on campus or more than 10 hours per week off campus. The strongest negative effects are associated with working off campus more than 20 hours per week, or working at both on- and off-campus jobs for more than 30 hours per week.

For part-time students, there is relatively little evidence of a relationship between on- or off-campus work and students' perceived growth and development (Table 5b). A noteworthy exception involves part-time first-year students' perceived gains in practical competence: Those working on campus for more than 20 hours per week reported moderately higher gains (about one fifth of a standard deviation). Among seniors, the results are mixed but again show few significant and meaningful associations with perceived gains. Like full-time seniors, part-time seniors who combined on- and off-campus work for more than 30 hours per week showed a small negative association with general education gains.

As with full-time students, the results suggest that working off campus can dampen grades. Part-time first-year students working off campus 11–30 hours per week earned lower grades than comparable peers who did not work. The same was true for those working both on- and off-campus jobs for up to 20 hours per week. Among seniors, working on campus for up to 10 hours per week paid a modest GPA dividend, while 21–30 hours per week of off-campus work resulted in slightly lower grades.

Discussion and Implications for Practice

As noted by King (1998) and authors of other chapters in this volume, working during college is now the norm for undergraduates in the United States. Nearly half of full-time first-year students and three quarters of seniors attending four-year colleges and universities responding to the 2008 NSSE reported working for pay. The numbers were even higher for part-time students, with 76% of first-year students and 84% of seniors doing so. Among first-generation students, one fifth of full-time first-years and two fifths of full-time seniors worked more than 20 hours per week. Because previous research suggests that where students work may have different effects, we isolated the associations between the effects of these two venues in our analysis. We also looked at first-year and senior students separately because focusing only on seniors would limit the findings to successful students. Even so, the results were quite consistent for the two groups, especially for those enrolled full time, suggesting few if any "survivor" effects are linked to work and study.[20]

The findings from this study both confirm and contradict conventional wisdom about the relationships between work and schooling. The good news is that working either on or off campus was positively related to several dimensions of student engagement, especially for full-time students. Those who worked on campus generally benefitted more than their counterparts who worked off campus. But contrary to expectations, some of the stronger positive effects on engagement were for full-time students working *more than 20 hours per week* on campus. Even more surprising, we found the largest net gains in engagement for students who reported working both on and off campus—a relatively small group whose surprising results beg further investigation.

The bad news is that, after controlling for student and institutional characteristics, we found some negative associations between off-campus work and students' perceptions of the campus environment. We also found that heavy work commitments on or off campus can undermine engagement for part-time students.

We also examined several outcome measures with statistical controls for levels of student engagement as well as student and institutional characteristics. For full-time students, working on campus for up to 10 hours per week was associated with slightly higher self-reported grades, while more than 20 hours per week of on-campus work corresponded to slightly lower grades. The GPA penalty was about twice as much for the same amount of work off campus. Given the positive relationships between work and several measures of student engagement and between engagement and selected educational outcomes, the benefits of work during college appear to be mediated by student engagement. This suggests that one potentially productive way to optimize the positive benefits of work and study is to induce students to intentionally connect what they are learning in class with experiences in the work setting. How might this be done?

The old story was that colleges and universities should create more on-campus employment opportunities to afford students a reasonable number of hours so that they can devote ample time to their studies while being in the company of educators and peers. Although this still seems to make sense, it is also the case that market forces coupled with changing student interests, habits, and attendance patterns markedly limit the effectiveness of such an approach, at least on a wide scale. In many instances, students need to earn more money to cover college and other expenses than on-campus employment will provide. Many students already hold jobs they do not want to give up while trying to earn a college degree. In addition, full-time students in good academic standing who do not work spend on average only about 12–14 hours on class preparation. This number has not changed over the past decade. Undergraduates who do not care for dependents or others have a significant amount of discretionary time; many of them spend an appreciable share of this time working, which is arguably at least as productive a use of their energy as other possibilities available to them. The bottom line is that a one-size-fits-all approach to promoting student success for students who work is not likely to yield the desired results, except perhaps with institutions located in small towns or rural areas where off-campus employment opportunities are extremely limited.

More difficult to enact but also more likely to be effective is a systemic effort to change the views of many faculty and staff that working during college is an unnecessary, unfortunate distraction from the only real business of undergraduate study, which is to engage fully in the curriculum and campus-based cocurriculum. The goal is to make faculty, advisors, and student life professionals full partners in helping students connect curricular and cocurricular experiences with student employment. It is beyond the scope of this chapter to describe a detailed campaign strategy to accomplish this. But one important step is to widely disseminate both national and institutional data about the number of students who work, why they work, and some ideas for how faculty can design assignments that require students to apply what they are learning to their work setting and, conversely, what they are experiencing on the job to their understanding of course material.

Another step is to ensure that students are well informed about the potential hazards and benefits of on- and off-campus work. Beginning with precollege orientation and continuing through first-year seminars and academic advising, students should be encouraged to think about how their work plans mesh with their academic program and other expectations for college life. It is especially important in these discussions to frame students' employment in a way that would facilitate achievement of their goals, emphasize the value of limiting work hours (at least until students fully understand their college workload), and encourage them to take positions either on campus or off that align with their academic or career interests (Luzzo, McWhirter, & Hutcheson, 1997). Part-time students and those who have flexibility in their off-campus employment could be encouraged to substitute a few hours of on-campus work for some off-campus hours to reap the probable benefits of higher levels of engagement.

Cuccaro-Alamin and Choy (1998) note that students make decisions that balance work, enrollment intensity, and borrowing to meet their college expenses. For students who take on heavy work commitments, counseling about alternatives may prove beneficial. Students may be able to offset some of their work hours with financial aid, and doing so may improve their chances of success. But given limited knowledge about costs and funding sources (McDonough & Calderone, 2006) and aversion to debt among some students (Cunningham & Santiago, 2008), ensuring that students and their families have full knowledge about all financial aid options is critical to their ability to make informed decisions.

Families could also benefit from a fuller understanding of the benefits and risks associated with on- and off-campus work.[21] Parent/family relations and orientation programs have been growing in popularity in recent years (Carney-Hall, 2008; Coburn, 2006). In light of the fact that first-generation students tend to work more hours than do their peers with college-educated parents, information about work and alternative financing strategies might prove particularly useful for this group. Lundberg and colleagues (2007) found that first-generation students had lower levels of campus involvement, peer involvement, and investment in learning, all of which might be further challenged by heavy work commitments. Arming families with accurate and clear information can create both a consistent message across venues of student support and can help families to better understand the best ways to support their students (Price, 2008; Taub, 2008).

Talking with students about how they are managing their commitments to school, work, and family also may have the salutary effect of helping them learn how to balance what are likely to be complex lives and multiple obligations. Further, as students reflect on the connections among their studies, current employment, and career aspirations, they may deepen their understandings about their values and long-term goals, behaviors that also are positively linked to student persistence and other measures of success in college (Chi, 1996; Chickering & Gamson, 1987; Cress, Astin, Zimmerman-Oster, & Burkhardt, 2001; Gerdes & Mallinckrodt, 1994; Light, 2001; Meara, Day, Chalk, & Phelps, 1995; Parker-Gwin & Mabry, 1998).

Conclusion

The contemporary college student experience is different from that which many faculty members and administrators remember. For better or worse, most students work, whether to pay tuition and fees or to buy discretionary goods and services such as automobile insurance, electronic equipment, and other items. With so many undergraduates today working while they pursue their studies, it is imperative that college and university leaders, faculty, academic advisors, student affairs professionals, and others committed to helping students succeed become more informed about the relationships between employment and both student engagement and educational outcomes.

Endnotes

1. For a review of literature that supports the effectiveness of these practices, see Kuh et al. (2005).

2. Roughly 184,500 first-year students and 194,900 seniors.

3. To compute total hours worked, we assigned the midpoint of each bounded response range; for the last response option (More than 30), we assigned a value of 35. The sum of on- and off-campus estimates determined the total hours category assignment.

4. Not just whether or not a student works, but also whether work was on or off campus and the number of hours worked.

5. A student was considered to be first generation if neither parent holds at least a bachelor's degree. This definition was deemed appropriate given our restriction to students attending baccalaureate-granting institutions.

6. Students who reported that they began postsecondary education at another institution were designated as transfers.

7. On-campus residence was defined to include campus housing, a fraternity or sorority house, or a residence within walking distance of campus.

8. The analysis sample represents 67% of first-year and 73% of senior respondents at eligible institutions (after removing special-focus institutions). All eligible institutions were included, though analyses of part-time students involved fewer

institutions because part-time enrollment is rare at some institutions, and no such students were in the sample. Three institutions were excluded from analyses of first-year students because of the absence of part-time students.

9. In Tables 2 through 3b, the complement of the first column (zero hours worked) is equivalent to the sum of the remaining columns and represents the proportion who worked.

10. These figures do not take work in the home into account, and many part-time students care for children or other dependents.

11. According to the U.S. Department of Education (2008), 1,263 private not-for-profit four-year institutions participated in the 2008–09 FWS program, compared with 563 public four-year institutions. Forty-three percent of FWS expenditures in 2007 went to private four-year institutions, and 37% went to public four-year institutions. Yet public institutions enroll about 65% of undergraduates at four-year institutions (Snyder et al., 2008, calculated from table 184).

12. The latter group includes students who reported living in campus housing, a fraternity or sorority house, or a residence within walking distance of campus. We use the terms *off-campus* and *commuter* interchangeably for those who reported living within driving distance of campus.

13. It should be noted that, as with our earlier discussion of the work variables, we know only *current* enrollment status. Some students in the part-time group may previously have been enrolled full time, and vice versa.

14. Complete results are available from the authors on request.

15. The last set of variables is necessary because some students reported working in both settings. For example, Table 2 indicates that 74% of full-time seniors were employed. But the percentages working on and off campus sum to 84% because 10% reported *both* on- and off-campus work.

16. Three exceptions are for academic challenge: There was no relationship for between 1 and 10 hours of work on campus for first-years and seniors, or for 11–20 hours of work on campus for seniors. There was also insufficient evidence of an effect of more than 20 hours per week of on-campus work on the supportive campus environment benchmark for first-year students.

17. Recall that only 1.5% of full-time first-years and 3.2% of full-time seniors work on campus more than 20 hours per week (Table 2).

18. In the last case, the effect is limited to 11–20 hours per week.

19. For a review of reliability of self-reported data, see Gonyea (2005).

20. As noted earlier, we are not able to assess the possibility of attrition prior to spring of the first year. We are also unable to assess the stability of students' employment patterns over time.

21. We use the word *family* rather than *parents* to acknowledge that important participants in these discussions may not be limited to students' parents but may also include students' spouses, siblings, or children.

References

Anderson, E. L., & Corrigan, M. E. (Eds.), *Changing student attendance patterns: Challenges for policy and practice* (pp. 69–83, New Directions for Higher Education, 121). San Francisco: Jossey-Bass.

Astin, A. W. (1999). Student involvement: A developmental theory for higher education. *Journal of College Student Development, 40*(5), 518–529.

Beeson, M. J., & Wessel, R. D. (2002). The impact of working on campus on the academic persistence of freshmen. *Journal of Student Financial Aid, 32*(2), 37–45.

Bradley, G. (2006). Work participation and academic performance: A test of alternative propositions. *Journal of Education and Work, 19*(5), 481–501.

Carney-Hall, K. C. (2008). Understanding current trends in family involvement. *New Directions in Student Services, 122,* 3–14.

Chi, M. T. H. (1996). Constructing self-explanations and scaffolded explanations in tutoring. *Applied Cognitive Psychology, 10,* 33–49.

Chickering, A. W., & Gamson, Z. F. (1987). *Seven principles for good practice in undergraduate education.* Racine, WI: Johnson Foundation.

Choy, S., & Berker, A. (2003). *How families of low- and middle-income undergraduates pay for college: Full-time dependent students in 1999–00* (NCES 2003–162). Washington, DC: U.S. Department of Education, National Center for Education Statistics.

Coburn, K. L. (2006). Organizing a ground crew for today's helicopter parents. *About Campus, 11*(3), 9–16.

Cress, C. M., Astin, H. S., Zimmerman-Oster, K., & Burkhardt, J. C. (2001). Developmental outcomes of college students' involvement in leadership activities. *Journal of College Student Development, 42*(1), 15–27.

Cuccaro-Alamin, S., & Choy, S. P. (1998). *Postsecondary financing strategies: How undergraduates combine work, borrowing, and attendance* (NCES 98–088). Washington, DC: U.S. Department of Education, National Center for Education Statistics.

Cunningham, A. F., & Santiago, D. A. (2008). *Student aversion to borrowing: Who borrows and who doesn't.* Washington, DC: Institute for Higher Education Policy and *Excellencia* in Education.

Curtis, S., & Shani, N. (2002). The effect of taking paid employment during term-time on students' academic studies. *Journal of Further and Higher Education, 26*(2), 129–138.

Dundes, L., & Marx, J. (2006–2007). Balancing work and academics in college: Why do students working 10 to 19 hours excel? *Journal of College Student Retention, 8*(1), 107–120.

Fjortoft, N. F. (1995, April). *College student employment: Opportunity or deterrent?* Paper presented at the annual meeting of the American Education Research Association, San Francisco.

Furr, S. R., & Elling, T. W. (2000). The influence of work on college student development. *NASPA Journal, 37*(2), 454–470.

Gerdes, H., & Mallinckrodt, B. (1994). Emotional, social, and academic adjustment of college students: A longitudinal study of retention. *Journal of Counseling and Development, 72*(3), 281–288.

Gonyea, R. M. (2005). Self-reported data in institutional research: Review and rec-ommendations. *New Directions for Institutional Research, 2005*(127), 73–89.

Harding, E., & Harmon, L. (1999). *Higher education students' off-campus work pat-terns.* Olympia: Washington State Institute for Public Policy.

Hey, W., Calderon, K. S., & Seabert, D. (2003). Student work issues: Implications for college transition and retention. *Journal of College Orientation and Transition, 10*(2), 35–41.

High, R. V. (1999). *Employment of college students.* Rockville Center, NY: Molloy College, Department of Mathematics.

Hodgson, A., & Spours, K. (2001). Part-time work and full-time education in the UK: The emergence of a curriculum and policy issue. *Journal of Education and Work, 14*, 373–388.

Hood, A. G., Craig, A. R., & Ferguson, B. W. (1992). The impact of athletics, part-time employment, and other activities on academic achievement. *Journal of Col-lege Student Development, 35*, 364–370.

Horn, L., & Nevill, S. (2006). *Profile of undergraduates in U.S. postsecondary educa-tion institutions: 2003–04: With a special analysis of community college students* (NCES 2006–184). Washington, DC: U.S. Department of Education, National Center for Education Statistics.

Hunt, A., Lincoln, I., & Walker, A. (2004). Term-time employment and academic attainment: Evidence from a large-scale survey of undergraduates at Northumbria University. *Journal of Further and Higher Education, 28*(1), 3–18.

King, J. E. (1998, May 1). Too many students are holding jobs for too many hours. *Chronicle of Higher Education*, A72.

King, J. E. (2002). *Crucial choices: How students' financial decisions affect their aca-demic success.* Washington, DC: American Council on Education, Center for Pol-icy Analysis.

King, J. E. (2003). Nontraditional attendance and persistence: The cost of students' choices. In J. E. King, E. L. Anderson, & M. E. Corrigan (Eds.), *Changing stu-dent attendance patterns: Challenges for policy and practice* (New Directions for Higher Education, 121). San Francisco: Jossey-Bass.

Kuh, G. D. (2001). Assessing what really matters to student learning: Inside the National Survey of Student Engagement. *Change, 33*(3), 10–17, 66.

Kuh, G. D. (2003). What we're learning about student engagement from NSSE. *Change, 35*(2), 24–32.

Kuh, G. D., Kinzie, J., Schuh, J. H., & Whitt, E. J. (2005). *Student success in college: Creating conditions that matter.* San Francisco: Jossey-Bass.

Light, R. J. (2001). *Making the most of college: Students speak their minds.* Cambridge, MA: Harvard University Press.

Lucas, C. J. (1994). *American higher education: A history.* New York: St. Martin's Griffin.

Lundberg, C. A. (2004). Working and learning: The role of involvement for employed students. *NASPA Journal, 41*(2), 201–215.

Lundberg, C. A., Schreiner, L. A., Hovaguimian, K. D., & Miller, S. S. (2007). First-generation status and student race/ethnicity as distinct predictors of student involvement and learning. *NASPA Journal, 44*(1), 57–83.

Luzzo, D. A., McWhirter, E. H., & Hutcheson, K. G. (1997). Evaluating career decision-making factors associated with employment among first-year college students. *Journal of College Student Development, 38*(2), 166–172.

McDonough, P. M., & Calderone, S. (2006). The meaning of money: Perpetual differences between college counselors and low-income families about college costs and financial aid. *American Behavioral Scientist, 49*(12), 1703–1718.

Meara, N. M., Day, J. D., Chalk, L. M., & Phelps, R. E. (1995). Possible selves: Applications for career counseling. *Journal of Career Assessment, 3*(3), 259–277.

Moore, J. V., III, & Rago, M. A. (2007, May). *The working student's experience: The hidden costs of working on college student success and engagement.* Paper presented at the annual meeting of the Association for Institutional Research, Kansas City, MO.

National Survey of Student Engagement. (2003). *Construction of the 2000–2003 NSSE benchmarks.* Retrieved March 20, 2008, from http://nsse.iub.edu/2003_annual_report/html/benchmarks_construction.htm

National Survey of Student Engagement. (2008). *Promoting engagement for all students: The imperative to look within. 2008 results.* Bloomington, IN: Author.

Nonis, S. A., & Hudson, G. I. (2006). Academic performance on college students: Influence of time spent studying and working. *Journal of Education for Business, 81*(3), 151–159.

Parker-Gwin, R., & Mabry, J. B. (1998). Service learning as pedagogy and civic education: Comparing outcomes for three models. *Teaching Sociology, 26*, 276–291.

Pascarella, E. T., & Terenzini, P. T. (1991). *How college affects students: Vol. 1. Findings and insights from twenty years of research.* San Francisco: Jossey-Bass.

Pascarella, E. T., & Terenzini, P. T. (2005). *How college affects students: Vol. 2. A third decade of research.* San Francisco: Jossey-Bass.

Perna, L., Cooper, M. A., & Li, C. (2006). *Improving educational opportunities for students who work.* Prepared for the Indiana Project on Academic Success. Bloomington, IN: Project on Academic Success.

Price, J. (2008). Using purposeful messages to educate and reassure parents. *New Directions in Student Services, 122*, 29–42.

Rago, M. A., Moore, J. V., III, & Herreid, C. (2005, June). *Disengaged and ignored: Are working students a lost cause?* Paper presented at the annual meeting of the Association for Institutional Research, San Diego, CA.

Raudenbush, S. W., Bryk, A. S., Cheong, Y. F., & Congdon, R. T., Jr. (2004). *HLM 6: Hierarchical linear and nonlinear modeling.* Chicago: Scientific Software International.

Rudolph, F. (1977). *Curriculum: A history of the American undergraduate course of study since 1636.* San Francisco: Jossey-Bass.

Snyder, T. D., Dillow, S. A., & Hoffman, C. M. (2008). *Digest of education statistics 2007* (NCES 2008–022). Washington, DC: U.S. Department of Education, National Center for Education Statistics.

Stern, D., & Nakata, Y. (1991). Paid employment among U.S. college students. *Journal of Higher Education, 62*(1), 25–43.

Stinebrickner, R., & Stinebrickner, T. R. (2003). Working during school and academic performance. *Journal of Labor Economics, 21*(2), 473–491.

Tinto, V. (1975). Dropout from higher education: A theoretical synthesis of recent research. *Journal of Higher Education, 45*(1), 89–125.

Traub, D. J. (2008). Exploring the impact of parental involvement on student development. *New Directions in Student Services, 122,* 15–28.

Tuttle, T., McKinney, J., & Rago, M. (2005). *College students working: The choice nexus* (IPAS Topic Brief). Bloomington, IN: Project on Academic Success.

U.S. Department of Education. (2008). *Federal campus-based programs data book 2008.* Retrieved March 19, 2009, from www.ed.gov/finaid/prof/resources/data/databook2008/databook2008.html

EFFECTS OF WORK ON AFRICAN AMERICAN COLLEGE STUDENTS' ENGAGEMENT

Lamont A. Flowers

National reports show that tuition has been rising at public two-year and four-year institutions (Choy, 2004; College Board, 2008a). The upward trend in tuition costs has occurred for several years and suggests a continual rise in tuition and fees in the years to come. Between 1978 and 1989, average tuition and fees rose by approximately 4.2% per year at public four-year colleges and 1.4% per year at two-year colleges (College Board, 2008a). From 1998–1999 to 2008–2009, average tuition and fees increased in constant 2008 dollars by $5,318, $2,209, and $307 at private four-year, public four-year, and public two-year institutions, respectively (College Board, 2008a). Average tuition and fees at public four-year colleges and universities were approximately 6% higher for in-state students in the 2008–2009 academic year than in the previous academic year (College Board, 2008a). At two-year public institutions, average tuition and fees were approximately 5% higher in the 2008–2009 academic year than during the 2007–2008 academic year. Concomitantly, over the past three decades, increases in family incomes have been substantial for the wealthy (e.g., 86% for the top 5%), yet extremely low for the poorest (e.g., 3% for the bottom 20%) of Americans (College Board, 2008a).

While tuition is rising, state appropriations for public colleges and universities and college enrollments are declining. State appropriations in current dollars for public colleges and universities were approximately $56 billion in 1999–2000 but $55 billion in 2003–2004 (Snyder, Dillow, & Hoffman, 2008). This decrease in state funding is intriguing considering that more college students are expected to enroll in colleges and universities throughout the next decade. National education projections forecast that, between 2006 and 2017, college enrollment will increase from 18 million students to approximately 20 million students (Hussar & Bailey, 2008). Thus, while the demand for a college education is rising, financial resources from governmental sources are declining (Hauptman, 2007; St. John & Paulsen, 2001). The decline in state funding has prompted many postsecondary institutions to develop creative ways to balance their budgets to maintain a quality educational experience for students (St. John & Paulsen, 2001). Despite the many financial strategies undertaken, many colleges and universities have chosen to raise tuition to cover expenses and provide a quality learning environment for students (Hauptman, 2007). In light of rising tuition and other expenses associated with attending college, many students and families must rely on the income that college students receive from working while enrolled to help defray the costs of attaining a college degree (College Board, 2008b; Furr & Elling, 2000; King, 1999; Miller, Danner, & Staten, 2008).

These trends may have especially important implications for African American students, given that the median income of African American families was approximately $40,000 in 2007, lower than for White ($77,133) and Asian ($69,937) families (College Board, 2008a). To meet financial needs, some African American college students who have not worked previously may be required to work, while students who are currently working may need to work additional hours or seek multiple employment opportunities while enrolled in college.

One major purpose of this book is to better understand the degree to which working in college detracts or enhances students' academic and social experiences in college. Accordingly, this chapter estimates the effects of working on and off campus on African American students' engagement in college to examine the extent to which working while enrolled in college provides African American students opportunities to pursue their studies in an educationally appropriate manner. This chapter focuses on African American students in large measure because of the lack of research that focuses on this issue among this student population. A focus on African American students is also warranted in light of racial/ethnic group differences in student employment. Data from the National Postsecondary Student Aid Study (NPSAS), shown in Table 1, demonstrate that African American students are more likely than White, Hispanic, Asian, and American Indian students to work full time while enrolled in college. African American students also average more hours of work per week (32) than White (29) or Asian (26) students. Moreover, Table 2 highlights that African American students are more likely to come from low-income families than are White and Asian students. African American students are also more likely than White, Asian, and Hispanic students to be financially independent and thus may be more likely to need to work full time. Taking into account these and other individual and

TABLE 1

Percentage Distribution of Undergraduates, by Their Work Status While Enrolled, Average and Median Hours Worked per Week, and With Respect to How They Defined Their Primary Role of Work and Study, by Race: 2003–2004

Race/Ethnicity	Did Not Work	Part Time	Full Time (35 or More Hours/Week)	Average Hours Worked per Week	Median Hours Worked per Week
White	25.0	43.7	31.4	29	29
Black	26.2	34.3	39.5	32	35
Hispanic or Latino	24.4	38.9	36.8	31	32
Asian	36.7	41.5	21.8	26	25
American Indian or Alaska Native	27.2	36.6	36.1	32	33

	Did Not Work	Student Working to Meet Expenses	Employee Enrolled in School
White	25.0	49.6	25.4
Black	26.2	42.1	31.7
Hispanic or Latino	24.4	48.1	27.5
Asian	36.7	44.6	18.8
American Indian or Alaska Native	27.2	41.7	31.1

Source: Adapted from the U.S. Department of Education, National Center for Education Statistics, *Profile of Undergraduates in U.S. Postsecondary Education Institutions: 2003–04* by L. Horn and S. Nevill, 2006, pp. 123, 125.

TABLE 2
Percentage Distribution of Undergraduates, by Their Income and Dependency Status, by Race: 2003–2004

| | Income Level | | |
Race/ethnicity	Low	Medium	High
White	18.6	50.9	30.5
Black	35.5	50.7	13.8
Hispanic or Latino	34.1	49.5	16.5
Asian	32.9	42.9	24.1
American Indian or Alaska Native	25.6	53.2	21.2

	Dependent	Independent
White	53.0	47.0
Black	36.0	64.0
Hispanic or Latino	46.8	53.2
Asian	56.4	43.6
American Indian or Alaska Native	35.0	65.0

Source: Data were accessed and analyzed via the U.S. Department of Education, National Center for Education Statistics, 2004 National Postsecondary Student Aid Study (Data Analysis System). Percentages may not sum to 100 because of rounding.

institutional characteristics, this cross-sectional study explores among African American college students the relationship between working on campus and off campus and engagement in activities that have been shown to promote intellectual growth and student persistence.

Students Who Work While Pursuing Postsecondary Education

Before addressing its primary purpose, the chapter begins by providing a snapshot of today's working college student to help situate the study in a larger context. As described in other chapters, recent national data show that the majority of college students work while attending college (41% work part time and 33% work full time; Horn & Nevill, 2006). On average, these students work approximately 29 hours per week (Horn & Nevill, 2006). At public four-year institutions, approximately 50% of the students work part time, 22% work full time, and 29% do not work. At two-year institutions, 38% work part time, 41% work full time, and 21% do not work. Of the students who work part time, 39% attend two-year institutions and 51% of these students attend four-year institutions (Horn & Nevill, 2006). For students who work full time (more than 35 hours per week), 53% attend two-year institutions and 36% attend four-year institutions. Smaller percentages of students in their third, fourth, and fifth years work part time or full time than their freshman and sophomore counterparts. Students who work part time are concentrated in business and management fields (25%), health disciplines (16%), and arts and humanities (14%). Likewise, students who work full time are more likely to major in business and management (25%), health disciplines (18%), and arts and humanities (11%).

African American Students Who Work While Pursuing Postsecondary Education

Although research describing the characteristics and experiences of African American students who work while attending college is limited, a plethora of data describes the work intensity of African American students who work while enrolled in college. Data from the NPSAS show that only 28% of African American male students and 26% of African American female students did not work while enrolled in 2003–2004 (Horn & Nevill, 2006). Table 3 shows that African American females are more likely than males to work full time and work more hours a week. African American students who attend public institutions are more likely to work part time than African American students who attend private institutions. African American students from low-income families are less likely to work while enrolled in college than are those from higher-income families. African American students from high-income families are more likely to work full time in college than are students from lower-income families. African American students whose parents have a bachelor's degree or higher are less likely to work, and less likely to work full time, while enrolled in college than are other students. African American students whose parents have no more than a high school diploma are more likely to work full time than students whose parents have higher levels of education. African American students who make mostly As are more likely to work full time than are African American students who make mostly Cs.

According to Table 4, African American students are more likely to consider themselves as students who work to meet expenses than employees who study while enrolled. African American female students are more likely than male students to define their primary role as an employee who studies. African American students who view their status as an employee who studies tend to be older than African American students who view their status as a student who works (not tabled). African American students who make mostly As are more likely to consider themselves employees who study, whereas African American students who make Cs and Ds or lower are more likely to perceive themselves as students who work.

TABLE 3
Percentage Distribution of African American Undergraduates, by Their Work Status While Enrolled, Average Hours Worked per Week, and Selected Institutional and Student Characteristics: 2003–2004

Characteristic	Did Not Work	Part Time	Full Time (35 or More Hours/Week)	Average Hours Worked per Week
Gender				
Male	27.5	36.1	36.4	31.4
Female	25.5	33.3	41.3	32.0
Income				
High	20.7	25.7	53.6	35.1
Medium	21.7	31.9	46.4	33.0
Low	35.1	40.6	24.3	28.2
Dependency Status				
Dependent	35.2	47.9	16.9	24.9
Independent	21.1	26.7	52.2	34.9
Parents' Education				
High school diploma or less	24.6	31.9	43.5	32.8
Some postsecondary education	26.8	34.9	38.3	31.8
Bachelor's degree or higher	27.8	37.8	34.5	30.2
Institution Sector				
Public	25.7	36.2	38.1	31.4
Private, not-for-profit	32.1	29.9	37.9	31.6
Private, for-profit	24.5	28.0	47.5	33.8
Grade Point Average				
Mostly As	24.8	26.2	49.0	35.3
As and Bs	25.7	29.0	45.3	33.2
Mostly Bs	26.4	31.9	41.7	32.3
Bs and Cs	25.9	37.3	36.8	30.3
Mostly Cs	26.6	36.8	36.6	31.1
Cs and Ds or lower	26.3	38.8	34.9	30.8

Source: Adapted from Horn and Nevill (2006) using data that were accessed and analyzed via the U.S. Department of Education, National Center for Education Statistics, 2004 National Postsecondary Student Aid Study (Data Analysis System). Percentages may not sum to 100 because of rounding.

TABLE 4
Percentage Distribution of African American Undergraduates, by Their Work Status While Enrolled, With Respect to How They Defined Their Primary Role of Work and Study, and Selected Institutional and Student Characteristics: 2003–2004

Characteristic	Did Not Work	Student Working to Meet Expenses	Employee Enrolled in School
Gender			
Male	27.5	43.8	28.7
Female	25.5	41.1	33.4
Income			
High	20.7	29.1	50.2
Medium	21.7	42.2	36.1
Low	35.1	46.9	18.0
Dependency Status			
Dependent	35.2	56.0	8.8
Independent	21.1	34.3	44.6
Parents' Education			
High school diploma or less	24.6	38.5	36.9
Some postsecondary education	26.8	45.1	28.1
Bachelor's degree or higher	27.8	46.2	26.0
Institution Sector			
Public	25.7	44.2	30.1
Private, not-for-profit	32.1	37.6	30.2
Private, for-profit	24.5	31.4	44.0
Grade Point Average			
Mostly As	24.8	26.2	49.0
As and Bs	25.7	38.2	36.0
Mostly Bs	26.4	39.6	34.0
Bs and Cs	25.9	46.0	28.1
Mostly Cs	26.6	45.9	27.5
Cs and Ds or lower	26.3	47.1	26.6

Source: Adapted from Horn and Nevill (2006) using data that were accessed and analyzed via the U.S. Department of Education, National Center for Education Statistics, 2004 National Postsecondary Student Aid Study (Data Analysis System). Percentages may not sum to 100 because of rounding.

Review of the Research on College Students Who Work While Attending College

As observed in other chapters in this volume, a number of cross-sectional as well as longitudinal studies have sought to estimate the impact of work on student learning and involvement in college (Furr & Elling, 2000; Pascarella, Bohr, Nora, Desler, & Zusman, 1994; Pascarella, Edison, Nora, Serra Hagedorn, & Terenzini, 1998; Pascarella & Terenzini, 1991, 2005). As a group, these research studies have helped to inform student affairs practitioners and higher education administrators on a variety of issues and topics. Together, the research literature on the effects of working while enrolled in college on student outcomes suggests that, while working in college may be essential for college students to help finance the costs of attending college, the potential impact of working on student outcomes is mixed. For example, Pascarella et al.'s study (1994), based on a single institution, showed that hours worked off campus resulted in small but negative effects on a standardized measure of reading achievement in the first year of college. In a later study, Pascarella et al. (1998), analyzing data from 23 postsecondary institutions, found that the number of hours worked per week negatively affected students' scores on a standardized measure of science reasoning. However, the same study also showed that hours spent working on and off campus resulted in small but statistically significant positive effects on a standardized measure of learning in the third year of college.

Other research suggests that working off campus and a high number of hours is negatively related to student outcomes. In his landmark study of the influences of college on student development, Astin (1993) found that working off campus was negatively associated with completing a bachelor's degree. He also found that working on campus was positively associated with college persistence and completing a degree. King (1999), analyzing data from the NPSAS, found that students who worked had higher grade point averages than did students who did not work while enrolled in college. King also showed that when the amount of hours worked per week exceeded 15 hours, a student's grade point average began to decline. Reporting findings from a national study, Horn and Berktold (1998) found that students who worked full time noted more negative academic experiences than did students who worked fewer hours per week. Furr and Elling (2000) demonstrated that students who worked extensively while enrolled in college were less likely to engage in academically centered student involvement activities than were those students who did not work or who worked less frequently. Miller and associates (2008) found that students who worked more than 20 hours a week were more likely to have lower grades and engage in unhealthy social behaviors (e.g., binge drinking) than were students who worked 10 or fewer hours while enrolled in college. In summary, existing research seems to support the contention that working while in college may lead to beneficial educational outcomes if students appropriately manage their work and study times while enrolled in college and do not work excessively (Astin, 1993; Furr & Elling, 2000; Horn & Berktold, 1998; King, 1999; Miller et al., 2008; Pascarella & Terenzini, 2005).

Although the existing body of research enhances our understanding of the impact on student outcomes of working while enrolled, additional research is needed. While other authors in this volume also note gaps in available research, this chapter focuses on the absence of knowledge about the experiences of African American students who work while enrolled in college. To address this gap, this chapter provides information on the relationship between working in college and African American students' engagement experiences. African American students make up approximately 12% of all students who work part time and 17% of all students nationwide who work full time. Because 34% of all African American college students work part time and 40% work full time (for approximately 32 hours a week), it is clear that many of these students expend a significant amount of time pursuing employment-related activities. In light of national data that show that African American students may not perform as well academically as students from other racial and ethnic groups (Horn & Nevill, 2006) and factoring in the amount of time these students devote to working in college, identifying the influence of working on student engagement for African American students is critical. Thus, given the lack of research estimating the influence of working during college on African American students' development and the apparent need for more culture-specific research on the impacts of college on students, this study uses nationally representative data from the National Survey of Student Engagement to examine the direct effects of work on African American students' self-reported academic and social engagement in college. Controlling for potentially confounding academic and nonacademic variables such as year in school, college major, enrollment status, college grades, Greek affiliation, residence status, and athletic participation, this cross-sectional study estimates the relationship between the number of hours African American students spent working on and off campus and their engagement in experiences that research has shown to enhance students' academic and social development in college. Accordingly, the major purpose of this study is to assess the direct effects of working on and off campus on African American students' self-reported engagement in college to yield findings that may generate suggestions for enhancing the educational outcomes of African American students who work while enrolled in college.

Methodology

Building on prior research conducted to examine the effects of college attendance on student development (Pascarella & Terenzini, 1991, 2005), this chapter addresses the following two research questions:

1. Controlling for student and institutional characteristics, to what extent does working on and off campus influence African American students' engagement in intellectually stimulating activities in college?
2. Do the effects of working in college on student engagement for African American students vary by gender, college racial composition, residence status, and athletic participation?

The conceptual framework that guides this study implies that students who are academically and socially engaged in college are more likely to develop in an educationally appropriate manner (Chickering & Reisser, 1993). Thus, many studies that examine student engagement utilize most of the same variables that researchers utilize to explore the impact of college on student development and educational outcomes (Furr & Elling, 2000; Pascarella et al., 1994; Pascarella et al., 1998; Pascarella & Terenzini, 1991, 2005). Thus, for the purposes of this study, *student development* and *student engagement* are used interchangeably to define desirable patterns of student involvement in college and meaningful personal and intellectual growth. Accordingly, the conceptual framework is based on extensive studies on the effects of college on student development. Because this study seeks to examine the relationship between work and student engagement, the conceptual framework highlights variables that will be used to statistically control for potentially confounding variables that may obfuscate the association between working in college and student involvement in beneficial academic and social experiences.

The conceptual framework for this study assumes that four sources influence students' engagement: (a) precollege characteristics, (b) institutional characteristics, (c) students' academic experiences in college, and (d) students' nonacademic experiences in college (Pascarella & Terenzini, 1991). One line of this research suggests that student background factors and precollege characteristics mediate the effects of college on postsecondary outcomes (Chickering & Reisser, 1993; Pascarella, 1985; Pascarella & Terenzini, 1991, 2005; Tinto, 1993). As such, the conceptual framework in this study is based, in part, on the notion that background and precollege characteristics (e.g., age, gender) influence African American students' engagement. Research has also shown that institutional differences affect student outcomes (Pascarella & Terenzini, 1991, 2005). Studies even indicate that students' perceptions of their institutional environments may play a role in determining the quality of their experiences and even contribute to or negatively affect their academic and social development (Pascarella & Terenzini, 2005). Thus, students' perceptions of their institutions are included in the analytical model.

Another line of college student development research suggests that students' academic experiences in college are important factors in understanding student development outcomes (Astin, 1993; Laird, Bridges, Morelon-Quainoo, Williams, & Holmes 2007; Pascarella & Terenzini, 1991, 2005; Terenzini, Springer, Pascarella, & Nora, 1995). Thus, proxy variables to account for these types of academic factors (i.e., grade point average, year in school) were included in the regression equations. As the conceptual literature on student development indicates, it is also important to take into account how a student spends his or her time outside of class (Chickering & Reisser, 1993; Pascarella & Terenzini, 2005). Of particular interest in this study were students' experiences in what may be characterized as nonacademic activities and experiences (e.g., working on and off campus). Additionally, as informed by prior research (Flowers & Pascarella, 1999; Pascarella, Flowers, & Whitt, 2001; Pascarella & Terenzini, 2005) to control for other potentially confounding nonacademic activities, the regression model includes variables such as Greek affiliation, residence status, and participation in athletics.

Data Source

The primary data source for this study was the 2004 administration of the National Survey of Student Engagement (NSSE). As described by McCormick, Moore, and Kuh in chapter 9, NSSE is designed to measure students' participation in educational experiences that prior research has connected to valued and desired educational outcomes (Chickering & Reisser, 1993; Kuh, 2001, 2003). This dataset contains data from a national sample of college students from participating institutions. In 2004, approximately 163,000 students were randomly selected from files provided by the 472 participating colleges and universities (National Survey of Student Engagement, 2004). In the current study, data from 4,598 African American students were analyzed. Of the total number, 38% worked on campus and 48% worked off campus.

Variables

Based on previous research (Furr & Elling, 2000; Horn & Berktold, 1998; Pascarella et al., 1994; Pascarella et al., 1998), the primary independent variables were students' self-reports of the numbers of hours they spent working on and off campus per week. The dependent variables in this study consisted of four composite measures of self-reported student engagement during college that were chosen based on their use in an extensive number of studies measuring student engagement in college (e.g., Kuh, 2001, 2003; Laird et al., 2007; National Survey of Student Engagement, 2004; Pascarella & Terenzini, 2005). The first scale, Academic Challenge, is an 11-item measure assessing how students expend their effort in engaging in academic activities (e.g., "Number of assigned textbooks, books, or book-length packs of course readings," "Number of written papers or reports of 20 pages or more," "Applying theories or concepts to practical problems or in new situations"). The second scale, Active and Collaborative Learning, is a 7-item scale assessing students' experiences in learning activities that foster student–student interactions and participation in a learning community (e.g., "Asked questions in class or contributed to class discussions," "Made a class presentation," "Worked with classmates outside of class to prepare class assignments"). The third scale, Enriching Educationally Experiences, is a 12-item scale assessing the degree of effort expended engaging in academic experiences (e.g., "Practicum, internship, field experience, co-op experience, or clinical assignment," "Participate in a learning community or some other formal program where groups of students take two or more classes together," "Study abroad"). The fourth scale, Student–Faculty Interaction, is a 6-item scale assessing students' interactions with faculty with regard to academic activities (e.g., "Discussed grades or assignments with an instructor," "Talked about career plans with a faculty member or advisor," "Discussed ideas from your readings or classes with faculty members outside of class").

Based on the conceptual framework and previous research (Pascarella & Terenzini, 1991, 2005), the present study incorporated a number of control variables. The first set of control variables consisted of two precollege and demographic characteristics: gender and age. The second set of control variables consisted of students' perceptions of the institutional environment: perceptions of the extent to which the institution provided academic support, perceptions of the extent to which the institution provided help with nonacademic issues, perceptions of the extent to which the institution provided assistance to enable students to excel socially on campus, and college racial composition. Students' academic experiences constituted the third set of control variables: year in school, college major, enrollment status, and college grades. The analytical model also included students' nonacademic experiences outside of the classroom: Greek affiliation, college residence, and participation in athletics. Precedent for using these control variables can be found in other research estimating the impact of college on student development and academic achievement (e.g., Flowers & Pascarella, 1999; Hayek, Carini, O'Day, & Kuh, 2002; Pascarella, Bohr, Nora, & Terenzini, 1995; Pascarella et al., 1994; Pascarella et al., 1998; Pascarella & Terenzini, 1991, 2005; Terenzini et al., 1995). Operational definitions of the dependent, independent, and control variables are shown in Table 5. Descriptive statistics of selected variables are reported in Table 6.

TABLE 5
Operational Definitions of Variables From the NSSE Included in the Analyses

Dependent Variable

Academic Challenge: An 11-item scale designed to assess the extent to which students engaged in academic work (Cronbach alpha = .72).

Active and Collaborative Learning: A 7-item scale assessing students' participation in various learning activities designed to promote learning (Cronbach alpha = .63).

Enriching Educational Experiences: A 12-item scale assessing the extent to which students participated in academic and social activities to enhance the college experience (Cronbach alpha = .56).

Student–Faculty Interaction: A 6-item scale measuring the magnitude and type of students' interactions of faculty (Cronbach alpha = .76).

Independent Variables

Hours worked on campus: An interval-scaled variable based on a student's self-report of the number of hours he or she worked on campus in a given week was coded: 1 = 0; 2 = 1–5; 3 = 6–10; 4 = 11–15; 5 = 16–20; 6 = 21–25; 7 = 26–30; 8 = more than 30.

Hours worked off campus: An interval-scaled variable based on a student's self-report of the number of hours he or she worked off campus in a given week was coded: 1 = 0; 2 = 1–5; 3 = 6–10; 4 = 11–15; 5 = 16–20; 6 = 21–25; 7 = 26–30; 8 = more than 30.

Control Variables

Gender: A categorical variable was coded: 1 = female, 0 = male.

Age: A categorical variable was coded: 1 = 19 or younger; 2 = 20–23 years; 3 = 24–29 years; 4 = 30–39 years; 5 = 40–55 years; 6 = older than 55.

Providing the support you need to succeed academically: An interval-scaled variable based on a student's self-reported assessment of the extent to which his or her institution offered academic support was coded: 1 = very little; 2 = some; 3 = quite a bit; 4 = very much.

Helping you cope with your nonacademic responsibilities: An interval-scaled variable based on a student's self-reported assessment of the degree of support he or she perceived when dealing with issues indirectly related to academic challenges was coded: 1 = very little; 2 = some; 3 = quite a bit; 4 = very much.

Providing the support you need to thrive socially: An interval-scaled variable based on a student's self-reported assessment regarding his or her perceptions of the magnitude of help the institution provided to support the student's social development was coded: 1 = very little; 2 = some; 3 = quite a bit; 4 = very much.

TABLE 5 (Continued)

Control Variables (Continued)

College racial composition: A categorical variable based on the college racial composition of the institution was coded: 1 = historically Black college and university; 0 = other college and university.

Year in school: A categorical variable based on a student's classification was coded: 1 = freshman; 2 = sophomore; 3 = junior; 4 = senior; 5 = Unclassified.

College major: A categorical variable based on a student's field of study was coded: 1 = Arts; 2 = Biology; 3 = Business; 4 = Education; 5 = Engineering; 6 = Physical Science; 7 = Professional; 8 = Social Science; 9 = Other; 10 = Undecided.

Enrollment status: A categorical variable based on a student's enrollment pattern during the academic year was coded: 1 = Full time, 0 = Part time.

College grades: A categorical variable based on a student's self-reported grade point average was coded: 1 = C– or lower; 2 = C; 3 = C+; 4 = B–; 5 = B; 6 = B+; 7 = A–; 8 = A.

Greek affiliation: A categorical variable based on a student's participation in Greek-lettered organizations was coded: 1 = Greek-affiliated, 0 = non-Greek-affiliated.

Residence status: A categorical variable based on a student's living arrangements in college was coded: 1 = lived on campus; 0 = lived off campus.

Athletic participation: A categorical variable based on whether a student participated in intercollegiate athletics was coded: 1 = participate in intercollegiate athletics, 0 = did not participate in intercollegiate athletics.

Analytical Procedures

The analytical techniques utilized for this study were based on previous research and scholarship produced on this topic (Pascarella & Terenzini, 1991, 2005). In the first stage of analysis, ordinary least squares regression (Pedhazur, 1997) was used to estimate the direct effects of working on and off campus on African American students' involvement in educational activities. Accordingly, the effects of working in college were determined by regressing each dependent variable on the two variables indicating the number of hours students' worked in college on and off campus while statistically controlling for demographic characteristics, institutional characteristics, and academic and nonacademic variables. The second stage of data analysis explored conditional effects (Pascarella & Terenzini, 1991) or interactions among the variables in the conceptual framework (Pedhazur, 1997) and the

TABLE 6
Descriptive Statistics of NSSE Variables

Variables	Mean	Standard Deviation
Gender	.72	.44
Age	2.28	1.38
Providing the support you need to succeed academically	3.23	.79
Helping you cope with your nonacademic responsibilities	3.02	.87
Providing the support you need to thrive socially	2.29	.99
College racial composition	.22	.41
Year in school	2.58	1.45
College major	5.42	2.83
Enrollment status	.84	.36
College grades	5.15	1.81
Greek affiliation	.07	.26
Residence status	.40	.49
Athletic participation	.07	.25
Hours worked on campus	3.41	2.89
Hours worked off campus	1.82	1.56

outcome variables. Accordingly, cross-product terms were produced by multiplying the variables of interest (e.g., gender, college racial composition, residence status, athletic participation) with the other variables in the regression equation to determine whether these cross-product variables significantly increased the variance in the direct effects models. Precedent for examining conditional effects in this manner can be found in other research exploring the impact of college on student outcomes (Flowers & Pascarella, 1999; Pascarella, Pierson, Wolniak, & Terenzini, 2004; Pascarella & Terenzini, 1991, 2005). Because of the large sample size utilized in the present study, results were reported significant at $p < .001$.

Limitations

This research study has several limitations. First, although this study sought to assess the effects of working on and off campus on African American students' academic engagement, no attempt was made to describe the unique features of individual work experiences or the quality of the work environment. Future studies may generate deeper insights by considering the actual experiences that college students encounter while working during college. As such, in the present study, the term *work* referred to all types of experiences in which students reported that they were paid by an employer. As a result, the generalizability of the findings to all working conditions and related contexts may be tenuous. Second, although the data come from a national database, institutions and students self-selected to participate in the data collection. The self-reported responses of students who participated in the study may differ from those students who were invited to participate but declined and from those students from institutions that did not choose to participate in NSSE.

Results

Using cross-sectional data from a national sample of African American college students, the study estimates the relationship between working in college and self-reported measures of engagement in educationally rich academic and social experiences. The student engagement variables measured the type and amount of academic work performed, frequency of class participation and collaborative learning, and the extent of interactions students had with faculty.

Table 7 summarizes the relationship between the hours students worked each week in college on and off campus on African American students' engagement. In the presence of statistical controls including demographic

TABLE 7
Summary of the Regression Analyses Examining the Relationship Between Working On and Off Campus and Engagement for African American Students

	Regression Coefficients		
	Working On	Working Off	
Student Engagement	Campus	Campus	R^2
Academic Challenge	.545*	.365*	.281
	(.060)	(.073)	
Active and Collaborative Learning	1.076*	.439*	.225
	(.096)	(.071)	
Enriching Educational Experiences	1.136*	.224	.303
	(.105)	(.038)	
Student–Faculty Interaction	1.975*	.305	.252
	(.152)	(.043)	

Note: Top number is the unstandardized regression coefficient, number in parentheses is the standardized regression coefficient. The full results are available from the author upon request.
*$p < .001$

characteristics and college grade point average, working while enrolled is positively related to student engagement in activities that enhance student academic development. Specifically, controlling for the other variables in the equation, regressing the working on-campus variable on each dependent variable resulted in statistically significant and positive regression coefficients for all four student engagement scales: Academic Challenge (b = .545), Active and Collaborative Learning (b = 1.076), Enriching Educational Experiences (b = 1.136), and the Student–Faculty Interaction (b = 1.975).

Table 7 also summarizes the direct effects of working off campus on students' engagement in college. Controlling for a wide array of factors including the number of hours students worked on campus, the number of hours students reported working off campus was positive related to two of the four scales: Academic Challenge (b = .365) and Active and Collaborative Learning (b = .439).

The second stage of data analysis considered whether the effects of working on and off campus on student engagement varied based on gender, college racial composition, residence status, and athletic participation (Pascarella & Terenzini, 1991; Pedhazur, 1997). Nonstatistically significant increases in R^2 (after the cross-product terms were introduced to the general models) indicate that the effects of working on student engagement among African Americans did not differ by gender, college racial composition, or athletic participation. However, a statistically significant increase in R^2 suggests that the relationship between working during college and student engagement is different for students who live on campus than for students who live off campus. More specifically, the relationship between working on campus and exposure to educationally enriching experiences was greater for students who lived on campus (b = 1.200) than for students who lived off campus (b = .947). Also, the relationship between working off campus and exposure to educationally enriching experiences was greater for students who lived on campus (b = .766) than for students who lived off campus. The relationship between working on campus and student–faculty interactions was greater for students who lived on campus (b = 2.222) than for students who lived off campus (b = 1.679). See Table 8.

Discussion and Implications

Likely reflecting the need to pay tuition and other costs, African American students expend a considerable amount of time working on and off campus throughout the academic year. This reality supports the need to provide students, parents, student affairs professionals, and other stakeholders with information regarding whether the financial benefits of working while enrolled in college are justifiable in terms of academic and social development.

TABLE 8
Summary of Conditional Effects of Working On Campus and Off Campus on Educational Experiences and Faculty Interactions for African American Students

Characteristic	Working On Campus	Working Off Campus
Enriching Educational Experiences		
Live on campus	1.200*	.766*
	(.121)	(.074)
Life off campus	.947*	.106
	(.081)	(.018)
Student–Faulty Interactions		
Live on campus	2.222*	.714
	(.177)	(.054)
Live off campus	1.679*	.196
	(.124)	(.028)

Note: Top number is the unstandardized regression coefficient, number in parentheses is the standardized regression coefficient. The full results are available from the author upon request.
*$p < .001$

The present study sought to address this important issue by estimating the impact of working while in college on African American students' perceptions of their engagement in college utilizing a national sample of students attending four-year colleges and universities that participated in the 2004 NSSE. Accordingly, this study was informed by extensive research on the effects of college on student development (Astin, 1993; Pascarella & Terenzini, 1991, 2005), which has demonstrated that the impact of working while enrolled in college on student development is best examined by controlling for demographic characteristics and institutional characteristics.

This study yields two major findings. First, controlling for other variables, African American college students' engagement is positively related to working on campus. Second, partialling out the influence of working on campus, working off campus also positively influences the extent to which students engaged in educational experiences on campus, but to a lesser extent.

These findings indicate that time spent working on and off campus is beneficial for African American students and is associated with participation in intellectually stimulating engagement opportunities. This result is consistent with previous research conducted on multiethnic student samples (Furr & Elling, 2000; Pascarella et al., 1994; Pascarella et al., 1998; Pascarella & Terenzini, 2005). However, the magnitude of the effects of working while enrolled in college seems to depend on whether the students work on campus or off campus. Consistent with other research (Pascarella & Terenzini, 1991), as the amount of time that students worked on campus increased, so did engagement in academic experiences regardless of how measured. Working off campus was positively related to only two of the four engagement scales (i.e., Enriching Educational Experiences scale and Student–Faculty Interaction scale). Moreover, the magnitude of the regression coefficients for the other two engagement scales was smaller for working off campus than for on campus, suggesting that hours worked off campus are not associated with the same types of engagement as is working on campus for African American students. Given previous literature (Pascarella & Terenzini, 1991, 2005), working while in college may provide students with opportunities to develop skills that enable them to integrate successfully into the academic and social community of their college or university. Working on campus may promote this outcome in a way that enables students to spend even more time engaging in activities that have been shown to enhance cognitive development in college. Based on an extensive review of the literature on the effects of working while attending college, Pascarella and Terenzini (2005) note:

> It may be that, for a substantial number of students who work during college, employment provides a context in which they acquire efficient organizational skills and work habits. As a result, they may be able to compensate for less study time by using the study time available more efficiently. (p. 133)

This quote seems to support the findings reported in this study and suggests that working in moderate levels has the potential to enhance student development for African American students. But, as research suggests (Astin, 1993; Furr & Elling, 2000), the effects of working on students' academic and social development in college vary based on the type of work (Horn & Berktold, 1998; Pascarella & Terenzini, 2005).

Conclusion

In terms of practical implications of this research, given the financial need for African American students to work while enrolled in college, student affairs professionals must provide students with information about the potential pitfalls of working in college. This study reinforces the importance of informing African American students about various on-campus employment options, given that on-campus employment is associated with greater benefits to student engagement than is off-campus employment. The findings also support the need for high school counselors to ensure that college-bound African American students receive information about successfully navigating the academic and employment culture in college to enable them to better understand the implications of working while enrolled as related to their academic development in college.

References

Astin, A. W. (1993). *What matters in college: Four critical years revisited.* San Francisco: Jossey-Bass.

Chickering, A. W., & Reisser, L. (1993). *Education and identity* (2nd ed.). San Francisco: Jossey-Bass.

Choy, S. (2004). *Paying for college: Changes between 1990 and 2000 for full-time dependent undergraduates* (NCES 2004–075). Washington, DC: U.S. Department of Education, National Center for Education Statistics.

College Board. (2008a). *Trends in college pricing.* Washington, DC: Author.

College Board. (2008b). *Trends in student aid.* Washington, DC: Author.

Flowers, L. A., Osterlind, S. J., Pascarella, E. T., & Pierson, C. T. (2001). How much do students learn in college? Cross-sectional estimates using the College BASE. *Journal of Higher Education, 72,* 565–583.

Flowers, L. A., & Pascarella, E. T. (1999). Cognitive effects of college racial composition on African American students after 3 years of college. *Journal of College Student Development, 40,* 669–677.

Furr, S. R., & Elling, T. W. (2000). The influence of work on college student development. *NASPA Journal, 37,* 454–470.

Hauptman, A. M. (2007). Higher education finance: Trends and issues. In J. J. F. Forest & P. G. Altbach (Eds.), *International handbook of higher education* (pp. 83–106). Dordrecht, The Netherlands: Springer.

Hayek, J. C., Carini, R. M., O'Day, P. T., & Kuh, G. D. (2002). Triumph or tragedy: Comparing student engagement levels of members of Greek-letter organizations and other students. *Journal of College Student Development, 43,* 643–663.

Horn, L. J., & Berktold, J. (1998). *Profile of undergraduates in U.S. postsecondary education institutions: 1995–96* (NCES 98–084). Washington, DC: U.S. Department of Education, National Center for Education Statistics.

Horn, L., & Nevill, S. (2006). *Profile of undergraduates in U.S. postsecondary education institutions: 2003–04, With a special analysis of community college students* (NCES 2006–184). Washington, DC: U.S. Department of Education, National Center for Education Statistics.

Hussar, W. J., & Bailey, T. M. (2008). *Projections of education statistics to 2017* (NCES 2008–078). Washington, DC: U.S. Department of Education, National Center for Education Statistics.

King, J. E. (1999). Helping students balance work, borrowing, and college. *About Campus, 4*(4), 17–22.

Kuh, G. D. (2001). Assessing what really matters to student learning: Inside the National Survey of Student Engagement. *Change, 33*(3), 10–17, 66.

Kuh, G. D. (2003). What we're learning about student engagement from NSSE. *Change, 35*(2), 24–32.

Laird, T. F. N., Bridges, B. K., Morelon-Quainoo, C. L., Williams, J. M., & Holmes, M. S. (2007). African American and Hispanic student engagement at minority serving and predominantly white institutions. *Journal of College Student Development, 48*, 1–18.

Miller, K., Danner, F., & Staten, R. (2008). Relationship of work hours with selected health behaviors and academic progress among a college student cohort. *Journal of American College Health, 56*, 675–679.

National Survey of Student Engagement. (2004). *Student engagement pathways to collegiate success: 2004 annual survey results.* Bloomington: Indiana University Center for Postsecondary Research.

Pascarella, E. T. (1985). College environmental influences on learning and cognitive development: A critical review and synthesis. In J. Smart (Ed.), *Higher education: Handbook of theory and research* (pp. 1–61). New York: Agathon.

Pascarella, E., Bohr, L., Nora, A., Desler, M., & Zusman, B. (1994). Impacts of on-campus and off-campus work on first-year cognitive outcomes. *Journal of College Student Development, 35*, 364–376.

Pascarella, E. T., Bohr, L., Nora, A., & Terenzini, P. T. (1995). Cognitive effects of two-year and four-year colleges: New evidence. *Educational Evaluation and Policy Analysis, 17*, 83–96.

Pascarella, E. T., Edison, M. I., Nora, A., Serra Hagedorn, L., & Terenzini, P. T. (1998). Does work inhibit cognitive development during college? *Educational Evaluation and Policy Analysis, 20*, 75–93.

Pascarella, E. T., Flowers, L. A., & Whitt, E. J. (2001). Cognitive effects of Greek affiliation in college: Additional evidence. *NASPA Journal, 38*, 280–301.

Pascarella, E. T., Pierson, C. T., Wolniak, G. C., & Terenzini, P. T. (2004). First-generation college students: Additional evidence on college experiences and outcomes. *Journal of Higher Education, 75*, 249–284.

Pascarella, E. T., & Terenzini, P. T. (1991). *How college affects students: Findings and insights from twenty years of research.* San Francisco: Jossey-Bass.

Pascarella, E. T., & Terenzini, P. T. (2005). *How college affects students: A third decade of research* (2nd ed.). San Francisco: Jossey-Bass.

Pedhazur, E. J. (1997). *Multiple regression in behavioral research: Explanation and prediction* (3rd ed.). Orlando, FL: Harcourt Brace College.

Snyder, T. D., Dillow, S. A., & Hoffman, C. M. (2008). *Digest of education statistics 2007* (NCES 2008–022). Washington, DC: U.S. Department of Education, National Center for Education Statistics.

St. John, E. P., & Paulsen, M. B. (2001). The finance of higher education: Implications for theory, research, policy, and practice. In M. B. Paulsen & J. C. Smart (Eds.), *The finance of higher education: Theory, research, policy & practice* (pp. 545–568). New York: Agathon Press.

Terenzini, P. T., Springer, L., Pascarella, E. T., & Nora, A. (1995). Influences affecting the development of students' critical thinking skills. *Research in Higher Education, 36*, 23–39.

Tinto, V. (1993). *Leaving college: Rethinking the causes and cures of student attrition* (2nd ed.). Chicago: University of Chicago Press.

II

IMPACT OF WORKING ON UNDERGRADUATE STUDENTS' INTERACTIONS WITH FACULTY

Paul D. Umbach, Ryan D. Padgett, and Ernest T. Pascarella

Three decades of research on college students indicates that faculty members play a central role in the development of undergraduate students (Astin, 1993; Kuh & Hu, 2001; Pascarella & Terenzini, 1991, 2005; Umbach & Wawrzynski, 2005). Studies suggest that out-of-classroom interactions with faculty are positively associated with gains in academic and cognitive development (Terenzini, Pascarella, & Blimling, 1996), personal and intellectual growth (Astin, 1993; Endo & Harpel, 1982; Pascarella & Terenzini, 2005), and student satisfaction (Kuh & Hu, 2001; Endo & Harpel, 1982). These interactions are frequently the best predictors of student persistence (Braxton, Sullivan, & Johnson, 1997; Pascarella & Terenzini, 1991; Stage & Hossler, 2000). Likewise, instructional approaches, such as cooperative learning, teacher organization and clarity, and high expectations for students, positively influence cognitive growth (Pascarella & Terenzini, 1991, 2005; Pascarella, Edison, Nora, Hagedorn, & Braxton, 1996).

Although we know a good deal about how faculty affect the student experience and student learning, we know relatively little about the extent to which working college students engage with faculty in ways that contribute to their growth while in college. Although many students must work to cover college costs and acquire career-related experiences, it is reasonable to assume that, because time is finite, working during college likely reduces the amount of time available for interacting with faculty and fully engaging in the collegiate experience (Pascarella & Terenzini, 2005; Stinebrickner & Stinebrickner, 2004). Relatively few studies have examined whether working inhibits

This research was supported by a generous grant from the Center of Inquiry in the Liberal Arts at Wabash College to the Center for Research on Undergraduate Education at the University of Iowa.

student relationships, both in and out of the classroom, and the amount of effort students put into their studies. In turn, little, if any research has examined whether experiences with faculty differentially affect the cognitive growth of working students.

Purpose and Research Questions

To address this knowledge gap, this chapter explores working students' experiences with faculty. The purposes of this study are fourfold. First, this chapter explores the relationship between working while in college and students' in- and out-of-class experiences with faculty members. Second, we examine whether working relates to growth in cognitive outcomes after the first year of college. Third, this study tests whether certain faculty approaches to instruction are particularly useful in reducing any differences in cognitive growth that we see after the first year of college. Finally, based on our findings, we suggest practical ways that policymakers, college administrators, and faculty can enhance the college experience and student learning for undergraduates who work. Three questions guide our research:

1. To what extent do students who work engage in best practices in education, particularly those related to college faculty, at the same level as their nonworking student peers?
2. After the first year of college, to what degree is working related to cognitive outcomes, such as need for cognition, critical thinking, and positive attitude toward literacy?
3. Are there particular best practices that ameliorate differences in cognitive outcomes between working and nonworking students?

The chapter begins by describing the best practices in undergraduate education that are said to contribute to student learning and an exploration of studies that apply these best practices to students who work while in college. We then describe the methodology and analytical approach we employ to answer our research questions. We follow our discussion of methods with a full explanation of the results of our analysis. Finally, we conclude the chapter with a discussion of our findings and of policies and practices that policymakers, administrators, and faculty can use to ensure a positive educational experience for working college students.

Background

The Seven Principles for Good Practice in Undergraduate Education highlight the importance of recognizing the complicated interaction between content and pedagogy (Chickering & Gamson, 1987, 1991) and serve as a guide for this study of students who work. These practices are encouraging cooperation among students, encouraging active learning, communicating high expectations, encouraging contact between students and faculty, giving prompt feedback, respecting diverse talents and ways of learning, and emphasizing time on task. As Chickering and Gamson (1987) suggest, faculty and their relationships with students are central to these practices. Yet, because time is finite, students who work likely do not have as much time to fully engage in the learning experience as do their nonworking counterparts.

Within this larger context of best practices in undergraduate education is the underlying value placed on pedagogical strategies and the incorporation of socialization as a mechanism toward active learning. Encouragement of student–faculty contact both within and outside the classroom is considered the most important principle in supporting student motivation and involvement within the collegiate environment (Chickering & Gamson, 1987). This principle focuses less on the role of the faculty member as a content instructor and more on the importance of interpersonal relationships between faculty and student. Interpersonal interactions with faculty are often viewed as an intricate and enduring part of the college experience (Pascarella & Terenzini, 1991). Moreover, the influence of faculty interactions is enhanced when contact moves beyond the classroom and into out-of-class experiences (Kuh, 1995; Pascarella & Terenzini, 2005). These interpersonal interactions can range from encouraging and supporting intellectual endeavors and future career goals to personal discussions unrelated to academics. However, evidence suggests that informal interactions that focus on intellectual and substantive material have a greater impact on student learning (Pascarella & Terenzini, 2005).

A substantial amount of research supporting the Seven Principles has focused on college teaching and the importance of student–faculty contact (Sorcinelli, 1991). Since Chickering and Gamson's work nearly two decades ago, a myriad of researchers have evaluated the impact of student–faculty contact on a number of college outcomes. The empirical evidence suggests that frequent student–faculty contact positively influences student learning and development (e.g. Astin, 1993; Kuh & Hu, 2001; Pascarella & Terenzini, 1991, 2005), cognitive development (Cruce, Wolniak, Seifert, & Pascarella, 2006; Pascarella & Terenzini, 2005; Terenzini, Pascarella, et al., 1996), and personal and intellectual growth (Astin, 1993). Examining the effects of student–faculty interaction during the 1990s, Kuh and Hu conclude that these interactions positively influence a student's effort to engage in other educationally purposeful activities during his or her undergraduate studies.

Surprisingly few studies have examined the effects of student employment on interactions with faculty in and out of the classroom. By definition, the amount of time allocated toward working hinders student involvement in other college learning experiences (Astin, 1993; Furr & Elling, 2000; Horn & Berktold, 1998; King & Bannon, 2002; Pascarella & Terenzini, 2005). It seems that working students must sacrifice key socialization opportunities because some time is absorbed by work. Weidman (1989) argues that to fully understand college impact, researchers must focus on the socialization of students. He cites Brim's (1966) definition of socialization: "the process by which persons acquire the knowledge, skills, and dispositions that make them more or less effective members of their society" (Weidman, 1989, p. 293). However, research suggests that working on campus may serve as a valuable mechanism of socialization. In particular, maintaining a part-time on-campus job increases the likelihood of working or interacting with faculty (Astin, 1993, 1999). In some cases, these arrangements have students working directly for or with a faculty member. Even if students do not work closely with a faculty member as part of their job, increasing the time spent on campus increases the likelihood that students will encounter faculty members on an informal basis. Employment opportunities that keep the student within the college environment allow the student to participate in out-of-class interactions and collaborations with faculty.

Two studies in particular examine the effects of student employment on the amount of time allocated toward faculty interactions; both find mixed results. Using data from the College Student Experience Questionnaire, Lundberg (2004) investigated the effect of working off campus on various levels of involvement in college experiences. Lundberg found students who work off campus more than 20 hours per week report significantly lower levels of interactions with faculty than do other students. However, working 20 hours or more per week off campus did not have a negative effect on learning. These results suggest that students working off campus compensate for their low levels of faculty interactions in ways that do not hinder their learning (Lundberg, 2004).

The second study was not limited to working off campus. Based on a single-institution sample, Furr and Elling (2000) surveyed undergraduate students on the relationship of work to their involvement in college. Furr and Elling found that working while in college is negatively related to frequency of interactions with faculty. Nonworking students were also more likely to establish a meaningful relationship with a faculty member. Examining the dichotomy of working on campus versus working off, Furr and Elling found that students who are employed off campus are less likely to interact with faculty. Conversely, student employment on campus had a positive effect on the levels of interactions with faculty.

The effect of working while in college on cognitive outcomes is also somewhat limited and inconclusive. Similar to the findings on the levels of engagement for working students, evidence on the impact of college employment on cognitive outcomes is inconsistent (Gellin, 2003; Padgett & Grady, in press; Pascarella & Terenzini, 2005). Some research suggests that working on campus during the first year of college is associated with gains in reading and mathematics skills, but unrelated to gains in critical thinking skills (Terenzini, Yaeger, Pascarella, & Nora, 1996). Others find no substantive difference in gains in reading comprehension, mathematics, and critical thinking between students who work on or off campus (Pascarella, Bohr, Nora, Desler, & Zusman, 1994; Pascarella, Bohr, Nora, & Terenzini, 1996; Pascarella, Edison, Nora, Hagedorn, & Terenzini, 1998). Some research shows that the number of hours worked on or off campus during the first year of college does not affect reading comprehension, mathematics, or critical thinking (Pascarella et al., 1994), while other research (Inman & Pascarella, 1998) suggests that working negatively affects the development of critical thinking skills.

From this research, we draw several conclusions that guide our analysis. First, relatively few studies have examined the extent to which working students engage with best practices as they relate to college faculty. Those that have explored these constructs have mixed results and often rely on limited samples or inadequate data. Many of these studies are limited because they rely on descriptive analyses of self-reported data or do not control for important precollege characteristics. Second, few studies have examined the relationship between working and cognitive development, and those that have find mixed effects. Third, it is important to examine both the place of work (on or off campus) as well as the number of hours worked. Clearly, where and how much students work affect their college experience. Finally, previous research provides little guidance to faculty about specific techniques or approaches that are particularly effective in providing a learning environment that encourages the cognitive growth of college students who work.

Method

Sample and Data Collection

We utilize student-level data from 19 institutions that participated in the Wabash National Study of Liberal Arts Education (WNSLAE), a longitudinal study investigating the effects of liberal arts experiences on various cognitive and psychosocial outcomes. The colleges and universities participating in the study represent a variety of characteristics including institution type and control, size, location, and patterns of student residence. However, because the study was primarily concerned with the experiences of students attending liberal arts colleges, liberal arts colleges were purposefully overrepresented. According to the 2007 Carnegie Classification of Institutions, 3 of the participating institutions were considered research universities, 3 were regional universities that did not grant the doctorate, 2 were two-year community colleges, and 11 were liberal arts colleges.

The initial sample was selected in either of two ways. First, for larger institutions, students were selected randomly from the incoming first-year class at each institution. The only exception was at the largest participating institution in the study, where the sample was selected randomly from the incoming class in the College of Arts and Sciences. Second, for a number of the smallest institutions in the study—all liberal arts colleges—the sample was the entire incoming first-year class.

The data collection was conducted in two waves. The initial data collection took place in early fall 2006 with 4,501 students participating.[1] Student demographic information, family background characteristics, high school experiences, and various precollege measures on cognitive and psychosocial outcomes were collected at time one. The follow-up data collection was conducted in spring 2007 and 3,081 students responded (approximately 68% of those who participated in fall 2006). Two complementary survey instruments were administered to measure a myriad of student college experiences, student engagement, and exposure to good practices: the National Survey of Student Engagement and the WNSLAE Student Experiences Survey.

In addition, a range of posttest measures on the cognitive outcomes were collected. Although all students completed most of the instruments chosen to measure college outcomes, there were two exceptions, one of which, the CAAP Critical Thinking Test, we use for this study. Because of concerns about the length of time required to complete the instruments, approximately half of the sample was selected to take the CAAP Critical Thinking Test while the other half took another assessment. Of the 3,081 students participating in both data collections, 1,485 had useable responses on the CAAP Critical Thinking Test.

After eliminating students with missing data, 2,994 students (97% of original completers)[2] remained in all of our analyses except the models of critical thinking (measured by the CAAP). A smaller subset, 1,431 students (96% of original completers) was used for a portion of the analyses because the CAAP was administered to approximately half of the larger group. Because men, students of color, and students with low ability responded at lower rates than their peers, we weighted the follow-up participant data to each institution's first-year undergraduate population by sex (male or female), race (Caucasian, African American/Black, Hispanic/Latino, Asian/Pacific Islander, or other), and ACT score (or COMPASS/SAT equivalent). This weighting cannot adjust for nonresponse bias but does make the sample more similar to the population from which it was drawn.

It is important to note that this chapter examines outcomes only after the first year of college and that the findings may differ if we explored these outcomes in subsequent years. Nonetheless, because the first year of college is very important to student success and development (Tinto, 1993; Upcraft & Gardner, 1989), particularly for students traditionally underserved by higher education (Terenzini et al., 1994), a snapshot of growth in the first year of college is particularly useful.

Analytical Approach

We conducted our analysis in three stages, each corresponding to one of our research questions. First, we ran a series of ordinary least squares (OLS) regressions to examine differences between working and nonworking students on nine best practices that faculty directly influence. We first ran these models with only the work variables to assess the effects of working without controlling for differences between students. We then ran our fully controlled models by adding measures of student background characteristics (precollege ability, gender, race, parental education, educational aspirations, precollege high school involvement) and the college student experience (institutional type, living on campus, student athlete status, and Greek status).

Second, we ran a series of OLS regressions exploring the relationship between working and cognitive outcomes. Our three dependent measures are a series of cognitive scores collected at the end of the first year of college. We used the same approach of entering variables into the regression in blocks. The first block includes only the work variables; the second block adds the control variables described previously, as well as a pretest measure for each of the cognitive outcomes.

Finally, we ran a series of models that extend the regressions of our cognitive outcomes models by adding interaction terms. For these models, we calculate cross-products of the nine best practices variables and the work variables to assess the possible differential relationship that the best practices have with the cognitive outcomes by different levels and types of work.

Dependent Measures

We use a variety of outcomes for the dependent variables, all of which were collected at both the beginning and end of the first year of college. For the first set of analyses, we used nine good practices, derived using factor analysis, that related to the faculty role in undergraduate education and that are linked to personal and intellectual growth. (A detailed description of all of the variables used in the models is available from the authors on request.) The first six are measures of good teaching and interactions with faculty: *Faculty interest in teaching and student development* (e.g., the extent to which faculty are interested in helping students grow in more than just academic areas, the extent to which faculty are generally interested in teaching, and the extent to which faculty are willing to spend time outside of class to discuss issues of interest and importance to students); *Prompt feedback* (e.g., how often faculty informed students of level of performance in a timely manner, how often faculty checked to see whether students had learned the material well before going on to new materials); *Quality and impact of nonclassroom interactions with faculty* (e.g., extent to which nonclassroom interactions with faculty have had an impact on intellectual growth and interest in items; personal growth, values, and attitudes; and career goals and aspirations); *Frequency of interactions with faculty* (e.g., how often students discussed grades or assignments with an instructor, how often students worked with faculty members on activities other than coursework such as committees, orientation, student life activities); *Overall exposure to clear and organized instruction* (e.g., frequency that faculty give clear explanation, frequency that faculty make good use of examples and illustration to explain difficult points, frequency that class time was used effectively, frequency that course goals and requirements were clearly explained); and *Cooperative learning* (e.g., in classes, students taught each other in addition to faculty teaching; participation in one or more study groups outside of class; how often one worked with other students on projects outside of class).

The final three good practice scales measure the extent to which faculty challenge students and have high expectations. These measures are *Academic challenge and effort* (e.g., how often students worked harder than they thought they could to meet an instructor's standards or expectations; number of hours a week spent preparing for class; extent to which the students' institution emphasizes spending significant amounts of time studying and on academic work; number of assigned textbooks, books, or book-length packs of course readings students read during current year); *Frequency of higher-order exams and assignments* (e.g., how often exams or assignments require students to write essays, compare or contrast topics or ideas from a course, argue for or against a particular point of view and defend an argument); and *Challenging classes and high faculty expectations* (e.g., how often faculty ask challenging questions in class; challenge students' ideas in class; ask students to argue for or against a particular point of view; ask students to point out any fallacies in basic ideas, principles, or points of view presented in the course).

In the second and third sets of analyses, we used three different cognitive measures as dependent variables. The first is the 18-item *need for cognition* scale. Need for cognition refers to an individual's "tendency to engage in and enjoy effortful cognitive activity" (Cacioppo, Petty, Feinstein, Blair, & Jarvis, 1996, p. 197). Those who have a high need for cognition "tend to seek, acquire, think about, reflect back on information to make sense of stimuli, relationships, and events in their world" (p. 198). In contrast, those with low need for cognition are more likely to rely on others, such as celebrities and experts, cognitive heuristics, or social comparison processes to provide or make sense of their world. The second cognitive outcome, *positive attitude toward literacy* (PATL), is a six-item construct designed to tap continuing motivation for lifelong learning. The PATL assesses students' enjoyment of such literacy activities as reading poetry and literature, reading scientific and historical material, and expressing ideas in writing. To assess *critical thinking*, we used the critical thinking module from the Collegiate Assessment of Academic Proficiency (CAAP) developed by the American College Testing Program (ACT).

Independent Measures

To account for differences in students' backgrounds and college experiences, we introduced several controls into our models. They include background variables such as sex, race, ACT composite score, and highest intended academic degree. We also include a measure of high school involvement. We also add a series of college experience variables including place of residence, working on and off campus, Greek affiliation, and member of a sponsored athletic team. We also control for institution type (e.g., community colleges, regional universities, and research universities) with liberal arts colleges serving as our reference group. In addition, pretest measures of educational outcomes serve as controls in our models. Because we have accounted for students' starting scores, we can more confidently attribute outcome scores to the college experience (Astin & Lee, 2003; Pascarella, 2006).

We represent student work and its various dimensions using a series of dummy-coded variables representing the amount of time students work on and off campus.[3] For students who work on campus, we code them as either working between 1 and 10 hours per week or more than 10 hours per week. Off-campus students are coded into three groups: working between 1 and 10 hours per week, working between 11 and 20 hours per week, and working more than 20 hours per week. The comparison group for all of the dummy-coded groups is composed of students who do not work.

Limitations

When examining our results, it is important to consider the limitations of our data. First, although the overall sample included a broad range of different kinds of postsecondary institutions from 11 different states, the inclusion of only 19 institutions that were not selected randomly means that we cannot generalize the results to the population of all two-year and four-year institutions in the United States. Indeed, because a major purpose of the WNSLAE was to estimate the impacts of liberal arts colleges and liberal arts education, liberal arts colleges were purposefully oversampled in the study. Although liberal arts colleges were oversampled in this study, it is important to note that 3 of the participating institutions were considered research universities,

3 were regional universities that did not grant the doctorate, and 2 were two-year community colleges. Our sample also includes only full-time, first-year students. As a result, working students represent only 55% of our sample, a substantially lower percentage than the national college student population.

A second limitation is that not all students who participated in the first (precollege) data collection participated in the second (follow-up) data collection. The 68.5% persistence rate in the WNSLAE from the first to second data collections is quite consistent with other large longitudinal studies requiring a substantial amount of participation in terms of time and intellectual effort (see, for example, the National Study of Student Learning; Pascarella et al., 1998). However, attrition from the first to second data collection is a limitation of the study. Although our weighting procedures adjusted the final sample for respondent bias by sex, race/ethnicity, tested precollege academic ability, and institution, the results may suffer from nonresponse bias.

Results

Working and Perceptions of Good Teaching and Interactions With Faculty

Table 1 summarizes the OLS regression results for the relationship between working and student interactions with faculty in and out of the classroom. Because the dependent measures in all of our models are standardized (mean = 0, standard deviation = 1), we can describe these coefficients as a proportion of a standard deviation difference between the target group and the reference group (nonworking students). We observed mixed results regarding the relationship between working and student perceptions of good teaching and their interactions with faculty. When only work is included in the models (see Model I), in general, working on campus less than 10 hours per week is positively related to student perceptions, and working off campus more than 20 hours per week is negatively related, relative to not working.

After adding controls for student background, college experiences, and institution type, many of the differences between students who work and those who do not disappear (see Model II). However, when differences persist, working on campus tends to have a positive relationship and working a large number of hours off campus tends to have a negative relationship with perceptions of teaching and interactions with faculty. Compared with students who do not work, students who work more than 20 hours per week off campus rate the quality of nonclassroom interactions with faculty lower and participate less frequently in cooperative learning. Students who work on campus, regardless of the amount, interact more frequently with faculty than do nonworking students. Interestingly, students who work off campus less than 20 hours a week also report more frequent interactions with faculty

TABLE 1

Summary Results of Relationship (Represented as a Proportion of a Standard Deviation Difference Between Target Group and Reference) Between Working and Measures of Good Teaching and Interactions With Faculty

Work:	Faculty Interest in Student Development and Teaching		Teaching Clarity and Organization		Cooperative Learning		Prompt Feedback		Quality of Nonclassroom Interactions		Frequency of Interactions	
	Model I[a]	Model II[b]	Model I[a]	Model II[b]	Model I[a]	Model II[b]	Model I[a]	Model II[b]	Model I[a]	Model II[b]	Model I[a]	Model II[b]
0 hours (reference)												
On 1–10 hrs/wk	0.165***	0.006	0.044	−0.071	0.184***	0.089	0.196***	0.059	0.210***	0.056	0.288***	0.216***
On > 10 hrs/wk	−0.032	−0.086	−0.060	−0.075	−0.053	−0.062	0.025	0.018	−0.009	−0.051	0.290***	0.226***
Off 1–10 hrs/wk	−0.016	−0.038	−0.099	−0.128	0.040	0.031	0.041	0.028	0.094	0.036	0.329***	0.243***
Off 11–20 hrs/wk	−0.011	−0.020	−0.049	0.070	−0.436***	−0.280***	−0.041	0.041	0.080	0.087	0.096	0.128*
Off > 20 hrs/wk	−0.059	−0.047	0.010	−0.061	−0.596***	−0.222**	−0.223**	−0.156	−0.268**	−0.228**	−0.202**	−0.057
R^2	0.005	0.079	0.002	0.052	0.042	0.153	0.011	0.084	0.014	0.099	0.032	0.133
N =	2,772											

[a]Model I includes only work variables with students who do not work as reference group.
[b]Model II has controls for precollege ability (ACT/SAT), gender, race, parental education, educational aspirations, precollege high school involvement, institutional type, living on campus, student athlete status, and Greek status.
*$p < .05$, **$p < .01$, ***$p < .001$

244

than their nonworking peers do. Perhaps these off-campus student workers are forced to effectively manage their time and, as a result, seek to take advantage of any opportunity to interact with faculty.

Working and Challenge, Effort, and Faculty Expectations

The models of academic challenge and student effort reveal similar patterns (see Table 2). In general, the uncontrolled models (see Model I) suggest that students who work a few hours on campus are more challenged and put more effort into their academics than nonworking students do. In contrast, students who work a lot of hours off campus generally put less effort into their coursework and are expected to do less. When we control for possible confounding variables (see Model II), many of these differences are erased, yet one troubling difference persists. Students who work off campus more than 10 hours per week report statistically significantly lower levels of academic challenge and effort than nonworking students do. Students who work 11 to 20 hours a week off campus score 0.16 standard deviation (SD) lower than nonworking students; students who work more than 20 hours per week off campus score one quarter SD lower than nonworking students on this measure.

Working and Cognitive Outcomes

Table 3 summarizes results of the relationship between working and cognitive outcomes of the first year of college. Similar to the results of the previous models, when we include only work variables in our models (Model I), we see substantial differences between working and nonworking students. Students who work on campus less than 10 hours per week score higher than nonworking students on all three of the cognitive measures. For two of the three measures (needed for cognition and critical thinking), students who work any amount off campus score lower than nonworking students.

In the fully controlled models (Model II), differences between groups disappear, with a few notable exceptions. Working more than 10 hours per week on campus continues to be associated with a more positive attitude toward literacy. More compelling are the relationships between working off campus and critical thinking. Even after controlling for the critical thinking pretest and a host of other variables, students who work off campus more than 10 hours per week score approximately 0.15 to 0.16 SD lower on critical thinking than do nonworking students after one year of college. We explore this relationship further in the following section.

Interaction Effects of Working and Good Practices on Critical Thinking

Because of the substantive differences observed between levels of work and critical thinking, we examined only critical thinking and possible conditional

TABLE 2
Summary Results of Relationship (Represented as a Proportion of a Standard Deviation Difference Between Target Group and Reference) Between Working and Measures of Academic Challenge and Faculty Expectations

Work:	Challenging Classes and High Expectations		Academic Challenge and Effort		Frequency of Higher-Order Assessments	
	Model I[a]	Model II[b]	Model I[a]	Model II[b]	Model I[a]	Model II[b]
0 hours (reference)						
On 1–10 hrs/wk	0.190***	0.034	0.135**	0.045	0.161**	0.041
On >10 hrs/wk	−0.013	−0.039	−0.012	−0.01	0.116	0.031
Off 1–10 hours/wk	−0.034	−0.043	0.005	−0.066	0.124	0.048
Off 11–20 hrs/wk	−0.185**	−0.087	−0.277***	−0.164*	−0.04	−0.097
Off >20 hrs/wk	−0.187*	0.034	−0.51***	−0.254**	0.392***	0.383***
R^2	0.001	0.078	0.026	0.159	0.013	0.073
$N=$	2,772					

[a] Model I includes only work variables with students who do not work as reference group.
[b] Model II has controls for precollege ability (ACT/SAT), gender, race, parental education, educational aspirations, precollege high school involvement, institutional type, living on campus, student athlete status, and Greek status.

* $p < .05$, ** $p < .01$, *** $p < .001$

TABLE 3

Summary Results of Relationship (Represented as a Proportion of a Standard Deviation Difference Between Target Group and Reference) Between Working and Cognitive Development After the First Year of College

Work	Need for Cognition		Positive Attitude Toward Literacy		Critical Thinking	
	Model I[a]	Model II[b]	Model[a]	Model II[b]	Model I[a]	Model II[b]
0 hours (reference)						
On 1–10 hrs/wk	0.131**	−0.053	0.250***	0.048	0.157*	0.007
On >10 hrs/wk	−0.017	−0.012	0.172**	0.135**	−0.037	0.079
Off 1–10 hours/wk	−0.215**	−0.048	0.033	0.015	−0.411***	−0.080
Off 11–20 hrs/wk	−0.352***	−0.051	−0.081	0.026	−0.779***	−0.158**
Off >20 hrs/wk	−0.190**	−0.104	−0.208**	−0.030	−1.088***	−0.154*
R^2	0.131	0.756	0.123	0.755	0.346	0.844
N	2,772	2,772	2,772	2,772	1,336	1,336

[a] Model I includes only work variables with students who do not work as reference group.

[b] Model II has controls for outcome pre-test precollege ability (ACT/SAT), gender, race, parental education, educational aspirations, precollege high school involvement, institutional type, living on campus, student athlete status, and Greek status.

* $p < .05$, ** $p < .01$, *** $p < .001$

effects of work and good practices. The intent of this analysis is to uncover possible practices that particularly enhance the critical thinking of working students who appear to score lower on the critical thinking outcome—that is, students who work more than 10 hours per week off campus. Table 4 presents the coefficients for measures of working, good practices, and the interaction of working and good practices on critical thinking.

The interaction terms suggest that many of the good practices contribute to critical thinking differently for working students than for nonworking students. In particular, the interaction between working more than 20 hours per week off campus and four good practice measures—cooperative learning, challenging classes and high expectations, academic challenge and effort, and frequency of higher-order assessments—has a positive interaction effect on critical thinking. In other words, the differences in critical thinking between nonworking students and students who work off campus more than 20 hours per week is greatly reduced when students who work substantial hours off campus participate in cooperative learning, are challenged by faculty, are given assignments and tests that tap into higher-order thinking, and put effort into their academic work.

The interaction effect of working and cooperative learning on critical thinking serves as a good example of how good practices may ameliorate the difference in critical thinking after the first year of college. See Figure 1 for a graphical representation of this interaction. At low levels of cooperative learning (–1 SD), the gap in the critical thinking score between nonworking students and students who work more than 20 hours per week on campus is substantial (more than 0.20 SD). As we move toward the mean of critical thinking the gap reduces substantially. When the frequency of cooperative learning is high (1 SD), the gap is quite small, and students who work more than 20 hours per week even score slightly higher in their critical thinking. The patterns for the challenging classes and high expectations, academic challenge and effort, and frequency of higher-order assessments are nearly identical to that of cooperative learning. This pattern suggests that, although students who work a large number of hours have lower gains in critical thinking in their first year of college, the differences between nonworking students and students who work more than 20 hours per week off campus can be reduced if faculty members structure their classes in ways that encourage cooperative learning and challenge students to do their best work.

Discussion and Implications

In this chapter, we seek to provide a comprehensive look at working students' experiences with faculty and the relationship between working and cognitive growth after the first year of college. Our findings offer both good

TABLE 4
Summary of Effects of Work, Good Practices, and Interaction of Work and Good Practices on Critical Thinking

	Faculty Interest Dev and Teaching	Teaching Clarity and Organization	Cooperative Learning	Prompt Feedback	Quality Nonclassroom Interactions	Frequency of Interactions	Challenging Classes/High Expectations	Academic Challenge and Effort	Frequency of Higher-Order Assessment
Work									
0 hours (reference)									
On 1–10 hrs/wk	0.005	0.001	0.005	0.007	-0.001	0.016	0.000	-0.002	0.001
On >10 hrs/wk	0.072	0.067	0.056	0.081	0.086	0.087	0.057	0.051	0.078
Off 1–10 hrs/wk	-0.084	-0.061	-0.071	-0.083	-0.073	-0.067	-0.047*	-0.062	-0.080
Off 11–20 hrs/wk	-0.154**	-0.166**	-0.158**	-0.160**	-0.154**	-0.153**	-0.151**	-0.150**	-0.173**
Off >20 hrs/wk	-0.169*	-0.168*	-0.072	-0.143*	-0.127*	-0.143*	-0.131*	-0.078	-0.174*
Good practice	0.056*	0.051*	-0.008	0.014	0.03	-0.015	0.019	0.007	-0.038
Interaction: Good practice × work									
On 1–10 hrs/wk	-0.056	0.023	-0.005	0.001	-0.087	-0.022	-0.052	-0.015	-0.007
On >10 hrs/wk	-0.052	-0.081	-0.107	0.016	-0.011	-0.063	-0.085	-0.084	-0.003
Off 1–10 hours/wk	-0.053	0.176***	0.044	0.096	0.157***	-0.072	0.233**	0.215***	0.201***
Off 11–20 hrs/wk	0.031	0.001	0.012	0.056	0.015	-0.037	0.004	0.029	-0.069
Off >20 hrs/wk	-0.115	-0.003	0.172***	0.025	0.086	-0.03	0.100*	0.135*	0.180**
R^2	0.845	0.848	0.847	0.845	0.847	0.845	0.848	0.847	0.848

Note: Model I has controls for outcome pretest, precollege ability (ACT/SAT), gender, race, parental education, educational aspirations, precollege high school involvement, institutional type, living on campus, student athlete status, and Greek status.

* $p < .05$, ** $p < .01$, *** $p < .001$

FIGURE 1
Interaction Effect of Working and Cooperative Learning on Critical Thinking

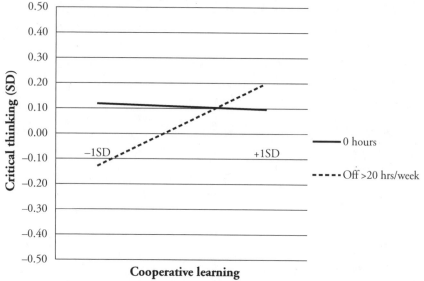

news and bad news about students who work. The good news is that, in most cases, college student employment does not appear to negatively affect student interactions with faculty or cognitive development. Working students are not significantly different from nonworking students in terms of their beliefs about faculty interest in student development and teaching, prompt feedback, teaching clarity, and in-class challenging activities and high expectations, regardless of the numbers of hours worked and whether they work on or off campus (Table 1). Students who work on campus and students who work less than 20 hours per week off campus more frequently interact with faculty off campus than nonworking students do. Perhaps more promising is the finding that working students were statistically similar to nonworking students on two of our three cognitive outcomes (Table 2).

However, our analysis raises some concern for those students who work off campus more than 20 hours a week, and to some extent those who work off campus between 10 and 20 hours per week. Students who work more than 10 hours per week off campus participate less frequently in cooperative learning and are less challenged academically and put forth less effort. This group also reports lower levels of critical thinking after the first year of college, when compared with nonworking students. In addition, students employed more than 20 hours a week off campus report fewer quality interactions with faculty than do unemployed students.

Although these findings contribute significantly to previous research, it is still far from clear whether working enhances or inhibits students' experiences with faculty or cognitive development. For many of the measures here, working seems to have little or no negative effect on relationships with faculty or cognitive outcomes. Students who work more than 20 hours a week off campus experience lower quality relationships with faculty and less growth in critical thinking. It is important, however, to keep in mind that these findings are based largely on a traditionally aged, full-time college student population. These findings may differ for adult populations and part-time students; future research should explore whether such differences exist. In addition, whereas the sample for this study includes students at liberal arts colleges, research universities, regional universities, and community colleges, a study with a more nationally representative sample may yield different results.

Nevertheless, in terms of the critical thinking reductions accrued by working many hours off campus during the first year of college, there is some hope. If these working students engage in above average levels of cooperative learning, are challenged by their faculty, put forth above average effort, and are given assessments that tap higher-order cognitive skills, the differences in critical thinking between nonworking students and students employed off campus for more than 20 hours per week all but disappear. The challenge is that on many of these measures, those working long hours in off-campus jobs are among the least likely to engage in the activities that will benefit them the most. Therefore, it is incumbent on faculty to be imaginative in creating an environment that fosters the development of these working students. Following, we outline some specific suggestions that will particularly benefit working students but will likely enhance the learning of all students.

Faculty members are encouraged to find creative ways to engage students in cooperative learning both in and out of the classroom. Because working students may not have time to work in groups outside of class, faculty who value collaborative work are advised to structure their in-class activities in ways that get students working together. Outside the classroom, faculty might rely on technology to get students to engage in cooperative learning. Asynchronous online discussion groups or places where students can collaborate on online documents are ways to engage students and can be done at any time of the day.

It is important that faculty members set high expectations and are clear about how much effort they expect from students in their classes. Effort does not appear to be a problem isolated to working students, but working students appear to put forth less effort and effort affects them differently from how it affects nonworking students. According to one national study (National Survey of Student Engagement, 2007), students spend approximately 13–14 hours per week studying, which is approximately half of what faculty believe they should. To what extent do faculty communicate these expectations and put in place procedures to ensure that students are putting forth the effort they need to be successful?

Similarly, faculty would be advised to create tests and assignments that require students to synthesize, analyze, and apply the things they are learning in and out of the class. These types of "deep learning" activities have been associated with a variety of positive outcomes (see Nelson Laird, Shoup, Kuh, & Schwarz, 2008). Essay assignments and exams that require students to defend an argument, apply something they have learned in class, and integrate ideas across classes are all useful examples. Requiring students to critique assigned readings is another example of a higher-order assessment. Whereas these assignments are particularly beneficial to working students, all students can benefit from the opportunity to use higher-order thinking skills.

Although we need to be cautious not to overgeneralize our findings given the relatively limited sample, the results of this study may have important implications for state, federal, and institutional aid policies. With the tightening of state and federal aid to students and the shift in emphasis to merit aid over need-based aid, students are increasingly reliant on income they generate while working in college. Students who gain access to college but who are forced to work long hours in an off-campus job have a markedly different collegiate experience than do those who do not work, particularly in terms of such important outcomes as critical thinking. Aid policies that completely fill the financial gap or reduce the number of hours students must work may free students' time to focus on their academic work. Because working on campus appears to have only a positive relationship or no relationship with measures of good teaching and interactions with faculty, institutions and policymakers might find ways to grow on-campus work opportunities.

Serving students who work is likely best accomplished in a campus-wide effort. Although this study focuses on student employment, all students can benefit from a campus culture that encourages faculty to engage in best practices described here. For more than a decade, scholars (see Austin, 1990, 1996; Feldman & Paulsen, 1999; Massy, Wilger, & Colbeck, 1994; Paulsen & Feldman, 1995; Umbach, 2007) have described ways to create a teaching culture and their suggestions may be instructive as we consider ways to best serve working students. For example, some suggest emphasizing teaching in faculty recruitment and hiring processes. Simple things, such as asking candidates to teach a class as part of their interview, are powerful symbols of the importance of teaching on a campus. Many institutions have faculty reward structures that place heavy emphasis on research. Colleges with a teaching culture have reward structures that more equally balance teaching and research or place greater emphasis on teaching. Some (Feldman & Paulsen, 1999; Paulsen & Feldman, 1995; Umbach, 2007) also argue that the creation or elevation of a teaching center is an important step in creating a teaching culture. Perhaps these centers could place special emphasis on how to best serve working students.

Whereas this study provides answers to some questions regarding student employment, it leaves many questions unanswered and offers direction for future research. For example, research that explores similar constructs using a more nationally representative sample, at both the college and student levels, is an important next step. This would not only allow for an exploration of part-time students, many of whom work, but would also create an opportunity to explore differences in college-level effects, such as climate and representation of working students on a campus, on the experiences of working students.

In addition to broader sampling, future research might extend the current body of literature regarding student employment by improving on the measurement of key work variables. As noted by other chapter authors, this study and many others rely on crude categorical measures of hours worked. The cut points used to designate hours worked in the survey data collection process are often randomly prescribed. A continuous measure would allow researchers to explore more fully nonlinear relationships between hours worked and the outcomes explored in this study and give a more complete picture of the effects of time spent working. Other studies might collect better information on the type of work students are doing and how it influences the college experience and cognitive growth. For example, do students who work in jobs that contribute to their career goals experience the same levels of development as students who do menial work?

Future inquiry might also pursue whether the Seven Principles for Good Practice in Undergraduate Education are appropriate and beneficial for all populations. This study suggests that these practices have differential effects on working students, but in many cases, do little to reduce differences between students who work and those who do not. As other chapters in this book suggest, college students are growing increasingly diverse. Who was once considered a nontraditional student may now in fact be traditional. Students are older and more likely to work than they were when Chickering and Gamson penned the Seven Principles. The Seven Principles, created nearly two decades ago, and related research tend to assume a one-size-fits-all philosophy that, on its face, looks like what was once a "traditional" college experience. Given the growing number of working students in college and the limited amount of time these working students have, perhaps there are other, more time-efficient practices that are effective at yielding positive outcomes. Perhaps it is time to revisit these principles and see whether other practices are more effective in enhancing the growth and development of today's undergraduates, particularly those who work.

Conclusion

This chapter tells a cautionary tale about students who work while in college and the faculty who teach working students. Although the story for college students who work is not entirely bad, colleges and their faculty should be on alert that working students often experience college differently from how their nonworking peers do. Students who work long hours off campus might not be getting a quality educational experience and are perhaps hindering their cognitive development. To serve these students better, faculty members and working students need to act in concert to create a culture that enhances the likelihood of success for all students. Because an overwhelming majority of college students work, seeking ways to enrich their experience will likely become a necessity to both working students and colleges and universities.

Endnotes

1. Of the 16,570 students who were invited to participate, 4,501 responded, resulting in a 27% response rate. This is a lower bounds estimate because ACT, the group in charge of the data collection, estimates that approximately one half to one third of the overall sample did not receive an invitation.

2. We analyzed the missing data but discerned no statistically significant relationship based on race/ethnicity, gender, ACT/SAT, and work. It is reasonable to expect that little bias is introduced when less than 5% of the sample is deleted because of missing data. Therefore, we used listwise deletion for the analyses.

3. We tested models including variables for the 101 students who work both on and off campus. None of these variables were statistically significant, perhaps because of low statistical power, and none substantively changed the effects of the other work variables. Therefore, we dropped them from the models.

References

Astin, A. W. (1993). *What matters in college? Four critical years revisited.* San Francisco: Jossey-Bass.

Astin, A. W. (1999). Student involvement: A developmental theory for higher education. *Journal of College Student Development, 40,* 518–529.

Astin, A. W., & Lee, J. J. (2003). How risky are one-shot cross-sectional assessments of undergraduate students? *Research in Higher Education, 44,* 657–672.

Austin, A. E. (1990). Faculty cultures, faculty values. In W. G. Tierney (Ed.), *Assessing academic climates and cultures* (Vol. 68, pp. 61–74). San Francisco: Jossey-Bass.

Austin, A. E. (1996). Institutional and departmental cultures: The relationship between teaching and research. In J. M. Braxton (Ed.), *Faculty teaching and research: Is there a conflict?* (Vol. 90, pp. 61–74). San Francisco: Jossey-Bass.

Braxton, J. M., Sullivan, A. S., & Johnson, R. M. (1997). Appraising Tinto's theory of college student departure. In J. C. Smart (Ed.), *Higher education: Handbook of theory and research* (Vol. 12, pp. 107–164). New York: Agathon.

Brim, O. G. (1966). Socialization through the life cycle. In O. G. Brim & S. Wheeler (Eds.). *Socialization after childhood: Two essays.* New York: John Wiley & Sons.

Cacioppo, J. T., Petty, R. E., Feinstein, J. A., Blair, W., & Jarvis, G. (1996). Dispositional differences in cognitive motivation: The life and times of individuals varying in need for cognition. *Psychological Bulletin, 119*(2), 197–253.

Chickering, A. W., & Gamson, Z. F. (1987). Seven principles for good practice in undergraduate education. *AAHE Bulletin, 39*(7), 3–7.

Chickering, A. W., & Gamson, Z. F. (1991). Applying the seven principles for good practice in higher education. *New Directions for Teaching and Learning, 47*, 1–104.

Cruce, T. M., Wolniak, G. C., Seifert, T. A., & Pascarella, E. T. (2006). Impacts of good practices on cognitive development, learning orientations, and graduate degree plans during the first year of college. *Journal of College Student Development, 47*(4), 365–383.

Endo, J. J., & Harpel, R. L. (1982). The effect of student–faculty interaction on student outcomes. *Research in Higher Education, 16*(2), 115–138.

Feldman, K. A., & Paulsen, M. B. (1999). Faculty motivation: The role of a supportive teaching culture. In M. Theall (Ed.), *Motivations from within: Approaches for encouraging faculty and students to excel* (Vol. 78). San Francisco: Jossey-Bass.

Furr, S. R., & Elling, T. W. (2000). The influence of work on college student development. *NASPA Journal, 37*(2), 454–470.

Gellin, A. (2003). The effect of undergraduate student involvement on critical thinking: A meta-analysis of the literature 1991–2000. *Journal of College Student Development, 44*(6), 746–762.

Horn, L. J., & Berktold, J. (1998). *Profile of undergraduates in U.S. postsecondary education institutions: 1995–96.* Washington, DC: U.S. Department of Education, National Center for Education Statistics.

Inman, P., & Pascarella, E. T. (1998). The impact of college residence on the development of critical thinking skills in college freshmen. *Journal of College Student Development, 39*(6), 557–568.

King, T., & Bannon, E. (2002). *At what cost? The price that working students pay for a college education.* Washington, DC: U.S. Public Interest Research Group.

Kuh, G. D. (1995). The other curriculum: Out-of-class experiences associated with student learning and personal development. *Journal of Higher Education, 66*(2), 123–155.

Kuh, G. D., & Hu, S. (2001). The effects of student–faculty interaction in the 1990's. *Review of Higher Education, 24*(3), 309–332.

Lundberg, C. A. (2004). Working and learning: The role of involvement for employed students. *NASPA Journal, 41*(2), 201–215.

Massy, W. F., Wilger, A. K., & Colbeck, C. (1994). Overcoming "hallowed" collegiality. *Change, 26*(4), 11–20.

National Survey of Student Engagement. (2007). *Experiences that matter: Enhancing student learning and success* (2007 Annual Report). Bloomington, IN: Author.

Nelson Laird, T. F., Shoup, R., Kuh, G. D., & Schwarz, M. J. (2008).The effects of discipline on deep approaches to student learning and college outcomes. *Research in Higher Education, 49*, 469–494.

Padgett, R. D., & Grady, D. L. (in press). Student development and personal growth in employment: A review of the literature. In B. Perozzi (Ed.), *Enhancing student learning through college employment.* Bloomington, IN: Association of College Unions International.

Pascarella, E. T. (2006). How college affects students: Ten directions for future research. *Journal of College Student Development, 47*(5), 508–520.

Pascarella, E. T., Bohr, L., Nora, A., Desler, M., & Zusman, B. (1994). Impacts of on-campus and off-campus work on first-year cognitive outcomes. *Journal of College Student Development, 35*, 364–370.

Pascarella, E. T., Bohr, L., Nora, A., & Terenzini, P. T. (1996). Is differential exposure to college linked to the development of critical thinking? *Research in Higher Education, 37*, 159–174.

Pascarella, E. T., Edison, M. I., Nora, A., Hagedorn, L. S., & Braxton, J. M. (1996). Effects of teacher organization/preparation and teacher skill/clarity on general cognitive skills in college. *Journal of College Student Development, 37*(1), 7–19.

Pascarella, E. T., Edison, M. I., Nora, A., Hagedorn, L. S., & Terenzini, P. T. (1998). Does work inhibit cognitive development during college? *Educational Evaluation and Policy Analysis, 20*(2), 75–93.

Pascarella, E. T., & Terenzini, P. T. (1991). *How college affects students.* San Francisco: Jossey-Bass.

Pascarella, E. T., & Terenzini, P. T. (2005). *How college affects students: A third decade of research* (Vol. 2). San Francisco: Jossey-Bass.

Paulsen, M. B., & Feldman, K. A. (1995). *Taking teaching seriously: Meeting the challenge of instructional improvement.* Washington, DC: George Washington University.

Sorcinelli, M. D. (1991). Research findings on the seven principles. *New Directions for Teaching and Learning, 47*, 13–23.

Stage, F. K., & Hossler, D. (2000). Where is the student? Linking student behaviors, college choice, and college persistence. In J. M. Braxton (Ed.), *Reworking the student departure puzzle* (pp. 170–195). Nashville, TN: Vanderbilt University Press.

Stinebrickner, R., & Stinebrickner, T. R. (2004). Time-use and college outcomes. *Journal of Econometrics, 121*(1/2), 243–269.

Terenzini, P. T., Pascarella, E. T., & Blimling, G. S. (1996). Students' out of classroom experiences and their influence on learning and cognitive development: A literature review. *Journal of College Student Development, 37*(2), 149–162.

Terenzini, P. T., Rendon, L. I., Upcraft, M. L., Millar, S. B., Allison, K. A., Gregg, P. L., & Jalomo, R. (1994). The transition to college: Diverse students, diverse stories. *Research in Higher Education, 35*, 57–73.

Terenzini, P. T., Yaeger, P. M., Pascarella, E. T., & Nora, A. (1996, May). *Work-study program influences on college students' cognitive development.* Paper presented at the meeting of the Association for Institutional Research, Albuquerque, NM.

Tinto, V. (1993). *Leaving college: Rethinking the causes and cures of student attrition* (2nd ed.). Chicago: University of Chicago Press.

Umbach, P. D. (2007). Faculty cultures and college teaching. In R. P. Perry & J. C. Smart (Eds.), *The scholarship of teaching and learning in higher education: An evidence-based perspective*. New York: Springer.

Umbach, P. D., & Wawrzynski, M. R. (2005). Faculty do matter: The role of college faculty in student learning and engagement. *Research in Higher Education, 46,* 153–184.

Upcraft, M., & Gardner, J. (1989). A comprehensive approach to enhancing freshman success. In M. Upcraft & J. Gardner (Eds.), *The freshman year experience: Helping students survive and succeed in college* (pp. 1–12). San Francisco: Jossey-Bass.

Weidman, J. (1989). Undergraduate socialization: A conceptual approach. In J. Smart (Ed.), *Higher education: Handbook of theory and research* (Vol. 5, pp. 289–322). New York: Agathon.

WORK AS A VEHICLE FOR IMPROVING EDUCATIONAL AND ECONOMIC ATTAINMENT

12

UNDERSTANDING THE RELATIONSHIP BETWEEN WORKING WHILE IN COLLEGE AND FUTURE SALARIES

Marvin A. Titus

As observed by authors of other chapters in this volume, the employment rate among undergraduate college students has risen substantially over the past few years. According to a report by Mortenson (2007), the percentage of college students who worked while enrolled increased from 45% to 55% between 1970 and 2006. Using data from the Current Population Survey (CPS) and the Bureau of Labor Statistics (BLS), Mortenson also reports that, over the same period, the employment rate of college students who were enrolled full time increased from 38% to 49%. According to a recent U.S. Department of Labor news release (2008), in fall 2007, 29% of all students who graduated from high school in 2006–2007 and enrolled in four-year institutions worked. A report by the American Council on Education (ACE, 2006) indicates that 78% of full-time college students who work are employed on a part-time basis.

College students who work would seem to be making time trade-offs with respect to the number of hours devoted to working versus studying. Nonetheless, some researchers (e.g., Baffoe-Bonnie & Golden, 2007) claim that, with regard to student outcomes, work time and study time may be complements rather than substitutes. Some analysts (Oettinger, 2005; Kalenkoski & Pabilonia, 2008) and authors of chapters in this volume (e.g., Flowers, chapter 10) attribute the increase in students working while enrolled in college to the rapid growth in the cost of attending higher education relative to family income and student financial aid.

An alternative explanation for students working while enrolled in college is that employment, particularly among traditional college-age (18-to 24-year-old) students enrolled at four-year institutions, further enhances the human capital that is being accumulated through their formal educational programs. Some studies (e.g., Stinebrickner & Stinebrickner, 2003) have used cross-sectional data to investigate the determinants of the number of hours that college students work, while other studies (e.g., Titus, 2006a, 2006b) examine the effects of working on persistence and degree completion. But little research examines the interconnections between hours worked while in college, bachelor's degree completion, and salary outcomes in the labor market. How working while in college affects student degree completion and labor market outcomes is of concern to policymakers. A recent report by the American Council on Education (2006) calls for more research in this area.

Guiding Framework

The framework for this study draws on concepts from the labor economics and college retention literature to examine students' decisions with regard to working while in college as well as how work influences the chance of college completion and salaries. This section discusses these concepts.

Several scholars (e.g., Ehrenberg & Sherman, 1987; Häkkinen, 2006) show that working while in college has a positive effect on the salary of graduates. This prior research suggests that college students may be participating in the labor market so as to maximize their initial salaries after completing college. College students who work may be faced with a work-time/study-time trade-off that is associated with possible risks and rewards. The risks may include reducing the chance of completing a college degree while the rewards may include a higher salary after graduating from college.

The student work-time/study-time trade-off may be viewed from the perspective of labor economics, specifically the microeconomic foundations of labor supply, and informed by the college retention literature. According to the microeconomics of labor theory, individuals are faced with the choice of allocating time between "renting their labor" (i.e., working) and nonmarket time such as leisure, or in the case of students, studying. This theory posits that a utility-maximizing college student chooses between spending time working and spending time on other activities, such as studying. For forward-thinking students, these choices may also be determined by the future costs and benefits associated with each activity. The future costs of spending additional hours working may include reducing the chance of completing a degree in a timely manner or increasing the likelihood of never completing the degree. The future benefits of allocating more time to working may include acquiring employer-valued skills and, consequently, increasing employer demand for the student, as measured by higher wages upon completion of college.

According to labor market theory, as the current wage rates increase, time becomes more expensive and students substitute less nonmarket time, such as the number of hours studied, with more hours worked. This increase in the allocation of time toward work is brought on by what is known as the substitution effect. The income effect, however, brought on by an increase in income beyond a certain level, may result in a decrease in the number of hours worked. The extent to which a college student works more or less hours depends on which effect dominates (see Figure 1). Because a student may increase leisure time as income increases (e.g., go to the movies with friends more often as income increases), this framework does not predict how a student will change her allocation of time devoted to study versus work in response to changes in current income. However, in general, the more hours an individual was working prior to a change in current wages, the larger the income effect. Because most traditional college-age students work part time, substitution effects are likely to dominate over income effects and result in an increase in the number of hours worked. The substitution effect may also result in the consumption of goods and services that require less time. For the college student, this may result in enrollment in courses that require less study time.

The extent to which a particular student works more hours and spends less time studying per week may also depend on the wage that is just sufficient for him to enter the labor market, or what is known as his reservation wage. In Figure 1, the reservation wage rate is equal to the steepness of the

FIGURE 1
Labor/nonlabor income versus hours of study/leisure

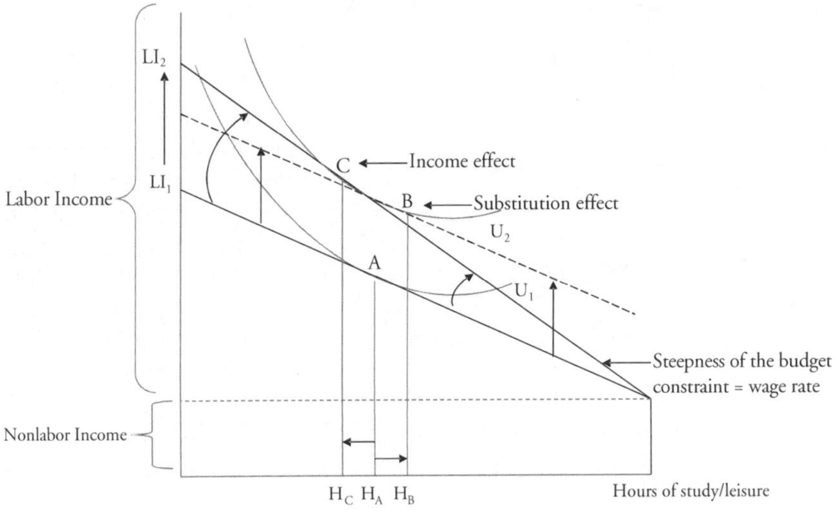

student's indifference curve, U_1 or U_2. When the market wage rate is more than the student's reservation wage, the student will increase his hours of work per week. Students with flatter indifference curves have lower reservation wages and a lower trade-off of income for nonlabor market activities, including studying. The steepness of a student's indifference curve also depends on preferences with respect to working. An individual's preference for working may be shaped by nonwage factors such as socioeconomic background.

While the number of hours worked per week by college students may be influenced by background characteristics and current income, future income may be influenced by college completion.[1] But the extent to which a college student works while enrolled may also influence the probability of completing a bachelor's degree.

The college retention literature (e.g., Astin, 1984, Bean, 1990; Tinto, 1993) addresses how students' chances of college completion are influenced by various factors such as student background characteristics, college experiences, and labor market participation, including the frequency of hours worked. With respect to such college student outcomes as retention, prior studies have produced mixed results. Using national data drawn from the first follow-up of the National Center for Education Statistics (NCES)–sponsored 1996 Beginning Postsecondary Students (BPS:96/98) survey and employing hierarchical linear modeling (HLM) techniques, Titus (2004) found that, among students who first enrolled as full-time freshmen at four-year institutions, the chance of retention after 3 years was positively related to the number of hours worked per week during the first year of college. Using the same dataset and statistical technique, a subsequent study (Titus, 2006b) showed that, for the same cohort of students, retention after 3 years was unrelated to the number of hours worked per week after controlling for financial characteristics of the institution attended. In a similar study, Titus (2006a) demonstrated that the chance of college completion 6 years after first enrolling in a four-year institution was negatively related to the hours worked per week in the first year of college.

The results of past research may be mixed because these studies treat the number of hours worked as an exogenous rather than as an endogenous variable.[2] Degree completion and labor supply decisions by college students may be considered singularly as well as jointly. To address this possibility, this chapter combines concepts from human capital theory (Becker, 1993; Mincer, 1974) and the student retention literature (Astin, 1984; Bean, 1990; Tinto, 1993) to examine how working while enrolled in college influences both the chance of bachelor's degree completion and salary outcomes in the labor market. Following the recommendation of Stinebrickner and Stinebrickner (2003), this study treats the number of hours a college student works per week as an endogenous variable.

Research Method

This study addresses the following four research questions:

1. What influences the number of hours worked per week during the first year of college among students enrolled at four-year institutions?
2. Taking into account the number of hours worked per week during the first year of college, what influences the number of hours worked per week during the third year of college among students enrolled at four-year institutions?
3. Taking into account the number of hours worked per week during the third year of college, what influences the chance of bachelor's degree completion 6 years after first enrolling among students enrolled at four-year institutions?
4. Six years after first enrolling in a four-year college or university, how is salary influenced by the number of hours worked per week during the third year of college?

This study draws on national data from the 1996 BPS (BPS:96/01) and the first (1998) and second (2001) follow-ups to that survey. This research examines the extent to which working while in college influences bachelor's degree completion and salary outcomes. In an effort not to confound the results of the study by including students who select to attend a community college and subsequently transfer to a four-year college or university, this study is limited to students who initially enrolled at four-year institutions. In this study, the initial analytic sample includes 3,116 students who first enrolled at a four-year institution in fall 1995 and earned at least $100 during 2001. The majority (66%) of the students in the sample were enrolled in public institutions; 34% were enrolled in private institutions.

Variables

This investigation uses four dependent variables in four separate models. In the first model, the dependent variable is the number of hours worked per week during 1995–1996, the first year of enrollment. Researchers (Stinebrickner & Stinebrickner, 2003) contend that prior studies on student employment and success do not take into account the endogeneity of hours worked while enrolled in college. Riggert, Boyle, Petrosko, Ash, and Rude-Parkins (2006) state that prior research examining the relationship between student success and working while in college has been beset by methodological limitations. This study addresses these limitations.

In the second model, the dependent variable is the number of hours worked per week during 1997–1998, the third year of enrollment. In the third model, the dependent variable is whether a student completed a bachelor's degree by the spring of 2001, 6 years after first enrolling. In the fourth model, the dependent variable reflects the annual salary in spring 2001.

In the first model, the independent variables measure the following student background characteristics: gender, race/ethnicity, socioeconomic status (i.e., parents' income and educational attainment), precollege academic ability (i.e., SAT scores), and unmet financial need. The second model adds cumulative grade point average and major field in 1997–1998 and the third model adds measures of involvement. Reflecting retention literature, student involvement is measured by whether the student lived on campus, participated in study groups, went out with friends, talked to an advisor, and talked to faculty outside of class, all during the student's first year. The student retention variables measure a student's academic performance in the first and third years, as well as satisfaction of the campus climate in the first year. It should be noted that like other variables described previously, satisfaction with the campus climate may be endogenous.

In the final model, the independent variables measure students' background characteristics, hours worked during 1997–1998, academic performance as of 2001, major field as of 2001, whether the student completed a bachelor's degree by 2001, and characteristics of labor market participation in 2001. Labor market characteristics are measured by whether a college degree was required for the job held in 2001, the number of hours per week worked in the job held in 2001, and job tenure (in months) as of 2001. To control for wage differentials between labor market areas, dummy variables for 54 U.S. jurisdictions (i.e., 50 states, the District of Columbia, and three territories) indicating the place of student resident in 2001 are included. Utilizing a Mincer-type (Mincer, 1974) approach to estimating wage equations, 26 different industries in which individuals are employed are also included to control for industry-specific differences in earnings. With the exception of number of hours worked, which is the focus of this study, all independent variables are treated as exogenous variables. Table 1 lists the variables utilized in the analyses.

With the relatively large number of cases and variables, as well as multiple data collections, the BPS is appropriate for examining the research questions. Nonetheless, despite its strengths, the BPS also has several limitations. First, because much of the BPS survey data are self-reported, the potential for measurement error exists. Second, the final follow-up to the 1996 BPS covers only 6 years after the student first enrolled in college. For some students, the time to bachelor's college degree completion may extend well beyond 6 years. Third, the BPS survey may not fully capture variables, such as family nonwage income or wealth, that may have an impact on such outcomes as college completion, occupational choice, or salary. To address the potential problem of omitted variable bias, a fixed-effects regression method

TABLE 1
Descriptive Statistics of Variables Used in the Analysis

Variables	Cases	Mean	Std. Dev.	Min.	Max.
Female	3,116	0.55	0.50	0	1
Asian	3,116	0.05	0.21	0	1
African American	3,116	0.09	0.29	0	1
Hispanic	3,116	0.06	0.23	0	1
White	3,116	0.79	0.41	0	1
Parents' educational background					
High school or less	3,116	0.28	0.45	0	1
Some college	3,116	0.17	0.38	0	1
Bachelor's degree	3,116	0.29	0.45	0	1
Master's degree or more	3,116	0.27	0.44	0	1
Parents' income (1995)	3,116	$64,929	$57,410	$0	$1,000,000
Unmet financial need	2,937	$2,136	$3,631	$0	$29,722
ACT/SAT score	3,116	960	202	400	1520
Declared a major during 1995–1996	3,116	0.71	0.46	0	1
Lived on campus during 1995–1996	3,116	0.73	0.44	0	1
Participated in study group during 1995–1996	3,116	0.24	0.43	0	1
Went out with friends during 1995–1996	3,116	0.70	0.46	0	1
Talked to advisor during 1995–1996	3,116	0.20	0.40	0	1
Talked to faculty during 1995–1996	3,116	0.24	0.43	0	1
Satisfied with campus climate during 1995–1996	3,116	0.87	0.34	0	1
Earned As or mostly As during 1995–1996	3,116	0.02	0.14	0	1
Earned Bs or mostly Bs during 1995–1996	3,116	0.38	0.48	0	1

TABLE 12.1 (Continued)

Variables	Cases	Mean	Std. Dev.	Min.	Max.
Earned Cs or mostly Cs during 1995–1996	3,116	0.43	0.50	0	1
Earned As or mostly As as of 1997–1998	2,808	0.39	0.49	0	1
Earned Bs or mostly Bs as of 1997–1998	2,808	0.55	0.50	0	1
Earned Cs or mostly Cs as of 1997–1998	2,808	0.06	0.24	0	1
Earned As or mostly As as of 2001	2,778	0.46	0.50	0	1
Earned Bs or mostly Bs as of 2001	2,778	0.51	0.50	0	1
Earned Cs or mostly Cs as of 2001	2,778	0.03	0.17	0	1
Declared a major during 1995–1996	3,116	0.71	0.45	0	1
Received a bachelor's degree by 2001	3,116	0.71	0.46	0	1
Hours worked per week while enrolled during 1995–1996	3,116	12	13	0	60
Hours worked per week while enrolled during 1997–1998	2,982	16	13	0	60
Major by 1997–1998					
Humanities	3,116	0.13	0.34	0	1
Social or behavioral sciences	3,116	0.16	0.37	0	1
Life sciences	3,116	0.06	0.24	0	1
Physical sciences	3,116	0.01	0.19	0	1
Math	3,116	0.01	0.10	0	1
Computer science	3,116	0.04	0.20	0	1
Engineering	3,116	0.07	0.25	0	1
Education	3,116	0.11	0.32	0	1

Major by 1997–1998					
Business	3,116	0.14	0.32	0	1
Health	3,116	0.07	0.26	0	1
Other	3,116	0.12	0.32	0	1
Undeclared	3,116	0.36	0.48	0	1
Enrolled part time any time during or after the third year	3,116	0.15	0.36	0	1
Major by spring 2001					
Humanities	3,064	0.16	0.37	0	1
Social or behavioral sciences	3,064	0.06	0.24	0	1
Life sciences	3,064	0.01	0.12	0	1
Physical sciences	3,064	0.01	0.10	0	1
Math	3,064	0.04	0.20	0	1
Computer science	3,064	0.07	0.25	0	1
Engineering	3,064	0.12	0.32	0	1
Education	3,064	0.20	0.40	0	1
Business	3,064	0.07	0.26	0	1
Health	3,064	0.03	0.17	0	1
Other	3,064	0.09	0.29	0	1
Undeclared	3,064	0.13	0.34	0	1
Completed a bachelor's degree by spring 2001	3,116	0.72	0.45	0	1
Labor market variables					
Job does not require a degree	3,015	0.49	0.50	0	1
Tenure (months)	3,115	147	124	1	1,103
Current job in 2001—average number of hours worked per week in	3,111	43	10	3	80
Annual salary in 2001	3,116	$31,361	$14,888	$100	$140,000

Source: BPS:96/2001

is used to estimate the salary model. A more detailed discussion of that method is provided in the following subsection.[3]

Statistical Methods

This study utilizes four statistical models, one for each dependent variable. Using ordinary least squares (OLS) regression, the first model examines the relationship between the number of hours worked per week while enrolled in college during 1995–1996 and students' background characteristics. Employing instrumental variable (IV) regression, the second model examines the possible endogenous nature of hours worked per week while enrolled in 1997–1998, instrumented by whether the student declared a major in 1995. IV regression techniques produce consistent parameter estimates when one or more of the independent variables are correlated with the error terms. Such correlation may be present when a variable that is related to an independent variable, but not to the error term, is omitted from the model. Omitted variables may cause OLS regression to produce biased and inconsistent estimates. IV regression, which involves using a predictor (an "instrument" for the variable in question), produces consistent parameter estimates.

Third, an IV probit regression investigates the relationship between the chance of completing a bachelor's degree within 6 years and the number of hours worked per week while enrolled during 1997–1998 as well as other variables. Because the number of hours worked is treated as an endogenous variable in this study, IV probit regression is employed. Similar to logit models, probit models allow for the estimation of binary outcomes when using regression techniques. Unlike logit models, which produce predicted log-odds, probit models utilize cumulative normal probability distributions and produce predicted probabilities. Stata, the econometric statistical software that is used in this study, does not have IV logit procedures. Therefore, IV probit regression is utilized for this research.

A fixed-effects IV regression model is used to analyze the relationship between annual salary in 2001 and the number of hours worked per week while enrolled in 1997–1998, taking into account labor market variables. The fixed-effects regression model takes into account unobserved labor market area and industry effects as well as individual heteroskedasticity, therefore providing rather efficient but conservative estimates of the pecuniary payoff to working while enrolled in college, completing a bachelor's degree, and other variables included in the analysis. The model's diagnostic statistics, specifically the Hansen *J* statistic, indicate that the number of hours worked per week in 1997–1998 is an endogenous variable that can be used to predict the annual salary earned in 2001 among individuals who first enrolled in four-year colleges and universities during fall 1995. The fixed-effects IV regression model is estimated via generalized methods of moments (GMM) techniques. GMM techniques allow analysts to take into account unobserved time-invariant individual-specific "fixed" effects when using panel or longitudinal data such as the BPS. To ease interpretation of the results, the coefficients of the variables in the fixed-effects IV regression are natural-log transformed.

All models are estimated using a technique that corrects for differences in the variance and standard errors resulting from intrainstitutional correlation. This technique produces robust standard errors, based on the clustering of students within institutions. Additionally, when analyzing data drawn from the BPS:96/2001, the appropriate NCES-provided sample weight is used. Consequently, all of the models described earlier produce parameter estimates based on weighted data.

Results

Descriptive analyses show that 64% of all students who first enrolled in a four-year college or university in fall 2005 worked during their first year of study. Among those students who worked in their first year, the average number of hours worked per week was 12. One third (33%) worked 10 to 20 hours per week, while 20% worked more than 20 hours per week and 12% worked 30 or more hours per week. Of those students who entered four-year institutions in fall 1995 and worked while enrolled during the academic 1997–1998 year, 72% were working in the third year after first enrolling. Among those students, the average number of hours worked per week was 16; 30% were working 30 or more hours per week.

Predictors of Hours Worked in the First Year

Table 2 shows that, among students who first enrolled at four-year institutions in fall 1995, the number of hours worked per week during the first year (1995–1996) was higher for Hispanics than for Whites. The number of hours worked per week was lower for students with parents who have a bachelor's or master's degree than for those whose parents did not attend college. Similarly, the number of hours worked was negatively related to parents' income. Students with ACT/SAT scores in the top quartile also averaged fewer hours of work per week than other students. Controlling for other background characteristics, the number of hours per week was negatively related to unmet need. This unexpected relationship may be explained by the possible offset that student earnings to financial aid received. In an effort to avoid experiencing a decline in financial aid, students with high unmet need may be working lower hours. Other analyses (available from the author on request) reveal that, among students attending four-year institutions, high unmet need increased the likelihood of working between 1 and 11 hours per week but was unrelated to the chance of working more than 11 hours.

TABLE 2
Predictors of Hours Worked per Week in 1995 Among Students Who Enrolled in Fall 1995 at Four-Year Colleges and Universities

	Beta Coefficient	Robust Std. Error
Gender		
Female	−1.026	0.536
Race/Ethnicity		
Asian	−2.073	1.038
African American	−1.557	1.082
Hispanic	3.040	1.319*
Parents' education		
Some college	−1.192	0.785
Bachelor's	−1.499	0.709*
Master's	−1.904	0.824*
Parents' income		
2nd quartile	−0.011	0.872
3rd quartile	−2.250	0.884*
4th quartile	−4.375	1.131**
ACT/SAT		
2nd quartile	−0.830	1.174
3rd quartile	−0.656	1.140
4th quartile	−3.777	1.256**
Unmet need ($1,000) during 1995–1996	−0.165	0.049***
Constant	17.980	1.470***
R^2	0.0509	
Number of students	2,812	

Note: Analyses conducted using OLS regression. Standard errors have been adjusted for clustering of institutions.
* $p < .05$, ** $p < .01$, *** $p < .001$
Source: BPS:96/2001

Predictors of Hours Worked in the Third Year

Taking into account the clustering of students within institutions, the endogenous nature of hours worked per week in the first year, and other variables, among students who were enrolled during the 1997–1998 academic year, the number of hours worked per week in the third year (1997–1998) was positively related to the number of hours worked in the first year (1995–1996). More specifically, Table 3 suggests that every hour worked per week in the

TABLE 3
Predictors of Hours Worked in 1998 Among Students Who Enrolled in Fall 1995 at Four-Year Colleges and Universities

	Beta Coefficient	Robust Std. Error
Hours worked in 1995—instrumented	0.966	0.398*
Gender		
Female	1.563	0.908
Male (reference group)		
Race/ethnicity		
Asian	−17.098	7.545*
African American	1.474	2.270
Hispanic	−3.295	2.336
White (reference group)		
Parents' education		
High school or less (reference group)		
Some college	0.521	1.119
Bachelor's	−0.067	1.316
Master's	−2.543	1.210*
Parents' income		
1st quartile (reference group)		
2nd quartile	−0.959	1.224
3rd quartile	−1.806	1.274
4th quartile	−2.027	1.627
Academic performance		
Earned As or mostly As as of 1997–1998	−3.225	2.954
Earned Bs or mostly Bs as of 1997–1998	−4.161	1.608*
Earned Cs or mostly Cs as of 1997–1998	−1.820	1.313
Earned Ds or mostly Ds as of 1997–1998 (reference group)		
Major in 1997–1998[a]		
Humanities	−7.554	3.403*
Social or behavioral sciences	−8.121	3.407*
Life sciences	−7.537	3.776*
Physical sciences	−9.493	5.673
Math	−1.364	7.339
Computer science	−6.026	3.852
Engineering	−17.743	5.345**
Education	−6.465	3.549
Business	−6.852	3.371*

TABLE 3 (Continued)

	Beta Coefficient	Robust Std. Error
Health	−7.183	3.679
Other	−7.137	3.459*
Undeclared (reference group)		
Constant	−45.865	44.259
Institution fixed-effects	Yes	
State fixed-effects	Yes	
Root mean square error	38.715	
Number of students	2,734	

Note: Analyses conducted using instrumental variable regression, which is estimated via generalized methods of moments (GMM). Standard errors have been adjusted for clustering of institutions. Instruments include independent variables listed in Table 1 and whether or not the student declared a major in 1995. The analysis is based on data weighted by the NCES-provided weight (B01AWT).
[a] Discrete change of dummy variable from 0 to 1.
* $p < .05$, ** $p < .01$, *** $p < .001$
Source: BPS:96/2001

first year, increased the number of hours worked per week in the third year by almost 1 hour.

Table 3 also indicates that, compared to those with undeclared majors, students who majored in humanities, social or behavioral sciences, life sciences, engineering, and business worked fewer hours per week in their third year. Students who earned mostly Bs in their third year worked fewer hours per week in that same time period than did students who earned mostly Ds. This finding, however, should be further examined for reverse causality. It is possible that hours worked per week influences academic performance. To test this hypothesis, using an IV regression model, academic performance in the third year was regressed against the endogenously determined number of hours worked per week in the same time period and academic performance in the first year. The findings indicate that the number of hours worked per week in the third year was unrelated to academic performance in that same year. One possible explanation for this result is that, by their third year, students may have figured out how much time to allocate between working and studying so that employment does not adversely affect their academic performance.

Predictors of Bachelor's Degree Completion

The instrumental variable (IV) probit regression analysis shows that the chance of completing a bachelor's degree within 6 years was negatively related to the number of hours worked during the third year, even after taking into account the endogenous nature of hours worked per week in the third year. Because the size of the estimated parameter for hours worked was quite small, the influence of the number of hours working per week in the third year had a negligible effect on the chance of completing a bachelor's degree within 6 years. Part-time enrollment any time after the second year was negatively related to the chance of degree completion by the sixth year. Other analyses, also using an IV probit regression model (results are available from the author on request), indicate that a student's chances of part-time enrollment in the sixth year were positively influenced by the number of hours worked per week in the third year. (See Table 4.)

Table 4 also shows that, after controlling for hours worked per week and other variables, the chance of completing a bachelor's degree within 6 years was higher for women than for men and for students who lived on campus during the last year of enrollment. The results suggest that faculty interaction with students in their first year had a lasting positive effect on the chance of completing a bachelor's degree within 6 years. The results also reveal that academic performance in the third year was positively related to degree completion.

Predictors of Annual Salary

The fixed-effects IV regression analysis shows that annual salary was positively related to the number of hours worked per week in the third year of college after taking into account the other variables in the model, among students who were employed during 2001. (See Table 5). Consistent with previous studies (e.g., Light, 1998; Neumark & Joyce, 2001; Ruhm, 1997), this finding suggests that, for college students attending four-year institutions, there is a future payoff in salaries to working more hours per week in their third year. The results from the fixed-effects IV regression also reveal that annual salaries were higher for those who completed a bachelor's degree than for other students. The economic payoff for working more hours per week while enrolled in the third year of college was higher than the payoff for completing a bachelor's degree within 6 years. This finding suggests that working while enrolled in college does have pecuniary benefits that accrue to students, even after taking into account other variables such as whether they complete a bachelor's degree within 6 years.

Annual salaries were also related to job- and labor market–related factors. Table 5 shows that, on average, salaries were 21% lower for individuals who were employed in a job that did not require a bachelor's degree than for other

TABLE 4
Likelihood of Completing a Bachelor's Degree by 2001 Among Students Who First Enrolled in Fall 1995 at Four-Year Colleges and Universities

	Beta Coefficient[a]	Robust Std. Error
Hours worked during 1997–1998—instrumented	−0.060	0.010***
Part-time enrollment any time after the second year	−0.628	0.172***
Gender		
Female	0.300	0.074***
Male (reference group)		
Race/ethnicity		
Asian	0.065	0.145
African American	−0.270	0.138
Hispanic	0.000	0.144
White (reference group)		
Parents' education		
High school (reference group)		
Some college	−0.155	0.108
Bachelor's	0.058	0.100
Master's	0.056	0.105
Parents' income		
1st quartile (reference group)		
2nd quartile	0.057	0.109
3rd quartile	0.013	0.102
4th quartile	−0.053	0.133
Lived on campus during last year of enrollment	0.364	0.149*
Student involvement		
Participated in study group during 1995–1996	0.109	0.094
Went out with friends during 1995–1996	−0.024	0.090
Talked to advisor during 1995–1996	−0.119	0.093
Talked to faculty during 1995–1996	0.210	0.101*
Academic performance		
Earned As or mostly As as of 1997–1998	2.083	0.894*
Earned Bs or mostly Bs as of 1997–1998	1.943	0.891*
Earned Cs or mostly Cs as of 1997–1998	1.274	0.891
Earned Ds or mostly Ds as of 1997–1998 (reference group)		
Constant	−.0225	0.950
Wald test of exogeneity		8.67**

TABLE 4 (Continued)

Log pseudo-likelihood	− 2016291.1
Number of students	2,494

Note: Analyses are conducted using instrumental variable probit regression, which is estimated via maximum-likelihood (ML) techniques. Standard errors have been adjusted for clustering of institutions. Instruments include independent variables listed in Table 1 and whether the student declared a major in 1995. The analysis is based on data weighted by the NCES-provided weight (B01AWT).
[a] Discrete change of dummy variables from 0 to 1.
* $p < .05$, ** $p < .01$, *** $p < .001$
Source: BPS:96/01

individuals. Average salaries in 2001 were also positively associated with the number of hours worked in the 2001 job. Additional analysis, available on request, using the same variables and statistical technique shown in Table 5, reveal that number of hours worked per week in 2001 was unrelated to the number of hours worked per week while enrolled in college during 1997–1998.

Table 5 indicates that students who earned As or mostly As had substantially higher average salaries than students who earned Cs or mostly Cs. The results also show that, compared to those who majored in education, the salaries of individuals who majored in math were 27% higher.[4] Individuals who majored in the humanities and the social sciences earned less than education majors.

Discussion

Together, the analyses suggest that hours worked per week in the third year of college is both negatively and positively related to student outcomes. On one hand, a college student who works more hours during the third year of enrollment has a lower likelihood of completing a bachelor's degree within 6 years. On the other hand, a student who works more hours during the third year of enrollment averages a higher annual salary 6 years after initially enrolling even after taking into account other variables including degree completion. The analyses further suggest that, in addition to a student's academic performance and completion of a bachelor's degree, employers also reward the time students allocate to work during enrollment in college. This employer reward for time allocated to work as a student may be one of the reasons students at four-year institutions are spending time in the labor market while enrolled in college. Despite the future economic benefits of labor market participation, working while enrolled in college has some risk for students. The analyses in this study show that the likelihood of earning a bachelor's degree within 6 years of first enrolling declines with the number of hours worked.

TABLE 5
Analysis of Annual Salary (natural log) in 2001 Among Students Who Enrolled in Fall 1995 at Four-Year Colleges and Universities

	Beta Coefficient	Robust Std. Error
Hours worked while enrolled during 1997–1998—		
instrumented	0.326	0.126**
Gender		
Female	−0.091	0.029**
Male (reference group)		
Race/ethnicity		
Asian	0.196	0.051***
African American	−0.039	0.053
Hispanic	0.032	0.050
White (reference group)		
Parents' education		
High school or less (reference group)		
Some college	0.004	0.034
Bachelor's	0.035	0.032
Master's	0.024	0.036
Parents' income		
1st quartile (reference group)		
2nd quartile	0.031	0.035
3rd quartile	0.009	0.032
4th quartile	0.098	0.043*
Completed a bachelor's degree by 2001	0.108	0.051*
Current job does not require a bachelor's degree	−0.207	0.029***
Job tenure (months)	0.010	0.011
Hours worked per week in current job during 2001	0.803	0.070***
Academic performance		
Earned As or mostly As as of 2001	0.193	0.069*
Earned Bs or mostly Bs as of 2001	0.083	0.071
Earned Cs or mostly Cs as of 2001 (reference group)		
Major as of 2001[a]		
Business	0.022	0.062
Humanities	−0.132	0.041**
Social or behavioral sciences	−0.162	0.069*
Life sciences	0.048	0.088
Physical sciences	0.044	0.084
Math	0.282	0.055***
Computer science	−0.074	0.047

TABLE 5 (Continued)

Engineering	−0.059	0.075
Health	0.021	0.050
Other	0.022	0.062
Education (reference group)		
Industry fixed effects	Yes	
Labor market area fixed effects	Yes	
Hansen *J* statistic	2.602	
R^2	0.376	
Number of individuals	1,702	

Note: The analyses are conducted using fixed-effects instrumental variable regression and estimated via generalized method of moments (GMM) techniques. Standard errors have been adjusted for clustering of institutions. Instruments include hours worked in 1997–1998 while enrolled and whether the student declared a major in 1995. The analysis is based on data weighted by the NCES-provided weight (B01AWT).
[a] Discrete change of dummy variable from 0 to 1.
* $p < .05$, ** $p < .01$, *** $p < .001$
Source: BPS:96/2001

The results of this study shed light on the short-term rewards and risks of working while enrolled in college. More research is needed to understand the longer-term implications of working while in college. Some of the unanswered questions include the following: How does a student's labor market participation while enrolled in college influence time to degree completion or the likelihood of completing a college degree beyond 6 years? How does working while in college affect salary outcomes more than 2 years after the expected time to degree completion?

More research is also needed to uncover how working while enrolled in college is shaped by precollege participation in the labor market. Students' precollege work experiences, specifically the frequency of work during high school, may be influenced by socioeconomic factors such as parents' education and income. More studies are needed to examine which criteria students use to allocate their time between work and study and how labor market participation decisions prior to entering college may shape decisions with regard to working during students' college career. This study should also be extended to examine the predictors of working and the relationship between working while in college and future earnings for different groups of students and for students attending different types of higher education institutions.

Although additional research is required to more completely understand these relationships, the results from this study may begin to provide answers to questions by college administrators and policymakers about why students make decisions with regard to allocating their time between working and studying while in college and how those decisions affect student outcomes such as degree completion and salaries in the labor market. At the very least, the results of this study have implications for campus programs with regard to facilitating the needs of students who choose to work while enrolled in college. Such programs may involve career planning and time management programs for students. As the results of this study show, the college experience of students attending four-year colleges and universities is interwoven with the world of work. Administrators and other higher education professionals may need to consider the development or enhancement of programs that help students successfully navigate through the landscape of college and the labor market.

Conclusion

The results from this study show that, compared to those with parents who did not go to college, students with parents who earned a master's degree work fewer hours per week in their third year. These findings suggest that working while in college may be shaped by cultural capital, which is reflective of an individual's social class (Bourdieu & Passeron, 1977). Although not a focus of this study, the findings from this research also indicate that students from high-income families realize higher salaries than other students even after controlling for hours worked while in college and college completion after 6 years. This finding suggests that college students' access to labor market information, a form of social capital, differs by social class. These class differences may shape how individuals enhance their human capital while enrolled in college through networks and information, or in other words, how students use social capital (Morrow, 1999) to transform their human capital into financial gains in the labor market.

Using qualitative techniques (along the lines of those used in other chapters in this volume), future research should seek to uncover how the cultural capital and social capital of college students may influence the relationship between work and salary outcomes. This study also has implications for future lines of inquiry using different research methods. Employing other statistical techniques, such as structural equation modeling (SEM), to examine the process of how college students gain workforce skills and dynamic panel modeling techniques to better understand how the process unfolds over time are other fruitful areas for future research.

Endnotes

1. More precisely, a college student's expected future income is her probability of college completion multiplied by the income of a college graduate with similar characteristics and labor market experience.

2. An endogenous variable is a variable that is related to one or more other independent variables. An exogenous variable can be described as a strictly independent variable that is unrelated to other independent variables in the model.

3. With the exception of the descriptive statistics shown in Table 1, this study uses the NCES-provided analysis weight B01AWT for all of the analyses.

4. Because it had the highest proportion of students enrolled in the major as of 2001, education is used as the reference group.

References

American Council on Education. (2006, May). *Working their way through college: Student employment and its impact on the college experience.* Washington, DC: Author.

Astin, A. W. (1984). Student involvement: A developmental theory for higher education. *Journal of College Student Personnel, 25,* 297–308.

Baffoe-Bonnie, J., & Golden, L. (2007). *Work-study: Time use tradeoffs, student work hours and implications for youth employment policy.* Paper presented at the IATUR—XXVIIII Annual Conference, Washington, DC. Retrieved October 5, 2009, from http://ssrn.com/abstract = 1078688

Bean, J. P. (1990). Why students leave: Insights from research. In D. Hossler & J. P. Bean (Eds.), *The strategic management of college enrollments* (pp. 147–169). San Francisco: Jossey-Bass.

Becker, G. S. (1993). *Human capital: A theoretical and empirical analysis with special reference to education* (3rd ed.). Chicago: University of Chicago Press.

Bourdieu, P., & Passeron, J. C. (1977). *Reproduction in education, society, and culture.* Beverly Hills, CA: Sage.

Ehrenberg, R. G., & Sherman, D. R. (1987). Employment while in college, academic achievement, and postcollege outcomes: A summary of results. *Journal of Human Resources, 22,* 1–23.

Häkkinen, I., (2006). Working while enrolled in a university: Does it pay? *Labour Economics, 13*(2), 167–189.

Heiselt, A. K., & Bergerson, A. A. (2007, Spring). Will work for a college education: An analysis of the role employment plays in the experiences of first-year college students. *Higher Education in Review, 4,* 83–106.

Kalenkoski, C. M., & Pabilonia, S. W. (2008). *Parental transfers, student achievement, and the labor supply of college students* (Working Paper 416). Washington, DC: BLS Office of Productivity and Technology.

Light, A. (1998). Estimating returns to schooling: When does the career begin? *Economics of Education Review, 17*(1), 31–45.

Mincer, J. (1974). *Schooling, experience, and earnings.* Brookfield, VT: Ashgate.

Morrow, V. (1999). Conceptualising social capital in relation to the well-being of children and young people: A critical review. *Sociological Review, 47,* 744–765.

Mortenson, T. (2007, June). Labor force status of college students ages 16 to 24, 1970 to 2006. *Postsecondary Education Opportunity, 180,* 11–16.

Neumark, D., & Joyce, M. (2001). Evaluating school-to-work programs using the new NLSY. *Journal of Human Resources, 36*(4), 666–702.

Oettinger, G. S. (2005). Parents' financial support, students' employment, and academic performance in college. Unpublished manuscript.

Riggert, S. C., Boyle, M., Petrosko, J. M., Ash, D., & Rude-Parkins, C. (2006). Student employment and higher education: Empiricism and contradiction. *Review of Educational Research, 76*(1), 63–92.

Ruhm, C. (1997). Is high school employment consumption or investment? *Journal of Labor Economics, 15*, 735–776.

Stinebrickner, R., & Stinebrickner, T .R. (2003). Working during school and academic performance. *Journal of Labor Economics, 21*, 473–491.

Tinto, V. (1993). *Leaving college: Rethinking the causes and cures of student attrition.* Chicago: University of Chicago Press.

Titus, M. A. (2004). An examination of the influence of institutional context on student persistence at 4-year colleges and universities: A multilevel approach. *Research in Higher Education, 45*, 673–699.

Titus, M. A. (2006a). Understanding college degree completion of students with low socioeconomic status: The influence of the institutional financial context. *Research in Higher Education, 47*, 371–397.

Titus, M. A. (2006b). Understanding the influence of the financial context of institutions on student persistence at four-year colleges and universities. *Journal of Higher Education, 77*, 353–375.

U.S. Department of Education, National Center for Education Statistics, 1996/2001 Beginning Postsecondary Students Longitudinal Study (BPS:96/01).

United States Department of Labor, Bureau of Labor Statistics. (2008, April). College enrollment and work activity of 2008 high school graduates. [Electronic version] News. Retrieved July 16, 2008, from www.bls.gov/news.release/archives/hsgec_04252008.pdf

CONCLUSIONS AND RECOMMENDATIONS FOR POLICY, PRACTICE, AND FUTURE RESEARCH

Laura W. Perna

T he chapters in this volume offer important insights into the phenomenon of the "working college student." The chapters describe the characteristics and experiences of undergraduate students who work and identify implications of working for students' educational outcomes. This final chapter summarizes the findings that cut across the volume and offers recommendations for public and institutional policymakers to improve the educational experiences and outcomes of working undergraduate students. The chapter concludes by identifying directions for future research.

Summary of Findings and Conclusions

While offering many insights for understanding the experiences and implications of students who work, the chapters in this volume together produce the following conclusions:

1. "Student" is only one of several roles and responsibilities for many undergraduates.
2. Work has both benefits and costs to students' educational experiences and outcomes.
3. Work should be reconceptualized as an experience that may promote students' educational outcomes.

"Student" Is Only One of Many Roles and Responsibilities for Many Undergraduates

Drawing on both quantitative and qualitative data from both single- and multi-institutional samples, the chapters in this volume consistently show that enrollment in college is only one of many identities, roles, and responsibilities for a substantial number of today's undergraduates (e.g., Kasworm, chapter 2; Levin, Montero-Hernandez, & Cerven, chapter 3; Ziskin, Torres, Hossler, & Gross, chapter 4; Rowan-Kenyon, Swan, Deutsch, & Gansneder, chapter 5; Pusser, chapter 7). Many students are not only enrolled in college but also working and assuming other roles including caring for children, parents, or other family members.

As the qualitative data poignantly illustrate, trying to meet demands of college, work, and other roles simultaneously can cause stress and other challenges. Rowan-Kenyon and colleagues describe the time-management challenges of adult students and the resulting trade-offs between work and school responsibilities that are required to meet multiple demands at the same time. Levin and colleagues contend that nontraditional students attending community colleges face anxiety and stress because of the conflict between their roles as student and worker, a conflict that occurs "in the midst of already strenuous [life] conditions." Pusser shows the tension between working while enrolled to reduce the opportunity costs of enrollment and engaging in academic experiences on campus in the context of time constraints imposed by working. Ziskin and colleagues describe the "delicate balances" of the lives of students attending four-year commuter colleges, noting that students' time is highly structured to meet the demands of work, family, and college.

The volume also documents the precarious nature of these "balances." Two chapters (Ziskin et al., chapter 4; Rowan-Kenyon et al., chapter 5) describe how one unexpected change (e.g., a sick child) can cause a cascade of problems in other areas of responsibility, including the ability to fulfill course requirements. Levin et al. conclude that a student's ability to manage the roles of student and worker often depends on a student's self-confidence and motivation as well as the availability of institutional and other support structures. Consistent with the notion of social reproduction, Ziskin et al. find that the students who describe the multiple demands of college, work, and family as "manageable" are those who have the income and resources needed to meet basic material, childcare, and other needs—that is, students from higher rather than lower socioeconomic status backgrounds.

Attention to employment as one of many identities, roles, and responsibilities sheds light on the differences in the implications of "work" among undergraduates. Although both traditional-age and adult students are employed, their experiences in postsecondary education are shaped by different experiences and perspectives because they "co-exist at the intersection of quite different life courses," where life courses are defined by roles and responsibilities that shift over time (Pusser, chapter 7). Whereas work may be a way for traditional-age students to test or explore career goals, work is a central identity of many adult students. Kasworm argues that the orientation toward and participation in higher education is fundamentally different for traditional-age and adult students because of differences in their "maturational world-view of themselves, their identity anchors, and their beliefs of the role of education for their futures." Using an economic perspective, Lynch, Gottfried, Green, and Thomas argue that nontraditional students differ from traditional students in terms of their utility functions, access to capital, and opportunity costs, and that the work experience of adult students may be an "input" into the educational production function that promotes the learning of both the individual student as well as the student's peers.

Work Has Both Benefits and Costs to Students' Educational Experiences and Outcomes

As noted in several chapters, employment provides the financial resources that many students require to enroll and stay enrolled. The chapters in this volume show that working while enrolled also is associated with other benefits, including greater engagement in effective educational practices and higher future earnings. McCormick, Moore, and Kuh find that, for full-time first-year and senior students, working on campus is positively related to measures of effective educational practices, regardless of the number of hours worked. Hours worked off campus are positively related to four of the five benchmarks (McCormick et al., chapter 9). After controlling for other student and institutional variables, Flowers finds that, for African American students, engagement in activities that are associated with intellectual growth during college increases with the number of hours worked on and off campus. Umbach, Padgett, and Pascarella show that, after controlling for other variables, perceptions of faculty interest in student development and teaching, timeliness of faculty feedback, teaching clarity, and in-class activities and expectations do not vary based on the number of hours or location (on or off campus) of work. Students who work in college earn higher salaries after college even after controlling for other variables, including attainment of a bachelor's degree within 6 years (Titus, chapter 12).

But working while enrolled is not without costs. As described in the previous section, several chapters demonstrate the tension that many community college students experience between their roles as students and workers. Levin et al. argue that this stress limits students' integration into academic life. Ziskin and colleagues suggest that working may limit students' opportunities to learn because time spent working while enrolled in college constrains the availability of time for studying and completing assignments.

Consistent with prior research (Pascarella & Terenzini, 2005), the quantitative analyses in this volume generally show the positive effects on several student outcomes of working a small number of hours and the negative effects of working a high number of hours (i.e., 20 hours per week or more) especially off campus. McCormick et al. find that, whereas working up to 10 hours per week on campus is associated with higher grades, working more than 20 hours per week on campus is associated with lower grades for full-time students. Working more than 10 hours per week off campus is associated with lower grades for both full- and part-time students. Umbach and colleagues show that, after controlling for other variables, working at least 10 hours per week off campus is associated with less participation in cooperative learning and lower levels of academic challenge and effort, as well as lower levels of critical thinking in the first year of college.

Working while enrolled—especially substantial numbers of hours—also reduces the likelihood of completing a degree. Using descriptive analyses, Levin et al. show that, although not working and working part time are positively associated with persistence for community college students, working full time is negatively related to persistence. Controlling for other variables and accounting for the endogeneity of work, Titus shows that working is associated with greater likelihood to shifting to part-time enrollment and reduced probability of completing a bachelor's degree within 6 years.

Moreover, the stresses and risks of working that are described in this volume are likely understated. The chapters in this volume consider only the perspectives and experiences of students who are—by virtue of their status as a currently enrolled student—"successful," at least to some extent, at simultaneously managing the demands of work, school, and other responsibilities. The voices and experiences of those who did not enroll or who left higher education because they were unable to manage these multiple responsibilities and subsequent stress are excluded.

Work Should Be Reconceptualized as an Experience That Promotes Students' Educational Outcomes

Despite the potential costs, the chapters in this volume point to the potential role of employment as an experience that may promote students' educational engagement and other outcomes. Recognizing that students are unlikely simply to stop working, the chapters call for a fundamental revaluing and reconsidering of the role of employment for today's undergraduates. As McCormick and colleagues (chapter 9) assert, public policymakers and institutional leaders can no longer view student employment as an "unnecessary, unfortunate distraction" from undergraduate studies given the prevalence and intensity of employment.

As the authors in this volume argue, working while enrolled in college has the potential to both reinforce and reduce economic and social stratification and inequality. Drawing on social reproduction perspectives, Ziskin et al. argue that institutional structures often play a role in replicating and legitimating social power structures by channeling students toward roles that reflect their class origins. The relatively higher rates of employment for students from disadvantaged backgrounds (e.g., first-generation college students) and for students attending community and commuter colleges signal the ways that employment during college reinforces stratification and inequality (Levin et al., chapter 3; Ziskin et al., chapter 4; Pusser, chapter 7; McCormick et al., chapter 9; Titus, chapter 12).

Because of insufficient financial resources, some students have been deterred from enrolling and others who have enrolled have needed to work (Advisory Committee on Student Financial Assistance, 2006; Flowers, chapter 10; Pusser, chapter 7). But, as Titus demonstrates, working while enrolled reduces the likelihood of persisting to degree completion. Therefore, the need to work reduces students' educational attainment, which limits both an individual's "life chances" (Pusser, chapter 7) and other individual benefits, as well as the societal benefits of higher education.

Clearly higher education plays a critical role in reducing economic and social stratification. Nearly half (45%) of adults whose parents are in the bottom quintile of income and who did not complete a college degree have incomes in the bottom income quintile compared with only 16% of adults whose parents are in the bottom income quintile but who complete a college degree (Haskins, Holzer, & Lerman, 2009). Only 1 in 20 adults from families in the bottom income quintile and who do not complete a college degree attain incomes in the top quintile compared with nearly 1 in 5 (19%) of those who complete a college degree (Haskins et al., 2009).

To ensure that all students—including those who work—have the opportunity to improve their economic and social attainment, the benefits of working must be maximized and the disadvantages must be minimized. Rather than viewing work only as a force that pulls students away from campus and reduces the opportunity for students to be engaged in campus life, this volume encourages institutional leaders to consider the educational benefits that may result from employment. As Lynch et al. argue, students' employment experiences may be conceptualized as an input into the educational production function that promotes student learning. Arguing that student employment typically does little to promote students' intellectual development—the primary purpose of higher education—Pusser calls for campus leaders to consider how to transform student employment to promote intellectual development not only by reducing student employment but also by "reimagining the role of employment in student development."

Implications for Public Policy

When considered in the context of the need to reduce stratification, improve the educational attainment of the nation's population, and maximize the public good aspects of higher education (Pusser, chapter 7), the prevalence and intensity of employment among the nation's undergraduates have important implications for public policy. Together, the chapters in this volume underscore the need to reconsider the roles of federal and state policies—policies that were constructed largely to address traditional patterns of enrollment—in promoting the educational success of working students. More specifically, the chapters in this volume suggest the need for policymakers to reduce students' financial need to work, change the treatment of work in federal financial aid policies and practices, and support institutions that serve large numbers of working students.

Reduce the Financial Need to Work

Despite the potential negative consequences, many students are working substantial numbers of hours out of financial necessity. These findings underscore the need for federal, state, and institutional leaders to identify ways to reduce students' financial need to work (Levin et al. chapter 3; Pusser, chapter 7; Umbach et al., chapter 11). Public policy is an especially important lever for addressing the financial need for students to work. As St. John (2008) argues, in a just society, if involvement promotes educational attainment, and:

> [i]f the opportunity to become engaged in college life is related to family income and the financial aid low-income students receive, then we should not ignore the effects of public finance when we consider inequalities in educational opportunity or explanations for variance in student academic success. (p. 205)

The primary instruments of "public finance" are federal and state government funding for student financial aid and state appropriations to higher education institutions. Therefore, the financial need to work may be reduced by (1) maximizing the availability of federal and state need-based grants for low- and lower-middle-income students, and (2) increasing appropriations to institutions so as to help slow tuition increases.

The positive effects of grant-based financial aid on enrollment, especially for low-income students, are well established (see Mundel, 2008, for a review). But less is known about the effects of increased grant aid on students' financing decisions, including the decision to work. Analyses of the effects of the Gates Millennium Scholars (GMS) program suggest the benefits of increased grant aid for students who work. Using descriptive analyses and a sample of African American students, Allen, Harris, Dinwiddie, and Griffin (2009) show that GMS recipients are as likely as nonrecipients to work, but that GMS recipients work fewer hours per week than do nonrecipients. Others conclude that the financial relief, including reduced pressure to work, provided by the GMS aid enables recipients to become more academically and socially engaged in campus life (Denson, Oseguera, & Hurtado, 2008; Hune & Gomez, 2008).

Change the Treatment of Work in Federal Financial Aid Policies and Practices

Policymakers should also reconsider the treatment of work in federal financial aid policies and practices. In chapter 1, Baum stresses two types of necessary changes: (1) eliminate work-study as a type of financial "aid," and (2) reconsider the treatment of student earnings in the needs analysis formula.

Noting the benefits of on-campus employment to student employment and persistence, other reports recommend increasing funding for the Federal Work-Study Program to increase on-campus employment (e.g., Perna, Cooper, & Li, 2007). Only 6% of all undergraduates in 2007–2008 received financial aid in the form of Federal Work-Study and the average award for Federal Work-Study recipients was just $2,300 (Wei et al., 2009). Only 1% of all aid dollars awarded to undergraduates from all sources in 2007–2008 was in the form of Federal Work-Study (College Board, 2008b). Although the total amount awarded for most other types of aid has increased in constant dollars over the past decade, Federal Work-Study dollars have remained unchanged ($1.17 billion in 2007–2008; College Board, 2008b).

In chapter 1, Baum recommends that work-study awards no longer be considered financial aid. As she notes, work-study not only masks the true magnitude of students' unmet financial aid but also reduces students' eligibility for other aid, particularly aid in the form of grants. She contends that income from on-campus employment should be viewed as earnings from hours worked, not a subsidy, because work-study employment requires the same effort as any other job. She concludes that Federal Work-Study is really a subsidy to employers, not students. For students, work-study earnings are merely compensation for services provided; whether the employer receives support from the federal government to pay these wages is irrelevant to the student (Baum, chapter 1).

Moreover, as Baum also notes, prior research does not establish whether the benefits of on-campus employment to student engagement and persistence depend on whether the position is funded via the Federal Work-Study Program. She argues that the benefits of on-campus employment to student integration and engagement may be achieved via on-campus employment that is funded from other sources.

A second recommendation for reconsidering the treatment of work in federal financial aid policies is to eliminate the work penalty from the federal needs analysis formula. As Baum describes, student earnings are currently "taxed" so that students who work more are penalized by receiving less need-based grant aid (assuming additional need-based aid is available). This tax is especially problematic for independent students without dependents because the earnings of these students are taxed at the same rate as the earnings of dependent students (Baum, chapter 1). The students who are hurt most by the work penalty are also likely those with the fewest financial resources (i.e., the students with the greatest need to work). As Baum recommends, the needs analysis formula should be revised so that students' financial aid is not reduced when students work more than 10 to 15 hours per week while in school and during the summer.

Provide Additional Public Resources to Encourage Institutions to Serve Working Students Better

Public policymakers should also allocate additional resources to encouraging institutions to serve working students better. These incentives should be directed toward institutions with the highest proportions of working students. The prevalence and intensity of student employment vary across institutions. Both are greater at public two-year colleges than at public and private four-year colleges and universities, although Ziskin et al.'s examination of the experiences of working students attending commuter colleges suggests variations among four-year institutions. In 2003–2004, 81% of all dependent undergraduates enrolled at public two-year colleges worked an average of 27.7 hours per week; at public four-year institutions 73% of dependent undergraduates worked an average of 22 hours per week; and at private four-year institutions 71% of dependent undergraduates worked an average of 20 hours per week (Perna et al., 2007).

Average family incomes are lower at public two-year colleges than at private four-year universities, suggesting variations in the financial need to work (Baum & Ma, 2007). But students attending private four-year institutions disproportionately receive Federal Work-Study awards. As Baum and McCormick et al. observe, because of the nature of the federal formula for allocating Federal Work-Study and other campus-based financial aid, students attending private four-year institutions are overrepresented among work-study recipients while students attending community colleges are underrepresented. In 2003–2004, 22% of undergraduates attending private four-year institutions held a work-study or assistantship position and 21% held a work-study position along with a regular job. In contrast, only 4.5% of undergraduates at public two-year colleges and 14% at public four-year colleges and universities held work-study or assistantship positions (2% and

7%, respectively, held only a work-study or assistantship position) (Perna et al., 2007).

Public two-year colleges not only have fewer Federal Work-Study dollars to distribute but also serve populations that have greater challenges to academic success. As Kasworm and Levin et al. describe, community colleges tend to serve students who are older and who on average have the lowest academic preparation and the fewest socioeconomic resources. At the same time, community colleges also have fewer resources to meet students' needs because these institutions average lower state appropriations and lower endowments than other institutions (Levin et al., chapter 3). In 2005–2006, public two-year colleges received only 25% of state appropriations to higher education institutions and 8% of local appropriations to higher education institutions, but enrolled 47% of all students attending public colleges and universities and 34% of all students attending public and private colleges and universities (U.S. Department of Education, 2009).

Therefore, federal and state policymakers should adopt policies and programs that encourage colleges and universities to serve working students better. One approach to changing institutional behavior may be to reward community colleges and other institutions that successfully serve high numbers of working students with additional funding. Many community college students are enrolled with the goal of improving their economic and social status (Levin et al., chapter 3). But the need to work to pay the price of attendance reduces the likelihood of achieving this goal (Levin et al., chapter 3). In a step toward encouraging community colleges to better serve their students—students who are disproportionately disadvantaged and working—in July 2009 President Barack Obama proposed to award, over 10 years, through a competitive grant process, $9 billion to community colleges to improve job training and degree completion, $2.5 billion for improvement of community college facilities, and $500 million for instructional materials to support community colleges' distance education courses (Jaschik, 2009). Although not specifically designed to improve the educational experiences and outcomes of working students per se, this type of effort implicitly recognizes the role of community colleges in educating this population.

Implications for Campus Administrators

The chapters in this volume should also encourage colleges and universities to recognize and respond to the prevalence, characteristics, and implications of working for today's undergraduates. Given the diversity across higher education institutions, campus leaders should consider the nature of employment for students on their own campus as a first step toward identifying appropriate institutional responses.

Regardless of the prevalence of working on campus, the authors in this volume stress the need to shift away from viewing working adult students as nontraditional and thus needing to change to fit existing institutional structures—structures that were developed largely based on the needs of traditional students. Because work is one central role, responsibility, and identity of many working students, expecting working students to adapt to institutional norms and structures that were created to address the needs of traditional students is inappropriate.

Instead, institutions should not only identify ways to adapt institutional structures and resources to support the educational success of working students but also recognize the transformative potential of work. More specifically, the chapters in this volume suggest the following recommendations for campus administrators: reduce students' financial need to work; improve students' knowledge of financial aid and the costs and benefits of work; consider the role of on-campus employment in promoting attainment; structure employment to maximize student learning; create a campus culture that supports the educational needs of adult working students; and adapt the delivery of instruction and support services to recognize the needs of working students.

Reduce the Financial Need to Work

Like public policymakers, institutional leaders also have a responsibility to reduce students' financial need to work. Whereas public policymakers may increase federal- and state-sponsored financial aid and appropriations, institutions may reduce students' financial need to work by controlling tuition and fees and increasing the availability of institutionally sponsored need-based grant aid.

At least in part because of trends in state appropriations to higher education institutions (Trombley, 2003), over the past decade, tuition and fees at colleges and universities nationwide continued to increase substantially. Between 1998–1999 and 2008–2009, average tuition and fees increased in constant (2008) dollars by 15% at public two-year colleges (from $2,095 to $2,402), 50% at public four-year institutions (from $4,376 to $6,585), and 27% at private four-year institutions (from $19,825 to $25,143) (College Board, 2008a).

Colleges and universities have been an important source of funds for addressing students' financial need to work. In 2007–2008, 21% of all aid to undergraduates was awarded by colleges and universities (College Board, 2008b). Moreover, colleges and universities are the single largest source of aid in the form of grants to postsecondary education students (both undergraduate and graduate) because 42% of all grant aid awarded in 2007–2008 was from colleges and universities (College Board, 2008b). As a result of the availability of grant aid from all sources, net tuition and fees (tuition and fees less grants and education tax benefits) for full-time students declined by 44% in constant dollars between 2003–2004 and 2008–2009 at public two-year colleges but increased by 34% in constant dollars at public four-year institutions and increased by 7% in constant dollars at private four-year colleges (College Board, 2008a).

Nonetheless, even with this institutional aid, substantial numbers of students are working high numbers of hours. This pattern underscores the importance of continuing to allocate resources to institutional financial aid as well as continually evaluating the implications of tuition and aid policies for students at individual campuses.

Improve Students' Knowledge of Financial Aid and Costs and Benefits of Work

The financial need to work may also be reduced by improving students' knowledge of financial aid. As several chapter authors (e.g., McCormick et al., chapter 9; Flowers, chapter 10) contend, institutions should provide counseling so that students and their families can make informed decisions about the appropriate balance among work, enrollment, and borrowing. Such counseling might be provided as part of precollege outreach and college-transition programming, orientation, and academic advising and should include attention to the costs and benefits of working on and off campus.

Institutional leaders should also support the development of a comprehensive system for delivering early financial aid information to prospective college students and their families, as recommended by the Advisory Committee on Student Financial Assistance (2008). Such a system should include attention to benefits and disadvantages of work for students' educational experiences and the role of work in the federal financial aid system. Some students are likely working because they do not have sufficient knowledge or information about available financial aid. King (2004) found that, in 1999–2000, 1.7 million low- and moderate-income undergraduates who were enrolled for credit at higher education institutions nationwide did not complete the Free Application for Federal Student Aid (FAFSA). About one half of these individuals were estimated to be eligible to receive a federal Pell Grant. More than half of fall 1999 undergraduates submitted a FAFSA after the March deadline, likely limiting opportunities for state and/or institutional grant awards (King, 2004).

Consider the Role of On-Campus Employment in Promoting Attainment

Several chapters in this volume suggest the benefits to educational outcomes of working on campus. Both McCormick et al. and Flowers find higher levels of engagement associated with working on campus rather than off campus. McCormick and colleagues also find that working up to 10 hours per week on campus was associated with higher grade point averages for full-time students, whereas more than 10 hours per week off campus was associated with lower grades for both full- and part-time students. Umbach et al. show that the frequency of student–faculty interactions is greater for students working on campus and working less than 20 hours per week off campus than for other students. Lewis identifies several workplace experiences that are positively related to learning for students employed on campus.

These findings suggest the potential benefit of increasing the availability of on-campus employment. But before adopting this approach, institutions should consider the appropriateness of this recommendation for their particular campus. As McCormick and colleagues caution, increasing on-campus employment is unlikely to promote educational success for all students at all institutions, given limits on wages that may be earned from on-campus employment, the time that students have available to work, and the jobs that students may already have when they enroll in college. Rowan-Kenyon et al. warn that, if the number of hours is constrained, then on-campus employment may not provide students with sufficient financial resources to meet their educational expenses.

Although there is some variation across institutional types, the vast majority of students who work are employed off campus (Perna et al., 2007). In 2003–2004, 93% of working undergraduates were employed off campus, with the share of students working off campus ranging from 97% at public two-year and private for-profit institutions to 89% at public four-year institutions and 87% at private four-year institutions (Perna et al., 2007).

Several forces may contribute to the dominance of off-campus employment compared to on-campus employment, including differences in financial compensation and perceived relevance to future career goals (Perna et al., 2007). One strategy for increasing on-campus employment may be to increase the attractiveness of on-campus employment to students, especially students who are working off campus when they first enroll at the institution. While offering higher wages than off-campus employers may increase the attractiveness of on-campus employment opportunities, institutions may also successfully attract students to on-campus positions by promoting other benefits (Perna et al., 2007). Among the potential nonmonetary benefits of on-campus employment relative to off-campus employment are greater convenience, congruence with academic coursework, and promotion of career goals.

Some anecdotal data suggest that providing students with higher-quality on-campus employment opportunities not only benefits students but also reduces institutional expenses. Rhodes College, a private four-year college near Memphis, Tennessee, has created 100 "student associate" positions, designed to provide undergraduate students with opportunities to gain professional administrative experience on campus. Rhodes administrators estimate that each student associate is associated with an institutional savings of

$29,000 because student workers receive lower wages ($10/hour) and fewer fringe benefits (Bushong, 2009). Anecdotal data suggest that students gain useful work experience through this program because such responsibilities have included coordinating reunions, cataloguing art, and assisting in institutional research (Bushong, 2009).

Another potential strategy for increasing on-campus employment opportunities and reducing instructional expenses may be to employ undergraduates as teaching assistants (Coplin, 2005). Coplin contends that undergraduate teaching assistants may effectively assist faculty with such responsibilities as taking attendance, grading (after extensive faculty training), conducting structured group activities or workshops outside of class, conducting surveys on aspects of the class over the course of a semester, maintaining a course website, identifying course improvements, holding office hours, and providing tutoring. Coplin's examples draw on his personal experiences rather than any rigorous evaluation of effectiveness. Nonetheless, using undergraduates as teaching assistants may have benefits to both the quality of instruction (by increasing instructional resources at minimal cost) and to the undergraduates who serve in this capacity (by increasing their engagement in learning, providing valuable experience, and providing course credit or earnings).

Structure Employment to Maximize Student Learning

The chapters in this volume also suggest the benefits of intentionally structuring student employment to promote learning. For example, McCormick and colleagues show that the benefits of work to student outcomes are mediated by engagement and conclude that the benefits of work may be maximized by purposely connecting students' college and employment experiences.

Lewis identifies 12 workplace strategies that are positively correlated with learning for students working on campus: informal training, observation, collaboration and teamwork, feedback from peers, feedback from supervisors, informal interaction with supervisor, task repetition, problem solving, idea experimentation, reflection, intuitive decision making, and congruence between work and academics. In addition to focusing on these particular strategies, Lewis recommends that employers may advance student learning by ensuring that job descriptions identify the learning that is embedded in job tasks and focusing students' summative and formative performance evaluations to consider growth in learning that results from employment.

Because Lewis's study focuses on the workplace experiences and learning outcomes for traditional-age students working on campus, the applicability of these recommendations for off-campus employment is unclear. Nonetheless, the notion of transforming work into a mechanism for promoting students' intellectual development is consistent with ideas raised in other chapters (e.g., Lynch et al., chapter 6; Pusser, chapter 7).

One potential strategy for improving the connection between employment and learning is to incorporate attention to knowledge gained through work-based experiences into coursework. Lynch et al. offer several suggestions for building connections between employment experiences and course content, including using task-based learning and providing real-world applications of course topics. Faculty may also increase the engagement of working students through mechanisms that facilitate their participation such as online learning environments and group work that may be completed through virtual group meetings.

Another potential strategy is to pay students for engaging in work that promotes learning and other educational outcomes (Pusser, chapter 7). Pusser notes that students are typically not paid for engaging in activities that promote their intellectual development, such as service and leadership development experiences. Pusser also recommends that institutions conduct workshops to promote students' awareness of the implications of employment for their intellectual development, authority relationships, stratification and inequality, and the public good.

Institutions may also recognize the contribution of workplace experiences to student learning by awarding course credit for relevant employment experiences. Coplin (2005) suggests that institutions may make student employment worthy of course credit by supplementing employment experiences with relevant and regular class meetings, readings, and discussion.

Several organizations offer mechanisms for assessing and awarding course credit for work and other prior experiences. Potential alternative credit options include the College Board's College-Level Examination Program (CLEP) and the American Council on Education's (ACE) College Credit Recommendation Service (CREDIT) (Kasworm, chapter 2; Lynch et al., chapter 6). The College Board's (2009) CLEP program offers 34 examinations designed to evaluate knowledge students may have gained through "independent study, prior course work, on-the-job training, professional development, cultural pursuits, or internships." Examinations are offered in topics pertaining to business, science and math, history and social sciences, foreign languages, and composition and literature. The College Board claims that 2,900 accredited higher education institutions grant credit for passing scores on CLEP exams. Through CREDIT, ACE determines the amount of college credit warranted by particular training or other out-of-college experiences. ACE (2009) claims that it "has reviewed thousands of training courses for Fortune 500 corporations, associations, labor unions, government agencies, schools, and training suppliers." By awarding course credit for employment and other life experiences, institutions may also reduce students' time-to-degree and total price of attendance (Coplin, 2005).

Create a Campus Culture That Supports the Educational Needs of Working Students

The chapters in this volume also show the clear need to create a campus culture that supports the learning and educational needs of working students, particularly adult working students. Kasworm encourages higher education institutions to create new paradigms that are responsive to the multiple identities and psychological and cultural needs of adult working students. Umbach and colleagues call for a campus-wide effort to better serve students who work.

Student interactions with faculty and staff are a central component of a supportive campus culture. Through their review of prior research and qualitative data analyses, Levin et al. (chapter 3) show the importance of support from and interaction with faculty and staff to working community college students. Ziskin et al. find that the perceived availability of one-on-one personal interactions with college personnel is critical to commuter college students' satisfaction with the college experience. McCormick et al. conclude that faculty, advisors, and student life staff must be partners in helping students connect curricular and cocurricular experiences with their employment.

To create a campus culture that promotes the educational success of working students, faculty and staff must understand the learning and support needs of working students. Ziskin and colleagues conclude that faculty, institutional policymakers, and student services staff must understand students' engagement in work to fully support their educational success. McCormick et al. recommend that institutions educate faculty and staff about the prevalence of student employment and ways to make connections between work and college experiences.

Encouraging faculty and staff to engage in meaningful one-on-one interactions may be particularly important to the educational success of adult working students. From their qualitative analyses, Ziskin and colleagues conclude that the academic success of many adult students may be jeopardized by their perception that, because of their employment status, family commitments, age, and other characteristics, they are "out of place" on campus. Through individualized interactions, faculty and staff may promote adult working students' sense of belonging and validate their presence on campus, and subsequently promote their academic success.

Institutions should place particular emphasis on encouraging, rewarding, and supporting faculty to adapt their instructional practices to promote the educational success of working students. Titus shows that student–faculty interactions in the first year of college are associated with greater likelihood of completing a bachelor's degree within 6 years, net of other variables. But Ziskin and colleagues offer examples where faculty either do not realize challenges facing working students—and thus do not offer the necessary assistance—or recognize the different experiences of working students but do not offer any additional assistance.

From the results of their study, Umbach et al. (chapter 11) offer several recommendations for the types of instructional practices that may better serve working students. Using quantitative analyses of students attending four-year colleges and universities, Umbach et al. show that working off campus more than 10 hours per week is negatively related to critical thinking but that these negative effects are reduced for students who work more than 20 hours per week off campus and participate in cooperative learning, are encouraged by faculty, complete assignments that build higher-order thinking skills, and devote attention to their academic requirements. These findings suggest the educational benefits to working students of faculty efforts to encourage cooperative learning, set high expectations for students' achievement, and create assignments that require students to demonstrate deep learning. A campus teaching center may also support faculty efforts with working students (Umbach et al., chapter 11).

Institutions may also create a culture that supports adult working students through other efforts that explicitly recognize the experiences and needs of these students (C. Kasworm, personal communication, July 9, 2009). Colleges and universities may recognize the needs of adult working students by developing partnerships with regional employers and offering some coursework at employers' work sites. Colleges and universities may also signal the value of adult students' prior experiences by recognizing credits granted to these experiences through CLEP, CREDIT, and other programs (as discussed in the prior section), as well as by facilitating the transfer of credits earned at other higher education institutions.

Adapt Delivery of Instruction and Support Services to Recognize Needs of Working Students

The chapters in this volume illustrate the need for institutions to adapt the delivery of academic and social services to recognize the needs and many roles of adult students (Kasworm, chapter 2; Levin et al., chapter 3; Ziskin et al., chapter 4; Rowan-Kenyon et al., chapter 5; Lynch et al., chapter 6). Although student agency is important, institutional support is also required for students to meet the multiple demands of work, family, and school (Kasworm, chapter 2; Levin et al., chapter 3).

Time is a substantial constraint for many working students, especially adult working students. The qualitative data presented in this volume illustrate how tightly adult students are scheduled to meet demands of their families, employers, and schools (e.g., Ziskin et al., chapter 4; Rowan-Kenyon et al., chapter 5). Working full time limits the ability of students to access personal and institutional resources and take advantage of opportunities to engage academically and socially with other students (Kasworm, chapter 2; Levin et al., chapter 3). Other research suggests that students who work are less academically involved, have fewer choices of classes, and have less access to the library (Choy & Berker, 2003; Furr & Elling, 2000; King & Bannon, 2002; Pascarella, Bohr, Nora, Desler, & Zusman, 1994; Pascarella & Terenzini, 2005).

Therefore, institutions should adapt academic and social support services to better serve the needs and characteristics of working students. By adapting these structures, institutions may not only allow working students the opportunity to become actively engaged on campus, but also promote students' self-confidence and motivation to succeed in college (Levin et al., chapter 3). Such adaptations are particularly important to the educational success of adult working students.

The chapters in this volume offer a number of suggestions for helping students to meet the multiple demands of work, family, and school roles. These suggestions include offering curricula and courses in the evenings and on weekends and in distance education formats; establishing course schedules in advance; offering students access to academic, advising, and other support services at night and on weekends; offering online course registration and virtual academic advising; providing childcare options; and supplying space for students to study between work and school (Kasworm, chapter 2; Levin et al., chapter 3; Rowan-Kenyon et al., chapter 5; Lynch et al., chapter 6). Institutions should also consider the availability of supports to help working students connect their employment and educational experiences, including career counseling and planning and occupational placement (Levin et al., chapter 3; Lynch et al., chapter 6; and Titus, chapter 12).

Future Research

While providing a comprehensive examination of the experiences of working undergraduate students, the chapters in this volume also raise several additional questions for future research. Future research should build on the conceptual and methodological approaches offered in this volume to examine the following questions:

1. What lessons can be learned from institutions that successfully support the needs of working students and maximize the benefits of employment to student learning?
2. How can employers promote academic success for working students?
3. How do the nature and implications of work vary based on student characteristics?

4. Why are some outcomes better for students who work than for students who do not work?
5. How should "work" and the educational outcomes of work be conceptualized by institutional leaders and measured in future data collections?

What Lessons Can Be Learned From Institutions That Successfully Recognize the Needs of Working Students and Maximize the Benefits of Employment to Student Learning?

As several chapters note, variations in institutional missions and other characteristics limit the generalizability of findings across institutions. Kasworm argues that, because different institutional contexts attract different types of adult students and adult workers, students' understandings of their role as a student relative to their other roles and their understandings of "student involvement" vary across institutions. Variations in the nature and availability of employment on and off campus and the availability of institutional and community structures to support students' multiple roles (e.g., public transportation, childcare) likely also play a role. The role of institutional context suggests the need for institutions to identify strategies that reflect an institution's particular context, including the characteristics and consequences of employment at their particular campus.

The role of institutional context not withstanding, however, important insights for addressing the needs of working students may be generated by examining the institutional structures that promote learning and other educational outcomes for working students. Future research should seek to identify the lessons that may be learned from institutions that are successfully addressing the needs of working students and maximizing the benefits of employment to student learning. Community colleges and commuter four-year colleges may be especially important sites for understanding how institutions may effectively promote the academic success of students with multiple roles and responsibilities (Kasworm, chapter 2; Levin et al., chapter 3; and Ziskin et al., chapter 4).

"Work colleges" may also be a productive source for learning how institutions may promote linkages between education and real-world experience. One example of a "work college" is Berea College in Kentucky. Founded in 1855, Berea's (2009a) mission emphasizes "learning, labor, and service." Admission is limited to students from low-income families; most students are from Appalachia. Students pay no tuition but all must work between 10 and 15 hours per week on campus or in the community while attending classes full time. Berea claims that, through "opportunities for manual labor as an assistance in self-support," "students integrate productive work, disciplined learning, career exploration, and personal development" (Berea College, 2009b).

Future research should also consider the lessons that may be learned from institutions that offer internship and cooperative education ("co-op") programs. In its 2009 rankings, *U.S. News & World Report* (2009) identifies 14 colleges and universities that "require or encourage students to apply what they're learning in the classroom out in the real world—through closely supervised internships or practicums, or through cooperative education, in which a period of study typically alternates with one of work." The 14 institutions on this list are Alverno College, Berea College, Drexel University, Elon University, Georgia Institute of Technology, Kettering University, Massachusetts Institute of Technology, New York University, Northeastern University, Portland State University, Purdue University–West Lafayette, Rochester Institute of Technology, University of Cincinnati, and Worcester Polytechnic Institute.

For example, through the co-op program at Northeastern University, undergraduates alternate semesters of full-time (usually paid) enrollment with semesters of full-time employment that is related to their major or career interests. Through the program, students may acquire up to 18 months of professional experience (i.e., up to three co-ops over 5 years) (Northeastern University, 2009b). On its website, the institution argues that students should participate in co-op "because the combination of classroom study and real-world experience is the best possible way to develop the knowledge, capability, and leadership skills that lead to a lifetime of achievement" (Northeastern University, 2009a). The institution reports that undergraduate co-op students earn, on average, $15,268 for 6 months of employment during the academic year (Northeastern University, 2009c).

How Can Employers Promote Academic Success for Working Students?

The chapters in this volume also suggest the need for additional research examining the roles of both on- and off-campus employers in supporting the enrollment, learning, and other educational outcomes of working students. Lewis identifies strategies that on-campus employers may use to promote learning for student employees. Additional research is required to understand the challenges to implementing these strategies for on-campus employers as well as the potential transferability of these strategies to off-campus employers.

Future research should also examine the forces that contribute to an employer's support of a student's college enrollment. Some of the data in this volume suggest the benefits of a supportive employer to students' educational outcomes. For example, in their quantitative analyses, Rowan-Kenyon et al. show that, among adult students who work full time, those who report having a supportive supervisor and coworkers report higher grades than other students. Their qualitative analyses suggest the benefits to engagement for students who are supported by employers through tuition reimbursement and flexible work schedules.

Further research is also required to understand the implications of employer-provided tuition aid for working students. Only a very small percentage of employees use a tuition reimbursement benefit to pay college prices (Lynch et al., chapter 6). Qualitative data in this volume suggest some forces that may limit use of this aid, including students' concerns that, if they use the aid, then they have future obligations to the employer (Pusser, chapter 7). Other students point to concerns about the pressure to maintain academic eligibility for employer-provided aid (Rowan-Kenyon et al., chapter 5). Future research should build on these exploratory findings to better understand why only a small percentage of students use employer-provided tuition aid and the benefits and costs of this aid to both students (aka employees) and employers.

How Do the Nature and Implications of Work Vary Based on Student Characteristics?

The findings presented in this volume illustrate that the nature and implications of work vary based on some student characteristics. For example, the qualitative data suggest distinctions in the experiences of students based on the number of hours worked and the nature of competing roles and responsibilities. Flowers finds variations in the relationship between work and African American students' engagement in effective educational practices based on whether students live on or off campus. These findings suggest the need to better understand the ways that students' experiences mediate the effects of working on students' educational outcomes.

The chapters also suggest the possibility that the needs, experiences, and implications of working vary based on other student characteristics. Therefore, as suggested by several authors (e.g., Flowers, chapter 10; Titus, chapter 12), future research should further explore variations in the relationship between employment and student outcomes based on such student characteristics as race/ethnicity, socioeconomic status, and enrollment status. The examination of the employment experiences of African American students by Flowers suggests the value of in-depth attention to the experiences of other groups. The descriptive data presented by Levin and colleagues suggest differences in the relationship between working part time and persistence across racial/ethnic groups. Ziskin et al. show that the range and scope of students' daily obligations vary based on their individual family and financial circumstances, suggesting the potential implications of these variations for the relationship between working and student outcomes. Titus found that students who are more at risk for educational failure, that is, students whose parents did not attend college, students from lower-income families, and students with lower ACT/SAT scores, worked more hours per week in the first year of college than other students. McCormick et al. show variations in student employment based on class level (with seniors both more likely to work and working more hours than freshmen) and enrollment intensity (with students who are enrolled part time working more than students who are enrolled full time).

Attention to other student characteristics may also improve understanding of the phenomenon of the working undergraduate student. As Titus notes, his results raise questions of how students' precollege employment experiences—in addition to their during-college employment experiences—may influence student outcomes. Future research should also consider how employment influences the experiences of students attending colleges where working is not the norm (e.g., low-income students attending highly selective colleges and universities; Kaplan, 2010).

Why Are Some Outcomes Better for Students Who Work Than for Students Who Do Not Work?

Several chapters in this volume show unexpected positive relationships between work and particular student outcomes. For example, in their quantitative analyses, Rowan-Kenyon and colleagues show that adult students who are employed full time have higher grades than their counterparts who are not employed. McCormick et al. find that working more than 20 hours per week on campus is associated with higher levels of engagement than is working fewer hours.

Given the nature of the research designs and data sources, the analyses in this volume cannot determine the reason for the positive relationships or the direction of causality. In other words, the analyses do not reveal whether these students have other characteristics that promote their ability to work a substantial number of hours while attending school and realize positive educational outcomes or whether these students have particular employment experiences that promote their achievement and engagement. If the latter, the analyses do not reveal the characteristics of extensive employment that promote student outcomes—for example, time management skills, relevant on-the-job learning, or something else.

These findings demonstrate the need to continue using multiple research methodologies, both quantitative and qualitative, and additional research designs to understand the implications of employment for student learning and other educational outcomes. Titus shows the contribution of instrumental variable regression to account for the endogeneity of work when examining the relationship between work and such outcomes as bachelor's degree completion and future salaries. As Titus suggests, alternative methodologies, such as structural equation modeling, may also be useful for understanding the process of how students gain skills from working and then use these skills to influence their academic and labor market outcomes.

How Should "Work" and the Educational Outcomes of Work Be Conceptualized by Institutional Leaders and Measured in Future Data Collections?

Finally, future research should build on the findings from this volume to consider more comprehensive measures of "work" and additional outcomes of employment during college. Existing datasets and research tend to define "work" as "employment for pay," with little attention to other commitments that may have similar implications for students' educational experiences, including homemaking, working on a volunteer (i.e., not-for-pay) basis, transitioning from dislocated worker status, and returning from military service (C. Kasworm, personal communication, July 9, 2009). Moreover, as several chapter authors note (e.g., Kasworm, chapter 2; Levin et al., chapter 3; and Umbach et al., chapter 11), knowledge about the characteristics, prevalence, and implications of employment using national datasets is limited by the data that are collected. Available measures typically describe only whether students are employed, whether employment is on or off campus, the number of hours employed per week, and whether students consider themselves to be "employees who study" or "students who work." McCormick et al. speculate that contradictions about the relationship between work and student outcomes in prior quantitative research may be the result, at least in part, of the limitations on the measurement of work.

Some authors in this volume (e.g., Levin et al., chapter 3; Rowan-Kenyon et al., chapter 5) respond to this limitation by supplementing available quantitative data with qualitative data. Qualitative data are especially useful for generating deeper insights into the experiences of working students. Future research should use the insights generated from qualitative research to identify additional measures of work in survey research. Potentially useful new measures would consider where students work (in addition to only if on or off campus), the type of work that students conduct, the conditions of the work environment, and the reasons that students work (Levin et al., chapter 3; McCormick et al., chapter 9; Flowers, chapter 10). As McCormick and colleagues suggest, future research should also consider changes in the continuity and nature of work over the period of a student's enrollment.

In addition, future research should include attention to the implications of working while enrolled for other outcomes. The education production function proposed by Lynch et al. specifies additional outputs beyond the common measures of academic performance and persistence, including attainment of a certificate, job placement, job and career enhancement, and quality of life improvements. Pusser and Titus speculate that one potential explanation for the positive relationship between employment during college and future salaries is that work allows students to acquire and demonstrate employer-valued skills and competence. Additional research is required to document these potential relationships.

Concluding Note

This volume describes the need for both public policymakers and campus leaders to recognize the prevalence of student employment and adapt prevailing policies and programs to promote learning and other educational outcomes for working students. As Levin and colleagues (chapter 3) argue, although student agency is important to the success of working students, public policymakers and institutions can encourage agency and promote student success through supportive policies, practices, and structures. Adapting structures and policies to promote the educational success of students who work is an important step toward raising the educational attainment of the nation's population, reducing stratification and inequality, and promoting the public good aspects of higher education (Pusser, chapter 7).

References

Advisory Committee on Student Financial Assistance. (2006). *Mortgaging our future: How financial barriers to college undercut America's global competitiveness.* Washington, DC: Author.

Advisory Committee on Student Financial Assistance. (2008). *Early & often: Designing a comprehensive system of financial aid information.* Washington, DC: Author.

Allen, W., Harris, A., Dinwiddie, G., & Griffin, K. A. (2008). Saving grace: A comparative analysis of African American Gates Millennium scholars and nonrecipients. In E. P. St. John & W. T. Trent (Eds.), *Resources, assets, and strengths among successful diverse students: Understanding the contributions of the Gates Millennium Scholars program* (pp. 17–48). Brooklyn, NY: AMS Press.

American Council on Education. (2009). CREDIT: Frequently asked questions. Retrieved June 10, 2009, from www.acenet.edu/AM/Template.cfm?Section = Learners&CONTENTID = 18684&TEMPLATE = /CM/ContentDisplay.cfm

Baum, S., & Ma, J. (2007). *Education pays 2007.* Washington, DC: College Board.

Berea College. (2009a). Berea College. Retrieved May 31, 2009, from www.berea .edu/about/

Berea College. (2009b). Learning, labor & service. Retrieved May 31, 2009, from www.berea.edu/about/learninglaborandservice.asp

Bushong, S. (2009, May 8). Rhode's work program gives students experience and saves the college money. *Chronicle of Higher Education,* A22.

Choy, S., & Berker, A. (2003). *How families of low- and middle-income undergraduates pay for college: Full-time dependent students in 1999–00* (NCES 2003–162).

Washington, DC: U.S. Department of Education, National Center for Education Statistics.

College Board. (2008a). *Trends in college pricing 2008.* Washington, DC: Author.

College Board. (2008b). *Trends in student aid 2008.* Washington, DC: Author.

College Board. (2009). About CLEP. Retrieved June 10, 2009, from http://www.collegeboard.com/student/testing/clep/about.html

Coplin, B. (2005). Seven steps: Ways to reduce instructional costs and improve undergraduate and graduate education (pp. 20–31). In *Course corrections: Experts offer solutions to the college cost crisis.* Indianapolis, IN: Lumina Foundation for Education.

Denson, N., Oseguera, L., & Hurtado, S. (2008). A profile of Hispanic students transitioning to college: The impact of the Gates Millennium Scholars program. In E. P. St. John & W. T. Trent (Eds.), *Resources, assets, and strengths among successful diverse students: Understanding the contributions of the Gates Millennium Scholars program* (pp. 49–71). Brooklyn, NY: AMS Press.

Furr, S. R., & Elling, T. W. (2000). The influence of work on college student development. *NASPA Journal, 37*(2), 454–470.

Haskins, R., Holzer, H., & Lerman, R. (2009). *Promoting economic mobility by increasing postsecondary education.* Retrieved June 7, 2009, from www.economicmobility.org/assets/pdfs/PEW_EMP_POSTSECONDARY_ED.pdf

Hune, S., & Gomez, G. G. (2008). Examining the college opportunities and experiences of talented low-income Asian American and Pacific Islander Gates Millennium Scholars and non-recipients: A complex picture of diversity. In E. P. St. John & W. T. Trent (Eds.), *Resources, assets, and strengths among successful diverse students: Understanding the contributions of the Gates Millennium Scholars program* (pp. 73–105). Brooklyn, NY: AMS Press.

Jaschik, S. (2009, July 15). The Obama plan. *Inside Higher Ed.* Retrieved July 15, 2009, from www.insidehighered.com/news/2009/07/15/obama

Kaplan, E. (2010). *Peer social networks among low-income students at elite colleges.* Unpublished doctoral dissertation. Philadelphia: University of Pennsylvania.

King, J. E. (2004). *Missed opportunities: Students who do not apply for financial aid.* Washington, DC: American Council on Education.

King, J. E., & Bannon, E. (2002). *At what cost? The price that working students pay for a college education.* Washington, DC: State PIRGs.

Mundel, D. (2008). What do we know about the impact of grants to college students? In S. Baum, M. McPherson, & P. Steele (Eds.), *The effectiveness of student aid policies: What the research tells us* (pp. 9–38). Washington, DC: College Board.

Northeastern University. (2009a). Co-op at a glance. Retrieved May 29, 2009, from www.northeastern.edu/experiential/coop/howcoopworks/coopataglance.html

Northeastern University. (2009b). How co-op works. Retrieved May 29, 2009, from www.northeastern.edu/experiential/coop/howcoopworks/index.html

Northeastern University. (2009c). Quick facts. Retrieved May 29, 2009, from www.northeastern.edu/experiential/coop/quickfacts/index.html

Pascarella, E. T., Bohr, L., Nora, A., Desler, M., & Zusman, B. (1994). Impacts of on-campus and off-campus work on first-year cognitive outcomes. *Journal of College Student Development, 35,* 364–370.

Pascarella, E. T., & Terenzini, P. T. (2005). *How college affects students, volume 2: A third decade of research.* San Francisco, CA: Jossey-Bass.

Perna, L. W., Cooper, M., & Li, C. (2007). Improving educational opportunities for students who work. E. P. St. John (Ed.), *Readings on Equal Education, 22,* 109–160.

St. John, E. P. (2008). Financial inequality and academic success: Rethinking the foundations of research on college students. In E. P. St. John & W. T. Trent (Eds.), *Resources, assets, and strengths among successful diverse students: Understanding the contributions of the Gates Millennium Scholars program* (pp. 201–228). Brooklyn, NY: AMS Press.

Trombley, W. (2003, Winter). The rising price of higher education. *College affordability in jeopardy: A special supplement to National Crosstalk.* Retrieved June 10, 2009, from www.highereducation.org/reports/affordability_supplement.pdf

U.S. Department of Education. (2009). *Digest of education statistics 2008.* Washington, DC: National Center for Education Statistics.

U.S. News & World Report. (2009). Best colleges: Internships/Co-ops. Retrieved May 31, 2009, from http://colleges.usnews.rankingsandreviews.com/college/internships-programs

Wei, C. C., Berkner, L., He, S., Lew, S., Cominole, M., Siegel, P., & Griffith, J. (2009). *2007–08 National Postsecondary Student Aid Study (NPSAS:08), student financial aid estimates for 2007–08: First look* (NCES 2009-166). Washington, DC: U. S. Department of Education, National Center for Education Statistics.

ABOUT THE AUTHORS AND EDITOR

Sandy Baum is senior policy analyst at the College Board and former professor of economics at Skidmore College. Dr. Baum earned her bachelor's in sociology at Bryn Mawr College and her doctorate in economics at Columbia University. She has written extensively on issues relating to college access, college pricing, student aid policy, student debt, affordability, and other aspects of higher education finance. Dr. Baum is the coauthor of *Trends in Student Aid, Trends in College Pricing*, and *Education Pays: The Benefits of Higher Education for Individuals and Society* for the College Board. Other recent work includes studies of setting benchmarks for manageable student debt levels and of tuition discounting in public and private colleges and universities.

Christine Cerven is a doctoral candidate in sociology at the University of California, Riverside. Her dissertation examines how identity is linked to self-esteem via social integration, self-meanings, and identity verification. Her current research projects include the examination of women's identity development within the community college context and the development of a measure of ethnic identity using an identity theory framework.

Nancy L. Deutsch is assistant professor at the University of Virginia's Curry School of Education where she teaches qualitative research and program evaluation. She is affiliated with the Research, Statistics & Evaluation and Applied Developmental Science programs. Her research examines the socio-ecological contexts of development, particularly issues of adolescence, identity, gender, race, and class. Nancy's book, *Pride in the Projects: Teens Building Identities in Urban Contexts*, a 4-year study of teens at an inner-city youth organization, was published by NYU Press in 2008. She is collaborating on a second book about adult–youth relationships and organizational practices at after-school programs and is studying the Young Women Leaders' Program, a combined one-on-one and group mentoring program for girls that uses college women as mentors.

Lamont A. Flowers is the Distinguished Professor of Educational Leadership in the Department of Leadership, Counselor Education, Human and Organizational Development and the executive director of the Charles H. Houston Center for the Study of the Black Experience in Education in the Eugene T. Moore School of Education at Clemson University.

Bruce Gansneder is professor emeritus, Curry School, University of Virginia. He taught research methods, survey research, and statistics. He authored or coauthored more than 170 academic presentations including more than 100 refereed journal articles, more than 60 national presentations, 10 book chapters, and more than 50 research/evaluation reports. He has provided methodological assistance in a wide variety of areas including sports medicine and science education, and higher education. He has directed more than 50 evaluation projects. He has just completed a $100,000 grant from Lumina Foundation for Education, the Emerging Pathways Study. He is currently statistical consultant for the *Journal of Athletic Training*.

Michael Gottfried is a doctoral candidate at the University of Pennsylvania, studying Applied Economics at the Wharton School of Business. He is also an Institute of Education Sciences (IES) Pre-Doctoral Fellow. Michael's primary interests lie in applying tools from the economics of education field to education policy. He has researched policy issues at many levels of education, including K–12, higher education, and postsecondary adult learning. He is on the board of editors of the *International Journal of Educational Advancement*, and he earned a master's degree in Applied Economics from the Wharton School of Business at Penn and a bachelor's in Economics from Stanford University.

Wendy Green is a doctoral candidate in Teaching, Learning, and Curriculum at the University of Pennsylvania. Her areas of interest are workplace and adult learning as well as diversity in organizations. As a MetroMath fellow, she has researched the intersection of school culture and the implementation of school policies, procedures, and practices within urban school settings. She has also completed research in the area of training and development. As the graduate co-chair of the Native American student group on campus, she works toward furthering the visibility of Native people on the UPenn campus. She is also on the board for Penn's Center for Native American Studies. She has 13 years of professional experience in the fields of counseling and education.

Jacob P. K. Gross is associate director of research at the Project on Academic Success (PAS). He received his doctorate in history, philosophy, and policy studies in education, with a concentration in higher education, from Indiana University in 2008. His general research interests relate to the ways education policies reproduce and challenge social inequality. He focuses on academic success, particularly among underrepresented students, in postsecondary education. Specific areas of interest include financial aid, racial and gender equity policies, postsecondary financing, the effects of institutional contexts on student success, and student flow.

Don Hossler is professor of educational leadership and policy studies at Indiana University (IU), where he has served as vice chancellor for enrollment services for IU Bloomington, associate vice president for enrollment services for the seven campuses of the IU system, executive associate dean for the School of Education, and chair of educational leadership and policy studies. His areas of specialization include college choice, student financial aid policy, enrollment management, and higher education finance.

Carol Kasworm is professor of adult education and department head of the Department of Adult and Higher Education at North Carolina State University. Her research interests have focused on the adult undergraduate experience, including the nature of learning engagement and participation patterns of adult students, the situated influences of varied higher education contexts in relation to adult learners, and the role of adult higher education in a lifelong learning society. Her scholarship includes 5 books, 28 book chapters, and 75 refereed and nonrefereed journal articles, as well as numerous papers and presentations. Dr. Kasworm is currently coeditor of the forthcoming 2010 *Handbook of Adult and Continuing Education* and Fulbright senior specialist in Finland.

George D. Kuh is Chancellor's Professor of Higher Education at Indiana University Bloomington where he directs the Center for Postsecondary Research. George has written extensively about student engagement, assessment, institutional improvement, and college and university cultures, and has consulted with more than 250 colleges and universities in the United States and abroad. His two most recent books are *Student Success in College: Creating Conditions That Matter* (2005) and *Piecing Together the Student Success Puzzle: Research, Propositions, and Recommendations* (2007). In 2001, he received Indiana University's prestigious Tracy Sonneborn Award for a distinguished career of teaching and research. George received a bachelor's from Luther College, a master's from the St. Cloud State University, and a doctorate from the University of Iowa.

John S. Levin is the Bank of America Professor of Education Leadership and the director and principal investigator of the California Community College Collaborative (C4) at University of California, Riverside, in the Graduate School of Education. His books in this decade—*Globalizing the Community College* (Palgrave, 2001); *Community College Faculty: At Work in the New Economy* (Palgrave MacMillan, 2006), with Sue Kater and Richard Wagoner; *Non-Traditional Students and Community Colleges: The conflict of Justice and Neo-liberalism* (Palgrave MacMillan, 2007); and *Community Colleges and Their Students: Co-construction and Institutional Identity* (Palgrave MacMillan, 2009) with Virginia Montero-Hernandez—are empirically based examinations of community colleges. His current research includes examinations of contingent faculty in universities and colleges, graduate student career choices, and program practices at community colleges.

Jonathan S. Lewis serves as an academic advisor at Bentley University, in Waltham, MA. He was assistant director for the Office of the Reynolds Club and Student Activities at the University of Chicago from 2007 to 2009. In that role, Lewis worked with professional and student staff to oversee operations, event planning, audiovisual services, and facility management for the university's 109-year-old college union. Prior to that, Lewis served for 5 years at Northwestern University's college union, in Evanston, Illinois, where he also received his master's degree in higher education administration and policy. Lewis has published previously with *The Chronicle of Higher Education*, as well as the Association of College Unions International.

Doug Lynch is the vice dean of the graduate school of education at the University of Pennsylvania.

Alexander C. McCormick is associate professor of education at Indiana University Bloomington, where he teaches in the Higher Education and Student Affairs program. He also directs the National Survey of Student Engagement (NSSE), which more than 1,300 bachelor's-granting colleges and universities have used to assess undergraduate education and promote effective educational practices. As NSSE director, Dr. McCormick works to enhance the national discourse about quality and accountability in higher education, while also promoting institutional improvement. Prior to his current position, he served as a senior scholar at the Carnegie Foundation for the Advancement of Teaching. He holds a bachelor's degree in French from Dartmouth College and master's and doctorate degrees in education from Stanford University.

Virginia Montero-Hernandez is a doctoral candidate in the Program of Curriculum and Instruction in the Graduate School of Education at the University of California Riverside. She obtained her bachelor's degree in Education at the Autonomous University of the State of Morelos, Mexico. In 2005, she received an award from the National Council of Science and Technology in Mexico to study abroad. She is part of the research team of the California Community College Collaborative (C4) at the University of California Riverside and coauthor of a book along with John S. Levin, director of C4. Her research uses qualitative methodology to study academic identity, student development, and organizational identity in the higher education system both in the U.S. and Mexican contexts.

John V. Moore III is project associate at the Center for Postsecondary Research (CPR) at Indiana University Bloomington, where he is completing a doctorate in higher education and inquiry methodology. His research interests include college student identity development, the effects of working on college student outcomes, and the relationship between theory and research methods. Prior to CPR, where he has worked on projects including National Survey of Student Engagement (NSSE), Beginning College Survey of Student Engagement, and the Project on Academic Success, John completed a master's in College Student Affairs at the University of South Florida and worked as a director of academic support services at University of the Sciences in Philadelphia.

Ryan D. Padgett is a doctoral student in the Higher Education Program and research assistant at the Center for Research on Undergraduate Education at the University of Iowa. His research interests include college choice, student access, first-year college experiences, college impact, and persistence in higher education, particularly of diverse and underrepresented student populations.

Ernest T. Pascarella is professor and Mary Louise Petersen Chair in Higher Education at the University of Iowa, where he also codirects the Center for Research on Undergraduate Education. His work focuses on the impact of college on students, and he is coauthor (with Patrick Terenzini) of the 1991 and 2005 volumes: *How College Affects Students*. The two books synthesize approximately 5,000 studies of college impact conducted over a 30-year period. He has received a number of awards for his research from national scholarly associations, and in 2003 he received the Howard R. Bowen Distinguished Career Award from the Association for the Study of Higher Education.

Laura W. Perna is associate professor of higher education in the Graduate School of Education at the University of Pennsylvania. Her current scholarship focuses on understanding the ways that public and institutional policies enable and restrict college access and success especially for students from underrepresented minority groups and from low socioeconomic backgrounds. Her research has been supported by grants from the U.S. Department of Education's Institute for Education Sciences, Lumina Foundation for Education, and other sources and has been recognized by the Association for the Study of Higher Education's 2003 Promising Scholar/Early Career Achievement Award.

Brian Pusser is associate professor and director of the Center for the Study of Higher Education of the Curry School of Education at the University of Virginia. His research focuses on the organization and governance of higher education institutions, the politics of higher education, and the role of the state in higher education.

Heather Rowan-Kenyon is assistant professor of higher education in the Lynch School of Education at Boston College. Previously, she was an assistant professor and coordinator of the Student Affairs Practice in Higher Education program at the University of Virginia. Dr. Rowan-Kenyon earned her doctorate in Higher Education Policy and Leadership at the University of Maryland, a master's in College Student Personnel at Bowling Green State University, and a bachelor's in Secondary Education/Social Studies at the University of Scranton. Her research interests include issues of college access and student success.

Amy Swan is a doctoral candidate in higher education at the University of Virginia. She earned a master's degree in arts management at Carnegie Mellon University's Heinz College and a bachelor's degree in women's studies at the University of North Carolina at Chapel Hill. Her research interests include college student development and the experiences of female students in science, technology, engineering, and math (STEM).

Chris Allen Thomas is a doctoral candidate in Educational Linguistics at the University of Pennsylvania, Graduate School of Education. He has worked on a number of interdisciplinary projects that focus on language, culture, and adult learning. In addition, he has worked for 3 years with the Graduate School of Education and Wharton Executive Education on innovative programs, such as the Work-Based Learning Leadership doctoral program. As part of a research team, he has consulted for the Conference Board on issues related to maximizing the effectiveness of corporate sponsorship of education programs. His research interests include discourse analysis, organizational learning, and organizational language policies.

Marvin A. Titus is assistant professor of higher education in the Department of Education Leadership, Higher Education, and International Education at the University of Maryland College Park. His academic interests include the economics of higher education, state higher education policy, student persistence, the labor market outcomes of college graduates, and quantitative research methods. Marvin has published in the *Journal of Higher Education, Research in Higher Education*, and *Review of Higher Education*. He is an editorial board member of the *Journal of College Student Development* as well as *Higher Education: The International Journal of Higher Education and Educational Planning*. Marvin has a bachelor's in economics and history; a master's in economics; and a doctorate in education policy, planning, and administration.

Vasti Torres, director of the Project on Academic Success (PAS), is associate professor of higher education and student affairs administration at Indiana

University, where she teaches courses in student development theory, research in higher education, and student affairs administration. Her research focuses on the effects of ethnic identity on the college experiences of Latino students. In 2007–2008, she became the first Latina president of the American College Personnel Association. Prior to coming to Indiana University, she was a faculty member at the George Washington University Graduate School of Education and Human Development. During her 15 years of administrative experience, she was associate vice provost and dean for enrollment and student services at Portland State University.

Paul D. Umbach is associate professor of higher education at North Carolina State University. His research focuses on social and organizational structures that affect college students and the careers of college faculty. Central to much of his work are issues of equity and diversity. He has published more than 40 peer-reviewed articles, book chapters, and other scholarly publications. In 2007, the Association for the Study of Higher Education awarded him the Promising Scholar/Early Career Achievement Award.

Mary Ziskin is senior associate director of the Project on Academic Success (PAS) at Indiana University. She holds a doctorate from the Center for the Study of Higher and Postsecondary Education at the University of Michigan and conducts research on student academic success in college. Her research interests also include the racial stratification of educational opportunity, discourses surrounding academic merit, and critical research methodologies. She teaches qualitative methods, survey research, and action research at the Indiana University School of Education.

Note: Page numbers followed by f or t refer to figures or tables.